FOOD AID FOR DEVELOPMENT

FOOD AID
FOR DEVELOPMENT

Three Studies
by

**Gerda Blau
Mordecai Ezekiel
B.R. Sen**

FOOD AND AGRICULTURE
ORGANIZATION OF THE UNITED NATIONS
Rome, 1985

The three studies in *Food Aid in Development* were originally written in 1954, 1955 and 1962, respectively. In order to preserve the spirit of the original text, no substantial editorial changes have been made. It should therefore be borne in mind that the Organization's editorial policy toward spelling, language use and style has changed considerably in the meantime. In particular, country names and the terminology employed regarding developing nations are notably at variance with FAO's current perspective.

The designations employed and the presentation of material in this publication do not imply the expression of any opinion whatsoever by the Food and Agriculture Organization of the United Nations concerning the legal status of any country, territory, city or area or of its authorities, or concerning the delimitation of its frontiers or boundaries. The views expressed are those of the authors.

P-66
ISBN 92-5-102180-5

Printed in Italy

FOREWORD

The origins of food aid extend back over many decades. What began largely as a bilateral disposal operation to liquidate unwanted and burdensome surplus stocks of agricultural commodities in North America has evolved into an international food aid system with an expanding multilateral component. Today food aid accounts for one-tenth of the net official development assistance of countries of the Organisation for Economic Cooperation and Development. Although there is still a lively debate over the advantages and disadvantages of food aid, the opportunities it offers as a resource for development are now widely accepted.

Why did this transformation occur and how far is it complete? In the 40th Anniversary Year of FAO, it is appropriate to consider this question. The transformation referred to above began when the Seventh Session of the FAO Conference in 1953 agreed that the best way to absorb excess market supplies in a hungry world was through positive demand-creating measures rather than through negative policies to curtail production. This constructive approach was reflected in the secretariat's work, which has consistently focused on finding innovative ways to use food aid to promote development and alleviate poverty and malnutrition, without disturbing normal patterns of production and marketing.

The studies reissued in this collection by three FAO pioneers from three contintents – Gerda Blau, Mordecai Ezekiel and B.R. Sen – form part of the same tradition. Each study in its own way was a landmark on the road toward a multilateral food aid system. They showed clearly and compellingly the direction that the international community should take and led to decisive action. And unlike many of the series of reports, papers and documents issued by international organizations, they still merit perusal today as original contributions in developing new concepts in the food aid field and in laying the foundations for the whole subsequent project approach of the World Food Programme. This is not to say that they fully anticipated all the practical difficulties of using food for development or resolved all the problems of organizing a predictable, adequate and stable flow of food aid. In fact, in my view, many of the lessons of experience since these studies were first issued have still to be fully learned. The current flow of food aid, though approaching US$3 billion annually, is much less in volume than it was in 1965 and can scarcely match the challenge of the widening food gap and growing emergency needs of low-income countries, particularly in sub-Saharan Africa, even apart from development requirements.

This underlines the need not only to expand food aid supplies, but also to make the most effective use of food aid for the manifold purposes to which these early studies pointed, whether as balance-of-payments support, as a source of national budgetary revenue, as project aid, or as programme aid. Yet too often food aid is allocated to countries erratically from year to year, depending on availability rather than as a planned, multiyear resource that can be properly integrated into longer term programmes or strategies. Although food aid planning is being gradually improved, it is still insufficiently coordinated with other external aid and domestic resources in ways that avoid generating long-term dependence or distorting consumption patterns.

Another complex subject which deserves more attention is the role of food in improving the access of poor people to basic foodstuffs, a major aim of food security policies. How can increased equity be best reconciled with economic growth? There is a growing body of experience of food subsidy, rationing and food stamp schemes that operate in developing countries from which useful lessons may be drawn. Above all, the whole problem of ensuring a timely response to acute food shortages and preventing famine – whether by prepositioning stocks in disaster-prone areas, by improving the International Emergency Food Reserve, or by better early warning and preparedness programmes – needs to be thoroughly considered.

The enduring importance of the three studies reissued in this collection lies in the fact that, at a critical time in the early history of food aid, they demonstrated convincingly and cogently how food from developed countries could provide an additional resource to lift some of the constraints on economic and social progress in developing countries without significant adverse side-effects. They showed that, in this process, the recipient, the donor and the multilateral organizations each have their own distinct responsibilities. This remains the position today. With food surpluses periodically building up in high-income countries, I believe it is all the more necessary to continue the search for new and more efficient ways of taking advantage of all such potential development resources. I hope that the reissue of these path-breaking FAO studies will stimulate fresh thinking on the use of food aid to reinforce world food security, and will reflect the growing public concern over the human predicament in the less privileged parts of the world.

EDOUARD SAOUMA
Director-General

INTRODUCTION

With a vast and still growing literature on food aid, interest in this important yet controversial form of development assistance continues unabated. The reissue of three early FAO studies on this subject is justified not only because they can be regarded as classics but also because they make original contributions which remain relevant and topical today, 30 years after their completion. They aimed at shaping international and national policy attitudes, and they succeeded in this to a remarkable degree. They provided an economic rationale and institutional foundation upon which today's multilateral food aid system rests.

To understand the context in which these studies were drafted, it should be remembered that the 1950s was a period in which the accumulation of large-scale agricultural surpluses had led to widespread concern. The deliberate destruction of food in a poverty-stricken world was inconceivable. Hence the importance of these studies, which demonstrated the scope (and limitations) of transforming food surpluses into food aid, and set out the conditions under which they could play a legitimate and positive role in promoting development and reducing malnutrition in the developing countries.

To a large extent the three studies characterize ten years (1953-62) in the history of FAO in fulfilling its constitutional function of promoting national and international action with respect to the distribution of food and agricultural products. Earlier attempts had consisted of the 1946-47 proposal for the establishment of a World Food Board and, in 1949, for the creation of an International Commodity Clearing House.[1] These proposals were inspired by an overoptimistic evaluation of the degree to which governments would be willing to accept limits on national sovereignty through multilateral action in matters considered of vital national impor-

---

[1] For a description of these two proposals, cf. P. Lamartine-Yates, *So bold an aim*, FAO, Rome 1955; Gerda Blau, *Functions of a world food reserve, scope and limitations*, FAO, Rome 1956.

tance. Neither proposal was accepted by governments, although they left their mark on FAO structures.[2]

When it met in late 1953, the Seventh Session of the FAO Conference was faced with the problems posed by the reappearance of heavy surplus stocks after the end of the Korean War boom, particularly in North America. This led the United States of America to adopt measures and legislation which, if they had been applied solely in the light of national interests, could have disrupted international commodity trade. Fortunately, governments were far-sighted and requested the Committee on Commodity Problems to work on (i) the formulation of principles to be observed in the disposal of agricultural surpluses; (ii) the development of suitable methods of disposal; and (iii) the strengthening of intergovernmental machinery for consultations on these matters.

The first study reproduced here, by Gerda Blau, was prepared to guide the discussions of an intergovernmental working party which met under FAO auspices in Washington in 1954 to examine these questions. While frankly acknowledging the risks, this study demonstrates with rigorous economic logic the possibilities of bridging the gap between the immediate desire to find additional outlets for surpluses on the one hand, and the equally urgent need for long-term measures to foster growth and combat hunger on the other hand. To achieve this, two crucial conditions for food aid projects have been identified: In simple terms, the need for the food supplies to lead to "additional" consumption over and above what it would have been in the absence of the concessional transaction; and the need for the recipient country to take complementary measures which – in making full use of counterpart funds from the sales of food aid – ensure the expansion of development programmes, preferably through food-for-work schemes. Many novel ways of using food surpluses to expand consumption are critically examined and their limitations (such as heavy administrative costs and complexity of management) are carefully identified; many of the observations made in the study have been borne out by subsequent experience.

At the time, however, the major contribution of the study was its common-sense analysis of concepts and policy options which were subsequently used by governments in formulating the FAO Principles of Surplus Disposal, a code of conduct to which the international community still adheres today. A cardinal principle, which was identified and accepted by governments, is that unilateral or bilateral actions should not be taken without prior intergovernmental consultations, based on a few pragmatic guidelines.

---

[2] The World Food Board proposal led to the establishment of the FAO Council; that for an International Commodity Clearing House led to the setting up of the Committee on Commodity Problems.

Thus this study marked the beginnings both of a more systematic investigation of the developmental uses of food aid and of an international consensus on safeguards to reduce the dangers to regular trade and marketing. It signified, in fact, a step toward the international coordination of national agricultural policies. For, although not legally binding in themselves, the FAO Principles of Surplus Disposal were formally accepted by most of the major producing, consuming and trading countries, and were incorporated in legal instruments negotiated under the General Agreement on Tariffs and Trade (GATT) and embodied in the Food Aid Convention. In this way they have helped to make food aid internationally acceptable as a positive vehicle for promoting economic and social development and in providing emergency relief, rather than being opposed as *ad hoc* surplus disposals from unwanted stocks which threaten the stability of agricultural markets or, still worse, as tools to enhance the competitive position of financially strong exporting countries.

These ideas of using food surpluses were elaborated in a detailed field survey, commissioned by the FAO Council and carried out by Mordecai Ezekiel, which was issued in 1955. A pilot study was organized to look into the practical possibilities of using food to help speed up economic development, focusing on ways to expand labour-intensive projects, with India as the country model.

Results exceeded expectations. They demonstrated in detail how the enormous capital represented by food surpluses could be used to finance a general expansion of an investment programme; they set out specific illustrative projects covering such fields as milk marketing, road building and soil erosion and go on to explore how developing countries may use their own occasional domestic food surpluses in similar ways, thus providing useful guidance to future self-help programmes. Recognizing the limitations of these approaches, Ezekiel's study also explores the preconditions for avoiding damaging side-effects on domestic producers or third-party exporters.

The originality of this work is twofold. There is the systematic distinction it introduces between assistance to projects and assistance to general development programmes, and the emphasis on the effect of these activities being viewed as an addition to the capital resources of a low-income country for financing its economic development, and not from the negative viewpoint of lowering the "burdensome surpluses" of high-income countries. In this it was a forerunner of today's balance-of-payments and budgetary support roles of food aid. From the standpoint of the type of analysis applied, the application of the demand multiplier analysis in the discussion of "financing of a general development program" (Part I, V: 116) is probably the single most significant contribution. This analysis postulates first the spending of domestic funds to finance parts of a development programme and then the introduction into local markets of additional foodstuffs as food aid. It examines the effects and requirements of the programme approach of international assistance to development which was to be actively debated in subsequent years. It goes on to analyse the economic characteristics of various types of projects, such as those based on food distributed in kind, projects involving additional employment which create additional consumption, or projects earning rapid income. These, together with the concrete illustrative projects in Part II of the study, have lost little, if anything, of their validity as examples of possible actions by food aid bodies, be they multilateral, regional or national, governmental or non-governmental.

In October 1960, the UN General Assembly adopted Resolution 1496 (XV) on the provision of food surpluses to food-deficient peoples through the United Nations system. For the first time in its history, the establishment of a multilateral system of food aid was envisaged in the highest political body in the world and FAO was invited to establish the necessary procedures.

Responding to the call of the General Assembly, the then Director-General of FAO, B.R. Sen, undertook the third study in this collection to examine the feasibility of additional arrangements, including multilateral arrangements, to mobilize available food surpluses for developmental uses. With the assistance of a group of independent experts and of an inter-governmental advisory committee, a comprehensive programme of action was developed. This set out the requirements for an expanded programme of food aid for development, national food reserves and emergency relief, as well as possible multilateral functions and arrangements.

The emphasis of this report is on development and the role of food aid in development. It strongly supports the programme approach and stresses that it is essential that an expanded programme for surplus utilization for economic and social development include country planning on one side and aid coordination on the other. There must, it argues, be full recognition of the primacy of the development priorities of recipient countries. While recognizing the risks to domestic agricultural development, the report considers that these can be avoided, providing that there be appropriate price and income policies and institutions to provide production incentives which can reach farmers directly. Food aid is conceived as part of the larger flow of overall development assistance within which food aid should be coordinated in a multilateral framework. The report rightly stresses that the chief limiting factor lies in the absorption capacity of recipient countries and in the necessity for correlated domestic efforts.

This last report led directly to international action. The initiative was taken by the United States, which accepted a multilateral approach to food aid as a supplement to bilateral arrangements, and proposed an initial fund of $100 million to meet international emergency food needs and for pilot food-for-work or nutritional projects. Other governments supported this approach. By the end of 1961, the UN General Assembly and the FAO Conference, in separate and parallel resolutions, had approved the establishment of a new international food aid agency, the UN/FAO World Food Programme.

This, then, was the culmination of the ten years of pioneering economic exploration and analytical work contained in the three studies reproduced in this collection. There was – and still is – much work to be done, but the process by which surplus disposals were to be progressively transformed into food aid had begun.

DISPOSAL OF AGRICULTURAL SURPLUSES

By
Gerda Blau

CONTENTS

Figures in round brackets denote paragraph numbers

FINDINGS AND RECOMMENDATIONS OF THE SEVENTH SESSION OF THE FAO CONFERENCE

DIFFICULTIES ENCOUNTERED IN ABSORBING SUPPLIES

1. The Seventh Session of the Conference, in its review of the world agricultural commodity situation, gave special attention to the growing difficulties encountered in absorbing supplies of certain commodities. While recognizing that the term "surplus" was capable of varying interpretations and that so far only one government had stated that it had surpluses of some commodities, the Conference stressed the urgency and importance of a constructive approach to the problem of disposing of supplies of food and agricultural products for which no adequate effective demand exists.

2. It was recognized that these current distribution difficulties had to be seen in perspective and that they should not be allowed to interfere with the whole-hearted pursuit of well-conceived, long-term agricultural development programs. It was also pointed out, however, that the very progress of such orderly development could be seriously jeopardized by the deterrent effects of surpluses overhanging the market, particularly to the extent that they disturb patterns of production and international trade. In this connection, emphasis was laid on the delicate nature of world market equilibria which might be disproportionately upset by the effects of marginal excess supplies. It was noted, moreover, that curtailed production of one commodity might in some measure merely shift rather than solve the problem of surplus stocks.

CONFERENCE VIEWS ON POSSIBLE REMEDIES

3. In its review of possible remedies, the Conference stressed the fact that, in accordance with FAO's basic aims, the foremost remedy for the absorption of excess supplies was to be sought in courageous policies for increasing consumption. The narrowing of the gap between effective demand and adequate nutritional standards depends essentially on progress made in raising the efficiency of production and distribution systems to the

mutual benefit of consumers and producers, and, on the other hand, raising the levels of both general and external purchasing power, particularly in countries with low consumption standards.

4. Notwithstanding the importance of basic development and consumption programs, it was generally felt that full consideration had to be given in the period ahead to special measures for keeping consumption in step with expanding production. The Conference urged that full use should be made of the experience gathered on such special programs, both national and international, and that FAO should consider, together with UNICEF and WHO, possibilities of developing special distribution programs. Stress was laid on the importance of considering how far long-term development aspects could be reconciled with temporary measures.

INTERNATIONAL REPERCUSSIONS

5. The Conference noted further that intergovernmental examination of the movement of surpluses into consumption required full consideration of the possible international repercussions of such measures, including the effects not only on competing exporters of identical or related products but also on production and the economic development within receiving regions. To promote constructive action and to relieve the anxieties of all interested governments, the Conference, therefore, regarded it as highly desirable that FAO should try to draw up principles and standards which might be applied in the disposal of agricultural commodities in surplus supply.

NEED FOR AN INTERNATIONAL FORUM - CONFERENCE REQUEST FOR CCP ACTION

6. The Conference noted with interest the consideration given by the U.S. Government to international safeguards in the formulation of Section 550 of the Mutual Security Act. The provisions of this Section, while constituting only one of the existing special disposal measures, were of interest not only because of their topical importance but also because of their general significance. It was noted, moreover, that the application of these standards had been sincerely followed in negotiations initiated so far. Nonetheless, the Conference was concerned about the international repercussions of this and similar programs, especially if their application were widened. It was concluded that the effects of such measures should be considered in an international forum.

7. The Conference noted that the necessary machinery for such consultation was readily available within FAO through the medium of its Committee on Commodity Problems (CCP) which, on grounds of both past experience and current competence, was well equipped for dealing with these matters. It therefore concluded that progress could best be made by the CCP undertaking as speedily as possible a review and study of the questions involved, to serve as a basis for the formulation of principles. It passed the following Resolution (No. 14), on *Disposal of Agricultural Surpluses*:

The Conference

Recognizing the need to improve consumption levels for agricultural products, and in particular to raise nutritional levels in under-developed areas and among children and other vulnerable groups,

Noting the existence of surpluses of some agricultural commodities and the fears of many Member Nations that the disposal of surpluses might have harmful effects on the economies of many countries,

Recognizing the urgent necessity of finding ways and means of moving surpluses into consumption without harmful interference with normal patterns of production and international trade,

Recommends for the attention of Member Governments the following principles to be taken into consideration in the disposal of agricultural surpluses, with full regard to the need for active steps to raise consumption levels, as stated above:

(i) that Member Governments which have excess stocks of agricultural products should dispose of such products in an orderly manner so as to avoid any undue pressure resulting in sharp falls of prices on world markets, particularly when prices of agricultural products are generally low;

(ii) that where surpluses are disposed of under special terms, there should be an undertaking from both importing and exporting countries that such arrangements will be made without harmful interference with normal patterns of production and international trade.

Requests the Committee on Commodity Problems, at the earliest possible date, and not later than the end of June 1954, in elaboration of the findings of the Conference and with a view to making recommendations for transmission to Member Governments, to consider:

(i) the most suitable means of disposing of surpluses including proposals for setting up consultative machinery through which the disposal of agricultural surpluses can be facilitated;

(ii) the principles which should be observed by Member Nations in order that the disposal of surpluses be made without harmful interference with normal patterns of production and international trade.

CCP WORKING PARTY ON SURPLUS DISPOSAL

8. The CCP, acting on the Conference recommendations, decided to establish a Working Party of eight members, to meet in Washington in February 1954 for a period of about three weeks, the terms of reference to be as set out in the final paragraphs of the above-quoted Conference Resolution. The following Governments were invited to appoint representatives:

Argentina	Netherlands
Egypt	New Zealand
France	United Kingdom
India	United States

The Report of the Working Party, which has since been completed, will be considered by the main Committee on Commodity Problems at its next Session in early June.[1]

---

[1] See *Annex A*: Report of the Working Party on Surplus Disposal to the FAO Committee on Commodity Problems - Summary of Findings and Recommendations, and *Annex B*: Disposal of Agricultural Surpluses - Extract from the Report of the 23rd Session of the FAO Committee on Commodity Problems.

THE MEANING
OF "SURPLUS"

9. The meaning of "surplus", according to common usage, is "that which remains when use or need is satisfied".[1]

10. In economic thinking, the definition of surplus is a much wider one. Supplies of commodities may be in "excess" or "surplus", even though the needs of potential consumers may be far from satisfied.

11. The discrepancy between common usage and economic language arises from the distinction which must be made between the intrinsic usefulness of goods (i.e., their capacity for satisfying needs), as against effective demand (i.e., the potential consumer's ability and willingness to buy these goods at given prices and on given conditions of sale).

12. In a world of convertible currencies, the term "surplus", if it is to be meaningful as a basis for action, must thus mean surplus *at a price*. Short of extreme cases when sellers cannot clear at zero, there will always be *some* price and conditions of sale at which stocks of foodstuffs and other agricultural products can be cleared.

13. Even in the extreme case of offerings free of charge (or at nominal prices) finding no takers, it will generally be found, on closer inspection, that the obstacle lies in the lack of effective demand at a price; the only difference being that in such cases the "price" to be paid by the ultimate consumers, or by those who provide for them, will be composed solely of transport charges, internal distribution cost, or other incidental expenses other than the cost of the goods at sellers' delivery points. Moreover, while there have been instances of free offerings or sales at nominal prices finding little response, such instances generally arise only if the market to which the offers are made is restricted (e.g., for export only or for sales to specified groups and specified areas only). In the absence of serious currency limitations, they are most likely to arise where offerings have been restricted to low-income countries or low-income groups – as tends to be the case under

special distribution programs. There are few instances known of free offers to an unrestricted market (domestic plus exports) having found no takers.

14. If seller's currencies are scarce, commodities offered against payment in these currencies will, *cet. par.,* command lower prices than identical or comparable goods available against other means of payment. Short of absolute embargoes on currency uses for imports, however, effective demand in each of the currency sectors will still be demand "at a price".

15. The insistence on price as a major element in the definition of any surplus situation should not by any means be taken to imply, however, that all disequilibria between supply and demand can automatically be solved merely by leaving the market to look after itself. Indeed, the mechanism of free market prices may at times be a very inadequate instrument for regulating supply and demand, particularly in the case of agricultural products.

16. One fundamental reason for this inadequacy is that, owing to the low responsiveness of demand to price changes for some of these products (aggravated by rigid distribution margins), even moderate and temporary supply increases in excess of current demand may result in drastic price falls and thus discourage new production to an extent which is against the best long-term interests of both producers and consumers. This may happen particularly in cases of those annual crops where acreage variations or shifts can be effected with relative ease. Alternatively, in the case of some agricultural commodities, the responsiveness of supply to price changes may be so low (because of the length of production periods, lack of alternative profitable outlets, or large shares of overheads in total costs) that even drastic price falls, with the hardship they entail, will not automatically bring about sufficient downward adjustments of production, even though there may be a real structural need for such adjustments. These difficulties arising from the sluggishness of supply responses will again be particularly severe for commodities which have inelastic markets, and demand for which cannot, therefore, be stepped up easily by means of price reductions. In short, in cases of both strong and weak short-term responses of supply to price changes, reliance on price as the sole market regulator may not bring about the kind of adjustments which are the most desirable in the long run. This is one main justification for various forms of governmental interference with agricultural prices, production, and trade; though it remains to assess in each case, on its merits, whether such deliberate interference with the market does, in fact, help or hinder the equation of supply and demand at a desirable level both short-term and long-term. Yet, whatever conclusions might be reached in such assessments (which it is obviously impossible to undertake within the context of this study), the important practical point to be noted here as a "datum" is that

national price-support policies are largely here to stay; and so are the closely linked phenomena of recurrent stock accumulations.

17. In the light of these general reflections, let us now look at some concrete examples of current stock accumulations and attempt to determine whether or not these stocks are "surplus". Take, first, the example of current Canadian wheat stocks which now exceed one year's domestic requirement and exports. Are these stocks "surplus"? The Canadian Government officially takes the view that they are not. Instead, it argues that the main factors which caused this accumulation – i.e., record levels of the highly variable Canadian yields over the past two years, coupled with remarkably high levels of wheat production in other countries – could change very rapidly and might again call for much larger disposals of Canadian wheat at a time when output might be reduced by lower yields obtained from the fairly constant area planted to wheat in Canada.[2]

18. There is, indeed, a good case to be made for liberal governmental stockholding policies which can help to cushion short-term supply variations. But where is the limit? No doubt, all stocks can be described as "burdensome" in the sense that resources must be tied up in holding them. But at what point will stocks exceed the "economic" level (i.e., the level up to which the advantages of holding them justify the cost) and become a real burden or "surplus"? Is it up to each Government to define the point at which its stocks become "surplus"? Or are there any absolute criteria which can be applied in defining "surplus" stocks?

19. The FAO Conference, in the Report of its Fifth Session in 1949, (page 10, footnote 3) stated that:

"The term 'surplus' as used in this section refers to supplies of food and agricultural commodities for which no effective demand exists at current price levels, on the basis of payment in the currency of the producing country."

This definition may be regarded as a valiant first attempt to establish some of the absolute criteria for which we are searching. At the same time, it needs to be qualified in several important respects. First, while it is correct to say that lack of effective demand at given price levels must be regarded as an inherent feature in any surplus situation, it does not follow the other way around that *any* supplies of food and agricultural commodities for which no effective demand exists at current price level in the seller's currency can be correctly described as "surplus". For if this were true, any stocks of any kind which could not be absorbed by the market at current prices at any given point of time would have to be described as "surplus". From the viewpoint of the economy as a whole, this would not make sense.

One normal market reaction, in the case of offerings at current prices exceeding demand, is for the prices to be reduced. This is an everyday occurrence and it would seem wrong to conclude that in the absence of such price adjustments taking place, the resulting accumulation of unsold supplies should automatically be classified as "surplus". Moreover, there will at any time be *some* level of unsold stocks which, though finding no buyers at current prices, will neither call for immediate price reductions, nor deserve to be classified as "surplus". Instead, this portion of unsold supplies will constitute the normal carryover of the market. A merchant who cannot sell his stock at current prices in one week or one month, will not for that reason regard it as "surplus". Nor will a Government. At harvest time, stocks are stored to be disposed of gradually over the marketing year and no one regards them as "surplus" merely because they cannot all be sold right away at current prices. Moreover, there are other important economic functions which can be performed by unsold stocks. As has just been seen in the Canadian example, some governments hold large stocks against possible future supply/demand variations. These stocks are available for purchase but if they cannot be sold at current prices, they are not for that reason regarded as "surplus". While opinions may differ as to the point at which such stocks become excessive, it is obvious that there will always be *some* level in excess of current pipeline requirements up to which such holdings are useful or even highly desirable.[3]

20. Another inadequacy of the above-quoted definition is the ambiguity of the term "current prices". Does this mean "prices asked for"? - or "prices current for a particular type of transaction in the seller's country"? - or does it relate to some elusive concept of a representative free market price? In the latter case, the definition would be a *contradictio in adiecto* since in a free market the volume of effective demand in the currency asked for will, at given offerings, not only depend on, but also *determine*, current prices. Thus, there could never persist a situation in which effective demand at current prices falls short of the volume offered. For in such a situation, current prices could not remain what they were.

21. Having now discussed at some length the fallacies and inconsistencies which must be guarded against in any definition of "surplus", it seems time to attempt the formulation of a consistent definition. Perhaps the best way of doing this is to formulate not one but two definitions; or, in other words, to recognize the distinction which may have to be made between the meaning of "surplus" from the seller's, or owner's, point of view,[4] as against the viewpoint of the economy as a whole.

22. From the owner's point of view, a "surplus" at any given point of time is that portion of his stocks (i) which he wants to dispose of,[5]

(ii) which exceeds his own (subjective) idea of a reasonable level of stocks for sale but unsold; but which (iii) cannot be sold (or could not be sold, if offered) at the prices and on the conditions which he attempts to maintain.

23. From the viewpoint of the economy as a whole, stocks – by whomever and however held, whether for sale or not – are "surplus" if they do not fulfill an economic function (pipeline requirements; smoothing of the effects of supply/demand variations and insurance against risks resulting from these variations; strategic and other emergency reserves), or, more generally, if their existence and management do not help toward adjusting supply to demand, or vice versa, over time at a desirable level.

24. While the two definitions need not overlap either way, it will generally be found that the definition of "surplus" from the owner's point of view is the wider of the two. The case for segregating some "surplus" stocks into larger reserves held for stabilization purposes is an illustration, for instance, of stocks which may be "surplus" from the owner's point of view (in the sense that they cannot be sold at the prices which the owner wants to maintain) but not from the viewpoint of the economy as a whole.[6] On the other hand, if stock-holdings exceed those required for all purposes listed in para. 23, then they will be "surplus" both from the owner's point of view and from that of the economy as a whole. Conversely, it can be held that the marginal supply needed to meet the inflated demand for stocks at the peak of a speculative boom is a case of stocks which are not "surplus" from the owner's point of view but which the economy should try to do without by finding ways of lessening the incentives for such speculative dynamic stockholding operations.

25. The claim made for this dual definition is that it is consistent in logic. As can readily be seen, however, it is of little use as a yardstick against which supplies can be measured and the point of "surplus" neatly determined. Moreover, while the definition of "surplus" from the owner's point of view is at least fairly straightforward (though based on his own subjective values), the definition from the viewpoint of the economy as a whole cannot be applied without introducing some judgements of value, such as the determination of what constitutes a "desirable" level for balancing demand and supply, or the weighing of the economic or social benefits of support policies against their cost. This so-called definition cannot do more, therefore, than lay down, in very general terms, some of the main aspects which should be considered in a commonsense approach. Nor would it seem wise, or even possible, to seek for a definition which attempts to do much more than that. These limitations will have to be kept in mind, particularly in any endeavor to establish international standards, principles, and safeguards which should be observed in surplus disposal

programs. In establishing such principles and international machinery designed to ensure their observance, it will have to be concluded at the outset that the diagnosis of a "surplus" situation – just like the diagnosis of an "emergency" or "famine" situation – cannot be based on any rigid criteria but will have to be determined in each case in a careful and impartial approach, based on a number of commonsense criteria on the lines proposed in this paper.

[1] Webster.

[2] These points were made by the Delegate for Canada to Committee B of the Seventh Session of the FAO Conference. His statement concluded with the observation that, in the light of the above considerations and historical evidence in their support, Canada did not feel that it had a surplus problem which merited special disposal measures or international consideration at that time. It had no more than a third-party interest in any such special arrangements made by other countries.

[3] The definition used by the Conference in 1949 did not actually specify that the stocks which it described as "surplus" had to be offered for sale. It thus embraced all kinds of reserves; including strategic reserves, which could not, if offered, be sold on the conditions stated in the definition. But even if it is implied – as presumably its authors meant to imply – that the definition relates only to supplies available for purchase, it still ignores some of the important economic functions which can be performed by unsold stocks.

[4] The "owners" of the surpluses generally will be governments, but not necessarily so.

[5] Excluding reserves held for purposes other than disposal. Note, however, that under this definition stocks *not* offered for sale may also be "surplus" from the owner's point of view. The criterion is that they are stocks which he *wants* to sell, not stocks offered. On the other hand, the definition excludes stocks which may be held for the sole purpose of eventual disposal but which the owner does not *want* to sell *at the given point of time considered*; e.g., speculative stocks which are held in the hope of profiting from a change in the market.

[6] The case for large stabilization reserves has been well explained by Keynes who states: "It is an outstanding fault of the competitive system that there is no sufficient incentive to the individual enterprise to store surplus stocks of materials, so as to average, as far as possible, periods of high and low demand. The competitive system abhors the existence of stocks, with as strong a reflex as nature abhors a vacuum, because stocks yield a negative return in terms of themselves. It is ready without remorse to tear the structure of output to pieces, rather than admit them, and in an effort to rid itself of them. Its smooth and efficient working presumes in practice, as stringently as the static analysis presumes in theory, a steady rate, or steady growth, of effective demand. If demand fluctuates, a divergence immediately ensues between the general interest and the course of action in respect of stocks which is most advantageous for each competitive enterprise acting independently". From "The Policy of Government Storage of Foodstuffs and Raw Materials", *Economic Journal*, London, September 1938.

METHODS
OF SURPLUS DISPOSAL

26. The Conference, in its Resolution No. 14, quoted above, requested the CCP to consider

"The most suitable means of disposing of surpluses including proposals for setting up consultative machinery through which the disposal of agricultural surpluses can be facilitated."

27. When interpreted literally and in a rather narrow sense, this assignment relates to disposals of existing stocks which their owners cannot sell at the prices and on the conditions they want to maintain. It will soon be found, however, that in thinking about the most suitable methods of disposing of such stocks, some assumptions need to be made as to the underlying factors which caused their accumulation. If the surplus stocks are symptoms of continuing maladjustments, then clearly any attempt at a once-for-all solution – such as, for instance, the segregation of stocks in a special reserve – will not go anywhere near the root of the problem. Instead, it is necessary to determine to what extent and for what reasons the market is out of gear and how its basic equilibrium can best be restored. Thus, the question of "How to dispose of surpluses?" inevitably merges into a much wider question which must be posed from the viewpoint of the economy as a whole, namely; "What causes surpluses and how can they be avoided?" Put in this wider form, the question of how to deal with surpluses is, in fact, a challenge to search for the most suitable criteria and methods for programing the selective expansion of production, trade, and consumption of agricultural commodities; which again must be looked at as part of economic programing generally.

28. The Seventh Session of the Conference, in its consideration of "Policies in Regard to Food and Agriculture", gave considerable attention to these wider aspects and set down some main lines for consultations and action on agricultural programing over the next two years.[1] Some of the outstanding Conference findings and recommendations under these headings will be referred to later in this paper. They will not, however, form

part of the main subject-matter here presented. For, while the need for perspective must be constantly kept in mind, it is not possible to attempt to solve all the world's problems at one go. In the following notes, therefore, a modest beginning will be made by merely sorting out and describing, with the aid of illustrative examples, some of the main types of action which can be taken (and have been taken or, in some cases, are being taken) for disposing of stocks which are "surplus" from the owner's point of view. This description will in itself go some way in showing the scope and limitations of such methods and their effects on the various interested parties (sellers, producers, consumers, taxpayers, competitors). It will then be followed, in a later part of this study, by some observations on the principles and safeguards which may need to be observed, in international transactions, in the interests of importers and competing exporters.

ANALYSIS OF POSSIBLE METHODS OF DISPOSAL

29. In the following table (pp. 20-27), an attempt has been made to list the rather baffling variety of possible ways of dealing with surplus stocks under the following three main headings:

I. Holding or Segregation of Surplus Stocks
II. Measures Designed to Expand Markets
III. Restricting New Supply

The valid objection against the groups and sub-groups shown in the table is that any such classification of methods tends to lead to overlapping and over-simplications. It is clear, for instance, that no absolute distinction can be made between methods designed to raise consumers' purchasing power as against those attempting to promote sales through special price concessions; for, strictly speaking, the second category forms part of the first. Notwithstanding the obvious need for caution, however, an attempt will be made in the course of this review to demonstrate some practical advantages of thinking in terms of such admittedly imperfect groupings.

30. In selecting the particular headings and sub-headings shown in the table, the definition of "surplus" from the owners' point of view has been taken as a starting point. Thus, the main question posed for the purpose of classification was this:

What can owners do with supplies which (i) they want to dispose of; (ii) which exceed their own (subjective) idea of a reasonable ratio of stocks on sale but unsold; but which (iii) cannot be sold at the prices and on the terms which the owners attempt to maintain?

Holding or Segregation of Stocks

31. In essence, the owners who find themselves in this difficult position can do one or more of the following things. First, they can persist, at least for the time being, in adhering to the prices and terms which they want to maintain – in which case they may have to go on holding the stocks in the hope of a change in the market in their favor (I/1: *Support Holdings*). If, however, no such market change is in sight and if at the same time they are obliged to go on adding to their stocks at prices higher than those at which they can sell, the strain may reach breaking point. Where the breaking point will lie will be determined by the scale of financial resources and storage facilities at their disposal and also by the output responses of producers to the higher prices at which the holders of stocks may have to go on adding to their supplies.

32. Under another variant of "Holding or Segregation of Surplus Stocks", the owners can change their ideas as to what constitutes a reasonable ratio of stocks unsold but on sale. Such a change of attitude can take the form of declaring that stocks previously regarded as "surplus" should be held as a special reserve against the risk of possible future supply/demand variations (1/3 *Stabilization Storage*). The principle of "stabilization storage" differs from that of mere "support holdings" both in purpose and in modes of operation; "stabilization storage" calls for the smoothing of both peaks and troughs, as against "support holdings" which merely call for a floor, (though in practice national programs started for the declared purpose of stabilization have often concerned themselves almost exclusively with the operation of floors).

33. While views on national and international buffer stock operations may differ,[2] there is much more widespread agreement on the need for "stabilizing" reserves in a more general sense; i.e., for ample public stockholdings which are managed in a stabilizing direction, though not necessarily by prescribed modes of operation.[3] If such ample stocks are to be maintained at all times, it is in periods of plentiful supply that they must be built up. At the same time the immediate practical effect of such a strengthening of stabilization policies in a situation of supported surplus stockholding may not be large. It may, in fact, merely mean a change in dedication of a share of the stocks which, even in the absence of such new policies, would not have been offered freely in the market without some lower price limits.

34. Under other variants, stocks previously regarded as "surplus" can be withdrawn from the market and segregated in special reserves against *strategic risks* (I/3/b) or against other *emergencies* (I/3/c). Here

Table 1. Possible Methods of Surplus Disposal

METHODS	NATIONAL ACTION	EXAMPLES OF BILATERAL OR INTERNATIONAL ACTION
I. Holding or Segregation of Surplus Stocks		
I/1 *Support Holdings*		
Stocks held for sale to all comers, but at prices and on conditions which may impede their absorption.	*U.S.A.*; part of stocks presently held by CCC.	
I/2 *Stocks Held for Gradual Disposal*	*Cuba*; sugar, 1952: 1,750 million tons held for gradual disposal over 5 years to U.S. market.	*Joint Organization*; (U.K. and Dominion Wool Disposals Ltd.) gradual disposal of wool from stocks accumulated during wartime; 1946-50.
I/3 *Segregation of Stocks for Purposes of:*		
(a) *Stabilization Storage*	*Japan*; rice, 1927-35.	
(i) Central storage for "ever-normal granary"; i.e., evening out of fluctuations due to harvest variations or, more generally, for price stabilization.	*U.S.A.*; for wheat and cotton under Federal Farm Board, 1929-32; and later, under 1938 legislation.	
(ii) Through special inducements for private storage.	*Canada*; wheat pools in the 'thirties.	
	France; 1929, wheat: special subsidies to private traders for spreading sales (measures taken to reduce supply fluctuations: stocks not strictly surplus).	
(iii) Through regulations for maximum stocks at ports.	*Brazil*; coffee, since 1931: fixing of maximum stocks at ports on	

(b) *Strategic Reserves*

supplies.

U.S.A.; rubber, hard fibers, late 1940s onward.
U.K.; rubber.
U.S.A.; part-purpose of special "insulation reserve" under new farm program proposed by the President.

(c) *Emergency Reserves*

U.S.A.; part purpose of new special reserve, see (b) above.

International *Emergency Food Reserve* (proposal for international ownership or administration-held stocks for emergency famine relief; considered by FAO in 1951-53 but rejected; cf. C53/19)

I / 4 *Destruction of Stocks*

Brazil; coffee, 1931-44.

II. Measures Designed to Expand Markets

II / A *Without Concessions on Prices and Terms of Sale*

II / A / 1 *At Given Consumer Incomes*

(a) *Education or Publicity Campaigns*

U.S.A.; for protective foods; cotton.
France for rice from Indochina in the 'thirties;
Some *European exporting countries* for sugar in the interwar period.

International *Tea* Marketing Expansion Board; Pan-American *Coffee* Bureau; International *Wool* Secretariat.

continue: **Table 1. Possible Methods of Surplus Disposal**

METHODS	NATIONAL ACTION	EXAMPLES OF BILATERAL OR INTERNATIONAL ACTION
(b) *Development of New Uses*	*Australia, U.S.A.*: bread enriched with skim-milk powder. *Japan*; "man-made" or synthetic rice from wheat flour and sweet potato starch; *Philippines*; reconstituted milk prepared from skim-milk powder and fat.	International *Rubber* Development Board (foam, roads).
(c) *Compulsory Uses*	Maximum grain extraction rates; compulsory admixture of home grains.	
(d) *Discouragement (or Restriction) of Uses of Competing Products*	Taxing competing products; import restrictions on competing products. Discrimination by other means (e.g., coloring of margarine).	
(e) *Reduction of Distribution Margins*	Measures designed to increase marketing efficiency; lowering of marketing margins by decree.	
(f) *Disposals under Agreement*		
II / A / 2 Raising Purchasing Power		
(a) *General Purchasing Power*		
(i) Full employment policies	X	ECOSOC, etc.
(ii) Development programs	Investment programs, Point IV.	IBRD, FAO
(iii) Credits	X	X

(b) *Raising Importers' External Purchasing Power*			
(i) Loans		X	IMF
(ii) Liberalization of exporters' import policies		X	GATT, OEEC
II/B *Sales on Special Terms to Specified Market Sectors*			
II/B/1 *For Concessional Prices*			
(a) *Specified Consumer Groups*			
(i) *Children and Other Vulnerable Groups*	*School Feeding. U.S.A. National School Lunch Act of 1946; U.K., 1943; Egypt, 1942; Italy, Ceylon. Maternity and Child Welfare Centers. U.K., Italy, Australia, Ceylon.*		UNICEF School Feeding Programs; mainly dried skim-milk. UNICEF
(ii) *Low Income Groups*	*Children's Homes, Orphanages, etc. Direct distribution. U.S.A. since 1936 continuously with greatest intensity in 1939-41; most agric. commodities included, but since end of war until recently almost exclusively dairy products, fruit and vegetables; Italy.* *Conditional right to free purchase through commercial channels. Stamp plans in U.S.A.* *Low-Cost Feeding. Public Dining-rooms in Brazil and Venezuela. Industrial canteens in India.*		UNICEF UNICEF UNRWA Arab Refugee Relief

continue: Table 1. **Possible Methods of Surplus Disposal**

METHODS	NATIONAL ACTION	EXAMPLES OF BILATERAL OR INTERNATIONAL ACTION
(b) *For Specified (generally inferior) Uses*		
(i) Reinforced by making commodities unfit for human consumption	*Germany, Netherlands, U.S.A., France,* de-naturing of grains for feed.	
(ii) Compulsory quotas combined with subsidies.	Prewar: *Germany,* potatoes and rye for industrial alcohol. *France,* wine for alcohol. *Italy,* sugar for alcohol, maceration for confectionery.	
(iii) Subsidized new uses	*U.S.A.,* citrus, dried fruit, (e.g. prune juice manufacturing), cotton (for insulating material) prewar.	
(c) *To All Foreign Markets*		
(i) Export Subsidies, direct to traders or through centralized foreign marketing at a loss.	Prewar (in the 'thirties): *Germany, Canada, France,* (1938/39) wheat; *Poland and Danubian countries,* grains; *Indochina,* rice. Postwar: *U.S.A.,* cottonseed oil, dried fruits and wheat sales outsides IWA, recently. *Canada,* canned pork, 1954. *Argentina,* wheat and linseed oil recently. *Argentina and Australia* in the 'thirties, to stimulate agricultural exports, mainly wheat, Argen-	
(ii) As part purpose of exchange depreciation or multiple exchange rates		

tina mainly through multiple exchange rates; *Brazil*, cotton, through special adjustment of exchange regulations in 1953; *Greece*, partly to stimulate exports of tobacco and dried fruit in 1953.

(d) *To Specified Areas*
(e) *To Areas in Need of Relief*

U.S.A.: Emergency Relief to Friendly Nations, Law No. 216, 1953.

Under special bilateral contracts
UNRRA
UNKRA

II / B / 2 *Disposals Without Price Concessions but on Special Terms*

(a) *Sales Against Importers' Currencies*

U.S.A.: Sales under Section 550 of MSA (possibly combined with use of counterpart funds for development - II/A/2/ii).

(b) *Barter Deals*

ICCH Proposals

Brazil, surplus rice sold to Indonesia in exchange for American buses, 1951/52. Deals involving payment or part-payment in kind (e.g., part-payment in kind under contracts for the construction of U.S. military bases).

(c) *Financing of Commodity Purchase by Grants or Loans (Tied Loans)*

U.S.A.: Some credits under ERP, MSA, Exim-Bank, etc.

III. Aiding Surplus Disposals by Restriction or Discouragement of New Supply

III / 1 *Output Restriction*

Restriction of output by quotas under international commodity continue: Table 1. **Possible Methods of Surplus Disposal**

| | | EXAMPLES OF |
METHODS	NATIONAL ACTION	BILATERAL OR INTERNATIONAL ACTION
(a) Acreage Restriction (or Prohibition of New Plantings)	U.S.A.: grains, cotton, tobacco, under first AAA, 1934-36, re-enacted in modified form in the second AAA, 1938; wheat 1938-42, 1950; wheat, cotton, tobacco, 1954. Switzerland, tobacco in the 'twenties. Canada, tobacco, prewar and in 1949, 1950 and 1952. Pakistan, cotton, jute, 1953. Egypt, cotton 1953. Brazil, São Paulo, coffee, 1902-1911.	agreements (attempted for wheat in 1933 and used for sugar, tea and rubber in the 'thirties). Rubber and tea, under international agreements.
(b) Destruction in Growth or Unharvested Crops	U.S.A., cotton, 1933; potatoes and oranges at times. Cuba, sugar cane, a number of times.	

III / 2 By Disincentives

| (a) Taxation or Lower Support Prices | Brazil, coffee, 1931-36, by special taxes. U.S.A., linseed, 1953. Brazil, cotton and sisal, 1953 by reduction of price supports. | |

(b) *Discouragement of Production by Marketing Quotas*	*U.S.A.*: cotton, Bankhead Act; *Canada*, wheat.	Restriction of exports by quotas under international commodity agreements. *Sugar*, under International Sugar Agreement; *Rubber*, International Rubber Regulation 1934-38. *India, Ceylon, Indonesia*, under International *Tea* Agreement in the 'thirties.
III/3 *Output Variation by Other Means*	High quality plucking of tea (India 1952); in livestock production by variation in fattening or slaughter; prohibition of irrigation of vineyards (*France* and *Algeria* in the 'thirties). *U.S.A.*, variations in minimum grades permitted for marketing of certain vegetables and dried and citrus fruit.	*Sugar*, control of factory output.

again, however, the scope for any such measures will be limited by available finance and by future supply prospects. If production continues to exceed consumption, the segregation of stocks for whatever purpose will not provide an enduring solution for stemming the tide of surplus supplies. Moreover, the creation of such special reserves, whether for purposes of stabilization, security, welfare schemes or emergency relief, will not bring forth any real change in the market situation, not even temporarily, if the newly created reserves merely represent a shift of stocks previously held for similar purposes under other auspices or under another name. If, on the other hand, stocks are withdrawn from the market without, in fact, constituting special reserves for purposes which would have otherwise been left uncovered, such withdrawals will represent little more than the sterilization of stocks. From the viewpoint of the interests of the economy as a whole, there is less difference than might appear at first sight between the waste of resources entailed in the creation and holding of "sterilized" stocks on the one hand and the waste entailed in their destruction on the other (I/4). The destruction of coffee stocks in Brazil in the interwar period has done more perhaps than any other symptom of economic maladjustment to rouse the public imagination and to set people thinking on ways of overcoming the paradox of poverty in the midst of plenty. It is not always realized, however, that there may be other forms of economic waste which, though being less conspicuous, can be even more serious and far-reaching. The loss of goods and services resulting from a slight drop in employment in major industrial countries, would, in one year, exceed by far the cumulative loss caused by deliberate peacetime destruction of stocks at any time since the beginning of the century. Similarly, the accumulation of stocks in "sterilized" reserves can represent a greater loss to the economy than, say, the destruction of agricultural produce in process of growth; for, in the latter case, it may at least be possible to divert some of the freed productive resources to other uses and to avoid the cost entailed in the indefinite holding of excess stock.

35. To sum up: liberal and wisely managed governmental stock-holdings are important, or even essential, elements of a balanced economy. The segregation of surplus stocks into new reserves for special purposes otherwise left uncovered may help, on certain conditions, in relieving the immediate pressure of supplies. The mere segregation of stocks cannot provide an enduring solution in those surplus situations which have no reversal of the supply and consumption trends in sight. It may be of help, however, as a transitional measure facilitating adjustment.

Possible Methods of Expanding Consumption

36. In the circumstances, if supply continues to outrun demand and if the owners of surplus supplies continue to adhere to their policies of price maintenance for all or part of their potential market, attention will have to be centered on special methods designed to expand markets. These methods have been listed in the Table of Methods under two main sub-headings; Group II/A lists the measures which attempt to expand markets by measures other than concessions on prices and sales. Group II/B deals with examples of sales on concessional prices or special terms to some market sectors, while maintaining higher prices or more stringent terms in other sectors.

37. As was pointed out earlier, such groupings are bound to be arbitrary to some extent. There are two practical reasons, however, why this particular grouping was adopted. *First*, offers of sales on concessional terms to specified market sectors (whether specified in terms of particular consumer groups, particular uses, or particular areas) generally require special safeguards in the interests of competing sellers. Methods designed to expand consumption on regular terms may not call for such safeguards, unless releases from stocks are made in exceptional volume or at an exceptionally rapid rate. The grouping thus runs parallel with the main distinction made by the Conference in its formulation of principles and safeguards to which it asked the Working Party to give further attention.[4] Taking the definition of "surplus" from the seller's point of view again as a starting point, the examination proceeds by dropping, one by one, the conditions which ideally a seller would like to maintain. Thus, owners of surplus stocks will first want to look around – in their own interest and not only out of consideration for competing sellers – for all possible ways by which they can expand their sales at the prices and on the conditions which they would like to adhere to for the market as a whole. In doing so, however, they will soon come up against the *second* main reason for distinguishing between the two groups; namely that, with few exceptions, the methods available for expanding sales on regular terms are less likely to produce rapid results in a serious surplus situation than are methods operating through special concessions.

AIDING SURPLUS DISPOSALS AT GIVEN PRICES AND PURCHASING POWER

38. First, there are a number of measures which can be taken without either lowering prices or raising purchasing power (II/A/1). These comprise endeavors to increase consumption by means of education or publicity campaigns; the development of new uses; measures for

increased marketing efficiency and lower distribution margins; compulsory admixtures; or the discouragement of uses of competing products by means of taxation, import restriction, or various forms of discrimination. Consumer education, research into new uses, and steps to improve marketing, may have some considerable influence on consumption levels in the long run. They are not likely however to produce any quick effects in clearing surpluses. A stronger immediate impact may be made by compulsory uses or by the discouragement of consumption of competing goods; except that such measures, to the extent that they are effective, may merely shift the problem of disposal to those other commodities whose consumption is adversely affected by them. A vast number of examples could be cited of repercussions in other countries which resulted from the imposition or tightening of trade restrictions in such circumstances.

MAINTAINING OR RAISING PURCHASING POWER

39. Next, there is the fundamental category of measures designed to maintain or raise consumers' purchasing power (II/A/2). The paramount importance of full employment policies and development programs has often been stressed and need not here be repeated. Such policies clearly provide more fundamental solutions than any others to the problem of inadequate market outlets. Measures designed to avoid the impact of a cyclical decline in employment and purchasing power are of particular importance when the danger of an impending recession threatens to aggravate problems of surplus disposal. Development programs and other long-term measures for raising consumers' purchasing power are obviously fundamental for creating the conditions of healthy and expanding economies without which no satisfactory basic solution to international marketing problems can be found. Development programs are not likely, however, to generate sufficiently rapid increases in purchasing power to assist materially in immediate solutions of surplus disposal problems through the ready absorption of large additional supplies of foodstuffs and other agricultural products *on regular terms*. They are thus the example *par excellence* of the difficulties experienced in relying for rapid results on the methods available in the first of the two main groups.

RELATION OF SURPLUS DISPOSALS TO DEVELOPMENT PROGRAMS

40. Because of this dilemma between the seller's desire for immediate additional outlets for surplus disposals on the one hand, and the fundamental need for longer-term measures in the interest of development on the other, special interest attaches nowadays to all those measures which

attempt to bridge the gap; i.e. measures trying to promote immediate disposals of foodstuffs on special terms and conditions which in themselves will help to promote development as well. Such arrangements can take the form of contributions in kind to development programs (such as, for instance, contributions in wheat made to the Colombo Plan) or some forms of sales under Section 550 of the U.S. Mutual Security Act which, on certain conditions, provides for the possibility of using importers' payments for the financing of development programs in the importing countries. Such arrangements, it is often argued, are twice blessed; by moving surplus supplies into immediate consumption and by contributing at the same time to the creation of stronger and wider markets in the future. Thus, so the argument runs, the provision of "capital through food", while from the "surplus" seller's point of view it is tantamount to a gift or to a long-term credit on highly favorable terms to the borrower and with no immediate returns to the lender, will eventually yield good dividends through the aid it brings to development. While the idea is no doubt attractive, and deserves close consideration, the blessing requires some qualifications.

41. In defining these qualifications, a distinction must first be made between (i) all forms of contributions in kind (whether offered free or on special terms) which replace commercial imports by the receiving countries, and (ii) offers on special terms, on the understanding that the goods will be used solely for additional consumption in the receiving countries. In the first case, the contributions in kind will be an almost unqualified blessing from the receiving country's point of view. By freeing funds which would otherwise have been spent on imports for current consumption, the contributions in kind, like any other forms of gifts or development credits, will enable the receiving country to devote more of its resources to investment. A slight qualification of the blessing from the receiving country's point of view will have to be made only insofar as a merely temporary windfall of free or highly favorable imports may delay the basic adjustment of its economy to world market conditions. The main qualification, however, will come from competing exporters of the same or similar commodities, whose interests will obviously be affected.

42. In the second case, if consumption is truly "additional" to what it would have been in the absence of the special offer, the interests of competing sellers (whether exporters or home producers) will not be harmed. This will only hold true, however, if the term "additional" is defined in a sufficiently wide sense. If, for instance, free wheat imports lead to additional consumption of wheat in the receiving country but at the same time cause a drop in the consumption of rice or other foods, the interests of the sellers of other foods will be affected, either through a reduction of the country's total food imports (which affects sellers of food abroad) or

through a reduction in the consumption of home-produced foods. If, on the other hand, the additional consumption of imported wheat does not lead to any reduction in the consumption of either wheat from other sources or of rice or other foods, then the first blessing will come largely true. Additional wheat will have been moved into consumption without any competing sellers of the same or similar products having been harmed in the process. Meanwhile, however, the second blessing may have got lost on the way. For if the consumption of wheat is truly additional, it means that no funds will have been shifted from current consumption to investment. The sum total of the country's purchasing power will have been increased by an amount exactly equal to the additional consumption, except for the additional net gain to investment through the extra strength and well-being of workers who have had more to eat than before.

43. While a clear understanding of such qualifications may be essential for getting the facts straight, it is at least equally important to point out that some major advantages still remain. While additional consumption may not in itself help to provide extra resources for development, (except through building up strength), it will be no mean advantage in itself if poorly fed people are given additions to their diets; particularly where the strain of development projects proceeding apace may already have necessitated a serious tightening of belts to squeeze the required investment resources out of the country's meager current income. In order to ensure that consumption is truly "additional", the government of the recipient country will have to take simultaneous action, however, for subsidizing those other competing goods which would yield lower earnings than before, either because they would be consumed in lesser amounts, or because their prices in the market would fall. Thus, to make the transaction self-balancing, the government would have to use its internal net receipts from the sale of extra wheat for subsidizing the consumption of competing products.

44. There is one way in which, in the case of "additional" consumption the second blessing of "aid to new development" can be restored. There may be a contribution to the expansion or acceleration of development programs, if *concurrently* with the sale of the wheat, unemployed workers or under-employed farm people are put to work on internal development projects (dams, roads, or irrigation canals, for example) which require little or no foreign capital. Internal credit will be issued by the government to pay the wages of these new workers; most of their new expenditures will go for food; and wheat or bread may constitute a large part of their purchases. (If the surplus foods represent a wide selection of food - butter, cheese, some meat, as well as wheat, in good proportion to food habits of the workers in the country concerned - and possibly textiles also - nearly the entire

increase in worker's food expenditures may be balanced by the sale of the surplus food and textiles.) A large part of the public expenditures for labor and domestic materials on the new development projects will be offset by the current sales of foodstuffs (and other surplus products) imported at no current cost to the government; total food consumption will have been increased; and the increased domestic expenditures on development will have been made with little or no internal inflationary effect.

45. The crucial condition set forth in the preceding paragraph is that the additional wage expenditures on development direct and indirect are made concurrently with the domestic sale of the surplus products, and in proper balance between the two. If the sale of surplus products at one period were offset by the freezing of the resulting (counterpart) funds for expenditure for new development projects at a later period, the result would not be attained. The sale of the surplus products, with no corresponding current action to expand consumers' incomes, would divert expenditures from other products and so compete with domestic or imported foodstuffs; while the expenditures of the counterpart funds at a later period, with no current addition to the supplies of consumers' goods available for consumption, would then tend to create domestic inflationary pressures. While some slight improvement might be attained in better physical condition of the people, and ability to work, the other economic difficulties would be so great that only negligible progress would have been made toward expansion of food consumption, disposition of surpluses, or more rapid economic development.

46. Even in the case of partial displacement of competing imports (i.e. the first of the two main cases here considered) when weighing the advantages of additional resources of "capital through food" against the disadvantages for competing sellers, it may be that the balance will come out in favor of using such capital; since in the long run all interested parties, including the competing exporters, will benefit from the increase of purchasing power in the recipient countries.[5] Moreover, the technique of financing development through "food-capital" will make it possible for the government of the recipient country to syphon off resources which it could not easily have obtained in any other way. In practice, the consumers of wheat in any one country are much the same people as the taxpayers. If the government uses the net receipts from the sale of wheat for additional development; and if at the same time the consumers' total current purchasing power remains unchanged (since the effect of the extra development financed by the transaction will take some time to work itself out), the consumers will not be better off than before; but the government will have been able to divert internal resources (by means of consumers' payments for wheat) which otherwise could only have been obtained by additional

taxation; i.e. by lowering further the current living standards of the people who both consume wheat and pay taxes.[6]

47. To sum up: while the gradual rise of living standards resulting from economic development may not in itself provide major scope for immediate outlets for surplus disposal on regular terms, except on certain conditions, special attention should be given to those forms of surplus disposal on special terms which, by making use of the local currency proceeds from surplus sales for development purposes, may enable a country to expand or accelerate its development program and may thus help at least in some measures in providing stronger and wider markets in the future.[7] Such arrangements for special disposals of surplus commodities in aid of development, while they may need special safeguards in the interests of third parties, are nonetheless among the more hopeful alternatives of surplus disposal which may be of benefit to all interested parties in the long run.

EXTERNAL PURCHASING POWER

48. The comments so far have been concerned primarily with the relation of surplus disposal to means of raising *general* purchasing power, without considering more specifically whether such added purchasing power will be internal only or also external; i.e. whether or not it will help to strengthen the importers' foreign exchange resources. Yet, in considering ways of disposing of internationally traded agricultural staples which are in abundant supply in hard-currency exporting areas, special interest obviously attaches to means of raising the importers' *external* purchasing power. This aspect of surplus disposals was the one that particularly engaged the attention of the FAO group of experts who, in 1949, came forward with proposals for an International Commodity Clearing House (ICCH).[8] In 1948 and 1949, except for a brief recession round mid-1949, levels of prosperity and economic activity had been generally (relatively) high and rising in most parts of the world; supplies of foodstuffs and other agricultural products available from non-dollar sources fell short of importers' requirements: but the absorption of abundant supplies of dollar commodities in the world market was stifled by the world dollar shortage. It was this situation which prompted the Council of FAO (in June 1949) to entrust the Director-General with the task of calling together a group of independent experts to propose measures for the re-activation of world trade in agricultural products. In essence, the resulting plan for an International Commodity Clearing House, proposed the financing, by contributions from participating governments, of long-term credits in agricultural products. Exporters were to be reimbursed from this central fund while importers' payments could be made to the fund in the currencies of the importing countries. It

was not quite clear, however, how the accumulating soft-currency balances were to be utilized and how, in the absence of any basic improvement in importers' dollar earnings, continuity of transaction could be assured once the hard-currency fund was exhausted. The Fifth Session of the FAO Conference in 1949 rejected the ICCH proposals and instead decided to establish the Committee on Commodity Problems which at that time was set up specifically for the purpose of considering "commodity surplus problems arising from balance-of-payments difficulties". A brief account of the Committee's activities in its early period will be given later in this paper.

SALES AGAINST IMPORTERS' CURRENCIES UNDER SECTION 550

49. Under recent U.S. legislation (Section 550 of the Mutual Security Act),[9] the idea of stimulating surplus disposals by offering sales against payment in importers' currencies has been put into practice on a bilateral basis.[10] Its purpose is to facilitate U.S. exports which had previously been assisted less directly, but on a much wider scale by economic aid programs and provisions for export payments to overcome dollar shortages.[11] The law provides that not less than $100 million and not more than $250 million of funds authorized under the Act, shall be used, directly or indirectly, to finance disposals of U.S. surplus agricultural commodities. It authorizes the President to enter into agreement with friendly countries for the sale of such surplus agricultural commodities under conditions negotiated by him with these countries and against payment in their currencies. In negotiating such agreements, special precautions are to be taken "to safeguard against the substitution or displacement of usual marketings of the United States or friendly countries" and "to assure to the maximum extent practicable that sales prices of such commodities are consistent with maximum world market prices of like commodities of similar quality". Assurances must also be obtained that the purchasing countries will not resell or transship to other countries or use for other than domestic consumption commodities purchased under the program without special approval by the President. "Appropriate emphasis" is to be given under the program to "underdeveloped and new market areas". Private trade channels are to be used to the maximum extent practicable.

50. The proceeds of such sales are to be used with particular regard to the following six purposes:

(1) for providing military assistance to countries or mutual defence organizations eligible to receive assistance under the Mutual Security Act;

(2) for purchase of goods and services in friendly countries;

(3) for loans, to increase production of goods and services; including strategic materials, needed in any country with which an agreement was negotiated, or in other friendly countries;

(4) for developing new markets on a mutually beneficial basis;

(5) for grants-in-aid to increase production for domestic needs in friendly countries; and

(6) for purchasing materials for U.S. stockpiles.

In carrying out these provisions, special precautions are to be taken to safeguard against the displacement of foreign exchange earnings which would otherwise accrue to the United States or any friendly nations.

51. Another bill (*S.2475*) providing for the sale of stocks held by Commodity Credit Corporation against importers' local currencies up to a ceiling of a further $500 million, was passed by the U.S. Senate in July 1953 and will come before the House of Representatives during the 84th Session of Congress. These funds are intended to be additional to those provided by other legislation.

52. The provisions of Section 550 represent a rather novel combination of several features which are important in special disposal programs. Some safeguards to competing exporters (sales of additional quantities only and at no less than approximate world price levels, with provisions against resale) are combined with some assurances given to importers in regard to the uses of counterpart funds. In defining six purposes for which importers' payments can be used, Section 550 goes further than the ICCH proposals had done, in grappling with the problem of how to use such accumulating soft-currency balances. It is doubtful, however, to what extent transactions financed from counterpart funds under (1), (2), and (6) of the six specified purposes will not merely replace dollar earnings that would have accrued to importers under Section 550 in the absence of these special arrangements. If, on the other hand, the payments made in importers' currencies are to be used for internal development purposes in the importing countries, then the qualifying comments set out in paras. 40-48 above will apply. As was explained there in some detail, it is possible on certain conditions for imports of surplus commodities on special terms to go into strictly "additional" consumption (i.e., without displacing any of the goods which would have been consumed in the absence of such imports), while aiding the recipient country's development at the same time. As was also stated above, however, such arrangements will not yield the desired results unless their relation to a country's development program is carefully planned and synchronized.

53. It may be of interest to trace in some more detail the distribution of the financial burden entailed in financing transactions under Section 550. The following example assumes a sale of 100,000 tons of wheat to country X, with the payment in country X's currency being used (a) for financing an internal development project in country X, or (b) for U.S. purchases of strategic goods from country X.

Step 1: The CCC sells 100,000 tons of wheat to country X under Section 550 at a price of $70, i.e., at a price "consistent with maximum world market prices of like commodities for similar quality". Assuming that the wheat had been previously acquired by the CCC at the then ruling loan support rate of $90, the difference between the CCC's buying and selling price will have to be financed by the U.S. taxpayer in the form of a loss of $2 million ($20 x 100,000) to be debited against CCC funds. At the same time, the CCC is reimbursed to the extent of $7 million (100,000 tons at sales price of $70 per ton) by funds authorized for such transactions under Section 550 of the Mutual Security Act. This transfer from CCC financing to MSA financing does not, however, make much difference from the viewpoint of the U.S. taxpayer who finances both CCC and MSA.

Step 2: Meanwhile, the Government of country X pays the equivalent of $7 million in its own currency to a U.S. Government account. At the same time, the Government of country X sells the wheat in its internal market at the same price as that paid by it to the U.S. Government. The consumers of wheat in country X thus finance the payment made by the Government of country X to the counterpart fund. (Alternatively, if the wheat is sold to country X at prices lower than those paid by the Government of country X to the U.S., the funds paid into the counterpart fund will have been financed party by the wheat consumers, and partly by the taxpayers of country X.)

Step 3 a: The counterpart funds are expended for a new development project in country X.
Net effect: The $9 million received by the wheat producer in the United States have been financed by the U.S. taxpayer: $2 million through CCC funds and $7 million through MSA funds. To what extent the release for development purposes of the receipts obtained from the internal sale of wheat in country X will actually constitute the financing of *new* development, will depend on conditions set out in paras. 40-48 above.

Step 3 b: The counterpart funds are used for a U.S. purchase of strategic goods from country X.

Net effect: If the U.S. purchase of strategic goods from country X would have been made even in the absence of the special deal under Section 550, then the net effect of the special transaction under Section 550 will be that country X has sold its strategic goods against wheat instead of having sold them against dollars with which it could have bought either wheat or other things in the U.S. At the same time, the U.S. taxpayer will have been partly compensated by the value of the strategic goods by the U.S. Government, since had this purchase not been financed by funds authorized under Section 550, it would have had to be financed by some other U.S. Government funds. Under this alternative, therefore, $7 million out of the $9 million paid to the U.S. producer of wheat would have been financed by the wheat consumers in country X and the remainder of $2 million would have been financed by the U.S. taxpayer in the form of CCC funds. Thus, by the transaction under Section 550, the producers of strategic goods in country X will have been reimbursed by the government of country X; and country X will have obtained wheat instead of the dollars it would have received in the absence of the special deal.

54. The Seventh Session of the Conference "noted with interest the consideration given by the U.S. Government to international safeguards in the formulation of Section 550, of the Mutual Security Act. The provisions of this Section, while constituting only one of the existing special disposal measures, were of interest not only because of their topical importance but also because of their general significance. It was noted, moreover, that the application of these standards had been sincerely followed in negotiations initiated so far. Nonetheless, the Conference was concerned about the international repercussions of this and similar programs, especially if their application were widened. It was concluded that the effects of such measures should be considered in an international forum".[12]

55. The CCP, in discussing these new measures by the U.S. Government in the Report of its XXIInd Session (November 1953) emphasized the following points:

"(a) It was appreciated that the United States, after greatly increasing its agricultural production to meet the large demands of the war and post-war years, was now facing difficult problems of adjustment which it was trying to resolve without undue harm to producers.

(b) The Committee welcomed the provisions of Section 550 which were intended to safeguard the interest of other exporting countries.

(c) Some delegates questioned whether the safeguards against market disruption were adequate even for the present limited program.

(d) The view was also expressed that European markets in particular would be unable to absorb large quantities without affecting other exporters.

(e) ·Uncertainty regarding the scope and operation of these and other surplus disposal measures might have harmful effects on the markets and agricultural economies of some countries and might lead to a reduction in output.

(f) Certain delegates also indicated that they felt some concern over future U.S. action in the field of agricultural commodities." [13]

The CCP concluded that "FAO's main object must always be to maintain agricultural production and efficiency at such a level as to meet in the most practical manner the world's nutritional requirements. Consequently, in view of the uneasiness about the adequacy of the safeguards, and the limited absorptive capacity of some markets, the Committee draws the attention of the Conference both to the general question of surplus disposal and the role which FAO would play in seeking and recommending solutions". [14]

56. Having introduced the review of sales against importers' currencies under Section 550 in para. 48 of this paper under the heading of methods designed to raise importers' external purchasing powers, it now remains to conclude that such sales will represent a net addition to the importers' resources of scarce currencies to the extent that the use of counterpart funds will not replace transactions which would have increased the importers' earnings in these currencies. In making such a determination, the length of the period over which the possibility of displacement is being considered will be important.

LIBERALIZATION OF EXPORTERS' IMPORT POLICIES

57. In concluding these comments on methods of aiding disposals through the improvement of importers' foreign exchange positions, mention must also be made of the important and direct improvement of exporters' sales prospects which can result, on certain conditions, from exporters' liberalization of their own import policies (II/A/2/b).

SALES AT CONCESSIONAL PRICES (TABLE OF METHODS, II/B/1).

58. The common characteristic of the various methods of market expansion described so far has been the assumption that the owners of stocks for disposal will not make any concessions in the prices which they want to

maintain for the market as a whole. On this assumption, a brief review was made in the preceding sections of possibilities of expanding sales (*a*) by means of education, development of new uses, or other measures designed to expand consumption at given levels of purchasing power, and (*b*) by means of raising purchasing power, general and external. Some of the measures considered under these headings also contained elements of the second main category of measures which must now be considered more systematically; namely the composite group of all those measures which are primarily designed to expand sales by means of lowering of prices in one or more specified market sectors, while maintaining prices in the other sector(s).

59. The market sectors to which sales at concessional prices are offered, can be defined in various ways; by groups of consumers (vulnerable groups and low income groups); by specified (generally inferior) uses, or by specified areas (export price concessions to all or some foreign markets). In all these cases, however defined, the following common characteristics apply.

(1) Sales are made at prices lower than those maintained in other market sectors (which, for short, will be called the "commercial sectors").

(2) The system will work only if ways can be found of keeping the "concessional price" market sector strictly separate from the commercial sector.

(3) Sales at concessional prices will increase sellers' earnings even if only part of these sales are additional to those which would have been made in the absence of these concessions, provided that the reduction in price per unit sold is more than outweighed by the increase in the volume of sales.

(4) Competing sellers, on the other hand, will want to have assurances that *all* sales at concessional prices will be additional to the sum-total of disposals which they can count on, in the absence of such concessions, in all sectors of the market.

(5) If the concessional selling prices are lower than those at which the commodities were acquired, (or if the commodities are given away free), finance must be provided from somewhere for meeting the sellers' loss.

(6) Given the levels of total supply and effective demand in the market as a whole, the expansion of sales at concessional prices in one market sector and the resulting reduction of the pressure of supplies available for sale in the other (commercial) sector may, on certain conditions, have the effect of strengthening prices in the commercial sector.[15]

60. So much for some of the common characteristics of all sales at concessional prices to specified market sectors, however defined. The differences between the various special disposal methods which are here lumped together under the one main heading of "Concessional Sales" are, of course, at least equally great. It is hardly possible to think of measures which differ more widely in humanitarian purpose, scale, effects, and modes of operation than say a local school lunch program, the distribution of food to Arab refugees, the diversion of de-natured wheat to the manufacture of industrial alcohol, a subsidy on all cotton sales to foreign markets or a special bilateral deal for the concessional sales of surplus rice. Yet it is important, in the interest of straight thinking and close analysis, to recognize this heterogeneous selection of special disposal measures as all belonging to the same species of "Sales at concessional prices and terms". It now remains to examine the various types of such measures a little more closely.

SPECIAL FEEDING PROGRAMS FOR CHILDREN AND OTHER VULNERABLE GROUPS

61. Special distribution and feeding programs can, if rightly designed, play a major part in improving the nutrition of children and other vulnerable groups. Such programs are worthy of special consideration on welfare grounds, quite apart from any opportunities which they may provide for channelling surplus supplies into consumption. Indeed, with very few exceptions, they have been undertaken by governments primarily for public health and social purposes.

62. The importance of improving the nutrition of vulnerable groups by special measures where necessary, has been often stressed and reaffirmed by FAO. Particular value is attached in these recommendations to programs of school feeding, and emphasis is laid on the responsibility of governments in initiating and developing such programs. [16]

63. Interest in school feeding on the part of governments has grown since the Second World War. Among the main contributory factors has been the development of temporary relief feeding programs which were carried out first by UNRRA and then by UNICEF and which stimulated interest in the continuation of these measures on a more permanent basis. FAO collaborated with UNICEF in the development of relief feeding programs. After the emergency period, special attention was given by the two organizations to programs which could be maintained without international assistance in the form of imported foods. [16]

64. School feeding and other supplementary distribution programs to vulnerable groups, particularly in areas where living standards are generally low, are often suggested as the best and obvious solution for large-scale surplus disposal. Estimates of the numbers of children who could, in principle, benefit from such schemes, are indeed impressive. The following table, for instance, shows available data for ten selected countries containing populations of considerable size, in which school feeding schemes have been introduced on a significant scale. The total number of children attending primary schools in these countries are about 49 million, of which over 8 million benefit from some form of feeding schemes, according to the latest available estimates. As to the possible contribution of school feeding schemes to the disposal of food surpluses, the following calculations may be illustrative. On the basis of 35 grams of skim-milk powder for each child on every school day, the children, who are presently covered by the existing schemes, can consume about 59,000 metric tons or about 25 percent of current world stocks of dried skim-milk. An increase of about 10 percent in the utilization of the capacity of the existing schemes may be considered feasible, without greatly expanding the existing machinery for distribution. Nearly another 6,000 tons could thus be absorbed. If the schemes were enlarged to cover say half of the children attending primary schools in the given countries, existing world stocks of dried skim-milk could be absorbed in about two years.

School Feeding Statistics in Selected Countries

Country	No. of children enrolled in primary schools	No. of children covered by feeding schemes (latest available estimates)
	(......... *In thousands* ....)	
Egypt	1 341	704
Colombia	762	55
Mexico	2 881	30
Brazil	4 133	64
Ceylon	1 105	600
India	17 394	—
Japan	11 191	6 000
Philippines	3 812	85
Italy	4 978	650
Yugoslavia	1 552	200
TOTAL	49 049	8 388

65. These impressive-looking estimates bear no close relation, however, to the practical possibilities of developing school feeding schemes and of using such schemes as channels for surplus disposals. The main limiting factors are these.

(1) Supplementary feeding schemes call for considerable administrative machinery and expenditure of government funds. In many countries, available resources in respect to both funds and qualified personnel are inadequate. Such resources as could be devoted to the expansion of facilities and training of workers are unlikely to be forthcoming unless there is an assurance of reasonable continuity in the provision of cheap food supplies.

(2) On the whole, governments prefer to rely, for developing supplementary feeding, on indigenous food supplies rather than imports, in the desire to ensure continuity of supplies. Moreover, from the nutritional standpoint the use of local foods in supplementary feeding has the advantage that a closer relation exists between programs and local food habits and resources.

(3) The foods which tend to be in surplus supply are not all suitable for use in supplementary feeding, either because they are not of high nutritional value or because their introduction into school meals may create difficulties. Of the foods now in surplus supply, the most suitable for use in supplementary feeding is dried skim-milk. Moreover, even when surplus supplies are offered free of charge or at nominal prices, the cost of transport and other ancillary services may be too high to make full use of such offers. In the case of dried skim-milk, for instance, such costs are a multiple of the price of 1 cent per lb. ex seaport, currently offered by the U.S. Government for UNICEF purchases.

66. Funds currently allocated by UNICEF for the purchase and shipment of surplus dried skim-milk and other foodstuffs for child-feeding programs in needy areas represent a minor share of the total budget devoted by UNICEF to its child welfare programs.

67. Of the various factors preventing the wider-scale utilization of surplus supplies of suitable foods at concessional prices for feeding programs, probably the most fundamental, within given financial resources, is the hesitation experienced in relying on sources and conditions of supply which may not provide sufficient assurances for the continuity of these programs. Child feeding schemes are part of general welfare and development programs and they cannot easily be switched on and off, depending on extraneous circumstances. On the other hand, while the importance of some reasonable degree of continuity must be stressed, it

does not follow necessarily that offers of suitable food on favorable terms but without assurances of permanency cannot, on certain assumptions, be used with benefit for the maintenance, or even for the long-term development, of national feeding-programs. It may be, for instance, that the temporary availability of cheap imported supplies will not only help to tide over the period until other more permanent sources of supply have been developed, but can actually assist, or in a sense subsidize, the development of these sources. This may be the case, for instance, in some of the countries where UNICEF, in co-operation with FAO, is now developing internal facilities for the production, processing, and marketing of milk. Moreover, there are a number of countries where, for various reasons, the development of indigenous sources of supply may be less economical as a long-term solution than reliance on imports at reasonable, but not even necessarily concessional, prices. Thirdly, the stimulus given to a welfare feeding program in its early stages by the availability of supplies from abroad on exceptionally favorable terms may in some cases induce governments to maintain their programs, at least in part, once the exceptionally favorable market conditions have come to an end.

68. On the whole, therefore, while the essential welfare character of such programs, financial and other limitations, and the need for some reasonable continuity of sources of supply must always be kept in mind, it can be concluded that they provide important outlets for the utilization of surplus stocks of suitable commodities, offered on concessional terms and distributed under appropriate safeguards against the mere displacement of other foods and against the seeping-through into commercial channels.

69. As to the chance of making these safeguards effective, it can be concluded that school-feeding programs and other forms of distributing food through supervised centers to vulnerable groups probably offer better guarantees than most other forms of surplus food utilization for the channelling of food into *additional* human consumption.

70. Maternity and child welfare centers are at present being utilized in many countries as a means of providing small numbers of infants and small children as well as expectant and nursing mothers with supplies of nutritious foods such as milk and vitamins. Dried skim-milk has been frequently used for this purpose, especially with UNICEF supplies, but any rapid expansion of the numbers reached would be difficult for financial and other reasons. In under-developed countries, the amounts available for all aspects of their public health programs often are as low as 5 to 10 cents (U.S.) per caput.

SPECIAL DISTRIBUTION PROGRAMS FOR LOW-INCOME GROUPS

71. Much of what has been said in regard to special distribution programs for vulnerable groups, also applies to the operation of such programs
for low-income groups. There are, however, some qualifications. First, the
scope for centralized supervised feeding arrangements is generally more
limited. Secondly, if food on special terms is distributed direct for household use, it is more difficult to ensure that its consumption will not merely
replace, rather than be additional to, the food purchases normally made by
the consumers concerned in commercial markets. It is generally recognized nowadays, not only that the adequate nutrition of children, and particularly the adequate provision of protective foods in their diets, is of key
importance for their physical and mental development, but also that the
direct provision of such foods through child-feeding centers probably is a
better way than any other for ensuring that the children actually get these
foods. The provision of additional purchasing power to the children's families would be a less effective means towards an end about the special
merits of which there can be little doubt. On the other hand, when it
comes to the distribution of food or other goods in kind to low-income
groups, the benefit is to be seen primarily in the "tied" additional purchasing power which these goods represent, rather than in any assurance that
the low-income groups will derive any special intrinsic nutritional benefits
from consuming them. In the circumstance, the low-income adult beneficiaries may not only be inclined to barter the form of purchasing power
represented by these foods for other forms, but they may actually resent
the workings of an economy which cannot succeed in providing them with
these extra increments in their purchasing power in money rather than
kind. It is probably largely for these reasons that the provision of extra
relief in kind to adult low-income groups has often been found in practice
to be neither very popular nor very satisfactory in its operation.

72. This does not mean to say, however, that there is no scope at all for
programs of special food distribution to low-income groups in periods other
than emergency. This would go much too far. Even at the risk of its imperfect
functioning or qualified welcome, the distribution of food to low-income
families at concessional prices or free of charge will be desirable, or even
essential, where needs are great. Distribution through canteens or dining
rooms for industrial workers could be developed, on certain conditions, under
such programs. Moreover, there are many groups in each country for whom
the government assumes the responsibility for feeding them and, in these
cases, the use of surplus foods can be easily controlled. Inmates of prisons,
juvenile institutions and similar groups are not always given satisfactory
diets. Even the diets of the armed forces in many under-developed coun-

tries can be improved if supplies of nutritious foods could be obtained free or at nominal cost.

73. International Agencies like UNRWA (Arab Refugees Relief) are responsible for feeding large groups of unfortunate people and these could be used to a greater extent for the effective use of some of the surplus foods, though even in such cases, it cannot always be avoided that some of the foods intended for the needy people leak into trade channels.

FOOD STAMP PLAN [17]

74. A rather ingenious way of overcoming some of the difficulties encountered in special distribution programs for low-income groups was introduced in the United States in 1939 in the form of the Food Stamp Plan, followed in 1940 by a Cotton Stamp Plan.

75. The Food Stamp Plan allowed special categories of people on relief or in need of assistance, to purchase through authorized channels specified quantities of stamps which entitled the holders to buy any kind of food from any retailers taking part in the scheme. For every $1 worth of these 'Category A' stamps, the buyer received *free* in addition 50 cents worth of 'Category B' stamps which he could use for purchases of foods designated "surplus". The weekly minimum of 'A' stamps to be bought by one person was fixed at approximately $1, an amount which was taken to represent the average weekly expenditure of poorer families on food. Retailers participating in the scheme accepted both 'A' and 'B' stamps as cash and received from the government directly, or through the wholesalers, their full value redeemed.

76. The purpose of the Plan was to raise farm income and at the same time to improve the standards of low-income consumers. It provided consumers with a reasonable degree of latitude in the selection of their foods while, at the same time, seeking to direct their purchases to those foods in which their diets were most deficient or of which the surplus was greatest. It was also argued in favor of the Plan that, in the long run, a program allowing consumers some degree of free choice is most likely to encourage increases in the production of those foods that they want and need most and to discourage production of commodities for which there are chronic surpluses.

77. For attaining the main objectives of the Plan it was essential that as much of the free-stamp subsidy as possible should represent a net increase over the participants' former expenditure on goods subsidized under the Plan. The Plan tried to bring about this net increase by making the issue of free stamps conditional on the purchase of a minimum amount of other stamps

which had to be paid for, and by giving larger quantities of free stamps with increased purchases of paid stamps. The U.S. Department of Agriculture estimated that in 1940, the net average increase in total food expenditures was about 75% of the value of the "free" stamps.

78. On the whole, the Food Stamp Plan, as operated in the United States, was thus fairly effective in overcoming some of the main drawbacks cited above in regard to special distribution systems for low-income families; namely the difficulties encountered in making purchases truly additional, in preventing the seeping-back of supplies into the commercial sector, and in avoiding some of the resented features of direct relief distributions without any scope for consumers' choice.

79. The scope for introducing such plans in less developed countries, or on an international scale, is limited, however, by the necessary pre-requisites of highly developed administrative machinery and commercial distribution channels as well as by the extra cost entailed in using such commercial channels as against direct relief distribution.

80. At the same time, more thought might be given to the adoption of some of the features of Two-Stamp Plans, or supplementary ration coupons, for relief distribution systems on an international scale. Such administrative machinery as exists for relief payments and centers could be enlisted more widely for these purposes. Careful thought would need to be given to the kinds of surplus commodities to be selected for distribution under such programs.

DIVERSION TO INFERIOR USES

81. Next, some attention must be given to a very different form of sales at concessional prices in a specified market sector; namely the diversion of food supplies to inferior uses, such as the use of high-grade wheat for feed, or the use of grains, potatoes, sugar, or wine for industrial alcohol. To meet the condition of keeping the "concessional market sector" separated from the commercial sector, various supplementary devices have been used, such as the de-naturing (artificial coloring or other forms of multilation) of grains or potatoes to make them unfit for human consumption; or the combination of subsidies with compulsory quotas for such inferior uses. Varied as the forms of such diversions have been, both in regard to the range of commodities diverted and the methods used for "policing" the diversions, the analysis of this category of concessional sales in a separated market sector is, in fact, a simple one. Almost by definition, the diversion of foodstuffs to inferior uses implies that productive resources (or the products

which these resources helped to create, i.e., the diverted foodstuffs), are being utilized for purposes which, in a better-balanced economy, could have been met by the utilization of less, or less valuable, resources. Such diversion thus represents the acknowledgment of the economy's defeat in getting full value out of its resources. It is a way out which cannot be classed anywhere much higher than about mid-way between optimum utilization on the one hand and destruction on the other.

82. Having said all this, it must also be noted, however, that once a serious surplus situation has developed, the possibility of diverting supplies to inferior uses may, on certain conditions, represent a partial way out, deserving careful consideration. After all, it might not be quite fair to blame the process of diversion itself for the maladjustment of resources which has already manifested itself in the accumulation of surplus stocks for which no more legitimate uses can be found. Against this, it might be argued that more legitimate, or superior, uses could perhaps be found if only the price for the market as a whole were lowered somewhat instead of the market being split into a "regular" and an "inferior use – concessional price" sector. This is the kind of argument, however, that can only be judged on the merits of the case.

83. In international transactions, the possibilities of "policing" inferior end-uses by means other than the physical mutilation of the goods (i.e., denaturing) are more limited generally than in domestic markets. On the other hand, there may be special facilities in certain cases for ensuring the "policing" in recipient countries (e.g., governmental monopolies for alcohol manufacture, as in France); and the chances of effective policing will also be increased if the governments or producing interests in the recipient countries are themselves anxious to protect domestic sellers' interests. To the extent that exporters cannot ensure that goods sold for inferior uses at concessional export prices (i.e., at less than the regular export prices charged for these goods) will be used exclusively for the stipulated purposes, these sales may merely displace some of their regular exports. To the extent that the "concessional price" exports *are* used for the stipulated inferior uses, they may, of course, interfere with the interests of sellers of those other lesser goods which normally go into such inferior uses, and they may thus merely transfer the surplus pressure from one commodity to another.

SUBSIDIZED NEW USES

84. The story is a little different for subsidized new uses. In essence, the argument to be applied in favor of subsidized new uses for strictly com-

mercial purposes is the same as that in favor of aiding an "infant-industry" by tariff protection. The infant should eventually grow up and become self-supporting or even a family earner. If, however, the infant remains in a state of arrested development for an indefinite period, then the subsidized new use will begin to look like being a more inferior use.

85. On the other hand, even the possibility of *continuing* subsidization of some new food uses now being developed may deserve serious consideration on nutritional and welfare grounds. The following are two examples of new food uses which might usefully be developed on a larger scale in the utilization of skim-milk powder.

(i) *Protein-enriched Bread*: bread is a cheap food but one that is incomplete in the nutritional sense. Spreading butter or vitamin-enriched margarine would only add fat and vitamins A and D. The addition of non-fat milk solids or skim-milk powder to bread makes an excellent combination. Since more bread is used by the low-income groups, whose diet is usually deficient in many essential nutrients, enrichment of bread with skim-milk powder is nutritionally a great advantage. Moreover, it is clear that protein-malnutrition is now the most serious nutrition problem in the under-developed areas. The addition of skim-milk powder to a staple food like bread would thus be a convenient means of getting high quality animal protein into the diets of the ill-fed masses. The practice of enriching bread with skim-milk powder is already well established in U.S.A. and in certain other countries. Recent investigations in Australia show that, provided skim-milk is suitably processed before drying, up to 6 percent of the powder can be added to the dough without altering the bread-making process significantly. It is estimated that, if all bread in Australia is enriched with 6 percent of the powder, 35,000 tons of skim-milk powder, which represents about four times their present production, would be required. Smaller amounts of ordinary skim-milk powder can be added even to indigenous breads, like the Indian *Chapatti*, without seriously affecting their normal appearance and taste but improving the nutrition quality considerably. Even if only 1 percent of skim-milk powder is added to the flour, as much as 70,000 metric tons, or about a third of the total stocks in U.S.A., can be utilized in India alone. The possibilities of this outlet are thus unlimited but there is the formidable problem of distributing the skim-milk powder except where the flour is made in big mills. One attractive feature of the outlet is, however, that the powder does not have to be reconstituted, and therefore even the notorious "roller process" powder can be used without difficulty.

(ii) *Reconstitution of Milk*: one of the main difficulties in popularizing reconstituted liquid skim-milk is its limited acceptability as a beverage. As often pointed out by those concerned with the practical operation of nutritional welfare schemes, a great preference is often shown for whole milk.

Thus the preparation of reconstituted whole milk by reintroducing fat in the skim-milk has received considerable attention in many places. For instance, a plan for producing reconstituted milk from skim-milk powder and deodorized coconut oil was started some years ago in Madras, India, to augment the city's milk supply by about 3,000 gallons, or about 11,000 liters, a day. Another example is the famous Bombay Milk Scheme which includes the production of the so-called "toned milk" from cheap imported skim-milk powder. The powder is dissolved in water (1 : 8) and the reconstituted skim-milk is mixed with an equal volume of buffalo milk so as to give "toned milk", containing about 3.5% fat and 9% non-fat solids, but costing only about half the price of whole milk. In the Philippines, it has been reported that over 50% of the milk consumed consists of milk prepared from imported skim-milk powder enriched with fat. Thus a very interesting possibility of utilizing at once two of the main surplus foods, namely skim-milk powder and butter, would be to recombine them into whole milk. For this purpose, it would be better to convert the butter into butter fat before export since the latter would not require refrigeration and, therefore, would be cheaper to pack, ship and store. This outlet is obviously of great potentialities but the process is not simple enough to be done on a domestic scale. It is feasible only on a community scale and needs a central plant for production as well as means for distribution of the liquid milk.

EXPORT SUBSIDIES

86. Sales at concessional prices for specified, and generally inferior, uses are of relatively small importance in international trade compared with the much more comprehensive differential-price practices which it now remains to consider; namely offers of surplus goods at concessional prices to all foreign markets (Table of Methods, category II/B/1/c). Such concessions may be made in various ways. They may be operated by means of export subsidies direct to traders or by centralized foreign marketing at a loss. These may be described as "two-price systems" or, on certain conditions, as "dumping". Both the prewar and postwar histories of trade in agricultural products provide a multitude of examples of such export sales at differential prices.

87. The objections which can be heard against such arrangements are well known and need not here be discussed at length. The most pointed of the objections generally come from competing sellers (whether competing exporters or home producers in the importing countries) who find their interests harmed. Objections are also made at times from the viewpoint of the economies of the subsidizing countries themselves, since it is argued that the artificial maintenance of high internal price levels, coupled with

export sales at subsidized prices, merely tends to prolong the basic maladjustments of which the need for such special export arrangements may be symptomatic.

88. The question is sometimes raised whether there are any legitimate grounds for competitors' objections to a two-price system even when it merely operates in such a way as to allow export prices to find their own levels and without any attempt to undercut competitors in foreign markets. In answering this point, one of the possible distinctions which can be made is between cases where subsidized export sales are coupled with internal output restrictions, as against those where production is allowed to respond freely to internal support prices. In the latter case, it is argued, the competing sellers' interests are harmed even though export prices are left free to find their own levels because the stimulation of output and curtailment of domestic consumption due to supported internal price levels lead to an accumulation of abundant supplies for export sales which tends to depress the prices ruling in foreign markets below what they would otherwise have been.

89. The General Agreement on Tariffs and Trade, in Article XVI on "Subsidies" states that "if any contracting party grants or maintains any subsidy, including any form of income or price support, which operates directly or indirectly to increase exports of any product from, or to reduce imports of any product into, its territory, it shall notify the CONTRACTING PARTIES of the extent and nature of the subsidization, of the estimated effect of the subsidization on the quantity of (exports and imports) of the affected product(s), and of the circumstances making the subsidization necessary. In any case in which it is determined that serious prejudice is caused or threatened by any such subsidization, the contracting party granting the subsidy shall, upon request, discuss with the other contracting party or parties concerned or with the CONTRACTING PARTIES, the possibility of limiting the subsidization".

90. The GATT provision follows that of Art. 25 of the Havana Charter. The Charter's other provisions on subsidies (Articles 26-28), though not formally adopted by GATT,[18] are also of some interest in the context of this paper, especially in regard to the special treatment which they provide for primary commodities.

91. Art. 26, para. 1 of the Havana Charter states that "no Member shall grant, directly or indirectly any subsidy on the export of any product, or establish or maintain any other system, which subsidy or system results in the sale of such product for export at a price lower than the comparable price charged for the like product to buyers in the domestic market, due

allowance being made for differences in the conditions and terms of sale, for differences in taxation, and for other differences affecting price comparability."

92. Under Article 27 ("Special Treatment of Primary Commodities"), exports of primary commodities at prices lower than those charged at home shall not be considered to involve a subsidy if the situation results from a system for the stabilization of domestic prices or producers' returns and if it is found that:

"(a) the system has also resulted, or is so designed as to result, in the sale of the commodity for export at a price higher than the comparable price charged for the like commodity to buyers in the domestic market; and

(b) the system is so operated, or is designed so to operate, either because of the effective regulation of production or otherwise, as not to stimulate exports unduly or otherwise seriously prejudice the interests of other Members. "

In its next four paragraphs, Article 27 is mainly concerned with defining the relation of rights and obligations in regard to subsidies for primary products to the procedures set forth in Chapter VI of the Charter ("Intergovernmental Commodity Agreements").

93. Under Article 28 ("Undertaking regarding Stimulation of Exports of Primary Commodities"), Member Governments are to refrain from applying export subsidies for primary commodities "in such a way as to have the effect of maintaining or acquiring for that Member more than an equitable share of world trade in that commodity". If, after notification of the Organization, and consultations with interested Members, no agreement is reached, the Organization is to determine "what constitutes an equitable share of world trade in the commodity concerned". The formulation of criteria which, under para. 4 of Article 28, is to be taken into account in making such a determination, are of considerable interest for that part of the CCP Working Party's terms of reference which requests it to consider the principles to be observed for ensuring "that the disposal of surpluses be made without harmful interference with normal patterns of production and trade". The criteria established in Art. 28 will therefore be considered in more detail in the next section of this paper which will deal with the principles to be observed by governments in formulating special disposal measures.

EXCHANGE DEPRECIATION

94. Exchange depreciation may be a powerful weapon for stimulating exports. Its effects are in some respects similar to export subsidies but differ from them greatly in that exchange depreciation constitutes a general measure which applies to the whole trade of a country, and not only to particular commodities or commodity groups. Exchange depreciation not only encourages exports but discourages imports and may thus create serious problems in international trade, if applied as a surplus-disposal method by a creditor country.[19] Multiple exchange rates, by limiting the scope of a given exchange rate to a sector of trade, render the effects of depreciations less general; but they give rise to other objections in view of their discriminatory nature, and the IMF authorized member countries to apply them only in exceptional circumstances.

CONCESSIONAL (OR FREE) DISPOSALS TO AREAS IN NEED OF RELIEF

95. The use of existing surplus stocks for providing free relief to countries threatened or stricken with famine or other emergency shortages is universally regarded as a highly commendable form of using such reserves. The Seventh Session of the FAO Conference, in its Resolution No. 21 on Emergency Famine relief, stated that it:

"*Notes* with warm approval and commends to the favorable attention of Member Nations the action of the United States Congress in authorizing the President to use for emergency famine relief up to $100 million of government-held stocks,[20]

"*Expresses* the view that if similar steps could be taken by other nations, a great contribution would be made towards meeting such immediate needs,

"*Recommends* that FAO should be prepared to assist in coordinating such actions."

96. A full account of the conclusions reached by two successive Working Parties set up to explore ways and means of establishing an international emergency famine reserve, is given in the FAO document C53/19. The FAO Conference, after considering at its Seventh Session the results of these enquiries which had been undertaken in response to a request made by its Sixth Session in 1951, was faced with some difference of opinion as to whether the creation of an international emergency food reserve or fund was necessary. It recognized, however, notwithstanding this difference of opinion, "that in any case a pre-requisite to the creation of such a reserve or fund would be evidence that Member Nations would be in a position to

provide the necessary stocks or money resources and that in the absence of such evidence it is impracticable to create an international reserve or fund as contemplated by the Sixth Session of the Conference, so long as this situation continues".[21]

Restricting New Supply

97. The Table of Methods of Surplus Disposal includes, as a third main category, the indirect aid which can be given to the disposal of existing stocks by the restriction of new supply. Such restrictions can take the form of direct *acreage controls* or *prohibitions of new plantings* (Table of Methods, III/I/a, b); of *disincentives* (III/2) through taxation, lower support prices, or limitations of outlets by means of national or international marketing quotas; and of various other forms of *output variation* (III/3) – such as selective harvesting (e.g., high-quality plucking of tea), changes in fattening and slaughter rates, or the variations of standards of minimum grades at which marketings are permitted.

98. A full discussion of the role of output restrictions in agricultural policies and of the varying effects that can be obtained by means of different forms of such restrictions is essential in any attempt to analyse possible methods of *avoiding* surpluses. Since, however, the CCP Working Party's terms of reference and the scope of the preparatory document have been confined primarily to the study of possible methods of *disposing* of existing surpluses, it does not seem necessary to consider here in any detail the various ways in which production can be curtailed or discouraged. The main points relevant in the context of this paper are of a more general nature and can be stated briefly. *First,* output restrictions, unless applied to a wide range of crops competing for the same resources, may merely shift rather than solve problems of agricultural surpluses. *Second,* in line with FAO's policies and objectives, preference should be given to measures which help to overcome marketing difficulties by means of raising efficiency and expanding consumption rather than by restricting supply. These general directives are not meant to imply, however, that it should be the unqualified policy of governments to encourage the expansion, or even maintenance, of output levels for all agricultural commodities at all times. Expansion at uneconomic costs, or to levels which are excessive in relation to long-term marketing prospects at fairly remunerative returns, may, in fact, entail a waste of resources which could be more profitably employed in other ways; though shifts of such resources may be limited, in any case in the short run, by the lack of their mobility and by lack of alternative profitable uses. *Third,* to return again to two of the elements of the definition of "surplus" which has been used throughout as a basis for the descriptions

of possible methods of surplus disposal presented in this paper: if owners hold stocks (i) which exceed the level they want to maintain for all purposes, but which (ii) cannot be channelled into consumption by any of the methods listed earlier, at the prices and on the terms which the owners are determined to maintain, then the only remaining way out will be the reduction of total supply for all purposes. There are only two ways in which this can be done: (1) the destruction (or sterilization) of stocks, or (2) the restriction of new supply. Of these, the first will not provide a solution if there are no signs of a reversal of the trend of production exceeding current consumption. Thus the downward adjustment of output, coupled where necessary with measures designed to lessen hardships caused to producers, may be the only way of dealing with persistent surplus stocks under conditions of a continuing decline of demand for these products. Such a persistent decline may be caused by growing effective competition from substitute products, by the development of cheaper (or protected) supplies from other sources, or by changes in consumers' habits and other conditions of demand. A true solution of a prolonged surplus will often require, in addition to output restriction, positive measures to provide or make more attractive alternative employment for the resources concerned. For countries highly specialized in the production of the surplus commodities, national action may not suffice and international assistance would then become necessary.

Choices Before Governments

99. Which of all the *possible* methods are *suitable* methods? The main conclusions to be drawn from this review are the following.

(1) There is no one group of methods that will be fully effective in disposing of surpluses, while at the same time meeting all conditions of non-interference with the interests of third parties. Almost by definition, any such movements of surpluses are likely to cause *some* interference with existing patterns of production and trade.

(2) In the circumstances, if solutions are to be found, they will have to represent a compromise between those interested in moving the goods and those whose interests may be harmed by such movements. To the extent that interests of more than one or two countries may be affected, measures should not be taken by unilateral or bilateral actions without prior intergovernmental consultations.

(3) Since no one method is likely to be fully satisfactory in moving surpluses, the best possible combination will have to be sought in each case by determining the special characteristics of the surplus situation

and the methods best suited for these characteristics. A sketchy review of some such relationships can be given as follows:

List A: **Relation of Characteristics of Surplus Situations to Special Disposal Methods***

Characteristics of Surplus Situation	Methods
Surplus likely to be temporary ..	Stabilization storage; compulsory uses or restrictions on competing uses; inferior uses; direct relief distribution; emergency and strategic reserves.
prolonged	Education and publicity; development of new uses; development programs; institutional supplementary feeding schemes; sterilization; restriction of new supply.
Response of demand to price changes:	
strong	Stabilization storage; export subsidies.
weak	Compulsory uses.
Demand affected by near substitutes	Restriction of competing products; publicity campaigns; subsidies.
Commodity price small share of retail price	Reduction of distribution margins; *direct* relief distribution.
Response of demand to income changes:	
strong	Full employment policies; development programs; general credits.
weak	Tied credits; direct distribution.
Exports largely from dollar area ...	Loans and investment from dollar area; sales against importers' currencies; liberalization of exporters' import policies.
Scope for influencing consumer habits:	
good	Education; development of new uses; feeding schemes for low-income groups or vulnerable groups.

Characteristics of Surplus Situation	Methods
poor	Compulsory uses.
Commodity has special qualities:	
nutritional	Education; feeding schemes; subsidized new uses; emergency relief.
strategic	Strategic reserves.
Third parties' interests important or vulnerable	Special safeguards needed for all methods for expanding sales on concessional terms.
Rapid results needed	In general, methods for sales on concessional terms likely to give more rapid results.
Long-term development of consumption standards and of markets	All methods which directly or indirectly help development.

---

* The list shows relationships between characteristics and methods, without, however, necessarily recommending these methods.

100. In further studies, an attempt will be made to relate possible combinations of methods to the special characteristics of surplus situations for five commodities – wheat, rice, linseed oil, soft oil, and dried skim-milk. Meanwhile, a more general and very sketchy survey is given in the following list of some of the commodity characteristics of which special account will have to be taken in the determination of methods for clearing surpluses.

List B: **Selected Characteristics of Commodities with Surplus Indications**

Characteristics	Commodities
Surplus likely to be:	
temporary	Rice, linseed oil.
prolonged	Wheat, soft edible oils, cotton.

Characteristics	Commodities
Response of demand to price changes:	
strong	Butter, cheese, meat; rice within certain price range.
medium	Wheat for feed, coarse grains; skim-milk.
weak	Wheat for human consumption; tobacco.
Demand affected by near substitutes	Butter, edible oils, cotton, wool, rubber.
Commodity price small share of retail price of finished products ..	Sugar, tobacco, cotton, wool, rubber.
Response of demand to income changes:	
strong	Butter, cheese, meat, edible oils, cotton, wool, rubber.
weak	Grains for medium or high-income groups; skim-milk, tobacco.
Surpluses largely in dollar area	Wheat, coarse grains, skim-milk, butter, cheese, sugar, dried fruit, tobacco, cotton.
Commodities with special qualities:	
nutritional	Skim-milk, fats, cheese, meat.
strategic	Grains, sugar, cotton, rubber, linseed oil.

101. The criteria shown in Lists A and B will not, of course, be the only ones determining choices before governments. The illustrations shown in the lists are inevitably based on some oversimplification. Nevertheless, the setting of the lists against each other may be of some help in determining the most suitable selection of methods in each case. The points are illustrated further in the accompanying tables.

Selected Characteristics of Specified Commodities

Characteristics of Commodities	Grains — Wheat for human consumption	Grains — Wheat for feed	Grains — Coarse grains	Grains — Rice	Oils — Linseed oil	Oils — Edible soft oils	Livestock — Skim-milk	Livestock — Butter	Livestock — Cheese	Livestock — Meat	Sugar	Dried fruit	Tobacco	Cotton	Wool	Rubber
Reponse of demand to price changes — strong								×	×	×						
Reponse of demand to price changes — medium							×									
Reponse of demand to price changes — weak	×												×			
Demand affected by near substitutes		×	×			×		×					×	×	×	×
Commodity price small share of retail price					×	×		×	×	×	×	×	×	×	×	×
Response of demand to income changes — strong						×		×	×	×	×			×	×	×
Response of demand to income changes — medium				×			×						×			
Response of demand to income changes — weak		×	×		×											
Surplus exportable supplies largely in dollar area	×	×	×			×	×							×		
Tendency to surplus likely to be — prolonged	×		×										×	×		
Tendency to surplus likely to be — temporary				×			×			×						
Commodity has special value — nutritional	×						×		×	×						
Commodity has special value — strategic	×	×	×	×	×									×	×	×

Possible Methods of Surplus Disposal → / ↓ Characteristics of Surplus Situation		Segregation of Stocks			on regu[...] at given consumer incomes				
		Emergency reserves	Strategic reserves	Stabilization storage	Education and publicity	Development of new uses	Compulsory uses	Restriction of competing products	Reduction of distrib. margins
Response of demand to price changes	strong			×					
	weak							×	
Demand affected by near substitutes					×	×			
Commodity price small share of retail price									×
Response of demand to income changes	strong			×					
	weak								
Surplus exportable supplies largely in dollar area									
Scope for influencing consumers' habits	good				× ×	×			
	poor						×		
Tendency to surplus likely to be	prolonged				×	×			×
	temporary	×	×	×			×	×	×
Commodity has special value	nutritional	×			×	×			
	strategic		×						
Situation requires strong safeguards for protecting sellers' interests		×	×	×	×	×	×		×
Rapid results needed			× ×	×					

urplus Situations to Methods of Disposal

	Methods of Expanding Consumption														Restricting New Supply	
	...erms				on concessional terms to specified market sectors											
	by raising purchasing power				to specified consumer groups				to specified uses		to specified areas					
					vulnerable		low-income									
Full employment policies	Development programs	Loans	Liberalization of exporters' import policies	Institutional	Direct distribution	Institutional	Direct distribution	Inferior uses	Subsidized new uses	Export subsidies	International relief	Sales against importers' currencies	Tied loans	Disincentives	Acreage restrictions
				×	×	×	×		×	×	×				
														×	×
									×						
				×	×	×	×				×				
× ×	× ×	×	× ×												
														×	×
×	× ×	×	× ×							×	×	× ×	×		
				×	×	×	×		× ×						
								×						×	×
×	×	×	×	×	×	×	×		×	×	×	×		× ×	×
×		×								×	×	×			
				×	×	×	×		×		×				
									×						
× ×	× ×	×	×	×		×					×			×	×
	×	×				×		×		×	×	×	×		×

[1] *Report of the Seventh Session of the Conference;* see particularly Resolution No. 6 on "Selective Expansion of Agricultural Production" (para. 61, page 26), and Resolution No. 7 on "Expanded Consumption of Agricultural Products" (para. 62, pages 27-28).

[2] The Randall Commission on U.S. Foreign Economic Policy recently expressed itself against the operation of buffer stocks by the United States.

[3] See para. 24 and footnote.

[4] See FAO Conference Resolution No. 14 *op. cit.* (para. 7), which differentiates between principles to be taken into account by Member Governments (i) in all surplus disposals, and (ii) in disposals on special terms. The implications are considered further in a later section of this study, "Notes on Principles and Safeguards".

[5] Except insofar as shifts caused by the displacement of home production by temporary imports on special terms may be out of line with the desiderata of long-term programing and the maintenance of incentives to the expansion of domestic agriculture.

[6] The net gain to poor consumers of the extra wheat will be modified, however, by the extent to which the taxes imposed for financing the additional development in the absence of the extra wheat supply would have been progressive.

[7] It may be noted that we are here primarily concerned with the effects of one particular form of *sales on concessional prices* (group II/B/1) rather than with the effects of economic development as such. Hence the need for special safeguards which, as was pointed out earlier (para. 37) arises particularly for group II/B; although, as was also stated earlier (para. 29), it is actually not possible to make a clear-cut distinction between "sales on concessional prices" as against other forms of raising purchasing power. The merging of these two categories becomes clearly apparent in the case of "tied loans", i.e., loans granted for specified commodity purchases. Such transactions, while they are obviously means of raising current purchasing power, can also be looked at as "sales on concessional terms". In fact, when following this thought through to its logical conclusion, we must say that *any* form of transferring current purchasing power from the "surplus" seller to the "surplus" buyer on favorable terms to the latter, is tantamount to a "sale on concessional terms". Yet, commonsense dictates that a distinction should be made in practice between general forms of financial aid, including aid for commodity purchases on the one hand, and sales on concessional terms on the other; though the former may well be more important in scale and effects than the latter.

[8] *Report on World Commodity Problems,* (C49/10), presented to the Fifth Session of the FAO Conference, November 1949.

[9] The Mutual Security Act of 1951, as amended by Public Law 118, 83rd Congress, 1st Session.

[10] Strictly speaking, offers of sales against payment in importers' currencies are not in themselves a method of "raising external purchasing power" (II/A/2) but rather a form of "sales on special terms" (II/B/2). In the Table of Methods, both Section 550 and the ICCH proposals have therefore been grouped under the latter heading. It seems convenient however for the purpose of argument, to discuss them here in connection with group II/A/2 to which, in any case, they are very closely related. (See also footnote to para. 48.)

[11] In 1953, funds for purchase of agricultural commodities were available under Sec. 541 of the MSA Act of 1953 and under certain overseas defence programs. Export payments continue to be possible under authority of Sec. 32 of the Agricultural Adjustment Act. Other provisions existed for the disposal abroad, under certain conditions, of agricultural commodities acquired under price support programs. Cf. *Report of CCP,* Twenty-Second Session (First Section), November 1953.

[12] FAO, *Report of the Seventh Session of the Conference,* paragraphs 85-92, "Surplus Disposal".

[13] *Report of the Twenty-Second Session (First Section), of the Committee on Commodity Problems,* II, 3: "Views Expressed by the Committee on Surplus Disposal", para. 34.

[14] CCP Report, *op. cit.,* para. 35.

[15] This was one of the features underlying the Food Stamp Plan in the United States. It is also one of the reasons why countries relying on commercial imports may be averse to arrangements made by their suppliers for sales at concessional prices to other areas.

[16] Cf. also FAO Nutritional Studies No. 10: "*School Feeding - Its Contribution to Child Nutrition*", November 1953.

[17] For detailed accounts, see:

The Food Stamp Plan: A study in law and economics, by Samuel Herman. Reprint: SMA-EAS-1, Jan 1942.

Chart Book - Distributions Programs, U.S.D.A. Surplus Marketing Administration SMA-EAS-2, Jan. 1, 1942.

Economic Analysis of the Food Stamp Plan, by N.L. Gold, F.V. Waugh, and A.C. Hoffman, U.S.D.A. Special Report, Oct. 1940.

[18] Members of GATT, under Art. XXIX, have agreed to observe the general principles of the Havana Charter's Chapter IV, of which Articles 26-28 form part.

[19] While the Articles of Agreement of the IMF recognize the need for a change in the foreign exchange rate of a country faced with a "fundamental" disequilibrium in her balance of payments, one of the main objectives of the Fund, expressed in Article I (iii), is to "avoid competitive depreciation". In the November 1952 issue of the IMF Staff Papers an article by Mr. Gardner and Dr. Tsiang discussed the various aspects of competitive depreciation and showed *inter alia* how an attempt to promote exports of a primary commodity by means of exchange depreciation can inflict serious injury on other exporting countries and force them to follow suit. The final result of this competitive depreciation may be a diminution of foreign exchange earnings for all exporters concerned.

[20] Authorization provided under U.S. Public Law No. 216, Aug. 1953, *Emergency Relief to Friendly Nations.* The authorization referred to by the Conference was due to expire after March 1954, but has since been extended for another year.

[21] Excerpt from Resolution No. 21 of the Seventh Session of the Conference.

SOME NOTES ON PRINCIPLES AND SAFEGUARDS

102. The FAO Conference, in Resolution No. 14 [1] requested the CCP to consider, in elaboration of the findings of the Conference:

"(ii) the principles which should be observed by Member Nations in order that the disposal of surpluses be made without harmful interference with normal patterns of production and international trade".

103. Earlier in the same Resolution, the Conference recommended for the attention of governments "the following principles to be taken into consideration in the disposal of agricultural surpluses, with full regard to the need for active steps to raise consumption levels.

"(i) That Member Governments which have excess stocks of agricultural products should dispose of such products in an orderly manner so as to avoid any undue pressure resulting in sharp falls of prices on world markets, particularly when prices of agricultural products are generally low;

"(ii) That where surpluses are disposed of under special terms, there should be an undertaking from both importing and exporting countries that such arrangements will be made without harmful interference with normal patterns of production and international trade".

104. The following notes do not attempt to formulate the principles which the CCP Working Party had been asked to consider. They are merely designed, for the convenience of the Working Party, to define some of the underlying concepts and to bring together some of the relevant conclusions from earlier sections of this paper and some of the findings reached in intergovernmental consultations on related matters under FAO's and other auspices.

"Normal Patterns of Production and Trade"

105. Both the formulation of principles adopted by the FAO Conference and the request for further CCP study and recommendations refer to the need of avoiding "harmful interference with normal patterns of production and international trade". Some understanding as to the interpretation of this key phrase will thus be an essential premise for the formulation of principles.

106. There is no way of arriving at a precise internationally applicable definition of "normal" patterns of production and trade. Any definition based solely on a historical base period would clearly not be adequate since it would not allow for the crucial fact that change itself is normal and that it is neither possible, nor desirable, to freeze the *status quo*. Moreover, to define any average of trade over a number of years as normal would not take account of the width of the range between lows and peaks which, for some commodities and countries, may well exceed, within a period of say five years, a range of several hundred percent. For the same reasons, no one year could be taken as a base. At first sight, it might appear that some approximate definition could be found by taking the very width of the range between peaks and troughs as a measure. In other words, trade could be defined as "abnormal" if its volume was considerably larger (smaller) than the maximum (minimum) over a stated number of years. This definition, it might be argued, would be fairly flexible, while at the same time guarding against any sudden major distortions of trade. But here again there is a rub. The historical peak figure presumably will relate to a country's trade in a year of prosperity or boom. The same figure, when applied as base for measuring trade in a slump, may be quite "abnormal". Thus, the concept of a range between peaks and troughs as historical base for defining "normal" trade might lead to incongruous results.

"Harmful Interference"

107. These reflections may suffice to show that a more flexible commonsense approach must be found for ascertaining any "harmful interference with normal patterns of production and international trade". The operative word, it would seem, is "harmful". For, clearly, the release of surplus stocks in any market will always, almost by definition, cause *some* interference with normal patterns of trade. On the other hand, a ruling as to whether or not such interference is "harmful" implies some judgement of values and weighing of interests; i.e. a combination of the kind of criteria comparable to those proposed for the determination of "equitable shares of trade" under Article 28 of the Havana Charter. It was there provided that in the case of Members' disagreement on the effect of a subsidy for trade in a

primary commodity the Organization should, in certain circumstances, be called upon to determine what constitutes a Member's "equitable share" of world trade in that commodity; and that, in making such a determination, account should be taken of "any factors which may have affected or may be affecting world trade in the commodity concerned", with particular regard to:

"*(a)* the Member country's share of world trade in the commodity during a representative period;

"*(b)* whether the Member country's share of world trade in the commodity is so small that the effect of the subsidy on such trade is likely to be of minor significance;

"*(c)* the degree of importance of the external trade in the commodity to the economy of the Member country granting, and to the economies of the Member countries materially affected by, the subsidy;

"*(d)* the existence of price stabilization systems....;

"*(e)* the desirability of facilitating the gradual expansion of production for export in those areas able to satisfy world market requirements of the commodity concerned in the most effective and economic manner, and therefore of limiting any subsidies or other measures which make that expansion difficult."

108. These criteria, when applied to the interpretation of the clause coined by the FAO Conference, in regard to "harmful interference", might read approximately as follows.

In determining whether or not export of a surplus commodity on special terms to a given region[2] causes any harmful interference with normal patterns of production and trade, account must be taken of special factors affecting international trade in the commodity concerned, with particular regard to:

(a) the "surplus" exporter's share in the region's imports of the commodity concerned during a representative base period;

(b) whether the "surplus" exporter's share in the region's imports of the commodity is so small that the effect of special terms on such trade is likely to be of minor significance;

(c) the degree of importance of trade in the commodity to the economy of the "surplus" exporter, to the importing region's economy, and to the economies of competing exporters of the commodity concerned and of closely related commodities;

(d) the character and extent of the concessions offered and their probable effect on (i) the region's total imports of the commodity concerned and

related commodities, and on (ii) the "surplus" exporter's share in the region's imports of the commodity concerned;

(e) the degree, if any, to which effects of the kind mentioned under *(d)* above are likely to interfere with the stability, or desirable expansion, of production of the commodity concerned and of closely related commodities (i) in the importing region, and (ii) in competing exporting countries.

DISPOSALS "IN ORDERLY MANNER"

109. The FAO Conference also recommended that all surplus disposals (not only disposals on concessional terms) should be made "in an orderly manner so as to avoid undue pressure resulting in sharp falls of prices on world markets, particularly when prices of agricultural products are generally low".

110. This recommendation was obviously based on the assumption that harmful interference can be caused not only by surplus disposals on concessional terms, but also by disposals in exceptional volume, or at an exceptionally rapid rate. The problem of determination is even a little more difficult, however, in the case of "exceptional volume" than in the case of "concessional terms". In the latter case there is no difficulty, generally speaking, in ascertaining that the terms *are* concessional and the problem is thus confined to determining whether or not these concessional terms cause "harmful interference with normal patterns of production and international trade". In the case of sales "in exceptional volume", on the other hand, it is necessary to determine both whether (i) the volume (or rate) of surplus disposals is, in fact, exceptional and (ii) whether this very fact of extra-large releases causes "harmful interference". A clear-cut definition of "exceptional volume" of stock releases for offer to foreign markets hinges on auxiliary definitions, such as "normal exports". Since the latter is ambiguous, the former will be, too. Thus, the determination of both (i) "exceptional volume" and (ii) "harmful interference caused by such volume" cannot be based on precise definitions but can only be made in each case with the aid of a series of commonsense criteria similar to those listed in paragraph 108.

111. In the case of sudden drastic changes in governmental sales policies such as the sudden abandonment of price support measures and large-scale releases of stocks on foreign markets, it will not be difficult in practice, however, to ascertain that the volume and rate of offerings are exceptional, whatever the specific criteria adopted for such a detemination. There

may be a case, in the interest of international cooperation, for governments agreeing not to undertake such exceptional large-scale releases of stocks by unilateral action without prior consultation with interested countries.[3]

SAFEGUARDS

112. Concepts such as "harmful interference" with "normal patterns" of trade attempt to define *principles* primarily with reference to the effects of actions. By another approach, *safeguards* can be defined in terms of certain *conditions* which must be observed to ensure the observation of agreed principles. Examples of such safeguards, in the interests of various parties concerned, are the following provisions of Section 550 of the U.S. Mutual Security Act:

(1) *Trade on special terms to be "additional"*
Special precautions are to be taken under Section 550 "to safeguard against the substitution or displacement of usual marketings of the United States or friendly countries".

(2) *Prices to be in line with world prices*
Precautions "to assure to the maximum extent practicable that sale prices of (surplus) commodities are consistent with world prices of like commodities of similar quality".

(3) *Assurances against resales or trans-shipments*
"Assurances must also be obtained that the purchasing countries will not resell or trans-ship to other countries, or use for other than domestic consumption, commodities purchased under the program without special approval by the President."

(4) *Foreign exchange earnings not to be displaced*
In making use of counterpart funds, special precautions are to be taken to safeguard against the displacement of foreign exchange earnings.

113. These four main points provide an interesting combination of the kind of safeguards which may need to be observed, in the interest of all parties concerned, in certain types of sales on concessional terms. As has been explained in some detail earlier, however, it may be difficult for the "surplus" seller to adhere to these terms in practice and to be successful at the same time in disposing of his goods. The larger the scale of desired disposals under such a program, the more difficult it will be to find additional outlets under the prescribed safeguards.[4] Moreover, the second of the four conditions quoted above would obviously not be applicable to special sales at lower than world prices, for which other forms of safeguards would have to be developed.

UNDERTAKINGS

114. If principles and safeguards of the kind here enumerated are to be adopted as international standards, corresponding undertakings will have to be given by governments. This will involve pledges to adhere to those standards, and to cooperate in the development and maintenance of international machinery which would provide a forum for complaints from any member(s) who considered their interests harmed through the lack of observation of these standards.

115. The importance of establishing international standards and of suitable machinery for assuring the observation of these standards was stressed by several speakers at the Seventh Session of the Conference, notably the Delegates for the Netherlands[5] and for New Zealand.[6] The speaker for the Netherlands proposed that a *convention* should be drawn up under which "governments on the one hand would agree not to dispose of surpluses unless under certain rules, whereas on the other hand, governments of countries in the shortage areas would undertake to accept these surpluses also under rules to be agreed upon in the agreement". To this end he proposed that a meeting be convened under CCP auspices to prepare for a drafting conference which could agree upon such a convention.

116. The delegate for New Zealand requested that undertakings should be made on the following lines.

(1) While the present chronic balance-of-payments difficulties of many countries persist, the "creditor" countries should not pursue national policies which artificially encourage an output of food and agricultural products in excess of domestic demand if the "cost of production" price of such is higher than the general price levels in the world market.

(2) If, pending adjustment of their national policies, high-cost production is maintained in "creditor" countries, they should undertake:

   (a) that any surpluses will not be introduced into world trade at prices below the cost of production where such action would harm the interests of other exporting countries;

   (b) that quantitative restrictions, tariff increase or other governmental measures will not be adopted in respect of imports.

(3) Exceptions to the above general rules may be permitted where production in excess of commercial demand is maintained solely for a transitional period to ensure employment of labor which would otherwise be displaced and which cannot be diverted quickly to other industries, or again to make food and agricultural products available without

charge to "under-developed" countries not having the financial resources to purchase their full requirements on the commercial terms prevailing in the world market (but with adequate safeguards to ensure that any existing trade with other suppliers is not prejudiced).

(4) The disposal of surpluses should be the subject of international consultation in FAO, or, failing that, the U.S.A., or any other country which may become similarly involved, should be required to consult those countries which would be directly affected by the introduction of the surpluses into international trade.

(5) In the disposal of the surpluses, priority should be given to supplies needed for bona fide relief purposes and for programs designed to raise living standards in under-developed areas of the word.

(6) Distribution of surpluses should be made according to allocations recommended by an international body fully representative of producing and consuming countries, preferably under the aegis of FAO.

(7) Allocations should be on the basis of need without regard to race, creed, nationality or political beliefs.

(8) Distribution should aim at promoting increased consumption of food and agricultural products; there should be properly coordinated research and educational programs to aid the introduction of new foods in areas where there are nutritional deficiencies.

INTERGOVERNMENTAL MACHINERY

117. The Seventh Session of the FAO Conference expressed the following view on machinery.

(1) *Consultative Machinery for Facilitating Disposals*: The Conference requested the CCP to consider "the most suitable means of disposing of surpluses, including proposals for setting up consultative machinery through which the disposal of agricultural surpluses can be facilitated".[7]

(2) *Forum for Considering Effects and Possible International Repercussions of Special Disposal Measures*: The Conference concluded that the effects of certain special disposal measures and their possible international repercussions should be considered in an international forum. The Conference noted that the necessary machinery for such consultations was readily available within FAO through the medium of the CCP which, on grounds of both past experience and current competence, was well equipped for dealing with these matters. It therefore concluded that progress could best be made by the CCP undertaking as speedily as possible a review and study of the questions involved to serve as a basis for the formulation of principles.[8]

CCP ACTIVITIES IN REGARD TO SURPLUS DISPOSAL

118. It will be of interest in this connection to recall briefly the activities and experiences of the CCP during the early period of its operations. The CCP was created by the Fifth Session of the FAO Conference in 1949. By the middle of that year the work of the International Emergency Food Committee[9] had virtually come to an end and the emergence of some surpluses, particularly in North America, prompted the Council of FAO to ask the Director-General in June 1949 to call together a group of experts with a view to solving problems of trade in agricultural products. The experts proposed the establishment of an International Commodity Clearing House, but their proposal was not found acceptable by governments. Instead, it was decided to establish the CCP as a Committee of the Conference, to "address its attention primarily to the food and agricultural surplus commodity situation arising from balance-of-payments difficulties". As outlined by the Fifth Session of the Conference, the functions of the Committee were to consider the needs of countries experiencing difficulties in securing supplies, to examine the proposals made by governments for the disposal of surplus supplies on special tems, having regard to the effect of such disposal on the interests of other countries, and to initiate international action where desirable.

119. In its first report to the FAO Council in May 1950 (CL 9/7), the Committee indicated that, as one line of approach, it had addressed direct enquiries to Member Governments as to their needs or surplus disposal proposals. Lists were received from the United States of surplus commodities, mainly in the category of supplementary foodstuffs, which were offered for sale at specific prices. The Committee, after satisfying itself that such surpluses, on the terms offered, were not likely to prejudice the interests of other exporting countries, attempted to facilitate their disposal by informing importing countries and by promoting direct negotiations between importing countries and the United States. Owing to the acute dollar shortage, few importing countries were interested in the offers, although the prices proposed were in some cases below ruling market prices.

120. As a second approach, the Committee initiated discussion with a view to promoting international action. Though there were no surpluses of basic commodities at that period, some surpluses of supplementary foods had arisen or were likely to arise. The Committee, however, concluded that price reductions would not offer a general solution because of the shortage of dollars facing most countries. The granting of credits by the supplying countries to be repaid later in goods appeared to offer possibilities. The Committee also drew attention to possibilities of developing special nutritional programs at nominal prices as a means of disposing of surpluses.

121. The FAO Council recommended that the work of the Committee be actively pursued and requested it to seek export possibilities at concessional prices, to determine areas where additional food supplies might be required at special prices or for specific purposes and generally to seek methods of achieving price stability and the disposal of surpluses through international machinery.

122. During the period up to the Tenth (October 1950) Session of the FAO Council, the Committee studied various forms of nutritional distribution schemes and drew the attention of all Member Governments to the possibilities of utilizing in such schemes certain of the surplus foods offered at special prices.

123. The Committee also continued to notify all Member Governments, and interested organizations, of the surpluses available, emphasizing the condition that such surpluses should not displace normal commercial transactions or be re-exported. The Committee had to report, however, that only a few of these offers which, for most part were made by the United States, had been taken up. This result was apparently due to doubts whether purchases of such surpluses even at very low prices were the best use of scarce dollars, to the possibility that the conditions recommended by the Committee might prove burdensome, to the uncertainty of a continuous supply of commodities at such prices, and to the inevitable delay in establishing administrative machinery for carrying out large-scale feeding programs. It should also be noted, however, that the period during which these surpluses were available was rather brief, the United States having withdrawn most of its special offers after the outbreak of hostilities in Korea. Until that time the Committee reiterated in its Reports to the Council that current surpluses had arisen mainly in North America and that hard currency shortages, which had their roots in the general lack of balance in world trade and payments, prevented importing countries from taking up the available surpluses.

CCP's WIDENED TERMS OF REFERENCE

124. The Committee's original terms of reference were considerably widened by the Special Session of the FAO Conference in 1950 which resolved that the Committee should be regarded as "the instrument of FAO to analyse and interpret the international commodity situation and advise the Council on suitable action", and that it "should address its attention to commodity problems falling within the competence of FAO to consider, whether arising from balance-of-payments difficulties or from other causes." [10]

125. In reviewing its activities in 1952 and 1953 in the course of its pre-Conference Session in November 1953, the Committee "stressed the current practical significance, in the light of certain commodity indications and policies, of its original terms of reference which still form the nucleus of the present version; namely its assignment as an intergovernmental body for the consideration of problems of surpluses of agricultural products, and of methods for dealing with them." [11]

[1] For full text of Resolution, see Part I, para. 7.

[2] The "given region" may be either "all foreign markets" or a particular area.

[3] It may be of interest to note in this connection that the Havana Charter, in Article 32, established specific safeguards to be observed in the liquidation of stocks, though only "non-commercial" stocks. See also GATT, Art. XX (General Exceptions), which provides, *inter alia*, that nothing in the Agreement shall be construed to prevent the adoption by any contracting party of measures "essential to the orderly liquidation of temporary surpluses of stocks owned or controlled by the government of that contracting party"; provided that such measures are not applied "in a manner which would constitute a means of arbitrary or unjustifiable discrimination between countries", and that they shall not be instituted "except after consultation with other interested contracting parties with a view to appropriate international action."

[4] Related comments in other parts of text: concerning *interpretation of the term* "additional" – see "Relation of Surplus Disposals to Development Programs", paras. 40-47, and "Sales under Section 550", paras. 49-55; concerning *world prices* – see "Export Subsidies", paras. 86-93; concerning *displacement of foreign exchange earnings* – see "Relation of Surplus Disposals to Development Programs", paras. 40-47; concerning *"Sales under Section 550"*, – see paras. 49-55.

[5] C 53/1/7: "Statement by H.E. Minister Mansholt concerning Surpluses of Agricultural Commodities."

[6] C 53/1/B/3: "Statements by New Zealand Delegate in Committe B of Commission I."

[7] Resolution No. 14.

[8] *Report of Seventh Session of FAO Conference*, p. 46.

[9] The International Emergency Food Committee was the descendant of the International Emergency Food Council which had been set up in 1946 to provide machinery for voluntary allocations of commodities in short supply. It was a body serviced by FAO but autonomous in its membership. Following the creation of the Council of FAO in 1947, the work of the International Emergency Food Council was merged with that of the FAO Council. The International Emergency Food Committee (again known as IEFC) was established as a Committee of the FAO Council to carry on the work of allocation.

[10] Terms of Reference of the FAO Committee on Commodity Problems. (CCP 53/24, Section IV, and Report of the Seventh Session of the Conference, Resolution No. 15).

[11] CCP Report of XXIInd Session (First Section), Nov. 1953, para. 38. The CCP Working Party on Disposal of Agricultural Surpluses in its Report, which will be considered by the Committee in June, concluded that the CCP could be materially assisted by the establishment of a Consultative Sub-Committee on Surplus Disposal, to meet normally in Washington at periodic intervals of generally a month's duration.

Annex A

REPORT OF THE WORKING PARTY ON SURPLUS DISPOSAL TO THE FAO COMMITTEE ON COMMODITY PROBLEMS[1]

Summary of Findings and Recommendations

Terms of Reference

1. The Working Party on Surplus Disposal was established by the FAO Committee on Commodity Problems (CCP), in pursuance of recommendations made by the Seventh Session of the FAO Conference, to consider the most suitable means of disposing of agricultural surpluses, including the setting up of consultative machinery, and the principles which should be observed by FAO Member Nations, in order that the disposal of surpluses be made without harmful interference with normal patterns of production and international trade. The Working Party reports its findings and recommendations to the CCP. Governments represented on the Working Party are not committed to the views expressed in its Report.

Means of Surplus Disposal – General Comment

2. Despite the difficulties of finding a generally acceptable and precise definition of the term "surplus", the Working Party concluded that even in cases where a government has not itself declared its stockholdings as being in surplus, it will generally be possible to appraise the surplus element involved in a given market situation by reference to some commonsense pointers.

3. Substantial increases have occurred during the past year in the commercial and government stocks of a number of important agricultural commodities. The bulk of the stock accumulations is in North America, and particularly in the United States. Most of the additional stocks expected in the current marketing year will also be in that region. At the same time, the problem is fairly widespread. Furthermore, the immediate prospects indicate that the problem of excess stocks for some important commodities is growing in magnitude, and the number of countries affected may, therefore, be increased.

4. In the longer run, the outlook for stock levels will depend in considerable measure on agricultural policies, especially in the United States. The basic long-term solution of the surplus problem is clearly to be found in higher levels of consumption through increased incomes, particularly in less developed areas, and in the increased demand that will result from the growth of population, together with adjustments of production through selective expansion and the adaptation of farm production to changing needs. The Working Party wishes to stress the outstanding general importance of economic policies designed to maintain, or raise, both internal and external purchasing power as a means of improving marketing prospects. Meanwhile, however, there is also a great need for specific action to dispose of existing excess supplies and to prevent the accumulation of new surpluses.

5. The need for special measures to dispose of surpluses must not be allowed to overshadow the possibilities of disposal through adjustments of prices for the market as a whole and of incentives to producers. At the same time, it must be recognized that the mechanism of free market prices may be an inadequate instrument for regulating supply and demand, particularly for agricultural commodities which, for a variety of reasons, are characterized by relatively weak responses of production and consumption to price changes. Serious hardship to all sections of the economy and social problems could be caused if farm incomes were left solely to the free play of market forces, but it remains to assess in each case on its merits whether governmental intervention does, in fact, help or hinder the equation of supply and demand at desirable levels, both short-term and long-term.

6. Keeping in mind that changes in the prices of primary products can influence the ultimate consumers' demand only to the extent that they are reflected in the retail prices of finished products, the Working Party suggests that governments and appropriate international agencies, under both regular and technical assistance programs, should continue to explore means of improving the marketing efficiency of primary products at all stages, with a view to lowering distribution and processing costs.

7. Special consideration must be given to the problems of the economies of less developed countries which depend largely on receipts from the export of a limited number of primary products.

8. Countries holding surplus stocks should refrain, as far as practicable, from imposing any restrictions on their customary imports of these commodities. Improvements of exporters' sales prospects can result, on certain conditions, from the liberalization of their own import policies. Full consideration should also be given to the liberalization of trade by importers of

agricultural products. Prospects of continuing availabilities of exportable supplies at attractive prices and the assurance that surpluses will be disposed of in an orderly manner will make it easier for governments to adjust their own production programs and trading policies.

Special Disposal Measures

9. The Working Party considered a number of types of special disposal schemes, including use in aid of development, sales against importers' currencies, use for welfare programs, and for emergency relief. It also considered segregation of stocks and production disincentives as possible aids to the solution of the surplus problem.

Sales on Concessional Terms, or Grants, in Aid of Development

10. The Working Party attached particular importance to the determination of suitable means for special disposals in aid of development. The standards of living of growing populations in large parts of the world are still miserably low. The economic development of these areas, including underdeveloped parts of more highly developed countries, should eventually lead to a larger flow of consumer goods and services. In order to achieve this goal, however, a painfully large share of these countries' meager current resources must be diverted to investment purposes. To the extent that the additional consumer demand generated by the process of development can be matched by supplies of foodstuffs and other essential agricultural products on concessional terms, or grants, development schemes can make an immediate contribution to the problem of disposing of the current surpluses with which the Working Party is concerned. To turn these possibilities into reality will, however, require careful planning and timing of surplus disposal measures in relation to the development activities which they are to assist.

11. The Working Party believes that carefully planned sales on concessional terms, or grants, in aid of development hold better prospects than any other form of special export disposal measures, for moving substantial amounts of surplus agricultural commodities into truly additional consumption. Governments and appropriate international agencies should therefore give special attention to the possibilities of taking advantage of surplus supplies which may be made available on special terms, for the expansion or acceleration of development programs.

12. Consideration should be given to the possibilities of using technical assistance facilities, in particular for helping countries in the solution of the difficult and important problems of internal organization involved in the utilization of commodities supplied for development purposes.

Sales Against Importers' Currencies, to be Used for Special Purposes

13. In reviewing possible ways of disposing of commodities which are in surplus in hard-currency exporting areas, consideration should also be given to arrangements for sale against importers' currencies to be used for special purposes. The outstanding current examples of arrangements primarily used for such purposes are transactions under Section 550 of the United States Mutual Security Act of 1951, as amended. These possibilities are, however, limited and are diminishing insofar as purchases for purposes of stockbuilding and de-rationing are concerned. On the whole, the Working Party concludes that any disposal of substantially larger amounts against importers' currencies would have to be where there is large scope for additional consumption, and on terms which would link the use of local currency receipts to development programs, primarily in under-developed countries.

Sales on Concessional Terms, or Grants, for Special Welfare Distribution Programs

14. Special feeding programs for children and other vulnerable groups are worthy of special attention on welfare grounds alone, quite apart from any opportunities which they may provide for channeling surplus food supplies into additional human consumption.

15. The scope for using surplus commodities supplied on special terms for such programs depends on the suitability of the foods in surplus supply, on the prospects for reasonable continuity and on financial, administrative, and other factors. Within these limitations, supplementary feeding schemes for vulnerable groups can provide important outlets for the utilization of surplus stocks, offered on concessional terms and distributed under appropriate safeguards against the mere displacement of other foods and against disturbances of domestic programs in the recipient countries and the seeping-through into commercial channels of commodities sold on special terms.

16. There is also scope for additional consumption of foodstuffs and fibers in raw or manufactured form distributed under special welfare programs to low-income and other specified consumer groups.

17. The Working Party therefore believes that governments as well as appropriate international agencies, in developing special welfare distribution programs, especially in those areas where consumption standards are generally low, should fully explore the possibilities of taking advantage of surplus supplies of food and other agricultural products which may be made available on concessional terms.

Sales on Concessional Terms, or Grants, for Emergency Relief

18. There may also be scope, though it will be unpredictable, for the use of surplus commodities in emergencies. In determining whether or not a country is faced with an emergency requiring international relief, it is necessary to consider not only the existing or threatening physical deficit in the country's food supplies, but also its ability to obtain food on commercial terms. While each case will undoubtedly be considered on its merits, the Working Party believes that in cases of extreme urgency, humanitarian principles will prevail over commercial considerations.

Holdings, or Segregation, of Stocks

19. While consideration should first be given to means of expanding consumption, the present supply position for some commodities is such that, even in the best of circumstances, accumulated stocks together with new supply cannot easily be absorbed over the next one or two marketing seasons. The Working Party concludes that firm holdings of excess stocks for gradual disposal over an extended period may be essential to avoid the disruption of international markets. Governments should also keep in mind the present opportunities for building up stocks for various special purposes. The mere segregation of stocks cannot provide a real solution to surplus problems, however, unless accompanied by other measures to bring supply and demand into balance.

Restriction, or Discouragement, of Production

20. In general, the Working Party believes that the adjustment of supply and demand should be sought in the expansion of consumption, especially through increased incomes, rather than in the reduction of production, and that such output reductions as are required in the light of existing supply levels and market prospects should be brought about, as far as practicable, through economic disincentives rather than through physical restrictions. In presenting this general conclusion, the Working Party also

recognizes, however, that the practicability and desirability of adjusting output through disincentives are limited by a number of factors. Insofar as physical restrictions have to be applied, governments should keep in mind the possible repercussion of such policies on the economies of other countries and on international markets generally.

21. The Working Party concluded that price support levels, originally established to stimulate production to meet essential requirements, have recently led to unbalanced agricultural output in relation to effective demand. While concluding that, in general, price supports should be brought more in line with the objectives of economic production and expanded consumption, the Working Party recognizes that the problem of the adjustment of price supports differs widely for different countries and commodities. Exporting countries that are heavily dependent on the export of agricultural commodities will find it more difficult to change their support policies than those exporting countries whose exports are more diversified or which have less need to promote their exports for reasons connected with their balance of payments or economic development. Among importing countries, similarly, those which are under the necessity to maintain or increase their farm production on grounds of balance of payments, economic development or social reasons, will find it more difficult to revise their support programs.

Principles

22. The Working Party gave careful consideration to the principles which should be observed by governments, in order that disposals of agricultural surpluses be made without harmful interference with normal patterns of production and international trade. It concluded that there is no way of arriving at a precise internationally applicable definition of "normal" patterns of production and trade and that a more flexible commonsense interpretation must be found. In developing a more detailed formulation of the criteria which, in its view, should be taken into account by governments in all disposal measures on concessional terms, the Working Party gave special consideration to the extent to which commodities supplied on concessional terms are likely to be absorbed by *additional* consumption. To the extent that sales of the commodities supplied on special terms may constitute some danger of displacement of commercial sales of the same or related commodities, the Working Party concluded that that danger will have to be assessed in the light of the benefits or possible harm to the economies of both exporting and importing countries. (See Section IV of the Working Party's Report.)[2]

23. Harmful interference with normal patterns of production and international trade can be caused not only by sales on concessional terms but also by the quantity of the commodity sold and the rate at which it is moved, seen in relation to other market characteristics. The Working Party recommends that governments undertaking, or proposing to undertake, large-scale releases should, whenever practicable, consult with other countries interested in the possible effects of such transactions.

24. In bilateral transactions involving special concessional terms, the intended beneficiary country should make every effort to prevent resale or trans-shipment to other countries, or the use for other than additional domestic consumption, of the commodities supplied to it on special terms or of the same or related commodities which might be freed for sale abroad as a result of the country's imports on special terms. The same principle should apply when more than two countries are involved.

Machinery for Intergovernmental Consultations

25. The Working Party attached particular importance to the need of avoiding the creation of any new machinery for consultations which can be carried out effectively through existing channels. It fully concurred with the conclusions stated by the Conference concerning the suitability of the CCP as an instrument for consultations on problems and measures of surplus disposal. It concluded that the CCP, in addressing its attention to surplus problems generally as part of its established terms of reference, should give special consideration to:

(*i*) assisting FAO Member Nations in developing suitable means of surplus disposal; and

(*ii*) promoting the observance of the principles recommended by the Conference and developed in this Report for the attention of FAO Member Nations, in order to avoid harmful interference with normal patterns of production and international trade, and reviewing proposed, or actual, policies, programs or transactions, in the light of these principles.

26. The Working Party concluded that the work of the CCP in accordance with the guiding lines and principles set out in this Report could be materially assisted by the establishment of a Consultative Sub-Committee on Surplus Disposal. The Working Party believes that, notwithstanding the establishment of the Sub-Committee, direct consultations between governments will continue to be desirable.

27. To enable the Sub-Committee to conduct its work efficiently and speedily, the Working Party recommends that, as far as practicable, all Member Nations should communicate to the Sub-Committee, at the earliest possible moment, all plans for the special disposal of surplus agricultural commodities through exports. The Working Party recognizes that governments would remain free as to whether or not they accept any conclusions reached by the Sub-Committee in its reviews of proposed or adopted measures. Therefore, the main value of the work of the Sub-Committee should be seen in the opportunity offered for the exchange of information and for consultations. The value and effectiveness of this consultative machinery will depend primarily on the co-operation given to it by FAO Member Nations, in respect to both the communication of information and the consideration of the Sub-Committee's conclusions.

28. The Working Party finds that the consideration of membership of the Sub-Committee, if established, should more appropriately be left to the CCP itself. At the same time, it wishes to state that in its view: (*i*) the membership of the Sub-Committee should be representative of geographical areas and of countries with different interests in commodity disposals and at different stages of development; and (*ii*) whatever the CCP decides about membership, any FAO Member Nation which believed itself particularly affected by any surplus disposal measures, should have the right to bring the matter to the attention of the Sub-Committee, as well as to the main Committee, and to participate in the discussions on that matter.

29. Meetings of the Sub-Committee should normally be held in Washington at periodic intervals of generally a month's duration, with additional meetings being called on an *ad hoc* basis, as required.

Comments on Specific Commodities

30. Comments in regard to specific commodities are presented in Section VI of this Report.[3]

---

[1] The CCP Working Party on Surplus Disposal met in Washington from 23 February-18 March 1954. It was composed of the following eight members:

Argentina	Netherlands
Egypt	New Zealand
France	United Kingdom
India	United States

The full text of the Working Party's Report has been issued as FAO Document CCP 54/2.

[2] FAO Document CCP 54/2.

[3] *cf* FAO Document CCP 54/2.

Annex B

"DISPOSAL OF AGRICULTURAL SURPLUSES" EXTRACT FROM THE REPORT OF THE 23rd SESSION OF THE FAO COMMITTEE ON COMMODITY PROBLEMS, ROME, 3-11 JUNE 1954 [1]

Disposal of Agricultural Surpluses

12. The Committee considered carefully the Report of the Working Party on Surplus Disposal (document CCP 54/2) and expressed its high appreciation of it. The Committee was particularly glad to note that the Working Party, notwithstanding the different interests of its members in regard to surpluses, was motivated by the over-riding importance of common aims and found it possible to agree on a series of unanimous conclusions and recommendations in regard to suitable methods of surplus disposal, including the setting up of consultative machinery, and in regard to the principles to be observed by governments in special disposal transactions, so as to avoid harmful interference with normal patterns of production and international trade. In the Committee's view, the Working Party's Report constitutes not only an important contribution to the clarification of thought on these difficult problems but also a valuable guide for practical action by governments and a new step forward in the inter-governmental co-ordination of national programs, policies, and transactions relating to agricultural surpluses.

13. The Committee agreed unanimously that the Working Party's Report represented a carefully balanced whole and that this balance should not be upset by any amendments to its text. Indeed, such suggestions as were made in the course of the Committee's debate for slight changes in emphasis in one or the other direction merely supported the Committee's conclusion that the Report, as it stood, represented the best obtainable compromise between the views held by the members of the Committee. The Committee therefore passed the following general Resolution.

RESOLUTION NO. 1(23)

The FAO Committee on Commodity Problems,

Having Noted with appreciation the Report of the Washington Working Party on Surplus Disposal (document CCP 54/2),

Commends the findings and recommendations of the Working Party on Surplus Disposal to the serious attention of the governments of FAO Member Nations,

Requests the Director-General to transmit to the governments of FAO Member Nations the Report of the Working Party on Surplus Disposal, together with the Committee's own views and recommendations as set out in its report.

14. Within the framework of its general agreement with the findings and recommendations of the Working Party's Report, the Committee wishes to refer specifically to the following aspects.

A. General Comment

15. Measures to dispose of surpluses already in existence will not solve the surplus problem unless parallel measures are taken to avoid the accumulation of new surpluses.

16. In general, the adjustment of supply and demand should be sought in the expansion of consumption, especially through increased incomes, rather than in the reduction of production.

17. Such output reductions as may appear unavoidable, in the light of existing supply levels and market prospects, should be brought about, as far as practicable, through economic disincentives rather than through physical restrictions.

18. Steps for improving the international co-ordination of national policies must form an integral part of any sound program of surplus prevention.

19. The adoption of special measures to dispose of surpluses must not be allowed to overshadow the importance of price adjustments, of policies of full employment and of economic development, of less restrictive trade policies and of the discouragement of uneconomic production, as basic means of dealing with the problem of surpluses.

20. Special consideration must be given to the economies of less developed countries which depend largely on receipts from the export of a limited number of primary products.

21. Consideration must also be given to balance of payments problems.

B. Special Disposal Measures

Sales on Concessional Terms, or Grants, in Aid of Development

22. In its review of possible methods of surplus disposal on concessional terms[2] the Committee attached particular importance to the determination of suitable means for special disposal in *aid of development* and therefore resolved as follows.

RESOLUTION NO. 2(23)

The FAO Committee on Commodity Problems

> *Believing* that carefully planned sales on concessional terms, or grants, in aid of development hold better prospects than any other form of special export disposal measures for moving substantial amounts of surplus agricultural commodities into truly *additional* consumption,

> *Recommends* that governments and appropriate international agencies should give special attention to the possibilities of taking advantage of surplus supplies which may be available on special terms, for the expansion or acceleration of development programs,

> *Further Recommends* that consideration should be given to the possibilities of using, where necessary, technical assistance facilities for helping countries in the solution of the difficult and important problems of internal organization involved in the utilization of commodities supplied on special terms for development purposes.

23. The Committee attached particular importance to the benefits which in its view could be derived from close co-operation on these questions with the International Bank for Reconstruction and Development. It therefore resolved as follows.

Resolution No.3 (23)

The FAO Committee on Commodity Problems

Having Noted the findings and recommendations made in paragraphs 71-79, and particularly in paragraph 74, of the Report of its Washington Working Party on Surplus Disposal (document CCP 54/2) on "Sales on Concessional Terms, or Grants, in Aid of Development",

Requests the Director-General to invite the President of the International Bank for Reconstruction and Development to further elaborate the views expressed by the Bank's observer to the Washington Working Party on Surplus Disposals on the ways in which disposals of surplus commodities could assist new development programs, and accelerate existing programs, taking into account the additional need for the imports of capital goods and local expenses and also recognizing the usefulness of additional imports of agricultural products in avoiding the inflationary tendencies that may be caused by development projects,

Requests the Director-General to invite the President of the International Bank to indicate to him, whenever possible, for the information of FAO Member Governments, such possibilities as there may exist, in the opinion of the International Bank, for utilizing agricultural surplus commodities in aid of development programs in under-developed areas.

24. The Committee suggested that FAO Member Governments should indicate to the CCP Consultative Sub-Committee on Surplus Disposal (see para. 33 below) their additional requirements, if any, for supplies of surplus commodities on special terms in aid of the expansion or acceleration of development programs in their own countries, setting out the relationship between the proposed receipts of surplus commodities and the projected development plans.

25. The Committee noted that the term "new development expenditure" as used in the Working Party's Report should be interpreted as relating to both the financing of new development projects and to the acceleration of existing projects.

Other Special Disposal Measures

26. On the whole the Committee concluded that any *disposal* of surplus in very large volume *against importers' currencies* would in most cases have

to be where there is large scope for additional consumption and on terms which would link the use of local currency receipts to development programs, primarily in less developed areas.

27. Based on the Working Party's findings in regard to *special welfare distribution programs* the Committee resolved as follows.

RESOLUTION NO. 4(23)

The FAO Committee on Commodity Problems

Believing that there is scope for additional consumption of foodstuffs and fibers in raw or manufactured form distributed under special welfare programs to low-income and other specified consumer groups,

Recommends that governments as well as appropriate international agencies, in developing special welfare distribution programs, especially in areas where consumption standards are generally low, should fully explore the possibilities of taking advantage of surplus supplies of food and other agricultural products which may be made available on a concessional, or grant, basis.

28. There may also be scope, though it will be unpredictable, for the use of surplus commodities for *emergency relief.*

29. While consideration should first be given to means of expanding consumption, *firm holdings, or segregation, of excess stocks* over an extended period may be essential to avoid the disruption of international markets.

C. Principles

30. Based on the Working Party's formulation of *principles*, the Committee resolved as follows.

RESOLUTION NO. 5(23)

The FAO Committee on Commodity Problems

Having Noted the following principles which the Seventh Session of the FAO Conference, in Resolution 14/53, recommended for the attention of FAO Member Nations, to be taken into consideration in the disposal of agricultural surpluses, with full regard to the need for active steps to raise consumption levels:

(*i*) That Member Governments which have excess stocks of agricultural products should dispose of such products in an orderly manner so as to avoid any undue pressure resulting in sharp falls of prices on world markets, particularly when prices of agricultural products are generally low;

(*ii*) That where surpluses are disposed of under special terms, there should be an undertaking from both importing and exporting countries that such arrangements will be made without harmful interference with normal patterns of production and international trade;

Having been instructed to give more detailed consideration to the principles formulated by the Seventh Session of the FAO Conference and to make recommendations in regard to the observance of these principles by FAO Member Nations in special surplus disposal measures,

Recommends that in determining whether or not sales on concessional terms or grants to a given region[3] cause any harmful interference with normal patterns of production and international trade and prices, account must be taken of special factors affecting trade in the commodity concerned, with particular regard to the following aspects:

(1) the extent to which commodities supplied on concessional terms are likely to be absorbed by additional consumption (i.e., consumption which would not have taken place in the absence of the transaction on special terms);

(2) to the extent that sales of the commodities supplied on special terms may constitute some danger of displacement of commercial sales of identical or related commodities, that danger will have to be assessed in the light of relevant factors, particularly the following:

(*a*) the exporter's share in the region's imports of the commodity concerned during a representative base period, due allowance being made for factors which lessen the significance of such historical comparisons;

(*b*) whether the exports on special terms are likely to form so small (or large) a share of the region's imports of the commodity[4] that the effect of special terms on such trade is likely to be of minor (or major) significance;

(*c*) the degree of importance of trade in the commodity to the economy of the exporter concerned, to the economies of competing exporters of the commodity concerned and of closely related commodities, and to the importing region's economy;

(*d*) the character and extent of the concessions offered and their probable effect on (*i*) the region's usual total imports of the commodity concerned and related commodities, (*ii*) the exporters' share in the region's imports of the commodity concerned and (*iii*) the interference with implementation of treaties or agreements which deal with world trade in these commodities;

(*e*) the degree to which commercial market prices are, or are likely to be, affected in the importing region and in world trade;

(*f*) the degree, if any, to which effects of the kind mentioned under (*d*) and (*e*) above are likely to affect the stability, or desirable expansion, of production and trade of the commodity concerned and of closely related commodities in both exporting and importing countries;

Further recommends that in weighing the advantages to countries benefiting from special disposal measures against the possible harm done to other countries, account must be taken of the relationship of possible sacrifices to the economic capacity of the countries concerned, and in particular to the effects of such sacrifices on their rates of development,

Draws the attention of FAO Member Governments to a number of special aspects which are set out in paragraphs 123-128 of the Report of the Working Party on Surplus Disposal, and which should be taken into account in applying the general principles stated in this Resolution to the review of some of the most important types of transactions on concessional terms.

31. The Committee noted, in line with the Working Party's conclusions, that harmful interference with normal patterns of production and international trade can be caused not only by sales on concessional terms but also by the quantity of the commodity sold, and the rate at which it is moved, seen in relation to other market characteristics. It endorses the Working Party's recommendation that governments undertaking, or proposing to undertake, such large-scale releases, should, whenever practicable, consult with other countries interested in the possible effects of such transactions.

32. The Committee noted that the term "related commodities", as used in the formulation of principles by the Working Party and adopted in this Report, will need to be interpreted on the merits of each case, with special reference to established trade patterns of the countries concerned.

D. Establishment of CCP Consultative Sub-Committee on Surplus Disposal

33. The Committee agreed with the Working Party's conclusion that the establishment of a *CCP Consultative Sub-Committee on Surplus Disposal*

could be of material assistance in carrying out the Committee's responsibilities in the field of surplus disposal. The Committee, therefore, decided to establish such a Consultative Sub-Committee, to convene in Washington not later than the end of July 1954.

34. The Committee agreed that the *membership* of the Sub-Committee should be open to all FAO Member Nations who wished to contribute actively, and on a regular basis, to the carrying out of the Sub-Committee's mandate. Other FAO Member Nations could attend the meetings of the Sub-Committee as observers, and should have the right to participate fully in the Sub-Committee's discussions on any subject in which they are particularly interested. Any FAO Member Nation should also have the right to bring to the attention of the Sub-Committee any subject under the Sub-Committee's terms of reference.

35. The Committee requests the Director-General to ask FAO Member Nations to inform him within four weeks from the date of his letter whether or not they wish to serve as members of the Sub-Committee. In undertaking this enquiry, the Director-General should also explain the rights open to all FAO Member Nations as observers, with a view to limiting the Sub-Committee's membership to those FAO Member Nations specially interested in participating actively in its continuing deliberations. Those countries shall become members which, within four weeks of the dispatch of this enquiry, notify the Director-General of their desire to do so.

36. The *terms of reference* of the Sub-Committee were defined as follows, on the understanding that the Sub-Committee could make recommendations to the CCP but not to governments.

(1) To keep under review development in the disposal of agricultural surpluses, and to assist FAO Member Nations in developing suitable means of surplus disposal;

(2) To provide a forum for the discussion of proposals, programs, policies or transactions of Member Governments for the disposal of agricultural surpluses in the light of the principles recommended by the Seventh Session of the Conference and elaborated in this Report and in the Report of the Washington Working Party on Surplus Disposals, and to promote the observance of these principles;

(3) To report periodically to the CCP, it being understood that copies of its reports and summary records, including any conclusions, should be circulated to FAO Member Nations as soon as possible.

37. Any recommendations of the Sub-Committee shall be submitted to the CCP.

38. The Committee agreed that the Sub-Committee should establish its *own rules of procedure,* in conformity with the principles set out in Part V of the Report of the Washington Working Party on Surplus Disposals.

39. International organizations who are entitled to send observers to the CCP should also be entitled to send observers to the Sub-Committee. On matters of primary concern to other inter-governmental bodies, the Sub-Committee should invite the assistance of these bodies, and should co-operate with them in avoiding the overlapping of functions.

40. In interpreting its mandate, the Sub-Committee should view surpluses in perspective and bear in mind the continuing need for steps to raise consumption levels, particularly in areas in need of development and among vulnerable and low-income groups, and in line with policies of selective expansion of agricultural production and trade. In general, the Sub-Committee should interpret its terms of reference in a flexible way.

41. The Committee recognizes that governments would remain free as to whether or not they accept any conclusions reached by the Sub-Committee in its reviews of proposed or adopted measures. Therefore, the main value of the work of the Sub-Committee should be seen in the opportunity offered for the exchange of information and consultations. The value and effectiveness of this consultative machinery will depend primarily on the co-operation given to it by FAO Member Nations, in respect to both the communication of information and the consideration of the Sub-Committee's conclusions.

42. To enable the Sub-Committee to conduct its work efficiently and speedily, the Committee recommends that, as far as practicable, all Member Nations should communicate to the Sub-Committee at the earliest possible moment all plans and programs for special disposal of surplus agricultural commodities through exports.

43. Meetings of the Sub-Committee should be held in Washington. Meetings should be called by the Secretariat at periodic intervals of generally a month's duration, with additional meetings being called on an *ad hoc* basis, as required.

[1] The text of the full report has been issued as FAO Document CCP 54/13.
[2] Concessions in terms may relate to prices or to other conditions of sales or payment.
[3] The "given region" may be either "all foreign markets" or a particular area.
[4] If the "region" is "a particular area", the significance of the exports on special terms to world trade generally may have to be considered as an additional criterion.

USES OF AGRICULTURAL SURPLUSES TO FINANCE ECONOMIC DEVELOPMENT IN UNDER-DEVELOPED COUNTRIES

A pilot study in India

By
Mordecai Ezekiel

CONTENTS

94

ABSTRACT OF THE REPORT

Chapter I. To meet the standards for surplus disposal suggested in many international meetings under FAO auspices, surpluses can be used for financing development only if they meet two basic conditions. These are (1) that the country is already doing all that it can without the surpluses to carry out economic development, so that the surpluses make possible additional development; and (2) that the new projects using the surpluses expand domestic consumption of surpluses to the full extent of the surpluses added to the supply. Under Condition (1), the country's volume of activity must have been limited by lack of finance or by insufficient numbers of trained and skilled manpower; both these limitations can be helped by projects carried on through the use of surpluses. Condition (2) is the necessity of preventing the use of the additional surpluses from depressing either domestic or international prices.

Chapter II shows how these conditions apply to projects which use surpluses for consumption in kind (Type I) so that those receiving the food add all of it to the food consumption of themselves or their families.

Chapter III shows how the conditions apply in the case of projects where additional labor is put to work for pay and part of their additional consumption is satisfied by selling them surplus products (Type II). Calculations are made to show how much of the wages paid them is likely to reappear as increased demands for surplus products under the conditions existing in India for one assumed illustrative project. This proportion is found to run from one-third to one-half. The question of how the rest of the cost of the additional projects might be met, and what effect that would have on the consumption of surplus foods, is also examined.

Chapter IV shows how the conditions would apply in the case of a project like the previous one, which also tapped existing resources which could be developed so rapidly that they would help pay the investment costs of the project (Type III). By this combination of surplus products and self-financing, it would be possible, under favorable conditions, to pay the entire costs of the additional project without having to draw on other funds.

Chapter V shows how surplus foods might be used to finance a general increase in the level of the Indian Five-Year Investment Program, rather than considering the additional projects one by one. An illustrative example of an additional 240 million dollars worth of investment a year is examined. This would provide an increase of 20 percent in the existing level of investment. It is found that such an increase could be financed to the extent of about 100 million dollars a year from surplus foods, while the rest of the cost could be covered by additional deficit financing, which the Indian economy could then stand. The various advantages and difficulties of considering the extra investment on this over-all basis, instead of project by project, are also examined.

In the next three chapters, these methods and principles are applied to selected actual projects of each type. These projects are used as illustrations of what could be done, although in many cases more detailed technical study or administrative planning and preparation would be needed before they could actually be carried into operation.

Chapter VI examines a number of specific projects of Type I, including two which would help to raise the level of training and skill among Indian workers, and one which would help to finance an urban milk marketing scheme. The projects include educational food scholarships for rural children and for specially backward groups, and internship training for educated unemployed to give them the practical experience necessary to use their education effectively, as well as one project to help stimulate more voluntary labor on village community development work or on other local development projects, and a city milk scheme which would use surplus foods not only to help feed the workers building the necessary plant, but also to help feed the milking cattle for a period and to provide dry skim milk to help produce toned milk sold at specially low prices. In all these projects, the surplus foods alone would pay a large part – three-quarters to practically all – of the additional costs, especially if supplies of surplus products for these uses could be assured for a term of three to four years. Altogether, these projects – if all were implemented – would use about 30 million dollars worth a year of surplus foods.

Chapter VII examines a number of concrete illustrative projects of Type II. These include roads, irrigation and hydroelectric projects, and reforestation and erosion control. The proportion of costs which could be covered from surplus foods runs around one-third or a little better in the first year of operation, to half or more after the investment in that type of project has been continued two or three years. Over a four-year period, the projects presented would use an average of about 40 million dollars worth a year of surplus products, which would pay 46 percent of the total costs. Many more projects of similar types could be added, if desired, from projects in India now awaiting approval.

Chapter VIII presents one example of a project of Type III. This is a forest roads and industries development project in the Andaman Islands. The roads would open up new areas to sustained yield cutting, and help the project to pay its own way from the value of the timber cut. Surpluses would be used to help feed the additional workers on the project and their families, and also the additional elephants. Together with profits on the additional timber cut, the surpluses used would cover 100 percent of the investment needed, if in addition to four million dollars worth of roads, ten million dollars worth of forest industry plants were built in four years (sawmills, plywood factory, wood drying and treating plants, etc.) This would take an average of three and a half million dollars worth of surpluses a year.

Chapter IX discusses the relation of food surpluses to current conditions in India. Due to rapid progress in agricultural improvement and favorable weather in recent years, food production has increased faster than demand for food, and the government has had to intervene to prevent too extreme declines in farm prices and in incomes of farmers, with subsequent deflationary effects on the Indian economy. The government already holds some food supplies purchased to support prices, and may go further in acquiring more. As a result it is possible that there will be some domestic surpluses of farm products already withdrawn from the market and held in governmental hands, which could be drawn on to help finance additional devolopment projects, along with any foreign surpluses which might be obtained for the same purpose.

Chapter X summarizes the entire report very briefly. The individual projects presented add up to an average annual investment of $135,000,000, and would use $73,000,000 of surplus products, on an average over four years.

Four Appendices examine in more detail (1) the statistical and (2) economic problems in estimating the increase in surplus food consumption; (3) the possible inflationary or deflationary effects; and (4) related information on private efforts to improve rural education.

PART 1. ECONOMIC PRINCIPLES INVOLVED

I. Pre-conditions for the use of surpluses for development

SCOPE OF THIS REPORT

During the last two years there have been many international discussions of the problem of surplus farm products, and of the way future surpluses might best be prevented and present surpluses disposed of. There has been general agreement that the solution should be sought by expanding consumption and by selective adjustments in production, rather than by restricting output.[1] Further, in disposing of existing surpluses, there has been general agreement that disposal efforts by any one country should be so devised that they will not tend to discourage production in other countries, either by exerting a downward pressure on market prices in the country receiving the surpluses, or on international markets for exports from other producing countries. An international code of principles and guidelines to be followed in disposing of such surpluses was developed and recommended to Member Governments, and a number of them have already indicated their intention to abide by these principles.

In the standards recommended for the disposal of surpluses, attention was given both to preventing damage to producers in other countries, and to ways of making the most productive use of the surpluses themselves without causing such injury. Three ways of using surpluses were singled out as most desirable from this point of view: (1) aiding economic development in less developed countries; (2) assisting in special welfare feeding programs, and (3) providing emergency relief to countries or areas threatened with famine.[2]

Each of these topics is worthy of careful and detailed consideration. However, this report is concerned solely with the first one. Its task is to explore how surpluses can be used to aid economic development without upsetting market conditions in the recipient country or international markets. There are some projects where more than one point might be involved, such as school feeding programs which might be classified as both welfare schemes and as contributing to economic development. In this report, however, the primary concern is with the effects on economic development, with any other incidental effects considered only insofar as they also contribute to economic development.

The idea in using surpluses to aid economic development is very simple. In most under-developed countries there are many unemployed or under-employed farmers and other workers. There are a number of projects which could be undertaken by putting these people to work with local materials and local resources, or with only small amounts of foreign equipment. This would speed their country's development and increase its productive ability by building roads, wells, dams, irrigation canals, schools, warehouses, processing plants, etc. But when unemployed people are put to work they have to be paid, and their increased purchases of food, clothing, etc., raise the levels of demand. This increase in demand for consumer goods, coming into the market before the newly created facilities can begin to expand production, would tend to cause inflation. That is where the surplus farm products from other countries could come in. They could help to satisfy a large part of the increased demand from the extra people put to work until later expanding production satisfied it. This would thus make possible increased employment and consumption for the present, and higher productive power, demand for goods, and sustained employment for the future. But to do this, the surpluses would have to be made available without current expenditure by the country concerned as, for example, free grants or as long-term loans with low interest rates.

For agricultural surpluses to be fully effective and useful in financing additional development, two conditions must be present in the country concerned.

Condition 1:

Limiting factors preventing a more rapid rate of economic development must be lack of sufficient resources of skilled manpower and of finance. Projects financed by surpluses could help expand such resources, through providing more finance, and through speeding up the education and training of skilled manpower, or possibly even by feeding the workers better. But if the country is already doing all that it possibly could even if more finance, more training, or more food were made available, then there is nothing more that surplus products could do to help speed the progress or to increase the levels of consumption and of production. If surplus products were sold on the markets under such conditions, they would simply depress prices and tend to discourage farmers from expansion of output.

Condition 2:

The increase in the consumption of foods, of the same type as those added to the supply through the sale or distribution of the surplus products, *must be as large as those additions to the supply, or else the surplus products must be accompanied by other additional funds.* If the additional consumption resulting from the additional projects is not as large as the quantities added to the supply, then the excess will be added to the previously available supply on the domestic markets. This would have two possible undesirable effects. It might reduce the income of domestic farmers, and tend to discourage them from further expansion in production, and lead the government to add to its stocks or otherwise support prices. Or it might reduce quantities of farm products imported or increase quantities exported, and to that extent tend to add to the pressure of supplies on international markets, and so harm producers in other countries.

Even though consumption of surplus products should increase as much as supplies were added, local markets might still be disturbed. India is a very large country with limited transport facilities and many separate market areas, and sometimes with local shortages occurring in some regions at the same time as gluts are occurring in others. With these imperfections in the market, increases in consumption and in supplies would need to balance out in each local market area. These are the areas or regions in which prices are in general equilibrium with one another, and through which supplies move freely from local markets and district markets through to central markets at large cities. In order not to upset the price situation that would otherwise prevail, increased consumption of surpluses resulting from additional employment, and supplies added through the sale of surpluses, would thus have to balance in each such market area, both by area and by time periods.

As indicated earlier, schemes to speed economic development by special feeding programs to raise the nutritional level and general efficiency of the workers would meet Condition 1. It is difficult, however, to see how schemes restricted to such an objective could be organized without competing to some extent with other purchases of foodstuffs by workers, and thus failing to meet Condition 2. Accordingly, projects limited to this objective are not considered further in this report.

Applying these two pre-conditions to India, the following facts emerge.

A. *Finance and skilled manpower both seem to be limiting factors*

In the first three years of the Five-Year Plan, public investment expenditures compared with the levels planned were as follows:

Year	Actual	Planned	% of plan
	crores of rupees [1]		
1951-52	259.5	593.7[3]	43.4
1952-53	269.7	593.7	45.3
1953-54 [2]	355.6	593.7	59.9

[1] An Indian "crore" is ten million (10,000,000). One crore of rupees is a little more than $2,000,000.

[2] Estimated in September 1954, from Five-Year Plan, Progress Report for 1953-54.

[3] Estimated at one-fifth of the five-year total of the original Plan. This is somewhat unfair, as it was never assumed that this much of the total would be achieved in the earlier years.

Performance, as a percentage of the 5-year average, has thus steadily improved year by year, and the present expectation in India is that in the final two years of the Five-Year Plan performance will come substantially up to that called for in these years. Unexpectedly good crops, however, (due in part to more favorable weather than average) have eased the foreign exchange situation and helped make it possible to finance the activity that has occurred without any inflationary pressure on prices. This was true even though one-quarter of the investment was financed by an increase in the floating debt, the drawing down of cash balances, and the sale of securities held in reserve – activities which under less favorable circumstance might tend to have an inflationary effect. As stated in the *Indian Progress Report*[3]: "The economic situation in the country... has shown the need for quickening the tempo of activity through larger investments, and it can be said that *for the coming few months at least, the problem is more one of organization and administration* than of finance" (italics added). "There is, at the present time, no reason to fear that deficit financing, on a large scale, will cause inflationary pressures, and the foreign exchange position is such that the additional import demands arising in consequence of the increases in money incomes as a result of deficit financing can be taken care of. From all points of view, therefore, the implementation of the Plan to the fullest extent possible has to be the country's first concern."

While it is possible that the reasons for the present optimism will continue, one may ask, what will happen if future harvests should again be average or below average. The better crops are certainly due in part to favorable weather. They also seem due in substantial part (perhaps half or more) to improved practices, more use of fertilizer, more land under cultivation, an increasing area of irrigated land, and growing knowledge of how to use water more effectively. The current large food supplies also provide an opportunity to build up larger reserves against future catastrophes, both in farmers' own hands, and in commercial or public storehouses. With these developments, it seems less likely that future years of unfavorable weather could check economic progress as seriously as did the short crops immediately after the war.

From this brief review of conditions affecting the speed of Indian development it appears that achievement in recent years has been held back somewhat below the levels planned by lack of sufficient preparation and organization to carry programs into operation, by insufficient numbers of qualified organizers, administrators, and "doers", and to some extent by too much fear of inflation, or at least, by slowness to realize that increasing food supplies made it less necessary to be so cautious in the use of deficit financing. The second Five-Year Development Plan, now in the process of preparation, will no doubt be more ambitious in these respects. Even so, there will undoubtedly still be much more that could be done if additional resources were made available – more in speeding up the development of the necessary trained, skilled, and experienced personnel, as well as more in concrete projects involving physical construction. In other words, if advance arrangements were made for the use of food surpluses in development, they would make possible an increase in the total investment in economic development, and Condition 1 would thus be fulfilled in India.

B. *How much of the necessary finance can surplus products provide?*

Whether the second condition will be fulfilled, or how closely it will be fulfilled, is a much more intricate problem, and one that can only be briefly sketched here. (Most of the rest of this report will be devoted to trying to appraise it more clearly, from actual cases.) The need for this condition is seen by the apparently common-sense position of one Indian administrator who flatly declared there would be no sense in importing food grains under present conditions, when prices have been falling and the government is considering purchase and storage operations to support the price. He feared that any addition through imports would only complicate this problem. It is quite apparent that with existing food supplies and the present level of internal demand, supplies are pressing on the market. The government must cope with this problem in any case – either by price support operations, or more liberal investment or expenditure to increase employment, demand and comsumption. But additional projects based on surpluses would not make this situation any worse. If such additional development projects put some of the poorest people at work (such as some of the millions of landless farm workers), they and their families would eat better, and food consumption would rise. If imported foods were used to finance the additional development under such arrangements that the second condition was satisfied, exactly the same amount of food would be added to the supply, through imports, as was withdrawn from supply by additional consumption. The government's problem of what to do about the fall in domestic food prices would not be solved, but neither would it be made any worse, while the country would be better off both through the higher level of employment and consumption, and through additional real capital having been created by the additional development projects, thus increasing the country's future ability to produce and to consume. If the present domestic supplies are so excessive that the government finds it must intervene and withdraw them from the market, once that is done, such governmentally-held domestic stocks may also be used as "surplus" stocks to help finance additional development, and the quantity used of imported surplus foods would be correspondingly smaller.

But if consumption of food rose by say only one-third the amount imported or withdrawn from governmentally-held stocks, then two-thirds would be a net addition to the available supplies, and the problem of dealing with the price decline would be correspondingly increased (assuming that the increased supplies were so located that they affected farm prices in producing regions). If nothing were done to offset the price declines, farmers might be discouraged from further expanding their acreage, and the imports for development might thus tend to reduce the level of production in the country – a serious and undesirable result. Or, if the government compensated by reducing food imports below those which it would otherwise import, this would only shift the problem. The gain to India would then be offset by damage and possible discouragement to producers in other countries.

These considerations indicate how important it is that Condition 2 be fulfilled in any use of surplus stocks for development – and in fact, as FAO resolutions have repeatedly emphasized, in any disposal of surplus stocks for any purpose. Accordingly this problem must be examined with great care for the specific inter-relationships and factors involved.

EFFECTS OF DIFFERENT KINDS OF DEVELOPMENT PROJECTS IN FINANCING WITH SURPLUS STOCKS

The additional financing which can be represented by surplus products depends on two factors, the amount of the additional investment, and the composition of the additional investment – i.e., what kind of additional projects it involves. Let us first consider the various types of projects.

There are broadly three different types of individual development projects from the point of view of the absorption of surplus stocks, and a fourth type – increase in a development program as a whole. These are briefly:

I. Projects where the food is moved directly into consumption under such conditions that those receiving the food add all of it to their own or their family's consumption. This may apply where the labor is paid in kind in whole, or in part. These are projects where the direct effects alone are important (Chapter II).

II. Projects where additional labor is put to work, and part of the additional consumption is covered by surplus foods. These projects may take the form of surplus foods being sold for domestic currency (such as rupees), and the money used in turn to pay the labor. In these cases indirect effects on consumption may have to be considered as well as direct effects. Whether or not Condition 2 will be satisfied then depends upon the arrangements made for financing the increased consumption of surplus foods and of other consumer goods (Chapter III).

III. Projects which begin to be productive in an unusually short time, so that all the additional consumption from the labor put to work is covered either by surplus foods or by the profits from the project. These are really a special variety of Type II (Chapter IV).

IV. Finally, there is the possibility that imported surplus stocks might be used to finance an increase in the development program as a whole, without being focused on any single or particular project or projects. In that case, for Condition 2 to be fulfilled, the increase in total national consumption resulting directly or indirectly from a given net addition to the total amount invested in development would have to be equal to the amount of surplus foods sold, or be covered by other supplementary financing. For example, if investment were raised by an amount equal to the value of surplus products used; if total consumption increased by three times that amount, and if one-third the increase in consumption were in the kinds of products where surpluses were available and where these were being fed into the market, this condition would just be exactly fulfilled (ignoring other factors, such as savings in unemployment benefits, etc.). The conditions under which such a balance might be obtained, whether these conditions exist in India or are likely to exist in other under-developed countries, and other aspects of this general case, are also examined in a separate chapter (Chapter V).

Problems involved in each of these types of projects are examined in detail in separate chapters as indicated. Before proceeding to that examination, however, certain considerations which apply to all projects may well be examined.

COMMON CHARACTERISTICS OF ALL TYPES OF PROJECTS

Certain common characteristics must be present in any of these several types of projects, if they are to be successful in meeting the conditions already set forth.

1. The food surpluses must be available without current domestic expenditure for them. They may be either foods in stock and owned by the domestic government, from purchases already paid for; or acquired from abroad, either as grants or as a long-term loan with low interest rates.[4] If purchased under a long-term loan, the price delivered in the recipient country would need to be comparable with domestic prices. If priced far above domestic prices, the advantage of surplus financing to the under-developed country would be greatly reduced.

2. The investment from the new project or projects must be in addition to that which would be made in the absence of surplus foods to aid in the financing. This is easiest to judge in the case of Type IV, where it can be shown that the total financing under the development plan has been increased because of the additional projects added or of the increase in the total investment to be made as a result of the availability of surplus foods to assist in the financing. It is more difficult to judge in the case of individual projects, as assurance must then be given that implementing a new project does not result in cutting down or delaying some previously selected project. In some cases, it might be decided to defer a project previously planned, and to shift its financing to help assist in implementing a more costly project. If that were done, only the net excess of the new project over the old one could be counted as additional investment.

In other words the government must already be investing as much in development as it safely can, with its available resources, so that the projects which are added as the result of the availability of surplus foods contributing to their financing, increase the total of investment made.

3. There must be assurance of sufficient continuity in the availability of surpluses over a term of years to carry the project to a successful conclusion. While some projects can be completed in a single year, most development projects require a number of years to carry through to a point where increased production can begin to flow. Other projects, such as the educational fellowships discussed later, require several years continuous operation to be worth starting at all. In all such cases, use of surplus products to aid in financing will need to be based on a commitment covering their supply over several years together, if maximum effectiveness is to be obtained.

Besides these general characteristics, there are a number of special issues relating to each of the four types of projects.

106

[1] *Seventh Session of the Conference*, 23 November - 11 December 1953, FAO, Rome, 1954, pp. 15-31, 44-48.

[2] *Report of the Council of FAO*, 20th Session, 27 Sept. - 8 Oct. 1954, pp. 22-25, 80-86, Rome, November 1954; *Report of the Working Party on Surplus Disposal to the FAO Committee on Commodity Problems* (CCP 54/2), reproduced also as *FAO Commodity Policy Studies Series*, No. 5, Rome, April 1954; and *Report of the Twenty-third Meeting of the FAO Committee on Commodity Problems*, Rome, June 1954.

[3] *Five-Year Plan Progress Report for 1953-54*, Government of India Planning Commission, New Delhi, September, 1954, pp. 27-28.

[4] In this report, the discussion is not restricted to existing surpluses held by any one country, or to existing legislation and administrative practices concerning the disposition or the receipt of surpluses. Rather, it is directed toward the economic principles which might govern the utilization of present or potential surpluses, domestic or foreign, under the existing conditions in the country selected for the pilot study. Commodity situations change from time to time, and legislative provisions and administrative practices are subject to modification and change. Every effort is made in this study to state clearly the assumptions made, and the figures used in the illustrative examples, so that the same approach can be applied under other conditions and in other countries, by making appropriate changes in the method and in the basic data used here, as needed to fit the new institutional or commodity conditions.

II. Economic characteristics of projects with surpluses distributed in kind (Type I)

Where surpluses are distributed in kind directly to the workers engaged on particular development projects, as pay for their labor on that project in whole or in part, it might seem at first glance that the amount of surpluses distributed will be exactly equal to the amount of the addition to food consumption and that their value will equal the value of the additional consumption generated by the project. But this will be so only if two other conditions prevail, namely (a) that the surpluses received by the workers or members of their families are not resold by them, or substituted for foods they would otherwise purchase, and (b) that the project is paid for mostly with the surpluses, and does not absorb in overhead costs or in additional pay, funds that would otherwise have been used to finance other projects.

The possibility of the resale of food by the workers, or of its substitution for food that they would have consumed in any event, is obvious. If they do shift the food received in this way either directly or indirectly, not all of the food distributed is absorbed in their own increased consumption, but instead a part of it, large or small as the case may be, is added to the amount available on the general market. To that extent the second basic condition is not fulfilled. This difficulty might be overcome in various ways, e.g., by preparing the food and distributing it directly in cooked form ready for consumption, as in messes or lunch rooms, or in prepared milk delivered to children or others to drink on the spot. Under Indian conditions, the distribution of clabber prepared from dry skim milk or reconstituted milk might also meet the problem for that product, although even clabber might be resold or substituted for food that would otherwise be purchased. To be most effective, *the distribution of the surplus foods direct to consumers should be no larger than the increase in their consumption that would ordinarily be expected from the increase in their income resulting from their work on the project.* Possible ways in which these difficulties may be overcome will be examined as individual specific projects are discussed.

III. - Economic characteristics of projects with additional labor put to work and additional consumption covered partly by surplus foods (Type II)

Even if economically sound, the direct distribution of food involves many administrative costs and problems and might often mean much more use of scarce administrative personnel than would ordinary use of regular market mechanisms. It would be far simpler to sell the surpluses for cash and to use the cash receipts to hire the labor and pay the other costs of the project. How could Condition 2 be fulfilled under these circumstances?

First, on the direct effects, a number of points are involved. In such a large country as India, there is the question of where the surplus products are sold. If they were sold in the same community where the project was undertaken there would be no difficulty or burden on the market, as the increased supplies would be counter-balanced by the increased consumption (assuming for the moment that the two were equal in amount). But in India the projects are often likely to be located at interior points, hundreds of miles from the ports where foreign surplus products would arrive, and transportation costs to the interior would be heavy. Further, the interior regions will usually be sending food supplies to the big cities so that this would involve duplicate shipments. Where such conditions exist, the surplus supplies might be sold at the ports while the increased consumption in the interior balanced the sales without addition to the supplies. But, as already noted, that could be done only where the port and the development project involved were both in the same or related market areas. In some products, notably milk, the market may be of only very limited geographic extent. Even for such general products as wheat or millet, the degree of competition between local markets in ports and in internal agricultural areas may show wide variations in different regions of the country. This aspect must therefore be given attention with respect to the specific local market conditions affecting any particular project, and with respect to each surplus product involved in financing it.

A second more basic point is with regard to how far consumption will in fact increase as a result of the additional investment. For example, if one crore of rupees ($2,100,000) were invested in any particular development project, the money would be spent in many different ways. Some would go for labor directly on the project; some for locally produced materials; some for domestically produced materials from other parts of the country; some for imported materials; some for equipment and technical supplies, which in turn may be in part domestically produced and in part imported; and some for professional and administrative staff and services, domestic or imported.

The proportion which each of these types of expenditure makes of the total costs will vary from project to project; the proportion of amounts received which will be spent for food as a whole or for the kinds of food which can be obtained as surplus products, may also vary in the different parts of the country or with different types of labor employed, and certainly will vary from one type of expenditure to another. Direct labor costs, for example, range from 20 percent of the total cost or less on some projects requiring heavy industrial equipment, such as hydro-electric plants or the Sindri fertilizer factory, to as high as 80 percent on projects requiring largely human effort, such as canal works or the grading and construction of local roads.[1]

When an unemployed man is provided work on project construction, he not only has more money to spend but he also needs more food to provide the energy for the heavy work he will be doing, and also – usually in under-developed countries – to help make up for previous malnutrition. A proportion of the wages received will be used for purchases of food of the type which might be obtained from surplus supplies (taken here as wheat, millets, and all other bread grain, and rice; dairy products, from dried whole or skim milk, butter, cheese, and possibly canned milk; pulses; canned meats; vegetable oils, and dried fruits and nuts). This proportion may run as high as 60 to 70 percent of total consumer expenditures. But what we are concerned with here is not the question as to how the *total* income will be spent, but rather how the *additional* income resulting from the additional development project will be spent. In most cases this new income will be added to the income that the individual or family group concerned already receives in cash or in kind from farming or from other employment or occupation. Studies made especially to show how income earned on development projects is spent, plus other studies of the relation of income level to expenditure level, indicate that the proportion of project wages (i.e., of project labor costs) used for increased purchases of foods of surplus types would probably average about 40 to 45 percent in India.[2]

Even if 70 percent of the costs are for direct labor on the project, and if 40 percent of this additional labor income were spent for surplus foods, these foods would then represent only 28 percent of the total costs of the project. That would be at retail prices, out of which transportation and marketing costs would have to be deducted to get the portion covered by surplus foods as valued at the ports of arrival. These marketing costs may run as low as 15 percent in rural areas, where food is sold at retail largely in the same shape as sold by farmers. Deducting this 15 percent, the percentage of the costs covered by surpluses at port values would be brought down to about 24 percent, which may not be enough – unless for a group of several projects – to be worth the effort of making special arrangements to use them.[3]

Before reaching any conclusion on this basis now, we must first consider (a) what happens to the remaining part of the project expenditures which are spent for costs other than labor, (b) what happens to the expenditures made by the project employees for purchases other than surplus products, and (c) what becomes of the marketing and transportation costs on surplus products bought by the project workers. If we can trace through the direct and indirect effects of all these various kinds of expenditures, we will get a more complete picture of the probable effects of the project expenditures on the total additional demands for foods which could be supplied from surpluses.

The non-labor costs include expenditures for imported equipment and materials, and for domestic materials. The payment for imported goods can have only a very indirect effect on incomes and activities in India, and we will therefore make no allowance for their contribution to the Indian economy. In this illustrative project, let us assume that 10 percent of the investment is for imported equipment and materials. Out of 100 units of investment, only 90 units then remain to be considered. Of these, in our present example, 20 are spent domestically for materials and 70 are spent for direct labor on the project.

The 20 units spent for domestic materials make additional demands for cement, gravel, tools, transportation, etc. Similarly, although 70 units are paid out for direct labor, only 24 units of those wages are spent for surplus foods at wholesale, while the remaining 46 units are available to buy other things and to cover the marketing costs on the surplus foods.

The workers will use these 46 units to buy non-surplus foods, textiles, medicines, and a variety of other products. These increased purchases and the 20 units spent for materials and services for the project, will give increased income to the domestic producers of all this wide range of products, and a portion of their increased incomes will be spent for food, including surplus foods. (If the additional demands stimulate wider production of these other products, the increase might come from selling more goods at the same price; where production cannot be increased, it might either drive up prices, and so increase incomes of the producers affected, or stimulate increased imports, and so get out of the direct channels of Indian markets, and also cause foreign exchange difficulties.)

A part of the increased expenditures will be saved by those who receive them, rather than be respent for foods or services. Part will be used to pay taxes, and part will be used to buy imported goods.

We may assume that savings will run to 9 percent of the additional income, taxes to 9 percent, and additional imports for consumption to 8 percent,[4] and we must therefore deduct the total of these, 26 percent, from the sums spent for domestic products and services before we can estimate the resulting derived disposable income at the next cycle of expenditure. Subtracting this 26 percent from the 66 units leaves 49 units of derived disposable income at the next cycle of expenditure. Assuming that 35 percent of this will be spent for surplus food and that one-quarter of those expenditures will go for marketing costs, only 26 percent will go for surplus foods at wholesale values. Out of the 49 units of derived income, this would give 13 units spent for surplus foods. Adding this to the 24 units purchased by the direct workers on the projects, gives a total of 37 units of surplus foods purchased, even with a project where 70 percent of total expenditures go directly for labor costs. This would then cover a little over one-third of the investment needed for the project.

Of the 49 units of disposable derived income, 13 units are estimated as spent for surplus foods, leaving 36 units to be spent for other domestic goods and services. When this is spent it will produce further derived demand and result in further expenditures for goods and services and so on at each succeeding cycle of respending. When these effects are followed through for two to three years, by the methods set forth in more detail in Appendix 2 (assuming the investment is spread through the first year), it is found that 15 more units of surplus food will be bought at later cycles of expenditure, bringing the total use of surpluses up to 52 units, or just over half of the total investment in the project. Of this, two-thirds would be purchased in the first year, almost one-third the second, and the remainder in the third. Sales of surpluses to balance the increased consumption would need to be similarly distributed in time.

With the project carrying at most half of its costs through the use of surplus foods even under the assumed low direct imports and high direct use of labor, additional finance will have to be secured, for it cannot be financed wholly from surplus foods without failing to fulfill Condition 2. Such funds might be obtained by an International Bank loan or other external credit or grant; or, if the economy were not running to its full capacity, it might be covered by deficit financing.

This introduces one further difficulty. If all the additional costs were covered by external financing that financing would presumably be used to import consumer goods and services to satisfy the increased demand for domestic goods not covered by the use of surpluses, and there would be no significant derived demand after the first round of expenditure, either from laborers' or other workers' derived income. The total purchases of surplus foods would be the 24 units purchased by direct labor, plus that resulting from the expenditure of 20 units for project materials. After deducting the 26 percent for savings, taxes, and imports, and taking 26 percent of the remainder as spent for surplus foods, this gives only 4 units more for surplus foods, or a total expenditure of 24 + 4, or 28 units for surplus foods. If all the rest were financed, then, by external financing, at most 30 percent would be covered by surplus foods under the assumed conditions, while 70 percent would need to be covered by external loans. *The use of surpluses for this project would then vary between a minimum of about 30 percent and a maximum of about 50 percent, depending on whether the rest of the cost were financed externally or internally.* External financing could, of course, be used to cover the cost of imported equipment and materials, namely 10 units in this case.

With the possible minimum figure, 70 percent of the project costs would have to be covered by additional financing. This might not be so difficult to obtain, however, for with 30 percent already covered, the project would be a more favorable one for financing than with 100 percent to be covered. Ordinarily, however, only a part of a project's cost is covered by outside financing, while the rest is covered by domestic funds. Since in this case we have assumed that the country is investing all that it can afford to, except possibly a small margin left for additional deficit financing, there is little, if any chance of domestic funds contributing much of the balance. However, if any margin is left, the additional investment might be financed in part by additional deficit financing, and the rest by an external loan. The project might then be financed, say 40 percent from surplus foods, 30 percent from additional deficit financing, and 30 percent from an additional foreign or international loan.[5] There is a possibility that countries wishing to encourage the economic development of less developed countries, and with agricultural surpluses to dispose of, might be willing to make grants or loans for economic development, in this case 70 percent cash and 30 percent in surplus products, and thus themselves provide the additional investment necessary to utilize the surplus products without any danger of internal inflation in the recipient country.[6]

In any project such as that treated in this chapter, the amount added to national investment, and consequently to economic development, would be much larger than the amount of the surplus food consumed, assuming, of course, that the project and the rest of the projected program were carried through as planned. For example, if half the cost were covered by surplus foods, and if 5 crores of surplus foods were used for the project, (roughly ten million dollars) that would add 10 crores (twenty million dollars) to total investment, and thus would make a significant contribution to the country's economic development.

These various aspects of Type II projects will be explored in more detail in Chapter VII, where specific concrete projects of this type are examined.

[1] V. M. Dandekar: *Disposal of Food Surpluses*, Chapter VII. Mimeographed report, to be published later as a bulletin from Gokhale Institute of Politics and Economics, Poona 4, Bombay State, India.

[2] See Appendix 1 for a summary of the results of these studies.

[3] As shown later, 70 percent represents a rather high proportion of direct labor, and therefore is an unusually favorable case for financing through surpluses. In Appendix 2 a case is worked out with 50 percent direct labor, which comes nearer to representing an average development project in India.

[4] See Appendix 2 for bases of the Indian figures. This marginal import rate for India is much below those for most other under-developed countries, because of the exceptionally self-sufficient character of Indian agriculture and industry. In making calculations for other countries attention would have to be given to their special conditions in this respect.

[5] The exact proportions of surplus foods possible under such a combination would have to be worked out in detail by the methods of Appendix 2.

[6] A country such as India might not be able to finance additional investment without inflationary danger, but might be able to do so with the help of surplus foods. That result would follow if the country was not in a position to expand its production of basic foodstuffs promptly in response to increased consumer demand, but could expand its production of other products such as clothes and textiles without perceptible inflation if the increased demand for basic foods was covered by the use of surplus foods. (With the current supplies of foodstuffs in India, this may not be so true there, but the current position may not continue into later seasons.)

IV. Economic characteristics of projects which earn rapid income (Type III)

There is at least a theoretical possibility that projects may exist which could earn immediate income, even during the first year of the project, and thus help cover part of the necessary investment from their own income. Agricultural expansion projects (land development through irrigation, drainage, or reclamation) generally take several years to get into production after the initial physical construction is completed, and therefore would not qualify; factories take a considerable time to build and to install the equipment, and then take more time to get the working force recruited and at work, and therefore in general would not begin to earn fast enough to meet the requirement; even storage or marketing facilities take some time to complete and to get into successful operation. There may be some cases where some additional marginal equipment or construction is needed, which can be quickly procured and installed and which will at once solve a bottleneck and raise the volume and income of an industrial or commercial establishment. Even in these cases such additions would ordinarily require so much of purchased equipment, domestic or imported, that they would not be particularly attractive for financing through the use of surpluses. Further, if the additional equipment or capacity promised a large immediate return, it would ordinarily already be included in the regular investment program, private or public, and would not be available as a potential additional investment.

There are, however, other possibilities that may be more realistic. In some cases countries have large stocks of available natural resources, such as ores or standing virgin timber, that have never been exploited because of the lack of necessary transportation facilities. A project which provided such facilities through constructing road, rail, or water transport, might begin to produce and sell valuable products as soon as it reached the potential resource. Even during the first year it might begin to produce some net return above the direct costs of exploitation which could be used to help pay part of the investment costs. In that sense, projects of Type III resemble those of Type II, except that the necessary additional investment to cover the cost not coverable from surplus foods would be covered by net income earned by the project itself. That would mean, of course, that the investment would have to be very remarkably productive, as well as very rapidly productive. In the favorable project just considered under case two, for example, on the final calculation, 4½ lakhs of rupees would have to be earned by the project during the period of construction for every 5½ lakhs of surplus foods used – and a return on investment of 45 percent of the amount invested right from the first year would be remarkable indeed. There is again the possibility of combining other financing with that from the project and from surplus foods; as for example financing the project 55 percent from surpluses, 20 percent from the project's own income, and 25 percent from an external loan – which would thus be a hybrid of Types II and III.[1]

If the project were publicly financed, but involved privately owned resources or the private operation of publicly owned resources, it would also be necessary for arrangements to be made for the payment of royalties, taxes, or other payments to public agencies, so that the government could recapture enough from the increased production to recoup the funds necessary to finance that part of the project's cost not covered from surplus products. It is not necessary that the project add enough to the national income to pay all its own way, but merely that it add enough to public revenues to enable the government to pay its necessary part of the costs without recourse to other means of securing the necessary financing – that is, if the project is to be a pure project of Type III, and not one of the hybrid types mentioned in the preceding paragraph.

A concrete illustration of a project of this type is presented in Chapter VIII.

---

[1] In that case, however, the surplus food proportion would be reduced if foreign financing were used to meet other domestic demands.

V. Financing of a general development program (Type IV)

1. PROGRAM APPROACH VERSUS PROJECT APPROACH

The financing of a general development program by food surpluses will be referred to, for convenience sake, as Project Type IV. Since any individual investment project can only be really assessed as a part of a general investment program and since any investment program necessarily consist of many investment projects, the difference between the "program approach" and the "project approach" has only a practical but not a logical basis. Certain programming and economic differences are important enough, however, as well as certain advantages for practical administration, to deserve consideration. The advantages of the program approach may be summed up as follows.

(*a*) Any single project may or may not be a substitute for another project which would otherwise have been undertaken. If may change the composition of investment rather than increase the total amount of investment. It is thus difficult to say when and whether a single project represents *additional* investment. It is quite practicable on the other hand to estimate the increase in the total amount of investment.

(*b*) An increase in effective demand may induce an increased supply of foodstuffs from the poorer sectors and from the barter sector of domestic agriculture for whose potential offer there may have previously been no effective demand. Although it is difficult to estimate this factor quantitatively, it might be assumed for India that after a year's interval 10 percent of the additional surplus foods needed might flow from this source, increasing further during the third and fourth year of the program. We may thus assume that there is some excess capacity not only in the textile industry and in other non-food consumer goods but also in agriculture. This derived increase needs to be taken into account when we consider the economy as a whole.[1]

(*c*) An increase in total investment continued over a period of years will generate an increase in the rate of domestic capital formation, since the marginal rate of savings will be higher than the average rate of savings. This planned growth of savings should lead to a growth of investment; the growth of investment can then be considered as "induced" by the program, and will tend to produce a further increase in surplus food consumption. It will thus constitute another type of indirect effect which cannot be traced by the individual project approach.

(*d*) For the increase in the total amount of investment the assurance of continuity of aid is necessarily as important as the amount of aid. Additional employment of labor will require additional foodstuffs for several years before the projects for increased domestic food production will materialize. These projects for increased domestic food production must form a necessary counterpart to other projects;[2] they can only be assessed within the framework of an investment program as a whole. It would be undesirable to raise the level of consumption if there were no assurance that this higher level can eventually be maintained on a self-sustaining basis. Food surpluses can and should form an important part of foreign capital inflow during the interval period; they supplement capital in its original sense of a subsistence fund. Only an analysis of the investment program as a whole can provide a proof that they will not be required in perpetuity but only for a specified limited period of years.

Without an assurance of continuity for several years the painful and expensive process of preparing additional projects and co-ordinating them within the framework of a program will not be undertaken. Once, however, the assurance is given that capital support will be forthcoming, the programming effort will increase considerably. This assurance must precede the actual flow of foreign capital. A period of time of one to two years may be required in many countries for the elaboration of increased programs and additional projects.[3]

(*e*) For covering the inflationary gap due to additional investment, only the gestation period of additional investment need be considered, i.e., the interval before the flow of products of additional investment can reach the market. It may be assumed on the basis of the investment program as a whole that the long-run effects of increased investment can be more easily handled and solved by means of domestic monetary and fiscal policy.[4] This would be impossible, however, for the shorter-run gestation period.

Administrative advantages

(*f*) In practice important differences arise in the handling of end-use surpervision of projects as against an end-use supervision of an increase in an investment program.[5] End-use supervision, i.e., tracing the use of say, individual sacks of wheat, might be attempted for individual projects. This is possible for the direct effects of an additional project, but hardly for the indirect effects. For the investment program as a whole – i.e., for a whole group of additional projects, it is now generally recognized that indirect effects should be financed without attempting to trace the control and verify the use of single parts of resources. The indirect effects must be considered in calculating the necessary financing, however, if additional investment is not to cause inflation.

(*g*) A central administration might be set up to handle the selling and buying, reporting and supervising of food surpluses used for development purposes, as an important part of the instrumentation of a "food surpluses for development policy". For example, if surplus foods were being used as suggested elsewhere, and development activities in schools, irrigation, roads, forests, milk processing, etc., were in progress, foods would have to be received, stored, sold and shipped for the needs of each such program. It would obviously be wasteful and confusing for each agency concerned to set up its own administrative offices for these purposes. Instead, one central surplus food management agency, receiving and consolidating reports from each participating agency as to their needs and requirements, in time and in space, for surplus foods or for funds, could handle the operations far more advantageously.

If the difficulty, discussed under (*a*) above, can be overcome, i.e., if it can be assumed and demonstrated that each individual project is "additional", then there should be no difference between the "project" and the "program" approach. We have assumed accordingly that each of the projects of the Types I to III described in Chapters VI to VIII are examples of what an increase in the investment program might consist of. By treating them as illustrations of an over-all increase in investment we can attribute to each project its proportional part in those direct and indirect effects which are usually recognized only for the investment program as a whole.

2. CALCULATION OF SURPLUS FOODS NEEDED FOR DEVELOPMENT

In Appendix 2 a case has been examined for projects which require 50 percent labor costs, and 10 percent costs for imported equipment and supplies; under the following conditions (*a*) 40 percent of direct labor costs is spent on surplus foods at retail prices, equivalent to 34 percent at wholesale prices; *(b)* 35 percent of derived income is spent on other surplus foods at retail, equivalent to 26 percent at wholesale prices; and *(c)* the marginal propensities to save, to tax and to import are 9 percent, 9 percent, and 8 percent respectively: under these conditions and assumptions the need for surplus foods is shown to represent 48 percent of total investment, ignoring derived effects after the third year. Including those, the total would be just over 50 percent.

Let us consider how much surplus foods might be used in a general increase in the Indian investment program as a whole. Let us take 20 percent as the assumed addition to the current program, now at about $1,200 million per year. The 20 percent addition would represent an additional annual investment of $240 millions. For such an increase in the overall program, it would probably be more realistic to have 25 percent in imported equipment and supplies, instead of 10 percent as assumed in Appendix 2. With that exception, we will assume that the other conditions stated in that Appendix still hold true. In addition, we will add two other assumptions not previously considered in discussing individual projects. Those are (1) that the increased demands resulting from the increased investment will stimulate sufficient expansion in Indian agriculture so that a portion of the increased demands can be satisfied by the increased Indian output, amounting to 10 percent of the increased demand for surplus foods in the second year, 20 percent in the third, and 30 percent in the fourth; and (2) that reinvestment of the increased savings resulting from the increased income will produce a further rise in investment and income, which in turn will produce a further rise in consumption of surplus foods. (It is clear that these two assumptions would produce effects in opposite directions, the first one tending to lower the additional current needs for surplus foods, and the second one tending to raise them.)

Under these new conditions, let us see what the effects might be for the economy as a whole.

A rough estimate of the increased demand for surplus food per 100 units invested may be made as shown at the top of page 120.

On this rough calculation, consumption of surplus foods would be increased 33 percent of the additional investment. Before deducting the estimated increased production of surplus foods, we must remember that this rough calculation has not considered the effect of derived income resulting from further re-spending of the remaining income at successive cycles of expenditure. This rough calculation is therefore a minimum which underestimates the total effect.

When that is calculated by the more detailed methods developed in Appendix 2, assuming that the $240 million is invested evenly over each year for four years, we find that the investment for these four years would produce a total increase in consumption of surplus products averaging 42

Units

1. *Direct effect of labor expenditure*
   Project labor — 50 units × 34 percent 17

2. *First derived effect*
   All domestic expenditures other than on surplus foods:
   (75 units — 17 units) × 26 percent = 58 × 0.26 15

3. In addition, we would need to consider the addition to demand
   from the investment of savings (which we have ignored above).
   Assuming that savings eventually come to 9 percent of all domestic expenditures whether for direct labor or materials, that would
   be:
   (58 units × 9 = 5.2 increase of investment
   (5.2 units × 0.26 1

Total estimated increase in surplus food consumption 33

percent of the additional investment, in the same four years, plus an additional 7 percent in the two subsequent years.[6]

The increased consumption of surplus foods resulting from the addition
of 960 million dollars to the Indian development program spread evenly
over a four year period, would thus be $471 million, largely concentrated in
the same four years. From this, however, we must deduct the part of these
increased demands which would be covered by further increased output
from domestic agriculture during the same period. When that is done, the
total increase in surplus food requirements comes out at an average of 36
percent of the investment for the first four years, with the subsequent
derived increase in consumption more than offset by the expansion in production.[7]

The annual savings at 9 percent of the additional income, if used for
further productive investment, would generate 18.5 further units of derived
income annually. With 26 percent of this spent for surplus food consumption, this adds an additional 5 percent of surplus foods on the average.
Adding this to the 36 percent net increase in surplus food consumption on
the average for the four years, calculated for the overall increase in the
national program, brings the total up to 41 percent of the additional investment. This is thus the final estimate, after deducting the increased
production of such foods and adding on the additional allowance for the
effect of investment of the savings.

With all these aspects taken into account, an increase of investment in
India of $240 millions per annum (20 percent above the previously pro-
grammed annual investment) might thus require – varying for different
types of composition of investment – an additional supply of surplus foods
equal to between 35 and 45 percent of the additional investment, or an
average addition of roughly $85 million to $110 million per annum. For

the whole four-year program, the additional amount of surplus foods needed would be roughly 350 to 450 million dollars' worth.

3. A Rough "Envelope" Calculation

The figures just given are based on the detailed formulae of how to handle different assumptions as to the percentage labor costs and the percentage foreign imports, and also as to the different values of the marginal propensities to import, to tax and to save, as given in Appendix 2. A shortened rough way of making such calculations is as follows:

Total increase in planned investment = $240 million

minus foreign imports   = $ 60 million

gives net domestic investment   = $180 million

Assuming the full income multiplier at 3.85, in the absence of the use of surplus foods, additional income created would amount to $693 million, requiring additional surplus foodstuffs of around $200 million (assuming an average of both direct and derived income spent for surplus food of about 30 percent). But since surplus foods used to satisfy additional demand do not generate additional domestic income, surplus foods must be treated in the same way as imported equipment, and the derived income reduced accordingly. This reduces the multiplier to a level which under the conditions assumed for India would generally average around 1.7. Applying this "damped multiplier" of 1.7, additional income from each year's investment would amount to $180 million × 1.7 = $306 million, and the additional food surpluses to around $100 million,[8] about the same as the average shown by the previous calculation.

4. The Composition of the Investment Program

The investment program, including any additions to it, must be carefully balanced to assure that the increased demands resulting from it will be satisfied from appropriately increased new production facilities. At present, there may be a margin of unused capacity to meet additional needs in some or even many wage-goods industries (e.g., textiles). The investment program should be so composed that if the future increase in investment is maintained according to plan, future increases in production from the programmed new capacities will just cover anticipated future increases in consumption and investment demands, with due allowances for foreign trade. In planning further additions to the investment program, this requirement would also have to be kept in mind. The need for external finance, both for surplus foods and for *complementary* foreign exchange to cover other unavoidable foreign expenditures will also have to be examined. This will provide the basis for "package deals" of surplus foods and foreign exchange. Even if these were negotiated and handled by different agencies, their over-all effect in the national program would still have to be coordinated for best results.

In the absence of such a detailed analysis it might be assumed that to maintain balance in the program as a whole the additions would be spread reasonably uniformly over all types of projects previously included, including those with low direct labor costs as well as those with high labor costs, those with high requirements for foreign imports as well as those with low requirements, and those with high cost for domestic equipment as well as low. On the average, the additions would thus follow the national average for all projects.

5. Use of Surpluses in a National Development Program

If a nation knew, when it drew up its future development plan (say for the next five years) that it could count on an annual contribution of x units of surplus foods (say 100 million dollars, for example) to use in financing additional development projects, it would thus first consider what its program would be if those supplies were not available, and second what additional projects it could add to utilize the additional funds.

The government would then have to consider whether an additional financing of 200-240 million dollars a year could be added to the plan previously devised, without too much danger of inflationary effects, in view of the relation of this additional financing to the whole proposed financial scheme for the development plan. With 30-40 percent of the investment financed (at a low rate of interest, or as a grant) from surplus foods, the loan for the balance of project costs should be more credit-worthy. Similarly, countries which have surpluses to dispose of and which are also willing to provide part of the funds for development, either on a grant or long-term loan basis at low interest cost, should be willing to consider a "package deal" in which they combined both the surplus products and part or all of the necessary supplementary financing. In the case just considered, for example, that might be 100 million of surplus products plus 60 million in foreign exchange annually, over an agreed term of years. In each such case, the "package" would have to be adjusted to the needs and possibilities of both parties concerned.

In adding on additional projects above the original program, the planning authorities would have to consider the effect of those additional projects on the balance within the plan as a whole. Too much emphasis on projects with a high labor intensity (where secondary roads and canals are among the best) might result in overburdening the program with projects which have a long gestation period and perhaps a long lag in showing a substantial effect upon subsequent increases in national production and income. Other balances, as between investment in agricultural and in industry, and as between different regions of the country and their potential labor supplies, would also have to be taken into account. Only if the net effect on the national program as a whole seemed desirable after all these aspects had been explored would it be worthwhile going ahead on the expansion.

Even though we approach the program as a whole, we must also consider individual projects or kinds of projects – but projects to be added to the previous program as a group, rather than one by one.

[1] See also Appendix 3.

[2] The same is true of projects for increased production capacity of other consumer goods, if and when the present unused capacity is insufficient.

[3] If, on the other hand, countries in a position to assist in financing economic development in other less developed ones preferred to make such contributions partly in cash (foreign exchange) and partly in foodstuffs, the assurance of such continuing supplies of foodstuffs and foreign exchange over a longer period would assist in preparing long-term programs. This would then give a different range of choice to the recipient country, with the possibility of placing more immediate emphasis on industrial expansion, and less on agriculture.

[4] See Appendix 3 for fuller examination of this point.

[5] "End-use supervision" means a check by country or agency on finance (or surplus products) to ascertain whether those resources have been used for the precise purposes specified when the agreement was made with the recipient country (or agency).

[6] With 100 units of annual investment distributed equally through each of four consecutive years under the conditions stated, the increase in consumption of surplus foods, from the total of 400 units of investment, would be as follows: 1st year, 28 units; 2nd year, 44; 3rd year, 48; 4th year, 49; 5th year, 22; 6th year, 5.

[7] Assuming that the induced increase in production (over and above that due to planned agricultural investment) lags one year behind the increased demand for surplus products which stimulates it, and increases by 10 percent each year, the net increase in units of food requirements is calculated as follows:

Year	Increase in demand	Increase in production	Resulting increase in supply	Net increase in requirements
1	28	10 %	–	28
2	44	20 %	3	41
3	48	30 %	9	39
4	49	40 %	14	35
5	22	50 %	25	–
6	5	60 %	13	–
			Total:	143

[8] This is computed by multiplying 306 by 30 percent, using the average of 34 percent surplus food for direct labor and 26 percent for derived income.

PART 2. CONCRETE ILLUSTRATIVE PROJECTS

The illustrative projects were selected from those which meet the following criteria.

i)   They are not being implemented under the current Five-Year Plan.

ii) They are projects with a relatively high direct consumption of foods, or with high direct labor intensity.

iii) The plans for the projects are either relatively simple, or have been developed in sufficient detail so that they could be put into action reasonably rapidly once financing was assured.

iv) Organizations to carry out the work exist, or could be developed, once financing is provided.

v)   The projects do not involve any heavy requirements of special technical skills, either of construction or of administration, and implementing them is unlikely to be hindered by any personnel bottlenecks.

In presenting these projects it should also be emphasized that their selection for use as examples here has no significance at all as indicating whether they are likely to be included in or excluded from the next Five-Year Plan. That plan is now under preparation and has not yet reached the stage of deciding which specific projects will be included. Projects given here are given solely as examples of projects not now under way or authorized which could be put into action even without waiting for the end of the Five-Year Plan now current, if arrangements for financing them as additional projects through food surpluses are developed and approved.

The projects thus selected include some individual ones which have been developed and proposed by various authorities in India as desirable projects for implementation, such as the specific irrigation and hydro-electric projects, or the Calcutta milk scheme. Others of a more general nature, such as the district roads proposal, have been suggested by competent experts as meeting a variety of local needs.

Still others were the educational, training, and local development proposals based on general ideas which evolved during the discussions with competent Indian experts and administrators on the local, state and federal levels. One project, that for reforestation and erosion control, was formulated in Rome on the basis of fragmentary discussions while in India. These latter projects (including most of those in Chapter VI) must be regarded as merely general schemes, only roughly and tentatively sketched, without detailed technical or administrative examination or development. They are included here as broad ideas or suggestions so that their possible implications for surplus financing might be explored. In some other projects the technical and administrative aspects have not yet been fully studied. The projects, therefore, are presented here merely as examples to suggest and explore how surplus products might contribute to their financing, without that meaning that they have yet been given sufficient technical, administrative, or economic formulation and appraisal.

If the Government of India should choose to develop any of these projects further, and to consider their actual possibilities for early initiation, it would no doubt first explore further their technical, economic and administrative aspects. If it wished to request external technical assistance in this connection, FAO, within the limits of its available resources, would do its best to provide such assistance for agricultural projects. Other UN agencies would no doubt stand ready to consider similar requests in other fields, and parallel assistance is also available from other sources, multilateral, bilateral, and private.

VI. Illustrative projects for surpluses distributed in kind (Type I)

Five specific projects are suggested which illustrate the possibilities of financing additional economic development through food surpluses distributed in kind.

A. Surpluses used to provide food scholarships for rural and other low-income youths to attend high schools and colleges, and thus increase the country's capacity to carry through rapid modern development.

B. Surpluses used to provide food scholarships for other special groups.

C. Surpluses used to provide fellowships for unemployed high school or college graduates, to serve as trainees or interns while they acquire the practical experience needed to supplement their theoretical training.

D. Surpluses used as an additional incentive to voluntary work in village community development projects or other voluntary labor activities, to increase the participation in such work by the poorest class in the villages, the landless labor, and thus to increase capital formation under such programs.

E. Surpluses used to speed the development of milk marketing facilities and the establishment of milk production colonies where needed, and thus improve dietary conditions, increase the demand and outlets for milk, and facilitate the development of this vital sector in improving the nation's productivity and health.

Proposals A to D are intended to illustrate certain possible methods of utilizing surplus foods for supporting educational and other development which in turn will help to accelerate the economic development of the country. They are not put forward as concrete plans, duly studied with respect to their difficulties and complications. It is fully realized that the mere availability of food is only one aspect of the problem of initiating supplementary feeding programs to benefit this or that group in the population. Attention must also be given to transport, distribution, buildings, equipment and administration, to the trained staff needed for organization and supervision and to the cost which all these may involve. Further, the social implications of such programs must always be borne in mind; that is, they must be adjusted to social customs and attitudes. Much experience indicates the importance of all these factors and the need for their careful consideration in planning and undertaking measures such as those outlined in the sections which follow.

A. EDUCATIONAL FOOD SCHOLARSHIPS

One of India's great bottlenecks in carrying out its Five-Year Plan is manpower, trained and skilled for the work needed to be done. This lack is especially great in administrative, organizational, supervisory, and technical competence, i.e. in the abilities needed to convert plans into realities. To fill this lack, people must be educated, trained, and given experience as administrators, technicians, supervisors, and foremen. Educational and training activity of all sorts, properly balanced with the expanding needs for trained minds to carry out the plans, is thus one of the key priorities in the whole scheme of development. India has made great progress in education since independence. The number of students in high schools has doubled, and more than doubled in primary schools and colleges.[1] Even so, expansion of educational activities has lagged behind the planned rate, especially for technical education. But unemployment among graduates is heavy, and provision is needed to provide practical experience to high school and college graduates as rapidly as they complete their courses, so that they can begin to acquire the experience necessary to make them effective employees, and eventually future administrators and managers. If necessary to this end, special arragements should be established for graduates to serve as trainees or interns in existing organizations or special projects, where by sharing in current actual work they can acquire the experience to help run the future expanding society (see section VI-C).

The need for a greatly expanded educated group to help operate a more advanced society is shown by the comparisons given in Table VI-1.

India thus has only about half as large a proportion of the population in administrative, professional and distributive occupations as has Japan or Italy, and less than a third as large as the United Kingdom and the United States.

Similarly, the proportion of workers in mining, industry, and transportation in India is only half as large as in Japan, and about one-third as large as in Italy and the United States. As India's economic development progresses in the future, all of these occupations will require more educated and trained workers and foremen, and highly skilled technicians, supervisors, organizers and administrators.

In addition to more persons with higher training and education, economic development also requires a much higher level of literacy among the entire population. Literacy is required (1) because it will help to speed

Table VI-1. Distribution of Economically Active Population, by Occupation

Occupation	India (1951)	Japan (1950)	Italy (1951)	U.K. (1951)	U.S.A. (1950)
			percent		
Agriculture, forestry and fisheries	69.8	48.6	41.3	5.0	12.4
Mining	11.1 }	1.6 }	36.1	3.8 }	1.6
Industry		19.8 }		43.9 }	32.0
Transportation	1.9	5.1 }		7.8	7.7
Trade and finance	5.7	11.8	10.4	14.1	22.1
Public administration and defence	2.1	4.2	6.6	8.0	6.2
Professional service	1.7	4.2 }	5.6	6.9 }	8.3
Personal, domestic and miscellaneous services .	7.7	4.7 }		10.5 }	9.7
Total	100.0	100.0	100.0	100.0	100.0
Total in administrative, professional and distributive groups[1]	9.5	20.2	[2]218.6	29.0	36.6
Total in mining, industry, and transportation ..	13.0	26.5	36.1	55.5	41.3

Sources

INDIA: Registrar General: *Census of India, Paper No. 3, Summary of Demographic and Economic Data,* 1951 Census. New-Delhi 1953. Based on sample survey study of the self-supporting population.

JAPAN: Bureau of Statistics: *Population Census of* 1950, Vol. III - October 1952 (p. 160-165). Figures are based on a 10 percent sample tabulation of the 1950 census; total excludes activities not classifiable and not reported.

ITALY: Istituto Centrale di Statistica: *Compendio Statistico,* 1954. Roma 1955. Figures are estimated for the census date based on a labor force sample survey.

U.K.: General Register Officer: *Census* 1951, Great Britain one percent sample tables, Part 1. London 1952. Excludes Northen Ireland. Figures are based on a 1 percent sample tabulation of the 1951 census. Total excludes activities not adequately described.

U.S.A.: Bureau of the Census: *1950 U.S. Census of Population* - P - B1 - pages 102, 104. Washington, D.C. 1952. Reprint of Vol. II, Part I, Chapter B. Total excludes industry not reported.

[1] Includes those in trade and finance, public administration and defence, and professional service.
[2] Including an estimate of 1.6 percent professional services (from 1936 census).

development, (2) because it is desired, and is desirable as an end in itself, to lead a fuller life, and (3) because it is an essential condition of modern political democracy. A modern technically advanced economy can be most effective only when every worker can read and write, and understands the basic sciences which affect the tasks with which he is dealing. This requires a great expansion in the work of basic education and in the numbers, quality, and training of the teachers and teacher training institutions.

Again, to carry through its new industrial revolution India must create a great new middle class of administrative, clerical, supervisory, technical and professional workers. Such workers must have at least a high school education; many need full college education, with a much higher proportion than previously having education with agricultural, commercial, and technical specialization. As matters are now, two obstacles stand in the way. First, a very large proportion of the population cannot afford to send their children to high school, still less to college. High school or college education is too dear for nearly all farm children. Second, there are not enough schools and teachers, and very few high schools are located in villages. The cost of room and board at a central town, say 15 rupees per month as a minimum, is prohibitive for most farmers' children. Similarly, a large proportion of urban industrial and commercial workers have incomes much too low to spare their children from work long enough to learn more than the barest ABC's. As a result, the predominant attendance in the high schools, and especially in the colleges, is drawn from one group in the society, most of whom have had little or no direct first hand contact with the realities of agricultural, industrial or commercial production. On the second point, the Five-Year Plan is bringing about a rapid and continuous expansion in schools and colleges, but the wages offered teachers are still insufficient to attract or hold the best-qualified people. If the developing Indian society is to have full vigor and effectiveness, it must correct these deficiencies by providing wider opportunities for the most able and promising people from all groups and walks of life to rise to positions of responsibility and to bring with them the varied knowledge, insight, and competence that the different groups can contribute.

To assist in attaining this end, surplus foods can be used to help establish a system of nation-wide educational feeding scholarships. Under the surpervision of the competent educational authorities in each school or college system, and in co-operation with qualified nutritional experts, existing messes can be expanded and new ones established, to cater for an enlarged number of students. Such expansion should be especially emphasized in high schools well situated to serve rural and low-income industrial youth, and in technical and professional colleges and universities. Such feeding arrangements are at present available for only a limited number of students in these institutions. Efforts might also be made to increase the proportion of rural girls in schools.

Selection of those to receive the food scholarships would be by ability, with no discrimination for race, caste or sex. Preferences should, however, be established in favor of children of landless agricultural labor, low-income industrial workers, and backward classes, who otherwise might find difficulty in obtaining a fair participation, and there might also be a "means test", as suggested later. Special emphasis would be placed on professional institutions, with few or no scholarships for arts institutions until the present unemployed graduates begin to be absorbed.

Before considering the plan for India as a whole, we may see more of what is involved by examining the educational situation in one of the most advanced States. The detailed educational data for Bombay State show the attendance of rural and urban youth in advanced education (high school, college, or university and professional schools) to be as follows.

Table VI-2. Advanced Education and Total Population, Bombay State[2]

	For rural youth	For urban youth
	.... *thousands*	
Number attending high school and college	138	424
Total population (1951)	24,790	11,170
Proportion of total population.......	0.55%	3.80%

Compared to the total numbers in the population, only one-seventh as many rural children are studying in advanced institutions as are urban children.[2]

The attendance of girls at school is generally much less than that of boys. While almost one-half of Bombay State's boys of school age (6-17 years) attend school, only one-quarter of the girls do. Generally throughout India, rural girls may attend primary school only the first year or two, and then be withdrawn to help in the home, while the boys stay on for a longer time. Yet women also need education, to understand and apply improved methods in child care, in selection, preparation and preservation of food, in caring for the family's health, and in the farm processes for which they are responsible, such as raising poultry and vegetables.

India already provides educational scholarships to help a limited number of the most promising youths to attend school, and provides school meals or lunches in some schools. The total number of scholarships is very limited, amounting in 1953/54 to 46 for "Public Schools" (private secondary schools); 27 for research in humanities, science and technology, plus a few hundred a year of scholarships for foreign training under various auspices.

These numbers, for the entire Indian Union, are exceedingly small. There were over 1,000 applicants for public school scholarships, yet only 46 could be granted. (Scholarships for backward classes are excluded here – they are considered in section VI-B.) These figures cover only scholarships awarded from central Government funds. In addition many States have scholarship programs of their own, aggregating much more than the central ones. Where school lunches are provided, they both improve the nutrition of the students and encourage their parents to keep them in school to take advantage of them.

Size of a possible program. To assist in correcting this situation by encouraging a larger attendance of rural youth and of girls at school, the authorities have suggested a program as follows.

In the colleges, universities, and technical colleges, where present attendance is about 600,000, to offer food scholarships for 10 percent, or 60,000 new students, who do not now attend.

In the high schools, with an attendance of roughly 6,000,000, to offer food scholarships for 10 percent, or 600,000 new students.

In the primary schools, with an attendance of about 25,000,000, to offer a single mid-day meal to 10 percent, i.e., to 2,500,000 new students. With the expansion in educational facilities already under way, the educational authorities believe that the existing and planned schools and colleges could enroll these additional students without difficulty.

The costs of the program have been estimated roughly as follows, on the basis of a nine-months' school year and present food costs in messes:

College students - 60,000 at 300 rupees each......	1.8	crores
High school students - 600,000 at 300 rupees	18.0	"
Primary students - 2,500,000 at 100 rupees.........	25.0	"
Total cost...	44.8	"

This full program would thus cost a stupendous sum annually for food, almost 100,000,000 dollars. Instead of starting on such a nationwide basis, it might be more practical to start on a smaller basis and proceed step by step. The food scholarships might be made available first in selected schools and colleges which already have some feeding facilities, which are teaching technical and professional subjects, and where the present capacity (or that soon to be made available) does not show promise of being fully used. Similarly, the additional school lunches might be made available first mostly in rural schools and in regions where some facilities and experience in providing such lunches already exist. The program could be expanded from time to time as more school systems and districts develop to the point of readiness to undertake such operations. The availability of the food scholarships might also encourage school authorities to move forward more vigorously to carry into action existing plans and budgets to expand schools for rural boys and girls, and for high schools and colleges for technical and professional subjects. With the fellowships and school lunches, there would be no difficulty in assuring full attendance of such students as rapidly as the expansions were completed.

In view of the large sums involved, we will take one-tenth of the proposed amount as a realistic proposal to be implemented at the start, with an initial annual cost of 4.5 crores, or 18 crores ($38,000,000) for a four-year period. If sufficient surplus foods were available to continue and expand this program over a longer period, the annual amount could increase gradually over a term of years to 10 crores a year (21 million dollars annually), or even higher.

Operating aspects. It would not be worth while starting on a program of this sort unless there was some assurance of continuity – at least of keeping it up long enough so that the students who left their homes to attend high school and college could stay to complete the four-year course if their work and progress was satisfactory. A four-year commitment from the authorities providing the surpluses, foreign or domestic, would therefore seem essential for starting such a program. The minimum commitment might be to enable those who start the first year to complete their courses. With allowance for 15 percent dropping by the wayside each year, so that 55 out of each 100 completed the four years' work, this would require a minimum commitment for the four years of just over three times the amount for the initial year – assuming all areas were able to start at the same time.

Except for tea, sugar and fruits and vegetables, most of the foods needed for an acceptable diet could be obtained from existing food stocks (and if the Indian Government adopts a policy of intervening to relieve part of the current gur market weakness, surplus gur from Indian sources might also be added). Some of the surplus products presently or potentially available from abroad, such as dry skim milk, butter, cheese, dried fruits and nuts, and canned milk, might be distributed in kind by the authorities operating the messes. Other imported products, such as wheat, rice, maize, sorghums, and oils and fats, might be sold at port cities and the receipts used to buy corresponding quantities of the same commodities in interior locations, thus saving transportation margins and much of the marketing charges. Sales should be regulated to sell at ports only as fast as corresponding quantities are purchased at interior points in the same market regions. The administrative difficulties of such a procedure should not, however, be underestimated, and methods of dealing with them were discussed in Chapter V. Funds other than from surplus products would be needed for tea, coffee, spices, fresh fruits and vegetables, but about 90 percent of the entire food cost could probably be supplied by surplus foods as thus defined. And if some minimum needs test were included (such as family income not to exceed say 30 rupees per person per month), the consumption of surplus foods would probably be largely a net addition to food consumption, as what the families would save on the students' usual food would be negligible compared to the students' new better diet, and would probably be largely taken up in increased consumption by the families themselves.

Although it would be left to the choice of the state school administration which products would be used in kind, and which products would be sold into local markets at ports and replaced by corresponding and concurrent purchases at local producing centers, the food scholarships themselves would always be in actual food supplied to the students to be consumed on the spot, to prevent diversion to other uses through sale.

A possible distribution of this food expenditure, in the light of the average composition of family food budgets in towns at diet levels of about these annual costs, but somewhat modified to meet school conditions, might be as shown in Table VI-3. (These money values alone do not provide a sufficient basis for calculating the nutritive adequacy of the diets, but such calculations lie outside the scope of the present report. The diets would presumably be somewhat more adequate than the average Indian food budgets on which they were based.)

Table VI-3. Illustrative Distribution of Foods Needed
for Food Scholarships [1]

	Total value in	
	Rupees	Dollars
	.... lakhs [2]	... millions ...
Food grains	153	3.2
Pulses	32	0.7
Edible oil	41	0.9
Vegetables	32	0.7
Milk and milk products	93	2.0
Meat, eggs and fish	31	0.6
Fruits, fresh and dried	19	0.4
Salt	2	—
Spices, tea, etc.	16	0.3
Sugar	29	0.6
Total	448	9.4

[1] AU-India data from expenditure studies, National Sample Survey.
[2] 1 lakh = 100 000.

Of these foods, all except fresh vegetables, part of the meat and fruits, and salt, spices, and tea might reasonably be obtained from foreign or domestic food surpluses.[3] Altogether, about 90 percent of the total foods involved might be so obtained.

Other sources of funds would be needed to buy non-surplus foods. If we assume that 20 percent would have to be added to the food costs for freight, and administration, and mess operation, that would mean that at best about 75 percent of the overall cost of the food scholarships could be covered through present or prospective surplus foods, foreign or domestic, while 25 percent would be carried in cash through school budgets. This amount would be about 4 percent of the amount spent by all educational institutions for their current operations (in 1954/55), so it would seem that it could be absorbed within the proposed increase in their budgets.

The costs would then be as follows.

	First year	4-year program
	(lakhs of rupees)	
Surplus foods	403	1 612
Other foods	45	180
Overheads and administration	89	356
Total	537	2 148

Some of the administrative costs, however, might be covered through surplus foods themselves, by arranging for the school teachers to share in the meals or noon lunches, and to handle the local arrangements in return for the food, without extra payment in cash. This in effect would pay a part of the additional administrative costs also in food. This supplement to the teachers' incomes would be especially desirable since their salaries are now so low compared to alternative employment that the school authorities find it very difficult to attract and hold the best-qualified people for this important work. At the very low salaries paid, the opportunity to earn part of their own food would be an important extra inducement. On the other hand it could put still more strain on the usually heavily overworked teachers, and might therefore be undesirable.

The surplus foods used in these programs would probably represent almost completely an addition to food consumption of the families concerned (except possibly for the part consumed by the teachers). This would therefore constitute a specially desirable use of food surpluses, so far as competition with the domestic market is concerned.

Used in the manner outlined above, food scholarships can supplement other activities already under way to improve and speed the preparation of Indian manpower and brainpower to play its necessary part in the future development of the country. The school feeding program itself would need to be worked out as part of the overall educational effort, with careful planning and organization, and close co-operation between educational, nutritional, and other authorities. By assisting in speeding up the preparation of properly qualified personnel, this school feeding program can help eliminate that limiting factor, and also contribute to greater production from the physical resources made available to industry and agriculture. While the contribution to economic development would be a long-time one, it would still be of real importance.

B. FOOD SCHOLARSHIPS FOR OTHER SPECIAL GROUPS

Besides rural youth and children of low-income urban population, there are two other under-privileged groups in India which have been specially recognized as in need of public help. These are the "backward classes" and the "displaced persons". The backward classes include two groups given special legal recognition. One of these, the "scheduled tribes", includes certain indigenous tribes, characterized by primitive and traditional tribal customs suited to a very early stage of development and environment and sometimes of nomadic habits. In some cases these tribes are in areas which were previously small princely States with both education and administration at a relatively rudimentary stage of development. The other group, the "scheduled castes" includes groups affected by religious and social prejudices, notably the "untouchables." These groups have been largely excluded from sharing in cultural advances in Indian life. According to the 1951 census these "backward classes" included 70,460,000 people, almost exactly one-fifth of the population. In addition there are other "backward classes" not yet specially enumerated, but their numbers and conditions are being studied by a Backward Class Commission. Similarly the persons displaced by partition numbered 7,300,000 in 1951. They have now been largely resettled and substantial sums are provided under the Five-Year Plan for their rehabilitation, but 77,000 of the aged, infirm, women and children among them have been accepted as the continuing responsibility of the Central Government.

Education bulks large in the program for improvement of the "backward classes", representing roughly three-quarters of the total budget. This includes establishing schools, providing scholarships and establishing hostels with free board and lodging.

In Bombay State for example, 10,347 "backward classes" students are lodged in hostels, at an expense to the State Government of 15 lakhs of rupees (1954-55). As compared to the total of almost 700,000 "backward classes" pupils attending school in this State, however, only about 1.5 percent are provided rooms and meals and even then, 40 percent of the total expenses are covered by private charity. With the government support ranging only from 10 to 15 rupees per student per month, varying by age and sex, the food provided is very inadequate both in quality and quantity, generally costing not more than 15 rupees per month, as compared to the cost of other students of 35 to 40 rupees per month for eating in usual college messes. Selected surplus foods could be used to improve the diet in these existing "backward class" hostels, including such foods as dry skim milk, pulses, oils and fats, butter and dried fruits or nuts. Without attempting to calculate specific quantities, an addition of 15 rupees a month of such foods to the average diet would bring them up much nearer to that enjoyed by other students, and would no doubt improve the health and vigor of these under-privileged pupils and also the progress and development in their studies. Such a supplement, on a 12-month basis would require 18.0 lakhs of surplus foods a year ($380,000) or 72.0 lakhs ($1,520,000) for a four-year program. In addition, transportation and distribution costs would have to be met. If programs of supplementary educational feeding for "backward class" pupils were developed for the other States with large numbers of these people, averaging the same amount as just estimated for Bombay, this might involve a total use of surplus foods totalling about eight times as much, yet it would reach only a small fraction of 1 percent of the "backward classes" youth in need of such assistance. Any expansion of the existing educational and hostel program for these groups could increase the use of surplus foods correspondingly.[4] Such aid to these students would make a corresponding long-time contribution to the economic development and modernization of their regions and States.

Scholarships for college work are awarded to a substantial number of backward class students from scheduled tribes and scheduled castes under the special legislation. In the current school year, 12,877 such scholarships were awarded. However, 20,664 applications were received from other "backward class" groups who did not qualify as "scheduled" tribes or castes, and of these, only 7,827 were granted scholarships. There were thus over 12,500 applicants for "backward class" scholarships who did not receive them. If food scholarships could be awarded them under the same conditions as suggested earlier for regular education scholarships, the other costs for tuition, etc., might be covered out of expansion in the "backward class" budget. Further, if high school food fellowships were established for additional "backward class" students (on the same proportion of ten in high school for every one in college shown by the total enrollments), that would mean another 125,000 food fellowships to be provided. If these were calculated at the same rate of 300 rupees a year used in estimating the program for the regular schools, that would mean an additional use of 4.1 crores annually. Assuming the same proportion of surplus foods to apply as in the general education program, 90 percent, that would mean using 3.7 crores of rupees

($8,000,000) worth of surplus foods for this food scholarships program for backward class student. Difficulties in housing such students would also have to be borne in mind.

The necessary additional funds for non-surplus foods, and the administration of the feeding and distribution programs, could probably be handled without difficulty within the expanding budgets for the "backward class" programs, since expenditure for these programs has run thus far well below the average rates anticipated in the first Five-Year Plan.

Using the minimum figures from each calculation, the program for backward class students would be as follows (in terms of food content of the proposed programs).

	Annual cost		Four-year cost	
	Total	Surplus food	Total	Surplus food
	.... lakhs of rupees			
Supplementary feeding in existing school hostels for backward class pupils	160	144	640	576
Food scholarships (in high schools and colleges) for backward class pupils	495	370	1 980	1 480
Total	655	514	2 620	2 056

In dollar terms, this would make effective use of surplus foods with a value of about $11,500,000 per year. These foods would represent direct additions to the food consumption of the youths concerned and would aid in providing education and strength to promising individuals from the most under-privileged groups in the nation; they would involve no perceptible substitution for other food which would burden domestic or foreign markets.

C. INTERNSHIP TRAINING FOR EDUCATED UNEMPLOYED

The need for opportunities for high school and college graduates to obtain practical experience has already been referred to. This need is underlined by the columns of newspaper advertisements offering positions of every type for graduates with two to five years' practical experience in engineering, commerce, industry and administration – but no offers of positions where new graduates can gain such practical experience.

There is substantial unemployment in India today among high school and college graduates, with 142,000 of the former, and 22,000 of the latter registered with employment exchanges. While perhaps half of those registered already have work of some sort, the remainder are believed to be wholly unemployed. Further, many unemployed – perhaps nine out of ten – are not registered at all. About 5 percent of the graduates registered are from engineering and medical colleges, but the great bulk are from arts colleges. Suggestions have been made that enrollment should be reduced in arts colleges, but increased in technical and scientific ones. In many cases college graduates have to wait several years before finding any suitable employment.

The existence of considerable unemployment among high school and college graduates is not inconsistent with the fact that a developing economy needs ever larger numbers of trained and skilled foremen, technicians, organizers, administrators, and scientists. In India today there are too many arts graduates, but insufficient graduates with specialized knowledge and skills. In addition, as the economy continues to develop, there will be continuous expansion in the need for persons competent to meet the manifold demands of the rapidly expanding line of activity – industry, transportation, trade and finance, construction, private and governmental administration, education and other governmental services and skilled professions. Higher education is a long process; present and planned expansions in educational facilities and school attendance are necessary to meet the future expanding needs.

Arrangements should be made to establish internship or trainee positions for many of these educated unemployed so that they can obtain experience in agencies for which they may work later, industrial and commercial concerns, transportation agencies, government departments, or as assistant teachers in schools and colleges. Messes would need to be established for them, since it would be difficult for workers living in lodgings in urban centers to prepare surplus foods themselves. In addition to their food, they should be paid a modest supplementary wage to cover their minimum out-of-pocket expenses, and budgets to this end should be provided in the institutions with which they worked. In addition, each institution or agency accepting such trainees or interns should be required to rotate them from one type of work to another, and to establish in-service courses or special training classes for them, to assist them in gaining both the experience and knowledge which would enable them soon to move ahead as fully employed professional, administrative, or educational workers. Through such means the program could be prevented from degenerating into a mere means of getting cheap labor, and made to serve an important purpose in bridging the gap between the theories and general knowledge acquired in college, and the nation's need for large numbers of skilled effective workers and leaders to speed its economic development. Special efforts would have to be made to insure that the trainees or interns were actually given experience in several types of work, received supplementary training and instruction, and opportunity to do work of gradually increasing responsibility, to prevent any abuses of the program by employers.

In view of the uncertainties as to the existing number of educated unemployed, it is difficult to suggest a figure as to the number of such food fellowships for interns which could be arranged and supervised at the beginning. Possibly 25,000 might be a minimum, though conceivably if a program were announced, there might be applicants for as many as 500,000. Perhaps an initial program of 25,000, at an annual cost of 1 crore for food (about $2,100,000) would be as many as could be placed in appropriate institutions, industries or offices for experience and training. This would probably require an administrative budget of 10 lakhs to cover the arrangements with the employers, and to administer the feeding arrangements, and probably a further 20 lakhs for the non-surplus foods. The surplus foods might then amount to 80 lakhs a year, or 80 percent of the food total. This additional use of about $1,700,000 worth of surplus foods a year, plus a regular budget of 30 lakhs for administration and non-surplus food ($620,000) would make a start towards closing a serious gap in the present arrangements for providing the skilled manpower needed for India's continued rapid development. At the same time it would help cure the frustration and despair of thousands of ambitious youngsters who have made sacrifices to complete high school or college, only to find that there seems to be no place for them, and no way to turn to start their careers.

Costs Summarized

	1 year	4 years
Surplus food	80 lakhs	320 lakhs
Non-surplus food and administration	30 lakhs	120 lakhs
Total	110 lakhs	440 lakhs

D. Use of Surpluses in Village Community and Other Development Projects

The Village Community Development Program now covers one-fifth of all Indian villages, and will be extended in 1955-56 to include 30 percent in all. In these projects, the villagers are encouraged and assisted both with technical aid and public grants to carry through projects which will improve local economic activity and standards of living. One condition of the work is that the villagers assist and participate in each project, either by themselves working voluntarily directly on the project, or by contributing to it in cash or subscribed capital. Projects conducted include the building or improvement of school houses, village wells or tanks, village privies; gutters and paving of village streets to end dust and mud; a community center for meetings, entertainment, etc.; village access roads, irrigation dams or weirs, or diversion dams in small water courses to spread flood waters over the land to be absorbed; irrigation canals, waterways, or drainage ditches; soil conservation terraces or "bunds"; storage warehouses for supplies for farm distribution (fertilizers, pesticides, etc., often in conjunction with establishing a local farmers' co-operative supply or selling agency); and sometimes small local warehouses or packing plants for stocking, sorting, or packing local products. These activities use local materials and local labor, plus skilled supervision and some skilled labor, such as masons or carpenters.

Although participation in these activities is entirely on a voluntary basis, the incentive to engage in them is much greater for farm owners than for rural labor without land, or with so little land that they are mainly dependent on work for others. There are 18 million such families in India, and in many sections they constitute around one-quarter of the total rural population, running even higher in Bihar and Orissa, and 40 to 60 percent in Hyderabad and Madras, but lower – about 10 percent – in the extreme north and east – the Punjab, Rajasthan and Assam. (Note Figure 1).

There is much less incentive for agricultural labor to contribute voluntary work to village development projects than there is for farmers having their own farms. Laborers do not profit directly from projects which increase economic productivity, and they are not certain to continue living in the village to enjoy the benefits of village improvement projects. Further, they are on the lowest level of the village living standards. Food alone usually takes 80 to 90 percent of their total expenditure, in most districts, and their average consumption of food is materially below that of landholding farmers. Yet there is much unused labor time in this group. In villages visited in Bombay State during this study, village leaders estimated that there was work for the landless laborers only about 3 months a year.

Possible Use of Surplus Foods to Encourage More Voluntary Labor. Surplus foods might encourage more participation in voluntary labor projects by using some selected foods to aid in providing a single meal to all workers on a project, with well-to-do farmers also contributing local supplies, or by the direct use of food for payment in kind up to about 80 to 90 percent of the wages which would otherwise be earned.[5]

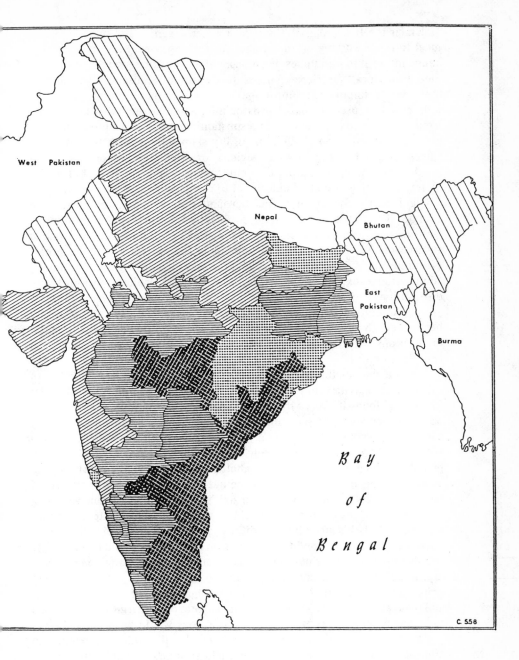

West Pakistan

Nepal

Bhutan

East Pakistan

Burma

Bay

of

Bengal

C. 558

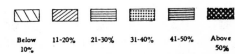

Below | 11-20% | 21-30% | 31-40% | 41-50% | Above
10% | | | | | 50%

Figure 1. Proportion of Agricultural Labor Families Among All Rural Families, 1950-51.

Under the first proposal, the village would organize and serve one solid meal to those working on the project each day they worked. In areas with abundant local food supplies of cereals, pulses, etc., these would be contributed from local supplies. Surplus foods would be used to supplement them and to improve the nutritional value of the meal. Surplus dry skim milk could be used to make curds or milk-based sweets (well known and liked in most parts of India), with a substantial portion served to each worker – say equivalent to about 1 oz. of dry skim milk powder for a serving. Cheese might be used in some regions, or dried fruits or nuts at times. Used in this way, the surpluses would not pay labor directly, but would merely offer an additional inducement to participate – and at the same time would increase the dietary efficiency and raise the level of health and energy. The surplus foods would go directly into increased consumption, with no significant displacement of other foods. Administrative costs and supervision, and distribution and shipping of the relatively small quantities of surplus foods used would be covered within the existing supervision and administrative expenses for development projects, while preparation and distribution of the foods would be handled by the local village authorities as a community activity. Considerable local effort and expenditure would be needed to organize communal meals as suggested, and their social implications with reference to existing village customs would have to be kept in mind.

Despite the small size of the amounts distributed, the large number of such village activities under way would make a very significant total outlet for surplus foods if every village participated. For example, if each village was given enough dry skim milk to provide such supplementary food to each of 200 workers 20 times in a year, that would require 250 pounds to a village. There are approximately 30,000 villages co-operating in such projects at the present time, and in another year there will be nearly 50,000. To provide this quantity of milk to one out of each ten such villages, would take 5,000 × 250, or 1,250,000 lb. or 625 short tons. At current values of about 1,200 rupees per ton, this would be worth 7½ lakhs of rupees – about $150,000. With this incentive to additional work, the increase of both the productive power and the conditions of living in each village would be materially speeded up. It would be desirable to have such a program started on the basis of a three or four year continuing grant, so that it would not be subject to being suddenly cut off, after the villages had become used to using the foods and to organizing their voluntary work in connection with a group meal. For a four-year program, a commitment of 2,500 tons would be needed.[6]

Dried fruits or nuts could be substituted for the milk at times, to an equivalent value – though they do not add so much desirable nutrition at such a small cost as does dry skim milk.

The second or alternative use of surplus foods in community projects would involve more elaborate arrangements. Here workers who would not otherwise engage in voluntary labor – especially the agricultural labor, and particularly those from landless families – would be engaged to work on particular projects over a considerable period when they were not otherwise employed. Some of such workers said "If you feed us, we will work", but others asked about food for their wives and children, and pocket money for clothes, salt, tea, etc. It would be possible to pay them directly in food, up to say 80 percent of their wages, and pay the balance in cash (say 5 annas a day, equal to one-fifth of a wage of 1½ rupees per day). This would involve actually transporting and distributing the equivalent food. Based on the average consumption of such families, and on the use made of additional income, their tendency would be to use not over two-thirds of the additional income for food, and to use the rest to improve other elements of their very meager standard of living. With 80 percent of their pay in kind as food, there would be some tendency to resell part of it. Further, not all of the total foods ordinarily consumed can be provided from food surpluses.

For administrative simplicity, it would be better to sell most of the surpluses at ports of arrival, at the same rate at which consumption was being expanded in the interior, and to pay the additional labor in cash, counting on their increased consumption to offset the additional supplies put on markets elsewhere. Additional labor on community development projects, if paid on a full-time cash basis, becomes the same thing as additional labor on any other project (Type II). As shown in Chapter III, not more than about 40 percent of the wages paid for such labor could be expected to reappear in the increased expenditures for surplus foods. The balance of the expenditures would have to be covered from other new resources.

The proposal for payment of cash wages for village development projects is also contrary to the philosophy of the Community Development program, which emphasizes the value of co-operative voluntary work to improve village living conditions and productive facilities. Some leaders in the movement fear that even the single joint meal might set a precedent, so that if later it were withdrawn for lack of surplus supplies, the whole voluntary labor idea might tend to wither away. On the other hand, the joint meal could be continued through contributions from village supplies, as the villages' production increased, and would provide a partial means by which the better-off farmers in the village could make some payment to the landless workers for sharing in the village work. Further, all the workers actually eating a meal together would be of value in helping to create a feeling of joint participation in joint activities and to break down caste and other prejudices.

The same idea might be used in a different way in connection with voluntary labor camps in regions and for projects outside of regular community development areas. Projects similar to those being built in the area are needed in other areas also. Many of these – especially those involving productive facilities, such as dams, roads, canals, etc. – are being built by voluntary work camps of various sorts. These usually are situated at a considerable distance from where the workers come, and housing and food are therefore normally supplied the workers who volunteer for the activity. Surpluses could be used for much of the foods supplied such workers, with very little displacement of existing food consumption, since if their families did not have to feed them at home, probably much of the food saved would go into increased family consumption. Furthermore, if educated unemployed were fed while in training, as proposed earlier in this chapter, many of them could be stationed at these labor camps, to help in performing the work, and to learn by doing. As they were gradually advanced to supervising fellow workers as foremen, to keeping the books and the accounts, to aiding the engineers and administrators in planning and conducting the activities, eventually they too would become fully qualified and experienced, and be ready to carry on useful and responsible work at good salaries.

The amount and value of surplus foods which could be used in feeding workers and trainees on voluntary labor projects would be limited only by the number of people qualified to plan, organize and conduct such projects, and the number of unemployed workers who would volunteer for such work. Probably as many as 100,000 volunteer workers would readily be recruited, plus say 5,000 unemployed graduates. If the necessary administrators and technical supervisory staff could be made available, the budget for the activity might run somewhat as follows.

Food for 105,000 men at 400 rupees each	4.2	crore
Of which: surplus foods (fed in kind)	*3.6*	"
other foods	*0.6*	"
Supervision	0.16	"
Purchased supplies, materials, freight, etc.	1.0	"
Total	5.36	crore

The project, as thus estimated, would use 3.6 crores of surplus foods (about 7.5 million dollars), and require a budget of 1.76 crores for other foods, materials and services. It should be able to complete a great deal of useful work for this expenditure.

The two types of activity may be summarized as shown in the table opposite.

E. Financing Milk Marketing Schemes Through Surplus Products

Milk marketing schemes may include arrangements for *(a)* the collection, chilling, processing, and shipment of milk from rural producing areas to central bottling and distribution plants; *(b)* the reception, processing, and

Estimated Cost for Stimulating Additional Voluntary
Labor in Local Development Projects

	1st year		4 years	
	Total cost	Surplus foods	Total cost	Surplus foods
	.... *lakhs of rupees*			
Supplementary foods in community development ..	[1]7.5	7.5	[1]30	30
Voluntary labor camps	536.0	360.0	2 144	1 440
Total	543.5	367.5	2 174	1 470

[1] Assuming administrative and transport costs assumed by regular community development personnel and budgets.

bottling and distribution in safe and sanitary form; *(c)* removing milch animals and their owners from cities and their suburbs, and re-establishing them, with their owners and workers, under more convenient, sanitary, and efficient conditions, in special "milk colonies" in suburban or rural areas, and *(d)* supplementing the local milk supplies by importing dry skim milk, whole milk powder, butter fat or butter-oil or other fats, and using them to produce liquid milk or milk substitutes made in whole or in part from the imported materials. Such schemes should include measures to improve the cleanliness and sanitation with which the milk is produced, handled, and distributed, to improve the methods of production on the farm, including feeding, breeding, disease prevention, production of roughages, and farm management; and to increase the use of milk in both rural and urban homes. The facilities for milk collection, bottling, and distribution may be operated by public agencies, by private enterprises, or by a combination of both, and financing may similarly be part public and part private. The production of milk is usually a private enterprise of farmers or dairymen, but may be assisted by public or corporate activities, such as the establishment of milk colonies.[7]

The Bombay Milk Scheme is the most fully developed example. Since this type of activity is less well-known than others discussed in this report, it will be described somewhat more fully.[8] A large tract of land at the edge of the city was acquired and equipped with a large modern milk plant with facilities for milk reception, weighing, testing, cooling, clarification, standardization, pasteurization, bottling and shipping, and capable of handling 500 maunds (40,000 pounds) of milk per hour. It also has 26 modern "dairy farm units", each consisting of well-ventilated sanitary barns for a large number of cows in milk, plus housing accommodations for the owners and milkers of the cows, and their families. A municipal order was passed under which the authorities could prohibit the keeping of milch cattle for profit in any specified area of the city, and could specify particular places in which they might be kept.[9]

Through the gradual application of this order, all cattle have gradually been transferred from Bombay City proper to the Milk Colony (at Aarey) where there are now about 12,000 milking animals, and 3,000 young stock. In addition, about 8,000 dry cattle are temporarily away in country areas until they calve and start yielding milk again. A country receiving station, with pasterization and chilling facilities, was also established at Anand (240 miles away) where milk is purchased from a region with about 23,000 cattle, and transferred in ice-cooled insulated wagons by rail to the central plant at Aarey. The milk is pasteurized and bottled, and trucked to distributing stations in the city, for sale to consumers. Two grades of bottled milk are produced, a full-cream buffalo milk, 7.3 percent fat, and a "toned milk" consisting of about 40 percent buffalo milk and 60 percent skim milk. Both are sold in ½ seer and ¼ seer bottles (about 1 pint and ½ pint respectively).

Substitution of dry skim milk for full milk in the hotels (undertaken at first as a measure to relieve an acute milk shortage) later helped finance the construction of the milk colony. The dry skim milk is imported at commercial prices, costing most recently about 90 pounds a ton, and resold to the hotels and restaurants under a public monopoly at a flat price of 1 rupee a pound. The substantial net profit to the Milk Department helped provide funds for the initial capital, and currently helps to subsidize slightly (to about ½ annas a seer) the production of toned milk. The tax thus levied on hotels and restaurants fell mostly on milk for use with tea and coffee, consumed largely by high-income people, where the amount used would hardly be influenced by the higher cost to the establishments, and thus provided a means of taxing a relatively high-income inelastic demand to help meet the needs of much poorer consumers with a much more elastic demand. The scheme now purchases about 3,000 tons of dry skim milk a year, of which two-thirds is resold to restaurants and hotels, and one-third is used for the production of toned milk.

The milk receiving and pasteurizing plant at Anand was built up by a local co-operative, with assistance given by the Bombay State Government and the Central Government of India. The United Nations Children's Fund (UNICEF) has now provided assistance of about $150,000 towards a milk pasteurizing and drying plant, on the usual conditions, which involve the co-operative in contributing considerably more than this in free milk to be distributed to Bombay school children over a term of years.

The present buying and selling prices are as follows (for buffalo milk 7.3 percent fat, except as noted).

	To producers at city milk colony	To producers at country receiving station	To consumers at retail
	.... *annas per seer*		
Price paid farmers	12	6[1]	
Costs delivered at plant	12	11-11½[1]	
Retail price, bottled (7.3%) ...			14
Retail price, toned milk (3%) .			6

[1] Equivalent of price paid for milk at 5 rupees per seer of butter fat (= 52.5 cents per lb. butter fat).

Originally the price of toned milk was 8 annas per seer (10½ per quart). In late 1954 the price was reduced to 6 annas a seer.[10] The change in milk sales per month since this change in price is reported to be as follows:

	Full buffalo milk	Toned milk	Total
	.... *thousands of pounds*		
Before price change[1]	6,080	2,120	8,200
After price change[2]	5,503	2,977	8,480
Change:	− 577	+ 857	+ 280

[1] December 1953 - February 1954
[2] December 1954 - February 1955 (Data for January and February preliminary)

The reduction of 25 percent in the price of toned milk thus caused an increase in toned milk sales of about 40 percent partly offset by a decrease about two-thirds as large in sales of full-fat buffalo milk. Presumably sales of toned milk will continue to expand, as the habit of using the product spreads further among low-income consumers. Many more people in Bombay are consuming milk, and the milk drinking habit is spreading to many who previously could not afford it. At the same time the total demand for milk produced by Indian farmers in the region has continued substantially unchanged. The present milk plant is now running to fairly full capacity. As soon as new plant facilities can be constructed and put into operation, the amount of bottled milk distributed in Bombay can increase further – especially if the price of toned milk can be dropped still more, as the result of larger volume and expected more economical operation in a projected new processing plant in the city proper.

Production of milk at the milk colony is conducted by the city milk producers who transferred their milking herds there. There are 115 "licencees" at the present colony. While the number of cows owned by each varies widely, the licencees milk an average of 110 animals. They are supplied concentrates and roughage for feeding their cattle by the colony administration at fixed prices. A considerable part of the roughages, especially green feeds, are produced at the colony itself, using the manure from the cattle (previously wasted in Bombay city), and the waste water from the dairy plant for irrigation. The dairy farm workers are paid by the cattle owners.

Before the scheme was established, the cattle, living right in the city and often in the streets, were a sanitary and traffic menace. The milk was dirty and frequently adulterated. The manure was wasted, and the cattle were sold for slaughter when they finished one lactation period and were replaced with others bought from the country. On all these counts the scheme has provided more sanitary, healthful, and efficient arrangements. Also, it has made toned milk available to a large group in the population who previously could not afford milk in any form. The scheme now supplies about half of greater Bombay's milk consumption (local dairies still exist in its suburban region, outside the area where cows have been banned). The total consumption of roughly 7,500 maunds a day (as reported by the officials concerned) for Bombay's population of over 3 million people, is an average of only 0.2 pounds of milk a day per person – just over one-third of a glass. This is far below the amount needed for minimum nutritional requirements, with practically no other source of animal proteins in the usual diet. Even that consumption is probably one-quarter larger than it was before the milk scheme was started. The "toned" milk has a composition similar to ordinary cow's milk. Previously the only milk available was buffalo milk, almost equal to light cream in fat, where genuine, but often adulterated and contaminated. Such high-fat milk is not easy for children to digest. Suitable milk for them has thus been provided for the first time at a price many more families can afford to pay, with corresponding increased health for hundreds of thousands of children who previously had no suitable, safe and economical milk available for their use.

Need for other milk schemes. Few other cities have exactly the same conditions for milk production and distribution as existed in Bombay before the scheme was introduced. (Calcutta and Rangoon are two cities with conditions similar in some respects.) Certain aspects of the scheme, however, such as modern bottling and distribution facilities, and dry skim milk powder to supplement supplies locally available, and the supply of special milk at a reduced cost, would be valuable in many other cities where the ability of consumers to pay high prices is limited, the arrangements for milk collection and marketing are antiquated, and (in many tropical or near-tropical conditions) there is fairly heavy dependence of local production on buffaloes.

In Madras a reconstituted milk is being produced by using dry skim milk and a hydrogenated vegetable oil, with added carotene. Butterfat and butter oil and dry skim milk might similarly be used for reconstitution. Other blended milk products might also be produced, where local milk supplies are insufficient, by mixing the available whole milk, either from cows or buffaloes, with appropriate quantities of butter or vegetable fats, dry skim milk, and water; such low-cost bottled products might be offered at two levels of fat content, such as 3 percent and 2 percent, to meet the buying power of various groups of consumers.

Use of surplus products in financing milk schemes. Regardless of whether a city needs solely a modern milk plant and country receiving and transporting facilities, or also needs a milk colony to house cows now located in the city or surburbs, a considerable part of the capital costs of the project might be covered by surplus farm products – especially if dry skim milk is to be used to produce toned milk.

Food surpluses might be used to help finance the costs in three different ways.

1. To provide part of the food for the additional workers given direct employment in erecting the plants, barns, etc., and for those employed in producing domestic equipment and materials for use in building such facilities.

2. To provide dry skim milk (and butterfat if needed) for a term of years to produce blended or other products.

3. In the case of city milk colonies, to provide feed grains, oilcake, and other concentrate feeds to be fed to the milking cows and buffaloes in the colony, above the quantities they were consuming prior to the establishment of the scheme.

The amounts that might be involved in such an undertaking will be illustrated by a specific case at Calcutta.

Dairy and milk conditions in Calcutta are somewhat similar to those which existed earlier in Bombay. The State authorities in Calcutta have established a large dairy and poultry breeding farm 36 miles from the city. This farm is equipped with a small milk plant which handles the milk produced by its own herd of over 400 cows, and also milk from producers in nearby villages and from a producing center 35 miles away, where a receiving and chilling station has been established. Plans are under way to build three dairy farm units at the farm to house (together with one already constructed) 5,088 milking animals, and to buy and irrigate 679 acres two and a half miles away, for additional fodder production.

The milk plant is bottling both full cow's milk (around 4.5 percent fat) and toned milk with less fat, sold at prices of 14 and 11 annas per pound, respectively. The milk is bottled at the farm and trucked into town, where it is supplied to all hospitals, some schools and colleges, and to some individual consumers through 75 local distribution points, open for two hours each morning.

A start has been made in building dairy units for the cows and dairymen at the farm; one unit for 1,272 animals is already completed, and three more will be built soon.

Plans have been prepared for establishing a large milk plant on the farm, with good transportation facilities, and also a milk colony to house the rest of the milking cows now being kept in the city proper. Of these cattle, all 23,000 would be housed at the present city-owned farm, and the rest – young stock and dry cows – on a dry-stock farm some distance away. The present farm of 2,000 acres (partly used for experimental and college purposes) would be supplemented by an additional 2,300 acres for fodder. The program differs from the Bombay Milk Colony Scheme in that the milk colony will be located in more rural sorroundings and will produce more of its green fodder, under irrigation on its own premises, and will depend less on forage shipped in from elsewhere. Funds for the other 18 units needed have not yet been provided, however, nor for the large central dairy plant and will not be made available before the Second Five-Year Plan starts in the 1956/57 fiscal year. If financing could be provided sooner through the use of surplus foods, work could start in 1955 instead, as plans have been drawn, and the administrative and operating authorities already exist and have gained experience from the present smaller pilot operations.

The plan now proposed by the Calcutta authorities is not necessarily the best method of improving the milk supply of Calcutta. Some technicians believe it would be better not to establish a milk colony for the cattle, but to encourage expansion of dairy cow numbers and marketing of fluid milk in farm regions around Calcutta, and to reduce and prohibit milch cattle in Calcutta as milk supplies from outside increased. This would involve establishing additional milk receiving, processing and shipment stations in appropriate rural centers, building a centrally-located milk processing plant in Calcutta, and providing milk distributing arrangements there. Another proposal is to build such a processing plant with the assistance of international organizations, and to provide part of the dry skim milk free from surpluses for several years to help establish welfare schemes. [11] There are also questions whether the processing plant should use pasteurization or sterilization. Regardless of which method, or combination of methods, is decided upon, the project would provide possibilities for the use of surplus products in the first two ways mentioned earlier, and possibly in all three.

The existing Indian proposals for the development of milk production and distribution in Calcutta will therefore be used here to illustrate how surplus products might contribute to the financing of such milk schemes, without that use meaning that the methods now proposed are necessarily the best or most desirable, either for Calcutta or for other cities similarly situated. If other methods of development and operation are decided upon after more extended study of the technical and economic issues involved, the calculations can easily be revised to show how far food surpluses could help finance such alternative arrangements.

The additional facilities needed under the present proposals are as follows.

Plant and Fixtures	Crores of rupees
22 dairy units (to accommodate 1272 animals each) ...	3.2
Fodder farm expansion, land irrigation and fencing	1.29
Dairy plant	0.73
Distribution facilities	.01,25
Workshop and central office	.10,72
Total:	5.33,97

By types of constuction, the expenditures envisaged are as follows.

	Lakhs of rupees
Land purchase	33.21
Reclamation and fencing	6.65
Roads	8.50
Flood embankment and irrigation canals ...	3.30
Construction of buildings	446.03
Machinery and equipment	65.45
Deep tubewells	9.70
Vehicles	16.70
Electric transmission line	3.30
Bulls	0.15
Total:	592.99

This total cost, 5.93 crores, is equal to about $12,500,000.

The distribution of these items into the classifications important for our analysis is as follows.

	Lakhs
Land purchase	33.2
Imported materials and services	56.3
Direct labor on project (including labor for sub-contractors)	284.8
Domestic materials and services	218.7
Total:	593.0

The three ways of employing surpluses, (1) for workers' increased consumption (2) for producing toned milk, and (3) for feeding cattle, will be considered separately.

Expenditures for land and for imports would not generate any appreciable increased consumption of food in India, and are therefore ignored. These total 89.5 lakhs of rupees.

(1) Since the direct labor would be employed largely in an urban or suburban environment, the proportion of the wages received being spent for foods which could be supplied from surplus may be estimated at the reduced figure of 35 percent, and an allowance of 25 percent marketing costs will be used, as on urban food expenditures.

The indirect expenditure, on the basis of the reasoning already set out in Chapter III, will similarly increase incomes and expenditure of other groups. Calculating the prospective effects on surplus food consumption by the methods presented in Appendix 2, assuming three cycles of spending and re-spending are carried through and that the investment is spread evenly through one year, the prospective increase in the consumption of foods of surplus types works out at 144 lakhs of rupees the first year, 74 lakhs the second, and 15 the third. (The small further derived effects after the third year will be neglected.) In these three years together, this comes to 233 lakhs, or about two-fifths of the total investment.

(2) In the case of the milk scheme, however, its heavy use of dry skim milk provides additional possibilities for financing through surpluses. The present pilot operations in Calcutta now use 180 tons a year of dry skim milk for the production of toned milk. The proposed new plant is expected to use ten times as much. In addition, supplementary facilities for the production of ice cream and other milk products may increase its use even more. If the authorities could be supplied 4,000 tons of surplus dry skim milk a year for the first three years of the project for use in the various products[12], how would that affect *(a)* the problem of paying for the plant *(b)* the fiscal situation in the country, and *(c)* domestic and international markets for dairy products?

At present prices of £90 per ton, FOB Indian ports, the 4,000 tons of dry skim milk would be worth about 48 lakhs of rupees, or over the three-year grant, about 144 lakhs. Adding this to the surplus foods under (1) brings the total cost to 377 lakhs, or about three-fifths of the total investment.

(3)   The third possible use of food surpluses is in feeding the cattle located on the colony, or even in country producing areas. After the cows are brought under the scheme, either in the milk colony or on farms supplying milk to the plant, they would be fed better than they were before in order to increase their production and efficiency. At Bombay, milch cattle are fed about 18 lbs. of dry concentrates a day. The cattle are largely buffaloes, producing about 15 lbs. of milk a day. If the cows at Calcutta were fed say 10 lbs. of concentrates a day, and half of that amount were supplied from surplus supplies, what would the value be per year?

About 23,000 additional milch cattle would be housed at the colony, with the expansion provided for. Five pounds per day for them for one year comes to 420 lakhs of pounds of feeds required annually. Assuming these feeds could be supplied in grains (maize, wheat, oats, sorghum) and in oil cakes, at an average value (at Indian markets) of 1.7 annas per pound, the total value for the 420 lakhs of pounds of feed would be about 44.5 lakhs of rupees. A grant of sufficient surplus feedstuffs to provide this amount of feed annually for three years would thus be worth 134 lakhs. The total value of the surpluses allotted to the project would then be:

	Lakhs
1. Increased food consumption by workers, directly and indirectly	233
2. Increased consumption of dry skim milk	144
3. Increased consumption of feedstuffs by cattle	134
	511 ($10,800,000)

The proportion of the total costs of 593 lakhs which could be covered by surplus food stuffs is thus 86 percent.

On the basis of these calculations, including using food surpluses to offset part of the labor costs and to·supply part of the additional dry skim milk concentrate feedstuffs for a three year period, it appears that it is possible to cover a much larger proportion of the total capital costs for milk schemes through surpluses than in any other type of construction scheme considered, except through the rare project of Type III opening up immediately very profitable production to repay the balance of the cost.

The magnitude of the scheme involved may be seen from the fact that, if the construction was completed in one year, it would put 19,000 men at work for a year on the direct construction, and make work for another 7,500 men for a year in producing and transporting the sand, gravel, cement, steel, and other domestic materials and equipment to be used in the construction. Altogether, then, it would provide employment for 26,500 men during that year, and also make continuing work for perhaps 5,000 people, whole and part time, on the production, processing, and distribution of the increased quantities of whole and toned milk going into consumption. These figures take no account of the additional employment generated in satisfying the further induced income.

Financial and Economic Effects of Financing the Milk Scheme through Agricultural Surpluses

Because of the use of surpluses in operating the scheme after the construction is finished, in addition to those used to offset the increased consumption during the period of construction, the milk scheme requires some additional special analysis of the probable effects.

1. *Effect on financing the plant.* The food offsetting that consumed by the workers in building the plant could be sold to local markets during the same period as the plant was being built and the proceeds become available for meeting current expenditures (except for the 89 lakhs which would become available in the second and third years). The funds from the milk powder used and the feed fed the animals on the other hand would become available, year by year, only after the increased facilities were put into use. Out of the 593 lakhs total cost, it may be assumed that the land, costing 33 lakhs, would be paid for in long-term installments, perhaps at the rate (including interest) of 3 lakhs per year. On this basis, it would be necessary to borrow money from some source to finance the part of the project which could not be covered from surpluses used during construction, the funds to be gradually repaid during the first 3 years of operation from the income from the use of the dry skim milk and the feedstuffs, and from the income earned from the project itself. The timetable of payments would then be about as follows.

	Expenditure	Receipts	Balance due on loans
	.... lakhs of rupees		
During construction period	560	144	416
During first year of operation	3	167[1]	252
During second year of operation	3	107[2]	148
During third year of operation	4	93	59

[1] Including 74 lakhs for increased use of surpluses in human consumption (effects of derived income in second year).
[2] Including 15 lakhs for increased use of surpluses in human consumption.

It would thus be necessary to have an initial loan of about 416 lakhs of rupees, which would be largely repaid in three annual installments, leaving the small balance and the payments on land to be repaid out of the income from the operations. With this favorable program for repayment, assuming the surplus products were obtained either as a grant or as a loan on a very long-term period of repayment at low interest rates, it should be possible to secure the short-term financing needed either from public or private sources at favorable rates of interest.

2. *Effect on the country's financial position.* The basic idea in using farm surpluses to finance additional development is that they should not affect the country's financial position, since the additional buying power put into circulation by the additional employment should be exactly offset by the additional buying power taken out of circulation by the sale of the products. In this case, the immediate capital investment is nearly all repaid by the sale of the surplus products within four years from the time that work on the project is first started. Since almost half the investment is repaid the first two years, the possible inflationary effect is reduced. But since each unit of investment can generate more than one unit of income and expenditure, due to the derived effects as the income circulates through several cycles of re-spending, there are still possible inflationary effects which would have to be counter-balanced by expansion in the general national production.

Thereafter, the project would more than pay its own way, and the repayments on its loans would help make possible greater investment in other projects. This offers an interesting possibility. If we think of not one single milk scheme of this sort, but of a series of schemes financed by surplus products in different parts of the same country, each started in a different year, the composite effect of all the schemes would have much less effect, either inflationary or deflationary, since the initial inflationary effects of the first year of one project could be offset by the repayments from other projects.

The same principle might be applied another way. The project might be split into units, some of which could be erected and put into operation each year for three or four years. For example, if both the Calcutta milk colony and milk plant could be erected and put into operation as three units, starting one-third each year for three years, its annual effect, either inflationary or deflationary, would be only one-third as large in the first year, and would be smaller and smaller in each successive year. The feasibility of such handling of the arrangements depends upon the technical possibilities of building and starting the central plant in installments, without loss of operating efficiency. For the milk colony, gradual removal of the cows from the city to the colony over years is probably more realistic than the earlier assumption of the entire operation being accomplished in one year.

It is obvious that even with all the support assumed from surplus products, milk schemes would still have some inflationary effect in the first year of the project, which would have to be offset by other fiscal or financial operations, or by general growth in the output of the economy.[13] This inflationary effect would be less if the project could be constructed in a series of annual installments. In addition there would be expenditures for imported investment and consumer goods to be covered in foreign exchange, amounting in the first year to about one-fifth of the total cost of the project, if built in a single year, or correspondingly less if spread over a term of years.

On either basis of calculation, however, it appears that financing a milk scheme through surpluses would place relatively less inflationary strain on a country's economy than would any other use of surpluses, except other direct distribution or immediately productive projects (Types I and III). In view of the great importance of improvement of milk supply and consumption to health and nutrition of the people of under-developed countries, this method seems an unusually attractive use of food surpluses.

3. *Effect on domestic and foreign markets for farm products.* Under the proposed arrangement, farm products would be used to help finance the operations through three uses of surpluses: (1) a broad range of foodstuffs to help feed the workers who were given employment during the construction of the plant; (2) dry skim milk (and possibly also butter fat) to be blended in the milk products sold; and (3) concentrate feed stuffs to help feed the milking cattle. Would such disposition of surplus products affect the concurrent supply, demand, or price position of farm products in India?

Here we must remember that we are operating on the assumption that in the absence of such financing from surplus products the plant would not be constructed (at least during the period involved), and that its activities would therefore represent a net addition to those which would otherwise be taking place in India at the same time. The surplus foods for the workers would be sold in Calcutta markets (or in markets at other metropolitan centers in India where employment was increased by work for the plant) at the same rate as the increased consumption of such foodstuffs resulting from the increased employment added to the increased demand on those markets. If the additions to supply and to demand exactly balanced in each market area in each period, no influence on price at all should result, either domestic or foreign. The workers might not, however, buy exactly as much additional food as had been estimated that they would, or might not distribute their purchases over the different commodities exactly as estimated. The differences involved would in any such case be small compared to the total quantities on the same markets, so these slight discrepancies should therefore have no measurable effect, either domestic or foreign.

The feedstuffs for the cattle, and the dry skim milk (and butter or butter oil, if used), are in the same position, in that they would supply a demand that would not have existed if the project had not been started. The concentrates supplied, half of those to be consumed by the milking cattle, are a net addition to the quantities they would have consumed if they had continued to be kept in the city. Similarly, the dry skim milk (and possibly butter) would help satisfy an additional demand that would not have existed in the absence of the operation. The experience of Bombay proves that when people are supplied pure sanitary bottled milk, both natural and "toned", at prices attractive to them, they will consume much more than before and thus enlarge the markets for the locally-produced milk and butterfat, and also for the imported milk products.[14] Further, the use of the surplus products would not displace any sale of foreign products, for we are assuming that if the surplus products had not been available to finance the project, the increase in consumption would not have occured at all.

The use of surplus food and feedstuffs to finance new milk schemes would not in any way tend to depress domestic or foreign markets. On the contrary, over the longer pull it would have a very definite tendency to raise demand for dairy products and to increase their consumption. The existence of the processing and distribution facilities, and the expansion of milk consumption resulting from the supply and sale of attractive milk at prices consumers can afford to pay, would enlarge markets for both domestic and foreign dairymen. Domestic producers in nearby areas would benefit from the increased demand for whole milk, and those in more distant areas from the increased demand for dry skim milk they could produce during periods of seasonal surplus (once proper plants were installed), such as have occured at Anand. Producers in other countries would benefit from the increased markets for imported dry skim milk and possibly even butterfat or butter-oil, once the three-years' supply has been used up.

After considering all three aspects – effect on financing the project, effect on country's financial position, and effect on domestic and foreign markets – it appears that there are no serious difficulties in using surplus products for financing milk schemes; on the contrary, there seem to be many sound and desirable advantages, both economically and nutritionally.

Other Indian Possibilities for Additional Milk Schemes

Besides the Calcutta proposals, there are other localities in India where similar new milk processing, bottling and marketing operations are needed, and might be carried out with the assistance of surplus foods for financing. At Bombay itself, a program has been considered to remove and centralize the remaining milch animals from the suburban portions of the city, and to establish an additional milk processing plant in a central location to handle and bottle the milk. This expansion would mean roughly doubling the present milk operations in Bombay, with an investment needed to cover it of roughly half that involved in the Calcutta program just discussed. Poona is another city where milk prices are relatively high and where a milk scheme involving the supply of toned milk at a much lower price might prove very effective and greatly increase the consumption of milk among the lower income groups in the community. In Northern India, on the contrary, milk is much cheaper and more plentiful, except during the hot dry summer period. While more efficient, modern, and sanitary milk handling and marketing arrangements are needed in many cities there, the possibilities of toned milk to widen the market are much less. In these regions, however, there is frequently a large surplus of milk and especially of skim milk during the flush season, with resultant very low prices and poor utilization of this valuable product. If the quality of milk was improved, and adequate installations for drying skim milk were installed at strategic locations, that should both increase dairymen's returns from this nutritionally valuable product and eventually also help supply at least part of the dry skim milk needed in other parts of India. This product is already widely used in India not only for the production of toned milk but also for the production of candies and sweets of many kinds, and if sold at retail prices in convenient small wrapped parcels in moisture-proof paper, it might also find an even larger demand for other uses such as in cooking in the home.[15]

Outside of India, especially in Southeastern Asia and other tropical regions, there may be a number of cities where similar milk schemes are needed and would be useful. The exploration of such possibilities is outside the scope of the present paper.

SUMMARY OF CHAPTER VI

The various projects of Type I discussed in this chapter would provide for the use of about 30 million dollars' worth of surplus foods and feeds, each year for 4 years, with the surplus product covering about three-quarters of the total costs involved. In addition to better education and food for thousands of school children and youths, useful activity or employment would be provided for 156,000 persons now unemployed or under-employed, and work and training of great value to the country's development would be accomplished. The figures shown for items A to D represent, in most cases, only small beginnings on much larger problems, and the volume of activity estimated could be greatly expanded later on, if resources should permit.

The Type I projects may be briefly discussed as follows.

	Total cost 4 years	Covered by food surpluses		Employment created (or unemployed benefitted annually)
		in rupees	in dollars	
	crores	crores	millions	thousands of men
A. Educational food scholarships	21.5	16.1	34	—
B. Food scholarships and feeding for special groups	26.2	20.6	43	—
C. Internship training for educated unemployed	4.4	3.2	7	25,000
D. Community and other local development projects	21.7	14.7	31	105,000
E. Milk marketing schemes	5.9	5.1	11	26,500
Total:	79.7	59.7	126	156,500

[1] *Seven Years of Freedom*, Ministry of Education, Pub. 160, 1954.
[2] *Annual Report on Education in the Bombay State for the year 1952-53*, and *Census Papers*, 1951, No. 2 (*Population*), and No. 5 (*Literacy and Education*).
[3] See Appendix 1, page 186, note 3, for a more detailed statement.
[4] For supporting details on "backward classes", displaced persons, and their education, see Dandekar, *loc. cit.* Chap. X and XI.
[5] See Dandekar, *loc. cit.*, Chap. III.
[6] From the point of view of nutrition alone, it is much more important to add milk solids to the diet of children than of adults. School milk programs, and other ways of improving the nutrition of children, thus are valid methods for the disposition of surplus skim milk, and are recognized as such under category 2, special welfare feeding programs, (see Foreword and Chapter I). This present report, however, is concerned solely with the use of surpluses for additional economic development, which does not include welfare plans as such. So long as large quantities of surplus skim milk are being diverted to feeding animals, (some of them to produce more milk to be fed to more animals), there is an obvious gain by feeding that milk to adults to encourage additional labor on development projects, and to promote better physical capacity of the workers to perform that work. Feeding programs for the children might well be developed at the same time, but on a welfare basis rather than on a development one.

[7] Starting a large municipal dairy scheme, and securing necessary supplementary financing for it, may be facilitated if arrangements are made for an experienced dairy firm or corporation in a more developed country to be affiliated with it in some way, such as under a management of technical-service contract. Many firms in other countries such as Denmark, the United States, the United Kingdom, and the Netherlands have had extensive experience in establishing and operating large-scale fluid milk plants under a wide variety of conditions and environments. By arranging to have an appropriate firm of this type associated in the undertaking many mistakes can be avoided and unnecessary expenses can be saved, and both the technical and financial resources of the firm may be made available.

[8] For further details, see Eric Shearer, "Milk for Bombay's Millions", in *Foreign Agriculture*, U.S. Department of Agriculture, Vol. XVIII, No. 9, Sept. 1954.

[9] *The Bombay Government Gazette*, Bombay Essential Commodities and Cattle (Control) October, 1946, and Bombay Cattle Control Order, 1949, 15 Oct. 1949 and 25 January 1955.

[10] At the same time the fat content in toned milk was reduced from 3.5 to 3.0 percent.

[11] *Progress Report on a Possible Form of an Understanding for International Cooperative Action to Increase Consumption of Dried Skim Milk*, (FAO) Committee on Commodity Problems, Consultative Sub-Committee on Surplus Disposal, Doc. CCP/CSD/55/20, FAO Rome. 30 March 1955, p. 6.

[12] In contrast to this figure the proposal for Calcutta referred to on page 150 estimated 6,000 tons a year as the probable Calcutta use for toned milk.

[13] See Appendix 3 for a more detailed discussion of problems of inflationary or deflationary effects during the process of development.

[14] The experience at the Anand Community may seem to run counter to this statement. Milk production at Anand has expanded so much under the stimulus of the prices offered by the Bombay Scheme that at flush seasonal periods of production the Scheme is unable to use all the Anand milk available, and a local surplus is left unsold which has to be used to produce the less valuable manufactured dairy products, ghee etc. Arrangements have recently been made with UNICEF to finance the construction of a small milk drying plant there to help use this surplus.

This does not mean, however, that the Anand producers are worse off because the Bombay Scheme has been started and is using dry skim milk to produce toned milk. On the contrary, the Anand farmers now have a profitable whole milk market which they did not enjoy at all before the Bombay Scheme was started and established the milk receiving and pasteurizing unit there. At the present time, the Bombay Scheme is drawing about one-third of its entire supply of whole milk from this region. When Anand has more milk available than the Bombay Scheme markets can use, in their regular proportion of full milk and toned milk, that does not mean that the milk plant could stop producing toned milk and could sell more whole milk to use up the surplus supply available from Anand. The Scheme's total demand depends on the total sales in both forms, and that depends in turn on the consumers' ability and readiness to buy milk of the two types. If the proportion of dry skim milk used was reduced, and the fat content of the blended milk was increased, its cost would have to be raised – and as the consumers' reaction to the recent decrease in the price of toned milk has shown, even a slight change in its price can mean a very large change in demand. Despite this situation, Anand producers are better off than they were before the Scheme was started and as the demand increases further, and the plant and bottling capacity to meet that demand are further increased, they will profit even more from it.

[15] See also *Report on the Marketing of Ghee and other Milk Products in India*, Marketing Series 56, Delhi, 1948; and *Report on the Marketing of Milk in The Indian Union*, Marketing Series No. 64, Delhi, 1950.

VII. Additional labor put to work and additional consumption covered partly by surplus foods (Type II)

The following are some important examples of labor-intensive projects which illustrate general types of development projects which could be financed in part by surplus foods.

A. ADDITIONAL ROAD CONSTRUCTION

Although much progress is being made on roads under the development program, only a start has been made in establishing the road system needed for full development and already laid out on the engineers' maps.

The national and State roads planned as the main highway network total about 75,000 miles, of which only a fraction has been built. In addition district and village roads are needed up to a total of about 257,000 miles. The current Five-Year Plan made little provision for roads, except for national highways, but some progress is being made on village roads under the Community Development Program.

A program of constructing 500 to 1,000 miles of district roads each year for a term of years (say four years) could be carried through without interfering with other work in this field. These would be single-lane metalled roads, built mostly by manual labor, with a water-bound macadam crust. They would be built at different points over the country where they could make the most useful addition to other roads, existing or programmed. In estimating the costs no provision is made for major bridges, so the roads selected would exclude locations requiring these.

The estimated costs of this construction (1,000 miles) per year, from the point of view of the categories significant for the present analysis, would be as follows.

	lakhs of rupees
Land purchase	100
Imported equipment and fuels	30
Direct labor (including labor employed by sub-contractors)	550
Other expenses	120
Total:	800

(about $17,000,000)

About 110,000 men, mostly unskilled or semi-skilled labor, would be directly employed for a year in carrying through this amount of construction.

From the point of view of using surplus products, this project has the following characteristics:

Expenditure for direct labor	69.0 percent
Expenditure for imported goods and equipment .	3.8 percent

The expenditure for land is a capital transaction and is not likely to lead to purchases of goods and services, so that it must be deducted, as must imports. On this basis, the expenditure on the project may be classified as follows.

		lakhs
Total cost		800
Less: imports	30	
land	100	
	130	670

Distribution of remaining cost:

Direct labor	550
Other costs	120

The direct effect of these expenditures on surplus food consumption then would be:

Direct labor, 550 lakhs at 34%	187 lakhs
Other expenses, 120 lakhs at 26%	31 lakhs
Increased consumption	218 lakhs

On this basis, a little over one-quarter of the investment needed to build the roads could be recovered by the sale of surplus products to offset the increase in food consumption by the families of those given work as a result of the project. Making this calculation by the more exact methods outlined in Appendix 2 and assuming the expenditure spread out through the year, this proportion would rise to 37 percent for the first year of the project, 46½ percent in the second year, and 49 percent thereafter. It would thus be necessary to supplement the surplus foods by financing from other sources, as already discussed in Chapter III, up to about 50 to 60 percent of the total cost.

Although the original proportion of direct labor on this project is very high, its effect on the use of surpluses is partly offset by the requirements for land purchase and for imports, leaving the roads program about the same as most other Type II projects.

B. Additional Irrigation Projects

A number of projects suggested for irrigation purposes are in regions consuming mainly wheat and millets, so that they could be financed in part from surplus foods without involving the possible use of surplus rice. These projects are as follows.

1. *Ramganga Project, Uttar Pradesh.* This involves construction of an earthern and rock-fill dam 330 feet high across the Ramganga river at Kalgash, a diversion weir 16 miles down-stream from the dam, and a feeder canal 146 miles long. The project would increase irrigation water supplies to 700,000 acres, generate 72,000 kw. of electricity, and help reduce flood damage. (Five years assumed as required to complete.)

2. *Gandah Project, Bihar State.* This is a major multi-purpose project involving a dam 2,573 feet long on the Gandah river at Bhasalotan, Champaran District; two main canals, one each side of the river, and a canal system totalling 243 miles long in U.P.. Bihar, and Nepal, together with several hydro-electric installations. Besides hydro-electricity and flood control, it would irrigate 2,640,000 acres in the two States of U.P. and Bihar, and take 11 years to complete, with 90 percent of the work completed in the first six years.

3. *Barna Project, Bhopal State.* This involves construction of a dam 1,240 feet long and 120 feet high across the Barna river at Bari, to irrigate 150,000 acres. (Four years assumed for completion.)

Table VII-1. Cost and Benefit Data for Illustrative Water-Use Projects

Project	Project costs			Estimated labor cost	Estimated benefits		Years to complete
	Imported goods and services	Domestic costs	Total costs		Acres irrigated	Electricity in kw.	
	.... lakhs of rupees				.... thousands		
Ramganga, U.P.	860	1,867	2,727	1,430	700	72	5
Gandah Canal, Bihar	650	2,750	3,400	2,125	2,640	35	6 (90%)
Barna, Bhopal	70	320	390	185	150	–	4
Tawa, Madhya Pradesh	200	1,500	1,700	890	590	22.5	9
Purna, Hyderabad	100	605	705	335	160	8	6
Mahanadi Delta, Orissa	200	1,300	1,500	975	1,576	–	3
Nandikonda, Andhra and Hyberabad	200	12,000	12,200	4,550	3,138	75	9

4. *Tawa Project, Madhya Pradesh.* A dam 6,230 feet long and about 200 feet high would be built across the Tawa river, near Ranipur, all of earth except a central concrete section 1,070 feet long for spillway and power-house. A left bank canal 90 miles long would irrigate 590,000 acres. A right bank canal might be added later. Nine years are needed for completion.

5. *Purna Project, Hyderabad.* This involves a storage dam at Yeldari on the Purna river, a second dam at Sideswar, and a lower diversion dam, plus 69 miles of canals. It would irrigate 160,000 acres, as well as generating electricity. Construction would take six years.

6. *Mahanadi Delta, Orissa.* This involves construction of canals for dis-tributing in this region water supplied by the Hirakud dam in northern Orissa, now under construction and nearing completion. Water would be supplied to 1,576,000 acres, making two crops of rice a year possible instead of one. Three years are estimated for doing the work.

In addition, one project was suggested in a rice and millet consuming area, as follows.

7. *Nandikonda Project, Andhra and Hyderabad.* This includes a high dam (350 feet) 8,860 feet long across the Krishna river near Nandikonda, and two lined canals one each side of the river, one about 140 miles long in Hyderabad State, and the other 276 miles long in Andhra. The project would irrigate 3,140,000 acres in the two States, and also generate much electric power. It would take nine years to complete.

The cost and other data are shown in Table VII-1.

Without considering the relative costs and benefits of each project, or the amount of surplus foods each one might use to advantage, the aggregate amounts involved if all of these projects were implemented might be briefly considered, with the amount of expenditure and surplus food utilization. The data for this analysis are summarized in Table VII-2.

If these seven projects were all implemented at the same time, that would require an annual expenditure starting at 3,314 lakhs of rupees (about 70 million dollars) and declining gradually from the fourth year on as various projects reached completion. Of this initial annual amount, 416 lakhs would be in foreign exchange (for gates, power-house equipment, etc.) and would affect domestic consumption only slightly and indirectly, and its effect is ignored. Of the balance of 2,898 lakhs, the 1,637 lakhs for direct labor is especially important.

Since these projects are in rural areas and generally remote from large cities, the figure of 40 percent of labor expenditure from surplus foods at retail, and 34 percent at wholesale, will be used. Using the method of Appendix 2, and allowing for spreading the investment through the year, the expected consumption of surplus foods, including the direct and indirect effects on income, works out at 1,023 lakhs the first year, 1,617 the second, and 1,699 the third. These are equal to 29 percent of the total investment the first year, 46 percent in the second, and 48 percent in the third (and thereafter, if the program were continued at the same annual level of investment as in the first year).

Table VII-2. Approximate Annual Average Expenditures
for Illustrative Water-Use Projects

Project	Foreign currency	Domestic costs	
		Total	Labor
	.... *lakhs of rupees*		
Ramganga	172	373	286
Gandah	98	412	319
Barna	18	80	46
Tawa	22	166	99
Purna	17	101	56
Mahanadi	67	433	325
Nandikonda	22	1 333	506
Total	416	2 898	1 637

With the fairly high labor intensity, but also substantial costs for imports of equipment, from one-third to one-half of the total investment could be covered by sales of surplus foods without affecting local markets, if the sales of the surplus foods were properly adjusted between different commodities, localities, and in timing through the year. Only one-third to one-half of the investment would need to be covered by other types of internal financing. If covered by external financing, however, the part covered by surplus foods would be still lower, for reasons explained earlier.

Because of the long period of construction of these projects using largely manual labor, only two full projects and a portion of the others could be completed in an initial period of say four years. In the next two years, however, all except two projects would be substantially completed. If surplus foods were available to help finance construction for only the initial three to four years, they would still make a great contribution to the country's development and carry the projects on to a point where they could be completed under regular financing. At the same time they would put about 240,000 men and women at work directly on the projects, plus possibly as many more producing materials or services for the projects or doing other new work to fill demands created by the project expenditures.

C. REFORESTATION AND EROSION CONTROL

Reforestation and erosion control are major problems in India. Enormous areas of hill and mountain land, once wooded, are now denuded and eroding badly, while furnishing only sparse grazing for short periods for bands of sheep or, even more disastrously for the soil, goats. Where new dams are being built and reservoirs established, as the great Hirakud dam in northern Orissa, the eventual destruction of the dam by silting up is a constant menace, and one that would do almost irreparable economic damage, after the economy of the region had been expanded to depend on the project for water, electricity and flood control.

Some efforts have been made to establish nurseries of suitable trees, and to supply young trees to farmers and encourage them to plant them, and some small efforts at reforestation may have been made in community development projects. Planting of trees along roads is a more general practice. As a whole, however, fuller and better utilization of existing forests has been given priority over building new ones for the future, or replanting trees to protect watersheds.

On the side of direct erosion control, a great deal has been done to develop contour terraces, both to save water and to prevent erosion. "Bunds" have been built generally by tractor or bulldozers, on large areas of agricultural land, usually in part at the cost of the farmers benefitted, either as separate projects or, in some cases, as part of community development schemes. Small diversion dams or water-spreading schemes have also been built, frequently under this latter program.

The problem of preventing or controlling erosion in drainage basins or watersheds above dams has been given little attention, however.

The availability of surplus foods might make it possible to use unemployed workers on specific watershed protection projects above important dams, including both reforestation and small erosion control structures. The Hirakud dam, for example, will impound water from a vast lightly-settled drainage basin lying in three States.

A program to re-establish forests and control erosion in this vast region might well include building small dams and diversion weirs and ditches of local materials at selected points on many small stream and tributaries, creating forest nurseries of suitable species, protection of existing desirable seed trees, planting by hand as fast as suitable stock developed, and establishing grazing control and a forest protection system to protect the plantings from destruction until of sufficient size.

All that would be needed for this scheme would be necessary technical direction, labor, and small hand tools. At appropriate points, camps would need to be built, largely out of local stone and timber, and access roads or trails. The amount of work to be done is so vast that the labor which could be used would be limited only by the ability to supply (or train) the necessary staffs of foresters, engineers and erosion-control specialists, and to finance the portions which could not be covered from surplus foods. The whole undertaking might be organized something like the civilian conservation camps which were established in the United States during the 1930's, with "companies" of unemployed young men recruited to work on the project for specified periods of time.

Well-trained and competent forest services already exist in India, both in the central Ministry of Food and Agriculture and in the governments in each State. Their technicians would have little difficulty in supplying sufficient trained people to plan and supervise operations under the program proposed, and to train and direct the necessary subordinate personnel. Detailed plans for any specific project carried out under this general program would be worked out in co-operation with the conservator of Forests and Silviculture of the State concerned.

Without attempting to map the work to be done in more detail, we may examine the suitability of the project for financing through surplus foods on some rough assumptions. Let us assume that five percent of the total costs involved would be needed for imported equipment (jeeps, surveyors' instruments, etc.); ten percent for domestic materials (cement, tools, hardware, special shoes and clothing, seeds, etc.), and ten percent for administration and technical supervision. All the rest would represent payments to workers on the project who would build the necessary structures (houses, sheds, roads, etc.), nurseries, dams, ditches, fences, and grow and plant the trees.

If one crore of rupees were expended on this operation each year for a period of four years (about $2,100,000 a year), that would involve employment of roughly 12,000 young men, plus possibly another 1,000 as technical, clerical, and administrative personnel. In addition, perhaps two to three hundred trainees or interns as suggested in Chapter VI-C, might also be used on the project. With this much manpower, it should be possible to grow and plant trees on at least one hundred thousand acres of denuded forests each year, or to do a corresponding amount of work on upstream water control projects.

The total sum of 100 lakhs of rupees would be then distributed as follows.

Total annual cost .... 100 lakhs
Imported equipment .... 5 lakhs
Domestic materials .... 10 lakhs
Administration and technical supervision .... 10 lakhs
Direct project labor .... 75 lakhs

With these annual expenditures for domestic materials and services, spread out through each year, increased consumption of surplus foods might be expected to be as follows (following the methods and assumptions of Appendix 2).

If the additional food (other than surplus products), and the additional materials and domestic industrial products to meet the increased demand could be produced by expansion in the domestic economy (i.e. to that extent the corresponding additional costs could be covered by additional deficit financing), the increased consumption of surplus products would be 39 percent of total costs in the first year, 54 percent of total costs in the second, and 56 percent in the third year and thereafter. On the other hand if all the additional costs, other than surplus foods, were covered by external financing and imported goods, so that there would be no further derived expansion in the domestic economy (until the project itself began to help increased production, which in this case would be after many years), then only 30 percent of the costs each year could be covered by the sale of surplus products. So surplus products would cover 30 percent of the annual costs of such a project, on the minimum, and on more favorable assumptions, from 39 percent in the beginning year up to 56 percent in later years.

While the project is one with a very long period of gestation before significant increased output would begin to be recovered, its long-time effects on soil erosion, timber production, water flow, and eventually possibly even on temperatures and climate, would make it of very great eventual value.

Other possible projects. Besides the projects examined above, almost any type of development project involving substantial employment of unskilled labor could be considered as a Type II project. Projects of this type could be developed to supplement special projects considered elsewhere in this report, such as in building school houses, mess halls, or dormitories or hostels, in connection with various projects discussed in Chapter VI. Also, as discussed in Chapter V, it might be necessary to have additional food storage capacity, both at ports and at some interior points, to hold the surpluses, imported or domestic, assigned to financing economic development – until the time came to dispose of them. Such warehouses might themselves be paid for in part with food surpluses, as a Type II project.

Further, India might decide to build up and hold much larger reserve stocks of foodstuffs, as an "Ever Normal Granary" or a "Famine Reserve", to be drawn on in later years of unfavorable weather, or of expansion in industrial employment running temporarily ahead of current food supply. Such supplies might be built up in part from foreign surplus foods obtained for that purpose (under the general FAO recommendations of using surpluses to relieve famine conditions and not under the economic development recommendation, with which this report is concerned), and in part from domestic surpluses. In this case, too, construction of the needed additional storage facilities might be financed in part as a Type II project.

Three types of projects are outlined here for financing in part by funds obtained from the sale or surplus foods. The projects presented may be roughly summarized as follows.

Projects	Annual investment	Surplus foods used	Additional employment created
	.... lakhs of rupees		
Roads	800	300 — 400	110,000
Irrigation and hydro-electric projects	3,300	1,000 — 1,700	240,000
Reforestation and erosion control	100	40 — 56	13,000
Totals	4,200	1,340 — 2,156	363,000
Totals in dollars	88,000,000	$28,000,000 — 45,000,000	

The estimates of the part covered are conservative ones. In cases where workers are fed in canteens or project messes, or supplied through project stores, the use of surpluses might be materially increased by favoring the commodities which are available from surpluses.

If both surplus products and additional financing to meet the part of the costs not covered by the surplus products could be provided, these projects could make a very substantial contribution toward India's economic development and toward effective use of under-employed workers.

VIII. Surpluses supplemented by immediate earnings: Illustrative project (Type III)

Projects of this type depend on the existence of resources, such as forests, minerals, etc., which are not now being exploited, but which can be opened up and reached if suitable extraction and transportation facilities are provided. To meet fully the two conditions desirable if surplus foods are to be most effective, the value of the products tapped and the speed of reaching them should both be so great that the project's net income produced during the same year as the construction would be sufficient to cover fully that part of the construction costs which cannot be met directly by surplus foods.

One promising project of this sort was found in India, i.e. the extension of the existing roads on the Andaman Islands, and the construction of a set of integrated forest industries to utilize more fully the timber resources thus tapped. The local public forest administration is already engaged in the exploitation of the valuable forest, on a sustained-yield basis. A port and a large sawmill have been built, and shipping and marketing arrangements for the export of the logs and sawn lumber have been developed, both to continental India and to European and other countries. Much of the lumber is a dense tropical hardwood, some of which compares well with teak in all respects, which is finding an expanding market in many countries and helping to earn needed foreign exchange for India.

About two-thirds of the present forest stand is of species for which there are no immediate markets, but among which is timber suitable for the production of plywood, processed blanks, boxes, flooring, etc. Drying kilns, dipping plants, a pressure treatment plant and a plywood factory would improve the quality and allow expanded marketing of the "softer" and more perishable species. The development of such integrated forest industries would thus make it possible to utilize more of the available timber, and greatly improve the returns from the operations.

The Andamans are a long narrow chain of islands, lying 750 miles from Calcutta, the nearest point in India, and nearer to Burma. The main islands make almost one continuous strip, divided by narrow straits. The southernmost island was originally used for a penal settlement, and part of it was settled by prisoners who were permitted to take up farming and engage in other occupations. Port Blair is the center with roads for some distance from it (roughly 30 miles), port facilities, a sawmill, etc.

Since 1949, some effort was made to settle here displaced persons from Calcutta, but it was found that much of the islands was too rolling for the rice cultivation to which they were accustomed, and this colonization scheme made little progress.

Exploitation of timber on the islands is carried out largely by the Forestry Department of the Indian Ministry of Agriculture. In the absence of other means of communication, the exploitation is limited to points which can be reached by water. Trees are cut to a few miles from the water's edge, using a combination of L.C.T. vessels, light portable tramways up to two miles from the water (the cars are hauled by elephants, down with the help of gravity and up with empty trucks) and tractors to haul logs on steep slopes up to a mile or two beyond the end of the rails or tractors. Elevated cable ways are being introduced, also, for use on steeper slopes. These methods have made it possible to extend the exploitation up to four to five miles from the water's edge, but not to reach the interior. At the same time the water communication is slow and not well suited for exploitation on a sustained yield basis, especially as in many places the water's edge is a tidal marsh, with repeated flooding for considerable distances.

It is proposed to develop the three main islands by extending the present roads until they run the length of the three islands, using ferries to cross the major rivers and the straits. This will involve a total construction of 120 miles of road, at an estimated cost of about 142 lakhs. Feeder roads, of a less expensive type, would also be constructed later. The first year's program would provide 40 miles construction, 15 miles in the southern islands, extending the existing road from Port Blair, and 25 miles in the center of the large middle island, and the development of a new port connecting with it. The main road program would be completed in three years, and the feeder roads would be built at the same annual rate. At the same time, a series of wood products processing plants would be constructed in two or three centers, including drying kilns, wood preservation and treating plants, additional sawmills where needed (the existing sawmill at Port Blair has a large unused capacity there), a plywood plant, and a fresh water basin for the storage of valuable plywood logs, up to a total cost of ten crores.[1] The industrial plants would take four years to complete and get into operation, but some units could be completed and start operating earlier. The first year's road construction would open up new territory to exploitation, so that annual production of saleable logs could be increased by 150,000 tons, with half the increase in production being reached in the first year.

Surplus products from foreign countries, or from Indian supplies acquired by the government on price-supporting operations, could be used (a) in feeding the additional men put to work on constructing the roads and factories and other industrial and transport facilities; (b) in feeding the men and elephants put to work in the expanded logging operation; and (c) in feeding the men engaged in building and eventually in operating the increased shipping, mercantile, educational, power, and other facilities which would be needed in the Andamans to keep pace with this general industrial development. Only the first two of these three possible outlets will be examined here.

The economic aspects of the operation, from the point of view of this present investigation, are as follows.

Cost of annual road construction (40 miles, main road): 47 lakhs, of which 37 would be for direct labor, two would be for imported equipment and fuels, and eight for domestic materials, supervision, transportation, etc.

Cost of annual construction of forest industrial plants: 250 lakhs, of which direct labor would be 83, imported equipment, 125, and domestic equipment, materials, and supervision, 42.

Additional annual product (before the new factories were utilized) 150,000 tons of logs, with a value at the port of 150 rupees a ton, and an extraction cost of 130 rupees per ton; with full volume of production achieved in the second year.

The workers on the project come largely from Behar in northern India, with their families remaining behind. (Behar is a wheat and millet-consuming area.) It is assumed that 34 percent of the direct labor expenditure (wholesale values) would be represented by increased consumption of foods of surplus types (food grains, pulses, edible oil, preserved meat, egg powder, milk and milk products, and dried fruits), partly in food used directly in feeding the workers on the project, and partly by increased consumption by their families in India. In addition, 200 more elephants would be needed for the logging and road construction, and food for them consisting of 25 pounds of grain per day (maize, millets, sorghum, or wheat or rice) could also be supplied from surpluses, while roughage would be obtained locally.[2]

On these bases, the possible increased consumption of surplus foods resulting from the project is calculated, for the first and second years of the project as shown in Table VIII-1.

For the second year and thereafter till the plants were completed, the figures would be as shown in Table VIII-2.

Under the conditions assumed, the additional surplus foods consumed during the first year would amount to 86.3 lakhs. In addition, the value of the timber produced, 112.5 lakhs, would exceed by 15 lakhs the cost of logging.[3] This net profit added to the value of the surplus foods, would come to 101.2 lakhs, or 34 percent of the entire investment that year of 297 on the industrial plant and the road. For the second year, with timber exploitation reaching full volume, the value of surpluses consumed, 117.1 plus the net profit on the logging, 30, comes to 147 which is 49 percent of the

Table VIII-1. Rough Estimate of Surpluses Used, First Year

Item	Industrial plant	Road construction	Additional logging	Total	Prop. from surplus food	Surplus food values
	....	.... lakhs of rupees, except as noted otherwise				
Total cost	250	47	97.5	394.5		
Direct labor	83	37	78	198	34%	67.3
Domestic materials and equipment	38	7.5	12	57.5	26%	17.3
Supervision	4	0.5	4.5	9.0		
Imported equipment and services	125	2	3	130		
Feed for elephants .... (1,825,000 lbs at 1½ annas						1.7
Total						86.3

Table VIII-2. Rough Estimate of Surpluses Used, Second to Fourth Year

Item	Industrial plant	Road construction	Additional logging	Total	Prop. from surplus food	Surplus food values
	.... *lakhs of rupees, except as noted otherwise*					
Total cost	250	47	195	492		93.8
Direct labor	83	37	156	276	34%	
Domestic materials and equipment	38	7.5	24	69.5 ⎫	26%	21.6
Supervision	4	0.5	9	13.5 ⎭		
Imported equipment and services	125	2	6	133		
Feed for elephants						1.7
Total						117.1

year's investment on industrial facilities and road. If the computations were figured leaving out the industrial plant, the value of surpluses consumed amounts to 47.1 lakhs for the first year, and 77.9 for the second, or well in excess of the cost of the road construction. Adding the net profits of the logging, the net returns from the operation above total investment is as follows.

Year	Value of surpluses consumed	Profit on logging	Total	Road cost	Net balance above investment
	.... *lakhs of rupees*				
First	47.1	15	62.1	47	15.1
Second	77.9	30	107.9	47	60.9

We can also see from the calculations that 16 percent of the cost of the industrial plant is covered by the additional use of surpluses resulting from the plant construction, so that it would only be necessary for the net balance from the road and logging to cover 84 percent of the industrial plant to have no deficit at all in the financing (assuming, of course, that the food surpluses used for the operation were available as a grant in aid of the development, or on a very long-term loan at low interest rates). If the plant construction had been undertaken at a slower rate, of 18 lakhs investment the first year ($380,000), and 72 the second and thereafter ($1,500,000), the entire cost of the investment in both roads and plant could be covered through the value of food and feed surpluses consumed, and through the net profits from the expanded logging operations. And as the new plants came into production and began to increase returns from the logging operations as well as from the industrial activities, the net income would increase and the rate of plant construction could be expanded – if surplus foods continued to be available to aid in the development.

It is believed that much of the additional plant required to develop the islands' timber industry could be built up and installed quite quickly and without great difficulty, but detailed investigation on the spot is necessary, particulary to establish priority of installation in relation to the developments foreseen. Expert technical advice through a mission to undertake this task should be started in ample time before plans are finalized.[4]

The favorable results estimated above were secured without making any allowance for additional increases in income produced in subsequent periods, as the income disbursed in the project is reflected in increased incomes, and in increased expenditures for surplus foods by those receiving these derived incomes (assuming some expansion possible in the Indian economy with basic food demands covered by surpluses). When allowance is made for this, by the methods explained in Appendix 2, almost 800 lakhs of the project's total investment of 1,188 lakhs, including both the road and the full industrial plant, could be covered from surplus foods and from net logging profits. It would be possible to construct and pay for 4.9 crores of industrial plant during the first four years of operation entirely from the surplus foods and feed used and the logging profits.[5]

The effect of the project on increased employment may be briefly calculated as follows, assuming average wages of 500 rupees per year for the men put to work directly on the project in the Andaman Islands, and of one man put to work a year for each 1,000 rupees spent for domestic materials, equipment, and supervision.

With the full project, roads and integrated wood-using industrial plants (including credit for derived income), the increased employment would be: in the first year, on the islands, almost 40,000 men; in continental India, 6,650; in the second year, 55,000 on the islands, and 8,300 in India. After the construction was completed in four years, there would be continuing new jobs, in logging and in the plants, for about 34,500 men on the islands, as compared to the employment there before the project was initiated. These are remarkable increases to be attained at a total investment of 1,188 lakhs of rupees over a period of four years (about 25 million dollars). At the same time, with the assistance of grants of surplus food totalling 797 lakhs (about 17 million dollars) over the four years, two-thirds of the entire cost of the project could be paid off in that period, leaving one-third (391 lakhs) to be covered from other financing, or from profits from the industrial plants. If the project were built more slowly, at the rate at which all investment costs could be completely covered through food surpluses and profits, all of the major roads and about one-half of the processing plants could be completed in four years, with the aid of 679 lakhs of surplus food (about 14 million dollars).

Launching such a big program of development in the Andaman Islands would involve many difficulties. On the human side, there are the dual problems of the indigenous native tribes, and of the settlers around Port Blair prior to the forest development. The native tribes include one tribe, only a handful in number (probably 1,000 or less), who live by hunting and fishing, and are experts with bow-and-arrow. They have been badly treated in the past, both by the early settlers and by the Japanese during the war, and as a result are very aggressive and hostile, shooting woodsmen and workers whenever opportunity offers. As they speak an unknown language, and little contact has been established with them, the problem of settling them and educating them has not yet been solved, but efforts to this end are continuing. Meantime, they create an additional hazard to the risks involved in opening up virgin tropical forest.

The settlers around Port Blair are largely descendants from the penal colony. They have some inferiority complexes as a result, and require education and social development to make them effective citizens of a modern society. Work is proceeding on this also, and it does not constitute an insoluble difficulty. Moreover, the original establishment of the islands as a penal colony still tends to stigmatize it from an employment standpoint; this attitude also needs to be overcome.

The development sketched would need to be accompanied by many others to utilize fully the resources of the islands. At present there is only one ship every three weeks between the islands and Calcutta, and no air service. Water transport would need to be materially increased and air facilities developed for passengers and mail, if a large industrial development of lumber and wood products is to be carried through. A shipbuilding industry might be established to build from native woods the many small coastal vessels and even sea-going ships needed; electricity, schools, water supply, and many other basic facilities would have to be established. In fact, an entire development plan for the Andamans would need to be set up, paralleling and supporting the basic wood industries provided for here. And with the islands opened up by these developments, suitable areas could be developed for special types of agriculture, with the possibility of promising returns from such products as rubber, oil nuts, and especially coffee and cocoa, depending on findings of experts and of experimental work on the spot.

It may be that the project could not be launched as rapidly as estimated. Recruiting the workers, preparing the details and plans, and expanding the first exploitation might require two to three times as long as estimated, because of the many operational and administrative problems involved. If that should prove to be the case, the annual rate of investment, manpower, and surplus utilization would have to be scaled down accordingly, but the basic relations would still hold true.

There are probably not many projects in any one country which can pay all their own way with the help of surplus foods as well as the one on the Andaman Islands for roads and associated industries promises to do. But careful examination of the possibilities may reveal good opportunities in other countries as well.

SUMMARY OF CHAPTER VIII

On the basis of these calculations, and taking into effect derived income, the Andamans operations could be carried forward on two different bases as shown in the table opposite.

On the first basis, one-third of the cost (391 crores), would have to be covered by other financing, especially in the earlier years. For example, 500 crores of imported equipment for the plant is estimated to be needed, and part of this might well be covered by an external loan. On the second basis, the industrial plant would be constructed more slowly, and all the cost – including the rupee value of the needed foreign exchange – would be covered by surplus foods and feeds.

Item	Investment		Total cost	Total investment covered by use of surpluses	Percentage of cost covered
	Roads	Plants			
	. . . . *lakhs of rupees*				
Complete industrial plant in 4 years	188	1,000	1,188	797	67
Part of industrial plant in 4 years	188	491	679	679	100

[1] It was also suggested that a paper mill or a fiberboard plant be established to use species not otherwise saleable, and small branches, sawdust, and chips not otherwise utilized. These industries, however, require large amounts of fresh water which apparently do not exist in the Andaman Islands, and other, better opportunities and materials for establishing pulp and paper plants exist elsewhere in India (Arne Sundelin: *Report to the Government of India on a Preliminary Pulp and Paper Survey,* Expanded Technical Assistance Program, FAO Report No. 268, Rome, March 1954). Accordingly paper and pulp plants have not been included in the present report. For details as to needs and methods for the improvement and further development of sawmilling, see V. Hasek: *Report to the Government of India on Sawmilling in the Andaman Islands,* Expanded Technical Assistance Program, FAO Report 145, Rome, October 1953.

[2] This number of elephants is based on Hasek's report, that one elephant can extract, on the average about 720 tons of logs a year. See Hasek, *loc. cit.,* page 19.

[3] This is based on present costs of logging and on export of the product as round logs at 150 rupees a ton. As rapidly as the sawmill and other treatment plants are put into use, the profit will rise. Wood exported as semi-finished and finished products, for example, is worth about more than twice as much per ton of logs.

[4] Basic alterations and improvements in the existing arrangements have been suggested as necessary if full progress is to be achieved. Among these are:

(a) A reorganization of the islands' timber industry – with some decentralization of administrative responsibility – in order to give the industry greater flexibility, increased efficiency and, thus, a better opportunity to meet competition from private enterprise. (This might involve establishing an operating organization under public control, similar to those set up for the Sindri Fertilizer factory and the Damoder Valley development.)

(b) An improvement in the arrangements for labor, with provision for a basic wage, an efficiency bonus, and continuing employment on a more permanent basis for those who prove satisfactory.

[5] Assuming that the entire plant were constructed in four years, and that the additional demand for other goods than food surpluses could be covered within the Indian economy, the percent of investment covered by food surpluses and logging profits would be 40 the first year, 68 the second, 79 the third, and 81 the fourth. If only as much plant were built as could be covered in full by the resulting surpluses and logging profits, the annual amount of processing plant construction would be, by years, from the beginning, 32, 123, 165 and 171 lakhs.

IX. Current economic conditions in India as related to use of surplus products for financing

At the time this study was started, it was assumed that the only food surpluses which might be available for use in India would be those obtained from abroad. Before the study was completed, however, the situation had changed to such an extent that it began to seem possible that India itself might soon have some domestic surpluses in governmental ownership which would also be available to assist in financing economic development. It seems useful to explain how this change has come about.

Agricultural production has increased much more rapidly than was expected when India's first Five-Year Plan (1951/52 to 1955/56) was drawn up. By 1953/54 grain production had shown an increase 50 percent larger than the increase expected by 1955/56. As shown in the following table, this increase continued into 1954.

All-India Production of Cereals and Grain[1]

(in million long tons)

1945/46 .... 45.7	1948/49 .... 47.8	1951/52 .... 46.2
1946/47 .... 46.1	1949/50 .... 49.7	1952/53 .... 53.4
1947/48 .... 48.2	1950/51 .... 45.3	1953/54 .... 60.7

[1] *Bulletin on Food Statistics,* Directorate of Economics and Statistics, Ministry of Food and Agriculture, Delhi, January 1955.

The increase was due both to favorable rainfall and to improved practices.

Some seven percent of the reported increase from 1950/51 to 1953/54 is estimated to be due to methodological changes in ascertaining the yields. Acreage in cereal and grain increased in this period by 8.1 percent and crop acreage under irrigation by an estimated three percent. Thus, of the ascertained real increase in total production, half appears to be due to favorable rainfall and improved practices, and the other half to increased acreage and increased areas receiving irrigation.

With the better crops, prices fell sharply in many regions in the first half of 1954, then started falling again in late 1954 and early 1955, with a total decline at local wholesale markets ranging from 20 percent for food grains up to 40 percent for pulses and even 50 percent for oilseeds. Stocks accumulated in the hands of dealers in local markets, in many cases in excess of the capacity of local warehouses; extreme local declines in prices followed where local markets were glutted. Prices of fibers and other specialities were generally firm. Wholesale prices of non-agricultural products were firm, with little or no change, and prices for farm products compared to prices of other products are apparently well below long-time average relations, especially in certain centers. With prices declining by much more than production or even saleable quantities had increased, farmer's net incomes and real buying power declined sharply. Wages of agricultural labor also fell.

Despite the continual expansion of public expenditures and employment on development projects under the Five-Year Plan, the decline in rural buying power and employment has had a depressing effect upon the whole economy. While the quantity of industrial output has generally continued to expand with new heavy goods plants coming into production, textile employment has declined gradually. In cotton-mills which provide one-third of all industrial employment, the number of workers in late 1954 was 4 percent lower than two years earlier, despite the concurrent growth in the population and in real national income. Even so, production of textiles continued to expand.

As usual, retail food prices, especially in the cities, have not fallen proportionately as much as prices to farmers, due to intervening fixed charges for transportation, taxes, commissions, etc. But retail food prices have still fallen materially. Consumption has increased somewhat and the people of India are somewhat better fed than in the recent scarcity years, especially so far as calories go. This has meant a real gain in health and morale. The accumulating heavy stocks are tangible proof, however, that only part of the increased supplies are moving into consumption, and the problem remains of how to achieve continued expansion in food consumption without generating a deflationary downward spiral in the economy as a whole.

Facing these difficulties, the government has released the last controls on the internal movement of food grains, and has taken steps toward supporting markets through government purchase and storage operations. It is also encouraging additional warehouse construction, under the Community Development Program and other programs, and is considering steps to improve local facilities and arrangements for warehousing, grading, inspection, and short-term loans on stored commodities, as recommended by its Committee on Rural Credit in its recent monumental report. It is hoped that these long-term measures, and the immediate programs which may be developed to check the fall in farm prices, will improve the income of farm people and the demand for non-farm products and thus help convert the unexpectedly large supplies of farm products into an expansive force in the economy, instead of as recently a deflationary and contractive force. The funds necessary for these operations can readily be raised by deficit financing under these circumstances, since what the country faces today is not too much money compared to the quantity of the goods, but rather the quantity of goods expanding faster than the quantity of money.

As part of this program, more and more farm products will come under governmental ownership or control. While part of these may be set aside as a storage reserve (or ever-normal granary) against future short crops, part will be available for immediate use – especially if, as now seems quite likely, the 1954/55 crops also prove to be large ones.[1] In view of these facts it seems probable that in addition to surplus supplies potentially available from abroad, there will also be Indian surpluses, already withdrawn from the market, available for use in financing economic development projects where they can be used for that purpose without burdening domestic markets. Accordingly, in this report potential Indian surpluses have been considered as well as surpluses already existing in other countries.

The postwar experience of India indicates that the problem of maintaining balance between agriculture and industry can be a severe one even in an expanding economy. If agricultural supplies are unexpectedly low as a result of short crops, acute food shortages and high prices may limit economic progress. If supplies are unexpectedly large, the resulting abundance does not automatically produce increased consumption and higher standards of living. Instead it may produce falling prices and declining real incomes in agriculture with deflationary repercussions throughout the economy. The effects are intensified if facilities and institutions for storing and financing the carryover of the increased supplies are lacking or greatly deficient. Governmental intervention to absorb the increased supplies without decline in rural buying power and to divert them to other current or future uses where they will not burden markets or check continued economic growth may thus become imperative. The use of surpluses for financing additional development as outlined in this report may be one useful link in this complicated process.

---

[1] In view of this situation, the use of surplus foods to help finance the construction of storage warehouses might well have been considered in Chapter VII.

X. Summary and conclusions

After considering ways in which surpluses might be used to finance increased economic development either through individual projects or through general expansion in national development programs as a whole, this report briefly summarizes individual projects, not now under way, which might usefully be financed through the use of surpluses. These may be summarized as shown on page 184.

From these figures, there appears to be a large volume of projects potentially suitable for financing through surpluses, in whole or in part, either as individual projects or as part of the general development program.

The longer the period for which the project can be assured surplus financing, usually the greater the proportion of total cost which can be financed in that way. On a four-year program basis, the average proportion of the cost covered by surpluses varies from as low as 46 percent for projects of Type II, up to 75 percent for those of Type I, and 100 percent for Type III (on alternative B).

The individual projects summarized here suggest possible uses for food surpluses in economic development which would employ 62 million dollars' worth of surpluses the first year, and use an average of 73 million dollars per year over a four-year period. The total increase in national investment would average 134 million dollars a year for the four years. If larger resources of surplus food and administrative personnel were available, many more such projects could be suggested in the several types.

In contrast to these individual projects, Chapter V has considered a general expansion in the Indian development plans based on the use of surplus foods, which would use an average of 100 million dollars worth of such foods per year, and increase total investment by $240 millions per year, on the average. That chapter sets forth the economic and administrative advantages of considering the problem as a general increase in the national development program, rather than project by project.

In practice, not all the additional projects listed here are ever likely to be implemented at any one time. Before actual steps could be taken to carry them on, either as individual projects or as part of a general expansion in the national development plan, the relative advantage to the econ-

Project type	Total cost		Amount covered by surpluses	
	1st year	4 years	1st year	4 years
	.... millions of dollars			
TYPE I - SURPLUSES LARGELY CONSUMED IN KIND (CHAP. VI)				
Educational food scholarships	11.3	45	8.5	34
Scholarships for special groups	13.8	55	10.8	43
Internship training for educated unemployed	2.3	9	1.7	7
Village community and other local development projects	11.5	46	7.8	31
Milk marketing scheme	12.4	12	3.0	11
Subtotal	51.3	167	31.8	126
TYPE II - SURPLUSES SOLD AND LABOR HIRED COM- MERCIALLY (CHAP. VII)				
District roads	16.8	69	6.3	31
Irrigation and hydroelectric projects	69.7	278	21.1	127
Reforestation and erosion control	2.1	8	0.8	4
Subtotal	88.6	355	28.2	162
TYPE III - PROJECTS HELPING TO PAY THEIR OWN WAY (CHAP. VIII) Forest roads and industries (Andaman Islands)				
Alternative A - full industrial development	6.2	25	2.5	17
Alternative B - partial industrial development	1.7	14	1.7	14
GRAND TOTAL (including Type III Alternative B) ..	141.6	536	61.7	302

omy of the various projects would have to be studied both over-all and with respect to their regional and local impacts, and the possible availability of surplus foods to finance them and of additional funds to cover the non-surplus costs would have to be determined. Further, India, the country which has served as the "guinea pig" for this exploratory study, would have to decide whether it wished to act along these lines, and to negotiate with possible donor countries for the gift or loan of the imported surplus products involved. Only after extended further investigation and action of this sort could these suggestions, or any part of them, become part of India's actual development program.

At the same time, this investigation, and the methods of analysis developed in connection with it, may serve a useful purpose in suggesting parallel possibilities to other countries, and in indicating ways in which some of the necessary information may be assembled and analyzed.

APPENDIX 1

Statistical problems in estimating the increase of food consumption

When new development projects are undertaken, more men and women are put to work both directly on the project, and at other points, producing materials for the project, or transporting and merchandising those materials en route to the project. How much of the increased income received is likely to be spent for food, and how much of that food is likely to be of types that could be obtained from existing surplus stocks?

To answer this question, it is necessary to know (a) the income group from which the newly employed workers are drawn; (b) how people at such income levels will probably use additions to their income; and (c) what foods and other products might be available from surplus stocks.

Each of the four agro-economic institutes made special studies for this survey on the labor employed on a number of different Indian development projects. On the two development projects where detailed data were collected these studies showed that the project labor was overwhelmingly drawn from the agricultural labor group, and information obtained on other projects was similar. [1] In most cases agricultural laborers constituted about three-quarters of the workers on the project. On four types of development projects in Madras State, for example, one type, bridge-building, employed nearly half non-agricultural labor, and one-third non-farm-owning agricultural labor. On the remaining three kinds of projects agricultural workers constituted from 65 percent to 85 percent of the total labor. On most projects examined the modal amount earned per family per month from project work fell between 10 and 40 rupees, and the total expenditure per caput ranged from 7 to 15 rupees (i.e., the equivalent of 5 to 10 U.S. cents per person per day, for all food, clothing, and other expenses. Prevailing prices, however, are materially lower in India than in the U.S.). We may therefore conclude that the workers on the projects in India come mostly from under-employed agricultural labor, with incomes prior to such employment in the very lowest income groups.

DIFFERENT METHODS OF PREPARING THE ESTIMATES

There are three ways which might be used to provide a basis for estimating how families will spend additional incomes from development projects. These will be designated the "before and after" method, the "with and without method", and the "income elasticity" method.

The *"before and after method"* comes nearest to reproducing what it is actually wanted to determine – the actual change in food consumption in a given community (or country) as the result of certain given increases in wages paid out on new development projects. This would involve measuring total income paid out, and expenditure for food by kinds, before and after the development project or projects were undertaken. This might be done as an operating experiment in some relatively isolated area, supplying concurrently the estimated amounts of surplus foods needed to prevent any change in prices up or down. Prices, weather conditions, general economic conditions and incomes received, however, change from time to time. It would thus be difficult to isolate the effect of the income changes alone. In any case, this method could be used for past events only where the necessary statistical observations had been made for some time. Such records were not available in India.

It would be possible to set up an experiment of the type described and collect the necessary information on incomes received and expenditures made over the period of the experiment, both before and after the development project was launched. Observation on development projects in India indicates that at the beginning increased incomes are used partly to pay off old debts, and only after a time does the full effect on food expenditures begin to appear. Accordingly, an experiment of this sort would need to operate for a considerable period, both before and after the increased incomes were paid, say, at least six months for each. The time available for making the present study was so short that it was not possible to use such an experiment. Countries considering the use of food surpluses to finance development on a considerable scale might well, however, set up several such experiments in different parts of the country. By using careful sampling methods to measure the average income, total expenditure, and expenditure by each class of foods for a carefully selected sample of families, interviewed possibly once each month through the period of the experiment, and with estimates of food used checked by objective measurements of the quantities actually prepared for family consumption by weight or measure, a well-based estimate of the result could be obtained. If there were changes in the general level of food prices or in other important economic factors during the period of the study, their effects also would have to be allowed for in interpreting the results.

The *"with and without"* method depends on comparing levels of income and of food consumption and expenditures in one community where an active development project is under way with levels in similar communities without such sources of extra income. By selecting the areas surveyed and the sample obtained in such a way as to secure close comparability both of local conditions, and of the composition of the sample as to size and type of families included, closely matched samples could be obtained. Differences in the averages of food consumption by types, and of income received, can then serve as a basis to estimate what proportion of the additional income disbursed to direct labor on the project goes into increased consumption of each kind of foods. Three special surveys of this "with and without" type were conducted in India for the special use of this present report. The results of these special studies will be presented later.

The *"income elasticity"* method depends on observing the differences in expenditure for food and other items between families with different levels of income, and the amount and composition of food expenditure at the different income levels. Then, on the assumption that with changes in income families will shift their consumption patterns to the same extent that families at different income levels show different patterns of consumption and expenditure, one can estimate the change in expenditure on food consumption by kinds of food that are likely to accompany given changes in the amount of income. In making such an estimate it is necessary to estimate the income class that will be affected by the increase in income and the extent of the increase that each class will receive. A good deal of scattered data is available in India on consumption patterns by income groups or by different levels of total expenditures, as will be summarized later.

STUDIES ON SURPLUS FOOD CONSUMPTION WITH AND WITHOUT A DEVELOPMENT PROJECT

For the purposes of this report, three special studies were conducted on food consumption and expenditure with and without development projects. In each case two matched samples were selected, one of families in a development area with members employed on a development project, and the other of similar families in other villages in the same region without employment from development projects. These studies were conducted for the use of FAO, one in Northern India by the School of Economics of Delhi University and two at different projects in Bombay State by the Agro-Economic Research Unit at the Gokhale Institute of Politics and Economics at Poona. In addition, less comprehensive studies of labor employed on various development projects in their regions were made by the Agro-Economic Research Units at Madras and Shantiniketan (Vishna-Bharati).[2]

Each of the three special surveys ran into unanticipated difficulties of various sorts. In one case, the agricultural workers drew heavily on credit for their consumption during the period surveyed, as it was just before harvest time and there was little current work to be had. In another, the information on farm production and farm income was incomplete, and while values of food consumed were obtained, there was no independent information on incomes. In another case the workers on the project proved to be largely refugees from distant regions, with quite different food habits from the families in the villages off the projects. In the case of the two southern regions, only expenditures for food were obtained, and it was necessary to estimate the total expenditure for all purposes from the usual regression of food expenditure per caput on total expenditure as shown in other studies (see Figure 2, page 193).

In the northern study objective measurements were made of food consumed by part of the families to check the survey estimates from the same families. There was reasonably good agreement between the estimates and the measurements, with the averages for individual foods from the two methods usually differing less than 10 percent for important foodstuffs, and the total estimated value of food consumption on the two bases agreeing even more closely.[3]

Despite the various difficulties and discrepancies, when the three sets of data were compared in terms of the percentage of change in total expenditure reflected in increased expenditure for foods of kinds which might be secured from surplus stocks, results were obtained as shown in the following tabulation.

Table A1-1. Proportion of Increased Income from Project Employment used for Increased Expenditure for Foods of Surplus Types, as Reported by Three Special Surveys[1]

Survey and Location	Number of households represented	Proportion of expenditures on surplus type foods
Ghod Project, Bombay State	180	56%
Ghataprabha Project, Bombay State	150	39%
Bhakra Nangel Project, Punjab and PEPSU States	251	26%

[1] Assuming income equals total expenditure.

There was thus a wide range in percentage of total expenditure for foods of surplus types, with the Bhakra Nangel project showing a much lower total percentage than the two southern projects, but with considerable differences between these two projects. For all three projects combined, the average proportion of increased expenditure going into surplus foods was 40.3 percent. The differences in this proportion between north and south India are consistent with the fact that average incomes are much higher in the north as follows.

Table A1-2. Average Expenditure per Caput among Families in Three Areas

Area	In selected villages without project employment	In selected villages with project employment
	.. rupees per person per month ..	
Ghod Project, Bombay State	7.8	13.3
Ghataprabha Project, Bombay State	6.7	14.1
Bhakra Nangel Project, Punjab and PEPSU States	17.7	37.6

In fact, the per caput expenditure in the villages without any project in the north average materially higher than in the villages with project employment in the two areas in the south.[4] The marginal increase in food consumption declines as the income is higher, as is clearly reflected in the differences between the averages for the northern area, and the two southern areas.

INFORMATION ON DIFFERENCES IN FOOD EXPENDITURE WITH HIGHER INCOMES

A great deal of statistical work has been done in India in collecting information on consumption, and in analysing the results. Unfortunately, however, little of this work has given much attention to the relation of income to consumption; in fact, in most cases separate data on income were not obtained, or, if obtained, were not used in the analysis. Accordingly it has been necessary to limit the analyses here to relations of total expenditure level to expenditure on food. This involves ignoring differences in savings, either positive or negative (going into debt). At the very low income levels important for the current purposes, however, it is not believed that this has made any serious difference in the results.

A survey of the conditions of agricultural labor in 1950-51, based on a selected sample of 11,000 families in 800 villages distributed widely through India, gives much useful background information about this important lowest-income group, which forms nearly one-third of all rural families. Although data were collected on both incomes earned and expenditure by kinds of food purchased, no tabulations have yet been made or published relating distribution of expenditure to levels of income.[5] The comparison of average family income with average expenditure, by States, shows generally very little difference between income and expenditure, with about as many States showing expenditure above income as show it below income.[6]

Another source of information on income, expenditure, and the distribution of various foods is the National Sample Survey, made at repeated intervals of about one-half year since late 1951. Full reports have been published only on the first three "rounds", those for October 1950-March 1951, April-June 1951, and August-November 1951.[7] Much interesting information on average family and per caput income, total expenditure, and expenditure on individual foods is included in the three published national reports. No analysis has been included in any of them, however, on the relation of differences in income level per consumption unit to expenditure on individual (or total) foods. In any case, the marked fall in the prices of many foods since 1951 would render analyses based on these earlier reports of doubtful value for the present use.

Fortunately, one report has been published based on a special survey in one limited area in early 1954 and containing an income-expenditure analysis which is useful for the present need. This study was a special survey of Farindabad Township, a suburban area near New Delhi where many refugees from the Partition had settled, and where a new town had been laid out for them. While the group was largely an urban group with urban occupations, there was much unemployment and a wide spread of incomes within the groups. A table analyzing the per caput expenditure for various items of consumption at given levels of total expenditure per caput is of special value for the present purposes, and accordingly pertinent portions of the table are reproduced here, as Table A1-3.[8]

In addition to the Farindabad report, there is much additional potentially useful material in the questionnaires from the subsequent rounds, which have not yet been tabulated or published. In response to a request for some special limited tabulations for the purpose of this present study, an exploratory analysis was made of the sample from the State of Uttar Pradesh, covering 297 selected households, classified into selected identical groups as to family composition, and showing differences in quantities of five groups of foods consumed in each group according to differences in income per household. While the number of cases was too small for fully stable results, the group averages showed generally consistent changes with change in income. Converting all the data into terms of expenditure and

Table A1-3. Per Caput Consumer Expenditure per Month in Rupees for Different Levels of Monthly per Caput Consumer Expenditure (Reference period: February 1954)

Items of consumption	Per caput consumption in rupees per month for February 1954 at levels of per caput monthly total expenditure								
	5-10	11-15	16-20	21-25	26-30	31-40	41-60	61-	all levels
All cereals	4.32	5.39	5.91	6.05	6.83	7.14	7.46	7.68	6.06
Pulses and products ...	0.32	0.48	0.59	0.70	0.73	0.82	1.10	1.19	0.64
Milk and products	0.67	1.25	2.22	2.88	3.33	4.11	5.94	11.50	2.74
Vegetables	0.31	0.66	0.78	1.10	1.14	1.58	2.04	4.30	1.04
Fruits and nuts	0.05	0.07	0.17	0.25	0.46	0.68	1.14	3.81	0.38
Meat, fish and eggs ...	0.01	0.12	0.16	0.21	0.35	0.36	0.90	2.22	0.28
Oils and products	0.52	1.09	1.37	1.62	1.01	2.06	2.36	3.35	1.51
Sugar and gur	0.51	0.88	1.12	1.38	1.59	1.71	2.05	2.44	1.26
Salt and spices	0.18	0.30	0.38	0.43	0.53	0.50	0.65	1.47	0.43
Beverages and refreshments	0.12	0.31	0.44	0.64	0.66	0.90	1.93	3.20	0.64
Total: food items	7.01	10.55	13.14	15.26	17.53	19.86	25.57	41.16	14.98
Total: all items	8.70	13.74	17.85	23.02	27.77	33.86	46.78	105.61	23.50
No. of persons	158	479	593	337	269	208	120	54	2218
No. of households	23	89	121	81	65	58	38	25	500

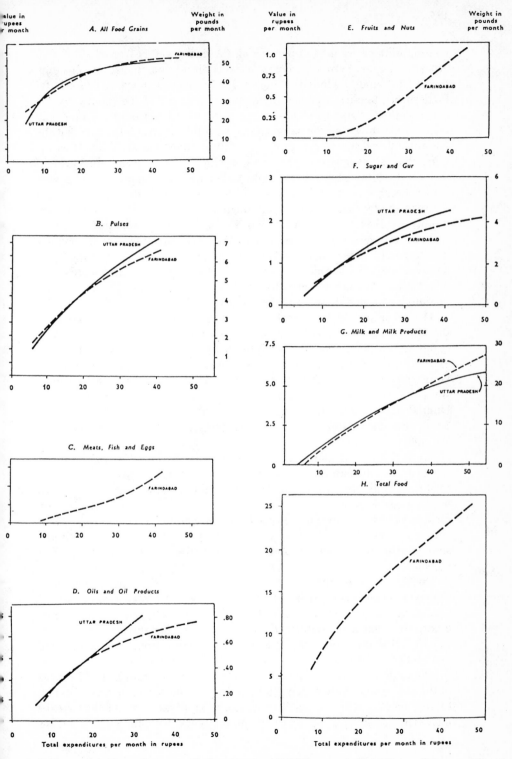

Figure 2. Differences in Expenditures on Various Foods with Differences in Total Expenditures, per Caput

consumption per caput and plotting all the data together from the different groups, relations between change in expenditure and change in consumption were found as plotted in Figure 2. (The curves shown here for Uttar Pradesh are free-hand curves fitted to the averages of the groups, by the usual method of free-hand smoothing.[9]) Similar data from the Farindabad analysis are shown on the same charts, with the scales adjusted so that the Farindabad measurements, in rupees, fall at about the same levels as the Uttar Pradesh averages, in physical quantities. (Value scales are shown at the left, quantity scales at the right.) For the lower income ranges with which the present study is concerned, there is surprisingly close agreement between the two sets of curves, although one is based on a suburban community in 1954, and the other on a largely rural State in 1953-54.

Requests were made to the Indian Statistical Institute, which conducts the National Sample Survey, for a sample tabulation from recent questionnaires covering a broader area than the two shown in the figures, and making the same tabulation as for the Farindabad records. The special tabulations requested have not been received.

Dandekar also made an analysis by expenditure classes of the data from the Ghod and Ghataprabha surveys. This provided a basis for obtaining regressions of food expenditure on total expenditure (after estimating total expenditure per caput from food expenditure per caput on the usual relation between the two, which is remarkably stable.) When these regressions were fitted and plotted on the same charts with the Farindabad and Uttar Pradesh curves, the regressions for pulses were much higher in the South (Bombay State) than in the two northern areas, and the regression for milk much lower.

Using the Farindabad regressions as a basis, therefore, we can estimate the expected increase in surplus food consumption for given increases in total food. First we must decide at what level of income, and for how much increase readings are to be made from the curves. As shown earlier, on most projects the average expenditure is about 11 rupees per caput per month for the entire family. The data from the "with and without" studies also showed similar low incomes in the villages without project incomes.

On the basis of these data and remembering that the Punjab area (Bahakra Nangel) is far richer than most of India, we may assume that 10 rupees per caput per month will represent the average family income before the project is established, and 15 rupees after the project is under way. Reading the corresponding expenditure figure from the curves fitted to the Farindabad data (Figure 2) we obtain the results in Table A1-4.

The table has been computed both for an increase from 10 to 15 rupees in the average monthly expenditure, per caput, and for an increase from 10 to 20 rupees. With the smaller increase, 55 percent would thus go for increased consumption of foods of surplus types; with the larger, only 48

Table A1-4. Estimated Surplus Food Expenditure at Given Levels of Monthly per Caput Income, from Farindabad Regressions (1954)[1]

	Income per caput			Increase in expenditure		Proportion of total increase in expenditure	
	10 Rps.	15 Rps.	20 Rps.	10-15	10-20	10-15	10-20
	rupees			*rupees*		*percent*	
Food grains	4.6	5.5	6.1	0.9	1.5	18.0	15.0
Pulses	0.37	0.51	0.63	0.14	0.26	0.8	2.6
Edible oil	0.72	1.19	1.49	0.47	0.77	9.4	7.7
Sugar and gur	0.62	0.95	1.24	0.33	0.62	6.6	6.2
Milk	0.90	1.75	2.4	0.85	1.50	17.0	15.0
Fruits and nuts[2]	0.03	0.05	0.10	0.02	0.07	0.4	0.7
Meat, fish and eggs[2]	0.03	0.06	0.10	0.03	0.07	0.6	0.7
Surplus foods				2.74	4.79	52.8	47.9
All foods	8.0	11.5	14.1	3.5	6.1	70.0	61.0

[1] For basis for considering these products as available from food surpluses, see footnote 3.
[2] Data entered are one-half of amounts shown on curves, as assumed portion which might be supplied through surplus products.

percent. (Even if sugar and gur were excluded as potential surplus foods, the total from surpluses would still be 50 and 42 percent, respectively.) These average marginal elasticities for surplus foods compare with corresponding elasticities of .70 and .61 for food as a whole. For the 10-15 rupee increase, 78 percent of the increase in food expenditure is for foods of surplus types; over the 10-20 rupee increase, about the same percent. The high income elasticity of milk, oil, and pulses offset the low income elasticity for grains. These results based on the income elasticity curves compare with the previous results based on the "with and without" comparisons as follows.

Percentage for
surplus foods

1. Averages from "with and without" studies

Ghod dam and canals project, Bombay State .   56   percent

Ghataprabha Canal project, Bombay State   39   percent

Bhakra Nangel combined resource project,
Punjab and PEPSU States   26   percent

Average   40   percent

2. Income elasticity data for Farindabad, Delhi State

With increase from 10 to 15 rupees per caput
per month   55   percent

With increase from 10 to 20 rupees per caput
per month   48   percent

Average ....   51.5 percent

The straight average of all these percentages is 45 percent. They include the Bhakra Nangel project, which is located in an exceptionally prosperous region, with incomes and standards of living much higher than in most regions of India, and especially than those where most of the underemployed agricultural labor is located (note again Figure 1 in Chapter VI). Accordingly, it appears that we might use 45 percent as a nation-wide estimate of the proportion of direct project labor payrolls which will be reflected in increased purchases of surplus foods. So as not to overestimate the increase, however, we will use 40 percent as the estimated proportion for project workers. Similarly, if we take a change from 15 to 20 rupees per month as representing the average increases in incomes resulting from derived increases in income off the projects (on the basis of the Farindabad tabulations, this would about represent bringing partially or wholly unemployed urban residents up to about modal incomes); 41 percent of this increase in expenditures would be reflected in increased purchases of surplus foods. We may therefore conservatively conclude as follows for India.

1. That 40 percent of the increased income from direct labor expenditures on a development project (including labor expenditures of subcontractors) will be reflected in increased surplus food purchases, at retail.

2. That 35 percent of the derived income increases will be reflected in increased surplus food purchases, at retail.

If other assumptions are made as to the foods available as surpluses, corresponding adjustments can be made in the percentages used.

Shifts in consumption patterns. One other point brought out by some of the "with-and-without" studies deserves mention. That is the possibility of shift in consumption patterns as between different types of food grains as income rises. For example, in some of the "before-and-after" studies, there were increases in wheat consumption with increased income and smaller increases in rice and pulses, partly offset by reduction in maize consumption.

These shifts indicate the possibility that increased incomes from development may not only lead to increases in consumption of some foods, but may actually lead to decreases in others. If this should occur over a wide region, markets for some products might be depressed by additional projects based on surplus food financing even though total food consumption increased. (The same is equally true of increased income from projects based on other financing, too, except for the effect of the sale of surplus foods on the markets.) In any actual operation, it would be desirable to determine as accurately as possible both the prospective and the actual effects of surplus financing and sale on the consumption of all the products affected (even including possibly some non-surplus products), and to adjust the selection of surplus products to be released or sold, by kind as well as quantity, as accurately as possible to offset or prevent any undesirable results due to such substitution between products.

[1] Dandekar, *loc. cit.*, Chapter VII.
[2] Dandekar, *loc. cit.*, Chapter VII.
[3] The food groups used here as possibly available from surpluses, imported or domestic, are as follows.
1. "Food grains" include wheat, coarse grains, rice, millets, and sorghums.
2. "Pulses" would include dry beans and peas.
3. "Fruits" might be supplied in part from dried fruits such as prunes, raisins and apples. The figures in the table include half of the expenditure for fruit.

4. "Sugar" is based on the use of domestic gur (low quality cane sugar produced in simple farm evaporation pans) of which there is a serious surplus in India at present.

5. "Milk" would be covered by the use of surplus dried skim milk, canned milk, butter, cheese, and other dairy products, which are already used in India in considerable volume. (Note Chapter VIII in this connection.)

6. "Meat" would be covered by the use of surplus tinned meats of various sorts, of dried eggs, and possibly in part by surpluses of dried or salted fish. As with fruits, this item is taken as only half of the expenditures reported.
(The "meat" item in Indian consumption surveys usually includes meats, fish, and eggs).

7. "Edible oils" are based on the possible use of surplus stocks of cottonseed oil, soybean oil, etc., either from abroad or resulting from domestic price-support operations.
Cotton might also have been considered, but was not included, due in part to limitation of much of the available statistical data to food alone. If any of the food groups mentioned should prove not to be available from domestic or foreign stocks held as surpluses, corresponding adjustments would need to be made in the resulting percentages of possible consumption of surplus foods.

[4] Standard errors were computed of the average expenditures for important food groups, for the matched areas, both with and without development projects. As a whole, they indicate that the differences in the averages have a good sampling reliability.

[5] Dr. B. Ramamurti, *Agricultural Labor, How They Work and Live*; Ministry of Labor, New Delhi, 1954.

[6] Dandekar, *loc. cit.*, Chap. III.

[7] *The National Sample Survey, General Report No. 1 on the First Round,* October 1950 - March 1951, Department of Economic Affairs, Ministry of Finance, Government of India, December 1952.

The National Sample Survey, No. 2, Tables with Notes on the Second Round, April-June 1951, Dept. of Economic Affairs, Ministry of Finance, Government of India, December 1953.

The National Sample Survey, No. 3, Tables with Notes on the Third Round, August-Nov. 1951, Ministry of Finance, Government of India, January 1954.

[8] *The National Sample Survey, No. 6, Survey of Farindabad Township,* March-April 1954, Department of Economic Affairs, Ministry of Finance, Government of India, December 1954.

[9] M. Ezekiel, *Methods of Correlation Analysis,* John Wiley and Sons, London and New York, 2nd edition, 1941, pp. 105-113.

APPENDIX 2

Economic problems in estimating the increase in consumption of surplus foods

Estimating the increase in food consumption which would result from a given increase in investment raises a number of new economic problems, since increased food consumption is to be supplied in part from stocks either from outside the country or already accumulated and in public ownership.

In the usual (Keynesian) analysis of the effect of increased investment on consumption, it is pointed out that an initial investment contributes more than the amount of that investment to increased demands, as the same sum is respent several times as it circulates from the original recipient and spender to one after another person or business concern in the economic system, each one using it in turn to make new expenditures. Factors that limit the amount of this multiplication are the fact that there is some delay in each case between the receipt of additional income and its expenditure, so that the income expansion is lower over a given period of time, as this period of respending is longer; and the further fact that at each cycle of respending there is some "leakage" due to part of the net income received being withheld as savings, being used to pay taxes, or being respent for imported goods. These "leaks" constitute deductions from the amounts which will be spent for consumption goods or services in the next cycle of expenditure. Ignoring the effect of the length of the time period, the total or ultimate effect of additional investment on increased income is:

$$(Eq. 1) \quad \Phi = \frac{1}{m + g + s}$$

where Φ is the investment multiplier and m, g, and s the marginal propensities to import, pay taxes (under the existing tax structure), and to save.

If we take 6 percent as the average saving rate in India, 8 percent as the average tax rate (including federal, state, and local levies, sales taxes, etc.) and 6 percent as the average import rate (each in terms of proportions of national income)[1] we may assume that the marginal rate (for the increases in income resulting from additional investment projects of the types discussed in this report) will average 9 percent for savings, 9 percent for taxes, and 8 percent for imports. Then, Φ (the Keynesian investment-income multiplier) would be 3.85, and the ultimate effect of an increase of 10 crores in investment would be to increase the national income by 38.5 crores.

This multiplier for India compares with a similar multiplier for Italy of 1.6. This was derived from a very detailed study, project by project, which followed the effects of an expenditure for wages, materials, consumers' goods and services, taxes, imports, etc., through several successive cycles, and made detailed estimates of the specific repercussions, both for the country as a whole and for different regions within the country.[2] It was estimated that imports for consumption would equal 17 percent of the resulting increase in national income, taxes 27 percent, and savings 10½ percent. These figures are based on an item-by-item and project-by-project appraisal of the repercussions and not on an overall calculation, as in Eq. 1. The much higher levels of these "leakages" (totalling 54 percent in Italy as compared with 24 percent estimated for India) explain the much smaller multiplier. In general it is to be expected that the less developed the country, with the usual higher consumption propensity and low development of the taxation system, the higher the multiplier will be.

The Italian study also considered the effect of the length of the income responding cycle, and the number of cycles completed, on the percent of the theoretical maximum expansion of income which would be attained by the end of given periods of time. Under Italian conditions, it found that with an income cycle of 3 months, a level of 81.8 of the theoretical would be reached in 24 months, and with an income cycle of 6 months, a level of 66.4 would be reached in the same period.[3]

EFFECT OF THE USE OF SURPLUS FOOD ON THE MULTIPLIER

The multiplier formula rests upon the assumption that *all* expenditures for consumption enter into a second cycle of expenditure, where the net income received, minus the reductions again of savings, taxes, etc., produce a second lower level of expenditure, and this is carried forward through successive cycles at a gradually declining level. When food surpluses are used to satisfy part of the consumption expenditure, however, the money spent for the purchase of such surplus foods becomes a "leakage" just as much as the money used for savings or taxes. Even if the surplus foods are taken from domestic food surpluses, previously acquired or underwritten by the government, they are in the same category as surpluses from abroad, for the payments for them do not raise the current incomes of farmers or increase their ability to buy more of other goods. This could be treated either as an addition to the import propensity (since the foreign surpluses are in fact imports, even if not currently paid for), or as a separate factor to be separately taken into account. The proportion of the consumption expenditures absorbed by food surpluses is higher for the direct labor expenditure at the first round than it is for the indirect expenditures based on other purchases at that round, or for the total expenditures at subsequent rounds. Accordingly, it may be well to follow the calculation through, round by round. We will assume that under Indian conditions three rounds of spending occur each year.[4]

We will first illustrate the calculation arithmetically for a project with certain specified conditions. (Other conditions are considered as specific projects are examined in the text.) We will assume (a) that the surplus foods are used to finance development projects of average labor intensity, where say 50 percent of total costs go into direct labor, including labor employed by subcontractors; (b) that 40 percent of such direct labor payments reappear as expenditures for surplus foods at retail, equal to 34 percent at wholesale; (c) that 35 percent of derived income net of saving, taxes and imports will be spent on other surplus foods at retail, equal to 26 percent at wholesale; and that the stated marginal propensities to import, to pay taxes, and to save apply;[5] and (d) that 10 percent of the project costs are for imported equipment and supplies, such as gasoline.

As mentioned, one aspect which must be considered in calculating the amount spent for surplus foods *at wholesale*, where imported surplus products would be sold to offset the purchases by consumers, is the distributing cost. This covers the fraction of consumers' expenditure which goes for distribution margins, and is thus diverted to paying transportation charges, labor, the profits of retailers, etc. On the basis of past studies in India by the Directorate of Marketing and Inspection, 25 percent may be taken as the average marketing margin for all surplus foods. For foods bought by general consumers, then, only 75 percent of the 35 percent spent for surplus-type foods at retail, or 26 percent, is taken as representing the wholesale market value of the surplus food.

Wages for direct labor on labor-intensive development projects go largely to landless laborers, who are the poorest rural people.[6] In these villages most of the food they purchase is grown locally, and is sold unprocessed and with only the simplest and least costly of marketing services or charges.[7] A selling margin of only 15 percent will therefore be used for the food purchased by direct project workers, reducing the 40 percent of income they spend for food at retail to 34 percent as the value of the food at wholesale.

The calculation of expected income and surplus food consumption will be carried out under two different sets of assumed conditions.[8]

a) *Assuming no respending of derived income for domestic goods*

Starting with 100 units of total investment, the amount spent for imported equipment and supplies, 10 units, must first be deducted, as that will have no significant effect on domestic demands or incomes.[9] Of the 90 units remaining, 50 units will be paid out as wages to project workers. Of this, 34 percent will be spent for surplus foods at wholesale, resulting in (50) (.34), or 17 units, increase in the consumption of foods of surplus types.

At the same time (neglecting temporarily the effects of workers' expenditures for other goods and services), 40 units will be spent on domestic goods and services for the project – cement, steel, transportation, etc. Deducting the portion of this set aside for taxes, savings, and imported goods, this will produce an increase in disposable income of

$$(40) \ [1 - (.09 + .09 + .08)] = (40) \ (.74) = 29.6 \ \text{units.}$$

Of this increased income, expenditure on surplus food will be

$$29.6 \times 26 \ \text{percent} = 7.7 \ \text{units.}$$

The total increase in domestic income to this point will be 50 + 29.6, or 79.6 units, and in surplus food consumption, 17 + 7.7, or 24.7 units.

Whether there are any further derived effects will now depend upon how the domestic costs of the project are financed. Costs of imported goods must in any event be covered by foreign exchange. The entire domestic costs of the project might also be covered by external financing, in part through surplus foods and in part by external grants or loans (as suggested in Chapters III and V). If that is done, foreign exchange will be available to import not only all the imported equipment needed on the project, but also all the consumers' goods for which there will be increased demands as a result of the project. The expenditure of the income remaining after surplus foods are purchased will be largely offset by the supply of imported consumers' goods placed on the market; there will be practically no further demands placed on the domestic economy or increase of jobs to meet those demands, and almost the total increase in consumption of surplus goods will be the 24.7 units just calculated – or ¼ of the total project cost.

In addition, 15 percent of direct labor expenditures, and 25 percent of derived disposable income, will have been spent for marketing services, which cannot be imported. This total of 15% × 50 + 25% × 29.6, or

15 units, will still have some derived effects, but this will be relatively small, and would add only 2.8 units to demand for surplus goods at the next cycle of respending.

b) *Assuming derived income respent for domestic goods*

On the other hand, the project may in effect be financed in part by surplus goods, and in part by additional production in the Indian economy, stimulated by additional income generated by the new project.[10] Where such additional "deficit financing" is possible, it will be necessary to take account of the income generated and the expenditures made at each successive step of spending and respending of the resulting increased incomes.

For the first round, starting with 100 units of additional investment, the 50 units of investment will be paid out to project workers as wages. This will be the total income respent in period 1, as purchases of materials, etc., will take a longer time to reappear in incomes than the assumed few months of the respending cycle.

From the income thus distributed, purchases of surplus food would be, at wholesale values (assuming taxes, savings, and purchases of imports are negligible for project laborers):

$$\text{from direct labor } 50 \times 34\% = 17 \text{ units.}$$

Income disbursed to other income receivers will equal total domestic investment, minus surplus goods purchased, or

$$90 - 17 = 73.$$

For period 2, induced income from income received in period 1 will result only from the expenditure other than for imports, or for surplus foods, since those are taken care of by the food withdrawn from previous surplus stocks, and do not generate any new income. Before calculating the expenditure for all types of domestic goods and services, we must deduct the fund set aside to pay taxes, as savings, or used to buy imported goods. These "leakages" total 26 percent on our assumed values, so the expenditures for other purposes for the second round of spending is

$$54.0 \times 26\% = 14.0 \text{ units}$$

and of this, expenditure on surplus food will be

$$54.0 \times 26\% = 14.0 \text{ units.}$$

The derived income for domestic expenditure in period 2 is then

$$54.0 - 14.0 = 40 \text{ units};$$

total expenditures for other purposes are

$$(40) (0.74) = 29.6 \text{ units};$$

surplus food consumption is 29.6 × 26% = 7.7 units and derived income is 29.6 − 7.7 = 21.9 units.

Continuing with subsequent periods, the calculations come out:

Period	Total expenditures excl. imports	Surplus food consumption	Derived income
4	(21.9)(0.74)= 16.2	(16.2)(0.26)= 4.2	16.2 − 4.2 = 12.0
5	(12.0)(0.74)= 8.9	(8.9)(0.26)= 2.3	8.9 − 2.3 = 6.6
6	(6.6)(0.74)= 4.88	(4.88)(0.26)= 1.27	4.88 − 1.27 = 3.61
7	(3.61)(0.74)= 2.67	(2.67)(0.26)= 0.69	2.67 − 0.69 = 1.98
8	(1.98)(0.74)= 1.47	(1.47)(0.26)= 0.38	1.47 − 0.38 = 1.09
9	(1.09)(0.74)= 0.81	(0.81)(0.26)= 0.21	0.81 − 0.21 = 0.60

The quantities from period 10 on become so small as to be negligible.

Summarizing the figures by years, on our assumption that three cycles of responding occur each year, the data are as follows.

Period	1st year		2nd year		3rd year	
	Derived income	Surplus foods	Derived income	Surplus foods	Derived income	Surplus foods
1st period	73.0	17.0	12.0	4.2	2.0	0.69
2nd period	40.0	14.0	6.6	2.3	1.1	0.38
3rd period	21.9	7.7	3.6	1.3	0.6	0.21
Total	134.9	38.7	22.2	7.8	3.7	1.28

The totals for the three years combined are thus 161 units for income, direct and derived, and 48 units for increased consumption of surplus foods. This shows how much the increased buying power generated by new investment may be modified by the use of surplus foods to meet some of the new demands.

Whereas without this effect being considered it may be estimated from the savings, taxing, and import propensities that in India additional investment would tend to generate additional income to the extent of 3.85 times the original investment, with the introduction of surplus foods the effect had been reduced to about 1.6 times the investment. This income multiplier, reduced because of the use of surplus foods, may be termed a "damped multiplier." The increase in surplus food consumption within the three years now comes to about 48 percent of the original investment, or much more than the figure of a little less than 25 percent calculated under the first assumption, where the effect of increased income at subsequent cycles of expenditure was removed.

The calculations just presented have involved one more implicit assumption not hitherto noted. That is that the entire investment for the year would be made in the first four months, and would complete its initial expenditure cycle in that period, while in the subsequent periods only the derived income effects would be felt. What difference would it make if we assumed that the year's investment was spread out evenly over the entire year, one-third in each four-month period? That question can be easily answered from the data just computed, assuming that the year's total investment be 300 units, 100 in each period. To show the full effect, the calculations are also carried through for the two succeeding years, to give full effect to the earlier investments. The data for the derived income work out as in Table A2-1.

Table A2-1. Derived Income, Investment each Period

Period	First year (by periods)			Second year (by periods)			Third year (by periods)		
	1st	2nd	3rd	1st	2nd	3rd	1st	2nd	3rd
Jan.-April ...	73.0	40.0	21.9	12.0	6.6	3.6	2.0	1.1	0.6
May-Aug. ...		73.0	40.0	21.9	12.0	6.6	3.6	2.0	1.1
Sept.-Dec. ...			73.0	40.0	21.9	12.0	6.6	3.6	2.0
Totals	73.0	113.0	134.9	73.9	40.5	22.2	12.2	6.7	3.7
Annual totals			320.9			136.6			22.6
Grand Total									480.1

Thus distributed, the income-expanding force of the investment of 300 units had been reduced to 320.9 units in the first year, or only 1.07 times the investment, and to 136.6 units in the following year, or 0.46 times the investment. For the years combined, it totals 480.1 units, or 1.60 times the investment, practically as much as before.

Similarly, the use of surplus products to meet the increased demands for surplus foods would work out as shown in Table A2-2.

Table A2-2. Increased Consumption of Surplus Foods, Investment each Period

Period	First year (by periods)			Second year (by periods)			Third year (by periods)		
	1st	2nd	3rd	1st	2nd	3rd	1st	2nd	3rd
Jan.-April	17.0	14.0	7.7	4.2	2.3	1.3	0.7	0.4	0.2
May-Aug.		17.0	14.0	7.7	4.2	2.3	1.3	0.7	0.4
Sept.-Dec.			17.0	14.0	7.7	4.2	2.3	1.3	0.7
Totals	17.0	31.0	38.7	25.9	14.2	7.8	4.3	2.4	1.3
Annual totals			86.7			47.9			8.0

On this calculation, the additional surplus foods consumed in the first year would cover only 29 percent of the investment that year, plus a further 16 percent in the next year – totalling 45 percent of the total investment in two years, or somewhat more than the effect in one year, with all the investment in the first period. The third year adds only 3 percent, bringing the total up to 48 percent. By an extension of the same procedure, we could test what the effect would be on income and on use of surpluses each year over a series of years, if the same amount of investment were made each year, in succession, and spread over each period, as illustrated in Table A2-3.

With 300 units invested each year, spread through the year, the increase in surplus food consumption thus works out at 29 percent of the annual investment the first year, 45 percent the second, and 48 percent the third. If the same investment were repeated each year, the maximum reached would be 49 percent.

All the results secured, of course, depend on our original assumptions, not only on the taxing, saving and importing propensities, and on the percent of income expended on surplus foods, but also on the assumed distribution of the investment in the particular project as between imports, direct labor, and other expenditures.

The process of applying this same procedure to other projects or to other countries with different values of the propensities and other constants

Table A2-3. Increased Consumption of Surplus Foods, Investment each Period for Three Years in Succession

Period	First year (by periods)			Second year (by periods)			Third year (by periods)		
	1st	2nd	3rd	1st	2nd	3rd	1st	2nd	3rd
Year 1-1	17.0	14.0	7.7	4.2	2.3	1.3	0.7	0.4	0.2
2		17.0	14.0	7.7	4.2	2.3	1.3	0.7	0.4
3			17.0	14.0	7.7	4.2	2.3	1.3	0.7
Year 2-1				17.0	14.0	7.7	4.2	2.3	1.3
2					17.0	14.0	7.7	4.2	2.3
3						17.0	14.0	7.7	4.2
Year 3-1							17.0	14.0	7.7
2								17.0	14.0
3									17.0
Totals	17.0	31.0	38.7	42.9	45.2	46.5	47.2	47.6	47.8
Annual totals			86.7			134.6			142.6

assumed, may be clarified by restating this procedure in more general algebraic terms, as follows.

a) *Assuming no respending of derived income for domestic goods*

On this simple assumption, the total income generated and consumption of surplus foods is given by the equations:

$$\text{(Eq. II)} \quad P = I_c + (I_k - I_c)(1-m-g-s) - S$$

$$\text{(Eq. III)} \quad S = I_c F_d + (I_k - I_c)(1-m-g-s) f_d$$

In these two equations the symbols have the following definitions:

P = income generated; (defined here as income net of savings, taxes, and expenditures for imported goods or surplus products);

S = total purchases of surplus products;

I_k = effective investment (investment minus investment expenditures for imported goods and services and for land purchases or other capital transfers);

I_c = investment used for direct labor on the project (including that employed by subcontractors);

F_d = proportion of wage payments to direct labor used for surplus food purchases at wholesale, after deducting marketing margin;

f_d = proportion of all derived income used for surplus food purchases at wholesale, after deducting marketing margin.

b) *Assuming derived income respent for domestic goods*

Under this assumption, the values of income generated and of consumption of surplus goods, are given for the first period by the equations:

$$\text{(Eq. IV)} \quad P_1 = I_k - I_c F_d$$

$$\text{(Eq. V)} \quad S_1 = I_c F_d$$

Here the symbols have the same meaning as in Eqs. II and III, except that P_1 and S_1 designate income generated and surplus purchases for the first period only.

For the second period, the equations are:

$$\text{(Eq. VI)} \quad P_2 = P_1 \, (1 - m - g - s) \, (1 - f_d)$$

$$\text{(Eq. VII)} \quad S_2 = P_1 \, (1 - m - g - s) \, f_d$$

If we use $K = (1 - m - g - s) \, (1 - f_d)$, then

$$\text{(Eq. VIa)} \quad P_2 = P_1 K$$

The value of additional derived income and of additional surplus food consumption in subsequent periods is given by the equations:

$$\text{(Eq. VIII)} \quad P_n = P_{n-1} K$$

$$\text{(Eq. IX)} \quad S_n = P_{n-1} \, (1 - m - g - s) \, f_d$$

each successive P, from P_2 to P_n, can be obtained by multiplying the previous one by the constant K. Similarly, for surplus foods, equation IX is as follows for periods 3 to 5:

For period 3, $\quad S_3 = P_2 \, (1 - m - g - s) \, (f_d)$
"   "   4, $\quad S_4 = P_3 \, (1 - m - g - s) \, (f_d)$
"   "   5, $\quad S_5 = P_4 \, (1 - m - g - s) \, (f_d)$

but $P_2 = K P_1$; $P_3 = K P_2 = K^2 P_1$; $P_4 = K P_3 = K^3 P_1$.

Substituting these values of P in the equations for S:

For period 3, $S_3 = KP_1 (1\text{-}m\text{-}g\text{-}s) (f_d)$
" " 4, $S_4 = K^2 P_1 (1\text{-}m\text{-}g\text{-}s) (f_d)$
" " 5, $S_5 = K^3 P_1 (1\text{-}m\text{-}g\text{-}s) (f_d)$

and from Equation VII, $S_2 = P_1 (1\text{-}m\text{-}g\text{-}s) f_d$.

So $S_3 = KS_2$, $S_4 = KS_3$, $S_5 = KS_4$ etc., or more generally,

$$(\text{Eq. X}) \; S_n = S_{n-1} K.$$

Each S can therefore be obtained by multiplying the previous S by the constant K_1.

Equation VIII holds true for all values of P from 2 to n, and IX holds true of all values of S from 2 to n. They do not hold true for P_1 which is uniquely defined by Eq. IV. Equation V is unique, since the value of S_1 in that equation differs from the general value for subsequent periods given by Eqs. IX and X. This is due to the separate allowances for surplus food consumption by direct labor, during Period 1.

We can now write general equations for the sums of these geometric series; for $n = \infty$

From equations IV and VIa,

$$(\text{Eq. XI}) \; \sum_1^n P = (I_k - I_c F_d) \frac{1}{1-K}$$

and from equations V, VII, and X

$$(\text{Eq. XII}) \; \sum_1^n S = S_1 + \frac{S_2}{1-K}$$

For finite values of n, the sums become

$$(\text{Eq. XIII}) \; \sum_1^n P = (I_k - I_c F_d) \frac{(K^{n-1}-1)}{K-1} \quad \text{and}$$

$$(\text{Eq. XIV}) \; \sum_1^n S = S_1 + S_2 \frac{(K^{n-1}-1)}{K-1}$$

For the illustrative case used earlier, where the values assumed were

$$I_k = 90, \; I_c = 50, \; F_d = 0.34, \; f_d = .26, \; K = 0.74$$

for the 9 periods covered in the earlier arithmetic calculations, equation
λIII becomes:

$$\sum_{1}^{n} P = (90 - 17) \frac{(0.74 \times 0.74)^8 - 1}{(0.74 \times 0.74) - 1} = (73)\,(2.1926) = 160.1$$

and from Equation λIV

$$\sum_{1}^{n} S = 17 + 14 \frac{(0.74 \times 0.74)^8 - 1}{(0.74 \times 0.74) - 1} = 17 + (14 \times 2.1926) = 47.70$$

The exact values thus calculated agree with those calculated arithmetically earlier, with insignificant differences due to the effects of rounding.

Since the successive values of P_3, P_4, P_5, etc., can be computed from each other by simply multiplying each preceding value by the constant K, and the corresponding values of S by multiplying the preceding S value by the constant K, the effects of any desired combination of investment, on any specified assumed conditions over any desired term of years, can be readily computed and examined, using the form of computation already illustrated in Tables A2-1 and A2-2. Various arithmetical shortcuts are also available in making such computations, but they will be obvious after a little practice in using the method.

The two sets of equations, under assumptions a) and b), provide lower and upper limits to the estimates for income derived and for additional surplus products purchased. It is also possible to make intermediate assumptions such as that imported goods will be used to satisfy half of the derived demand for consumer goods other than surplus products, while the other half is assumed to be satisfied by increased domestic production, with corresponding additional derived incomes. Estimated values for such modified assumptions can be calculated by corresponding modifications in the methods and equations just developed.[11]

---

[1] These estimates are based on the average rates shown in statistics for recent years, so far as available, plus estimates and forecasts of savings rate, as discussed in Chapter V. Imports have been declining and the figure for imports is based on an estimate of the future imports for consumption after imports for investment are allowed. Some Indian economists believe that marginal rates for savings and imports are even lower than those used here. If their figures were used, the estimates of derived income, and of additional surplus food consumed, would be raised correspondingly.

[2] *Economic Effects of an Investment Program in Southern Italy*, SVIMEZ – Associazione per lo Sviluppo dell'Industria nel Mezzogiorno, Rome, 1951.

[3] *Economic Effects of an Investment Program in Southern Italy*, pp. 66-69.

[4] While industrial production, in response to new orders, may be slower in India than in Italy, a much larger proportion of the total will be for relatively "soft" consumers' goods and less for heavy industrial products, than in Italy; and such goods can be produced and distributed in India without undue delays. Accordingly a four-month

period for each cycle of respending seems a reasonable assumption for Indian conditions.

[5] There are three reasons why the percentage of derived incomes spent for surplus products is lower than for direct project labor incomes.

(1) Less of the production costs of the goods purchased are represented by direct labor, and more by other costs (use of equipment, profits, etc.) which go to higher-income groups.

(2) The increased incomes are thus spread more generally over all groups in the economy, and higher income groups of course spend a smaller proportion of their total income for food than do lower-income groups.

(3) Surplus foods may make a smaller proportion of food consumption for higher income groups than for lower-income groups. Relatively less is spent for grains, and more for meat, dairy products, fruits, and vegetables. If the surplus products used are limited to grains, the effect will be considerable. For India, where it is assumed that surpluses of dairy products, dried fruits, nuts, and tinned meats might also be drawn upon, this point is not so important, for the relative consumption of these protective foods increases sharply with higher income groups, offsetting the reduced consumption of grains.

[6] See Dandekar, *loc. cit.*, Chapter VII.

[7] In a more careful investigation, the assumed size of this margin could be verified by a field investigation.

[8] See Appendix 3 for a fuller discussion of the reasons for these two different sets of assumptions.

[9] This ignores the possible second-order effects of increased imports on increased demand for Indian exports. For methods of estimating such second-order effects, see SVIMEZ, *loc. cit.*, pp. 69-76.

[10] See Chapter III for reasons supporting the validity of assuming that this can occur within the Indian economy. In addition to the points mentioned there, there is the further possibility of some expansion of agricultural products for sale, as a result of increased "monetization" of agricultural products formerly disposed of by barter, or consumed within a self-sufficient economy.

[11] For example, very conservative estimates have been used for the values of F_d, m, g, and s, in order to prevent over-estimating the additional consumption of surplus products. These might have been taken as 0.39 for F_d instead of 0.34, and (in line with suggestions of Indian economists) as 0.08 for marginal savings, 0.08 for marginal taxes, and 0.06 for marginal imports. If that had been done, and for the example given, over the first 9 periods the quantity of surpluses used would have been

$$S_1 = 50 \times 0.39 = 19.50$$

$$S_2 = (90 - 19.50)(1 - 0.08 - 0.08 - 0.06)\,0.26 = 70.50\,(0.78 \times 0.26) = 14.31$$

$$S = 19.50 + 14.31\,\frac{(0.78 \times 0.74)^8 - 1}{(0.78 \times 0.74) - 1} = 52.84$$

With the change in the values assumed for the constants the estimated proportion of investment covered by surpluses increases from 48 to 53 percent.

SELECTED REFERENCES ON THE USE OF INCOME MULTIPLIERS:

1) G. Haberler, *Prosperity and Depression,* New York, 1946, Ch. 8 Para. 4 and Ch. 13, Para. 1-7.

2) R.H. Goodwin, *The Multiplier,* in S.E. Harris, *The New Economics,* Knopf, New York, 1950, pp. 482-499.

3) F. Machlup, "Period Analysis and Multiplier Theory", *Quarterly Journal of Economics,* Vol. LIV, 1940, pp. 1-27.

4) F. Machlup, *International Trade and the National Income Multiplier,* Blakiston, Philadelphia, 1943.

APPENDIX 3

Surplus financing versus inflationary and deflationary dangers

This report has mainly been concerned with how far and how fast additional development projects would increase the consumption of surplus foods, and whether the value of surplus products could cover the whole or only a part of the entire costs of the investment in the project or projects. This issue is important so that surplus products thus used should really go into additional consumption, and not depress domestic or foreign markets for farm products. In this context there is another facet of this issue, which we have not faced directly or explored, which is also of importance. That is, whether the addition of the project or projects to the previous development program will tend to have an inflationary effect at first, and a deflationary effect in subsequent years. This appendix will examine that question.

The relations between savings, investment, imports, and level of national income are influenced by the means used in financing a nation's development. As W. Arthur Lewis has shown, the inflationary effect of a given investment program upon the country's level of prices depends not only on how much money is invested in the program, but also how it is raised – i.e., how investment is financed. It depends in other words, upon how much of that investment is covered by taxes, and by loans raised within the country, and based on genuine savings, to finance the program.[1] These propositions are somewhat modified, however, when the possibilities of using surplus products for financing are also taken into consideration. If the country is able to secure foreign assistance, public or private, (part of which may be in surplus products), and to use those external resources wisely to offset the increased demand for goods caused by the internal investment, it can raise its levels of production and consumption, without creating any inflation or balance of payment difficulties during the period the investment is being spent. Also, if the investment projects are wisely selected so that they increase the potential future levels of production in line with the increased income generated, they will help to sustain that increased level of national income in the future, without later inflationary difficulties and without requiring continued capital imports.

Let us examine these general propositions in somewhat more detail. We have seen already that when part of the increased demand for goods resulting from increased incomes is satisfied by the use of pre-existing governmentally-held stocks of goods (i.e., food surpluses, whether domestic or foreign), without any new income payments being created, that satisfies part of the new domestic demand without generating any new domestic income, and therefore the amount of additional derived income in the next responding cycle is reduced accordingly (see Appendix 2, especially equations IV, VIa, and VIII). Foreign loans can act in a similar manner, if the foreign exchange is used not only to cover necessary external expenditures for imported goods and services required directly by the project, but also to increase the imports of consumer goods to offset the increases in purchases of such goods resulting from the project. In such a case, the only inflationary effect upon the economy would be from payments for domestic services (transportation, marketing, etc.) involved in handling the materials for the projects and the imported goods. These would have to be supplied by expanding the relevant domestic activity, and cannot be imported. While they would generate derived income of a smaller amount at the next cycle of expenditure, most of this in turn would go for the purchase of commodities, which could be offset by corresponding imports. If the full amount of the original investment were offset by surpluses and by imported goods, that would thus offset practically all of the initial and the derived income, leaving only a very small residual effect (the fraction of the income from domestic services which would reappear as demand for other services) to have any inflationary effect.

In the discussion above we have neglected the fact that part of the immediate income would be diverted into taxes and savings, or ordinarily spent for imported consumer goods. The latter would cause no difficulty, as foreign exchange is assumed to be available to cover it. If the taxes and monetary savings were not re-spent currently as additional public expenditure or additional investment, that would reduce correspondingly the amounts of external financing that would have to be used to import consumer goods. For example, on our previous assumption of 9 percent for marginal savings, and 9 percent for marginal taxes (Appendix 2), expenditures for consumer goods and services would increase only 82 percent as fast as income paid out (excluding that part of direct project labor used to pay for surpluses at wholesale, which we have assumed to generate no taxes or savings), and the necessary foreign financing for additional imports to offset the additional consumer purchases would be reduced correspondingly.

Where surplus foods are available to satisfy part of the immediate increase in demand, and where additional foreign loans or investments can be secured to bring in additional goods to satisfy the rest of the demands, there will be no substantial further derived domestic income once these imported goods have absorbed the increased incomes, and no further inflationary effects. It follows from this that under these conditions, also, there will be no further derived expansion in domestic income at subsequent responding stages to increase further the consumption of surplus foods, as estimated under assumption b) in Appendix 2, but rather the entire effect on surplus consumption will be that calculated simply in the first expenditure of direct labor income, and in the first expenditure of all other derived income (plus the small portions remaining from services to provide further responding stages), as we have discussed under assumption a).

We can estimate the size of this addition by calculating the increased consumption for surplus goods under the example set forth in Appendix 2, and making the assumption that *all* domestic expenditures by consumers for goods at wholesale are covered by imports, and so are leakages, and that only the expenditures for marketing services produce derived income. The total personal income, direct and derived, produced by the additional domestic investment of 90 units is then only 93.6 units, and the total increased consumption of surplus products is only 28 units as contrasted to the 48 units calculated in Appendix 2 under assumption a). The total domestic personal income generated by the project, under the new assumption, is thus only 1.04 times the original domestic expenditure, and the total expenditure for surplus products is practically only the percent of that original expenditure reflected directly in surplus purchases (which in this case was $50 \times 34\% + 40 \times 26\% = 27.4$ units), when calculated without any allowance for saving or other leakages.

In the Indian economy there appear to be possibilities of increasing production of domestic consumer goods and services, especially when necessary additional basic foodstuffs are supplied from surpluses. Marketing services are largely transportation and labor. There is ample unemployed labor available, and the volume of railway traffic can be increased substantially with little additional cost for rolling stock or maintenance. In industrial products, textiles and clothing bulk the largest among consumer purchases. Existing plants can operate more overtime, more workers can be readily employed and cotton is in ample supply and production is expanding. While maintenance and repairs will increase, these items are small in proportion to the value of the additional goods turned out. It therefore appears reasonable to assume for the Indian economy that there is a good deal of elasticity in the potential production of marketing and other services, and of consumers' industrial products, which could be used to meet the initial expanding demand without immediate price inflation. And to the extent that this can be done, the calculated income multipliers and surplus expenditures discussed in Appendix 2 under assumption b) would hold good. We may therefore conclude that India will probably be able to produce the additional non-surplus goods, and turn to the next question, of possible inflationary effects.

This involves a dynamic aspect of the development process. As we have seen earlier, an investment of 100 units (as for example on roads and water use projects, as presented in Chapter VII) if continued year after year, will generate an expanding volume of income year after year for several years – even when part of the increased demand is satisfied from surplus products. Thus for the first two groups of projects given in Chapter VII combined, the increase in demand is as follows for each 100 units of additional total investment, domestic and foreign.

	1st year	2nd year	3rd year and later
Income spent for domestic products	96	137	144
Income spent for surpluses	28	42	45
Total	124	179	189

Not only is there a substantial uncovered excess above surpluses to be satisfied the first year, by expansions elsewhere in the economy as already suggested, but the size of that uncovered excess becomes larger each year. Would the net effect tend to be inflationary?

In considering this we must consider not only the expenditures because of the project, but the eventual effect of the project on the productive capacity of the economy itself. Individual projects differ very greatly in the time it takes for the work to be completed and for the use of the resultant factory, equipment, electricity, or irrigation water to begin to increase natural production. This lag in the effect of capital investments – or "period of gestation of investment" as it is sometimes called – may vary from as little as six months for some types of industrial or mercantile investment, (or for small installations in existing enterprises, such as an irrigation pump on a going farm), up to five to ten years, or even longer, for massive new structures requiring years to complete and to get into operation, such as irrigation or hydroelectric projects. Increases in working capital, making it possible to apply more fertilizer to crops, may have very rapid effects on productivity. Some large projects, such as roads, railways or canals, can be put partly into use as fast as portions are completed; others, like hydroelectric plants, must be fully or nearly completed before any contribution to production can be made. Averaging all these types together, and recognizing that the Five-Year Plan attempts to co-ordinate investments so that industries to use the new power and transportation are often being built at the same time as the hydroelectric plants or railway extensions to serve them, a gestation period of two years may be assumed as the average before new investment will begin to expand national productive capacity.

Another question is how much effect past investment may have on current capacity to produce, even after the gestation period is passed. This ratio of "increased production ÷ increased investment" may be called the "output-capital ratio".[2] In highly-developed economies, such as the United Kingdom or the United States, this ratio runs only about 0.3. In less developed economies, however, capital is much scarcer and there is a big gap between known technical possibilities and present technical methods which can be quickly overcome given both capital and effective educational and extension activities. There is some evidence that under these conditions the output-capital ratios will run substantially higher. For India, with its very low incomes, low level of literacy, and great shortage of capital, this ratio may be estimated at 0.6. That is, 100 units of capital applied in year 1 may be expected to raise potential output by 60 units in year 3 and later. It is not certain, however, that this higher output will be obtained, so we will also examine the consequences if the output investment ratio should only be 0.3, as in more developed countries.

We can see what either value might mean for a developing economy by working out an assumed case. Let us assume the economy starts at a level of 1,000 units national income, invests 5 percent of its national product each year in economic development, and has an output-capital ratio either of 0.6 or 0.3. We will examine the higher ratio first.

Assuming that investment was already being made at a gradually increasing rate in previous years, one may estimate the potential output of the economy as shown in Table A3-1.

Over ten years, with an annual investment of 5 percent of the national income, the annual productive capacity of the economy would rise 27 percent. If, during the same period, savings have also run at 5 percent of national income, then the materials and services required for investment would exactly equal in value the portion of current production not purchased for consumption. Assuming also that public expenditures (other than for investment) have exactly equalled public revenues, production of goods and services, and demands for goods and services, will have exactly balanced, and the investment and expansion of economic activity will have taken place without any inflationary effect.

In addition, there will have been an annual increment in production capacity, owing to the earlier investment, varying from 24 units in year 1 to 36.6 units in year 10, which can be translated into increased production, if demand is sufficient. To make that happen, the money in use must be increased each year to a corresponding amount,[3] either by expansion of credit by banks, or by deficit financing by governmental agencies. In the

Table A3-1. Estimated Dynamic Effects
of an Investment Program on National Income,
with Output Investment Ratio at 0.6

Year	Investment (5% of national income)	National income previous year	Effect of investment 2 years earlier	National income current year
- 1	40	—	—	—
- 0	45	—	—	976
1	50	976	24	1000
2	51.35	1000	27	1027
3	52.85	1027	30	1057
4	54.39	1057	30.8	1087.8
5	55.96	1087.8	31.5	1119.3
6	57.60	1119.3	32.6	1151.9
7	59.28	1151.9	33.6	1185.5
8	61.0	1185.5	34.6	1220.1
9	61.8	1220.1	35.6	1235.7
10	63.6	1235.7	36.6	1272.3

absence of such expansion in the circulating medium, either the increased production capacity would not be fully utilized, or a deflationary pressure would be created. (What has been happening in India recently seems to be a little of each.)

Additional investment projects might be added without inflationary effect if the full cost of these projects were covered by external loans or grants, as already discussed, or if fully and concurrently covered by increased consumption of surplus foods (as in the Andamans project, Chapter VIII). But what would be the effect if projects of Type II were added?

Assume that 10 units a year of Type II projects were added to the investment program just shown, beginning with year 1; that these projects had the same output investment ratio of 0.6 assumed before, had an average gestation period of 2 years, and involved 5 units of direct labor and 5 units of domestic goods and services. Over a term of years, these projects would have the following effects on the economy as shown in Table A3-2.

During the two years before the additional investment begins to affect national income, the additional projects have an inflationary effect of 1.2 percent of national income in the first year, and of 1.7 percent in the second. Thereafter, as the new projects begin to expand national income by their own effects, the inflationary force declines, practically disappears

Table A3-2. Effect of Additional Investment in Type II Projects

Year	Additional investment (I)	Productive Capacity		Additional buying power for domestic goods derived from added investment (IV)	Excess of IV over III (V)	Additional demand in % of national income (V ÷ II + III) (VI)
		Previous national income (II)	Additional national income (III)			
1	10	1000		12.2	12.2	1.2
2	10	1027		17.3	17.3	1.7
3	10	1057	6.0	18.6	12.6	1.2
4	10	1087.8	12.0	18.9	6.9	0.6
5	10	1119.3	18.0	18.9	0.9	0.1
6	10	1151.9	24.0	18.9	-5.1	-0.4

in the fifth year, and from the sixth year on would release production in excess of demand generated by the project.

If the economy of the country had sufficient unused capacity to increase output by 1½ percent or a little over, in response to increased demands in the first two years, it would be possible for it to absorb the effect of additional projects of this magnitude (1 percent of national income) without any measurable inflationary effect. If there was not this much unused capacity in the economy, then the projects would have to be financed in some other way, if inflation is to be avoided. If financed either by external credits or grants which would provide imported commodities to absorb all the increased domestic taxes which would reduce domestic expenditures for consumption or private investment, the expected use of surplus foods would have to be scaled down correspondingly. There would then be no significant additional derived income at subsequent cycles of respending to widen the demand for surplus foods, and only the increased consumption of food at the first cycle, without any multiplier effect, would enter into the calculations.

When the two tables are recalculated assuming an output capital ratio of only 0.3, the inflationary pressure in the first two years is substantially the same as shown in Table A3-2, but declines somewhat more slowly thereafter. The rate of expansion in the national income is of course slower, increasing by less than half as much with the output-capital ratio of 0.3, as with the ratio of 0.6.

The additional investment projects suggested for India, as outlined in this report, total about 150 million of dollars investment per annum. Of these, about 40 million are for projects of Type I (excluding milk schemes), where there are no significant multiplier effects. The remaining projects have an average total annual investment of 110 million, of which 60 to 70 million would be covered by food surpluses, and 15 million would be for imports. The balance of under 40 millions, which might have inflationary effects on the economy, constitutes one-sixth of one percent of the present level of Indian national income. This seems sufficiently small so that even if all the projects were implemented they could be absorbed without any appreciable inflationary effect.

This discussion leads to one other very important conclusion: that the income-multiplier effect of additional investment, after the first cycle of spending, cannot be expected to appear if the project is wholly financed externally, whether in cash or in surplus foods. The estimate of increased consumption of surplus foods resulting from a given project must therefore be adjusted to the way the project is to be financed, with a much lower percent in the case of projects financed externally than where the country itself can carry the investment from not-quite-fully-utilized production capacity.

¹ *Relations between Foreign Capital and the Mobilization of Domestic Capital*, paper by W. Arthur Lewis in consultation with the ECAFE Secretariat, Economic Commission for Asia and the Far East, doc. E/CN.11/1 and T/WP.2/L.9; 4 August 1952.

² This is usually stated as the "capital-output ratio", i.e., increased investment ÷ increased output. The reverse statement, as given here, seems a more useful way, by stating resulting output as a proportion of the investment required to produce it.

³ This is not necessarily to the same amount, as the money in use may be turned over several times each year.

APPENDIX 4

Private efforts at rural education

The need for better education for rural youth has been recognized for some time by many groups in India, and a number of efforts have been made by private or charitable groups to deal with the problem. Some of the most interesting and long-established activities in this direction are those of the Rural Educational Society of Satara, Bombay State.[1] This was established in 1953 as a result of the efforts of Karmaveer Bhaura P. Patil, who had long been interested in improving the condition of rural youth of all classes. Primary schools, and then high schools, were established in rural villages with the co-operation of the local people, and later teachers' training schools and a college were established in the villages especially for the rural people. As the activities expanded, public agencies gradually took over some of the schools, but in 1953-54 the Society was still operating 289 educational institutions altogether, with a total of 27,517 students attending.[2] Of these, about 1,200 were provided with hostel and boarding accommodation. The schools operated included 240 primary schools, 44 secondary schools, 4 teachers' training colleges and 1 arts college.

In these schools, special attention was given to two basic concepts which Mr. Patil had emphasized throughout his life – one, that the schools should be open to all, without any discrimination because of race, origin, or caste; and two, that all students should do at least one hour's work with their hands each day to contribute to the needs of the school – growing farm products, helping to build new buildings or wells, or other useful and productive work. In return, they receive a cash credit for the work that they do, so that they can pay part of their living and other expenses. In some of the schools, those who do productive work two hours a day can get further matching help from a loan fund, and can thus cover practically all their school expenses from their own labor and borrowings, which they can repay from their increased earning power after graduation.

The principle that educated men should know how to do manual work with their own hands, should not be afraid or ashamed to get their hands dirty or to earn part of their way through school, is one that is widely followed in many highly developed countries, especially in northwestern Europe and North America. In comparison to the idea widely held in many less developed countries that an educated man should only direct and surpervise others, but should never do part of the actual physical work himself, the other idea is that a man can never properly direct or surpervise other persons unless he himself is capable from first-hand actual experience of doing everything that they are to do, and therefore knows intimately what it is that he wants them to do. In educational work, especially in colleges, the experience in some highly-developed countries is that students who work part time to earn part or all their expenses while in college, are usually more serious students and make better use of the instruction they receive than are most of the other students who are supported by their parents. These principles have helped to give educated groups in these countries a practical and realistic approach to life that is often missing among such groups in less developed countries. These same principles, whose value and validity under Indian conditions have been so well demonstrated by Karmaveer Patil, might well be more widely adopted in Indian education and life.

The Rural Education Society operates many student hostels. Their officers are greatly interested in the idea of using surplus foods to increase the number of their students receiving this assistance. They emphasized, however, that it would do no good to provide additional school boarding for a single year, unless continuing support was assured over a term of years, so that students who left their homes to take higher education with this assistance would be assured of continuing through to graduation. A minimum program would seem to be one for four years, with a steady supply of surplus foods assured for that period. This would make it possible to award food fellowships for four years at high school or college, subject to satisfactory behavior and school progress, and thus assure the students receiving these fellowships that they could complete their work at that school.

[1] The earliest effort of this sort was the SRINIKETAN (Village Reconstruction and Rural Education Center), founded by Rabindranath Tagore about 1920. Located about 90 miles from Calcutta, it is still functioning, together with a rural university that gives special emphasis to education by correspondence courses.

[2] The Rayat Shikshan Sanstha, Satara, India, a brief report, 1953-54. 1 December 1953.

DEVELOPMENT THROUGH FOOD

A strategy for surplus utilization

By
B. R. Sen

CONTENTS

SUMMARY

1. More than half the world's population is undernourished or malnourished. Hunger, poverty and stagnation form a vicious circle. The situation is being aggravated by the acceleration of population growth which is in the nature of an explosion never before experienced in human history. Disparities in income levels are steadily widening between countries. While in the developed countries incomes annually increased at well over $20[1] per head from 1950 to 1957, in the underdeveloped countries they rose by $1 per head in the·same period. The awakening of the vast masses of underprivileged people all over the world cannot be contained by this slow rate of progress.

2. International efforts to deal with these problems have so far had very limited results. Most of the less developed countries have the natural and human resources needed for their own salvation, but they must mobilize them and use them more efficiently. This they can do, without having to make prolonged and far-reaching sacrifices on their present, almost intolerable, living standards, only if external aid is made available. The volume of public economic aid in the last ten years amounted to only about 0.4 percent of the gross national product of the developed countries. This is small, both in relation to what the underdeveloped countries need to make a real start on their economic and social development, and in relation to what the developed countries could afford to give without undue sacrifice or prejudice to their own economy or well-being. There is however a growing awareness among the developed countries of the problem of inequality between nations and the danger that it presents.

3. Apart from measures to expand aid, the stabilization of world market prices of the exports of less developed countries, and the elimination of barriers to these exports need greater attention. For though there has been very little progress in increasing the volume of exports of the less developed countries, the value of these exports represents about eight times the amount of the international aid they receive, and minor fluctuations in their value can have a great impact on their foreign exchange resources,

often nullifying the effect of aid. Some of these countries are accumulating stocks of exportable commodities which is a burden they can ill afford to carry.

4. It is only through economic and social development that the vicious circle of hunger, poverty and stagnation can be broken. Expanded aid must therefore be directed primarily toward this end. Emergency relief, however, needs more attention and a better international machinery than exists at present.

5. Food aid does and should play an important role in aid programs. The concept of food as aid and as a means to accelerate economic development in the less developed countries is not new. In the United Nations Resolution[2] it has been expressed as a consensus of world opinion and as a guiding philosophy.

6. Like all aid, food aid should be integrated in the over-all development programs of receiving countries and planned in such a way as to maintain adequate balance in the development of their economies.

7. Development programs involve an increase in investment and usually an increase in domestic incomes. The increment in incomes gives rise to an increase in demand for consumer goods, and especially for food. Because of the "stickiness" of the agricultural sector, of unpredictable bad weather or faulty forecasting, domestic supplies may be inadequate to meet this increase in demand. On the other hand, with exiguous foreign exchange resources, the possibilities of importing the additional supplies required are also likely to be limited. Under the circumstances, unless aid (including food aid) is available, there is a likelihood that inflationary pressures might be created which would jeopardize development.

8. Food aid used much in the same way as commercial imports has a counter-inflationary effect. Following sales to consumers of food received as aid, and the consequent withdrawal of purchasing power, the government would be in the same position as if there had been additional proceeds from taxation or larger voluntary savings. It is then enabled to finance expansion.

9. Properly planned timing and adequate composition of food aid to correspond to the demands of consumers are essential for the success of the operation.

10 If the pace of development is to be stepped up, the volume of investment will also have to be increased. The government is then faced with a

dilemma. Should the over-all rate of growth be restricted to the rate of growth of food supplies with a balanced allocation of development resources (including current imports) to that sector, or should the over-all rate of growth be raised and strict measures taken to curtail the demand for food which would follow increased investment? The alternatives, therefore, are inaction in the face of rising demographic pressure, or action which would initially lower even the present inadequate standards of living. Both are likely to lead to greater social tensions. Such tensions may be avoided with food aid, if concurrent steps are taken to fulfill certain conditions. Food aid can then serve as additional capital in its original sense of a subsistence fund. It can help implement labor-intensive projects, introduce land reform, launch long-term investments, and rationalize the livestock industry.

11. The utilization of food aid for the purpose of general economic development will depend on the availability as aid of resources other than food. It is estimated that food aid for economic development alone could not be expected to amount to more than one sixth to one fifth of the total capital aid required by underdeveloped countries. In certain countries this proportion might be more, in others less.

12. National food reserves should be established with the help of food surpluses, given on easy terms or as grants. Particulary in countries exposed to vagaries of weather and consequent speculative activity, these reserves would buffer seasonal and emergency fluctuations in the supply of basic foods, and also help governments to implement domestic price and income policies. It is essential that the reserves be on call in the recipient country if the latter functions are to be fulfilled. While absolute price fixation is not desirable, and selective price changes may be necessary, floor prices established one or two years in advance are essential if agricultural progress is to be stimulated and expanded use is to be made of food aid.

13. Food aid shoud also be used to help initiate or accelerate social development programs. Human investment is the most important investment of all. Food aid could be used to provide lunches for school children and students, and to give more attention to the needs of infants and expectant mothers. For these programs a larger supply of protein foods will be necessary. These foods will in the long term best be provided by the expansion of domestic livestock industries in the underdeveloped countries themselves. In the interim period, until such expansion occurs, provision should be made to supply foods under the expanded food aid program. Recent experience has shown that rather than restrict the volume of commercial trade in these products, such aid by stimulating the demand for foods in the less developed countries is likely to increase it.

14. Over the next five years, perhaps about $12,500 million worth of commodities will become available for use outside normal commercial channels. The *sine qua non* of an expanded program for surplus utilization for economic and social development, such as is now contemplated, is country planning on one side and co-ordination of aid on the other.

15. The governments of recipient countries will have to take responsibility for determining the uses to which surplus foods will be put, since it is their development which is to be promoted. National plans must constitute a charter of policy, and outline not only what the people may expect in time, but also the duties and the sacrifices which they have to undertake in order to achieve their objectives. The plans must be comprehensive. They must spell out not only targets, but also the policies and institutions required. Every effort must be made to strengthen the planning machinery in recipient countries. It is up to each country to decide on the general lines and objectives of its development programs; the technical elaboration of these programs, however, may well profit from assistance from abroad.

16. In every case care must be taken to see that the progress of agriculture in the recipient countries is safeguarded, and that agricultural policies and institutions (such as a national food agency) are so devised as to make sure 'that incentives reach down to the farmers.

17. The donor countries must so organize their aid as to devote more attention to the "areas of greatest need" referred to in the UN Assembly Resolution.

18. They must, if necessary, introduce policies enabling or amending legislation to expand aid and broaden its uses. They must be ready to make aid available on favorable terms, depending on the situation of the recipient country. They must also accept the possibility that some countries might prefer to receive aid through multilateral channels, and be ready to earmark an adequate portion of their surpluses for such channels. They must recognize the need for nonfood aid as a complement to food aid, and strengthen arrangements for co-ordination of aid, in which the United Nations system and FAO could also provide assistance. They must so adapt the food aid program as to secure its continuity for at least five to ten years, and its adequate composition. In the latter context, a conversion of surplus grains into protein foods would lead to greater acceptability of surpluses and also result in an increase in total economic aid to underdeveloped countries.

19. The larger the total flow of aid, the larger the quantity of surplus food that can be utilized without harmful repercussions on normal international trade in the commodities concerned.

20. According to the Expert Group, aid now runs at $3,600 million per year. It should, to achieve the objective we have in view, be increased to $5,000 - $6,000 million per year. This would represent one half to three quarters of one percent of the national income of the developed countries. The experts assumed that their global aid target corresponded to the absorptive capacity of the underdeveloped countries, and that it would be sufficient to achieve a rise in average income in these countries of two percent per year. Absorptive capacity, however, is not static and may increase with a rising volume of aid. Furthermore, recent official statements have suggested a figure of one percent of the gross national product as a possible rate of contribution from developed countries.

21. International arrangements for emergency food relief must be treated separately from the use of surpluses for economic development. Adequate arrangements do not exist to deal with such sudden disasters as earthquakes and floods which call for immediate action. For this purpose it would be desirable to establish an international emergency food reserve. FAO has given much thought to these problems, and in particular presented a plan known as the Three Circles Plan which was recognized as technically sound. If the United Nations Resolution, which also covers emergency relief, is to be implemented, some plan of action along these lines will have to be adopted.

22. The operations envisaged in the Report would involve the following activities and functions for FAO, in co-operation with the United Nations and other agencies as appropriate:

(a) assistance and advice, on request, to potential recipient countries in the programing of surplus food utilization for economic and social development, integrated with their general economic development programs;

(b) assistance and advice, on request, to recipient countries in the establishment and operation of institutions and policies required for enlarged programs of surplus food utilization;

(c) advice, on request, to potential donor countries, regarding the needs and requirements of recipient countries in terms of kinds and quantities of surplus foods and matching aid;

(d) appraisal, on request, of emergency or chronic food shortages in individual countries, and reporting to prospective donor countries on such situations requiring emergency assistance, and arranging with them for appropriate aid, or meeting such emergencies from reserve stocks already pledged to FAO;

(e) control and administration of the international emergency food reserve, constituted by pledges given by participating countries, for supporting and replenishing national food reserves after emergencies, and in meeting emergency food shortages caused by crop failures or other disasters;

(*f*) liaison and collaboration with international lending agencies and *consortia* (or committees) including national agencies, which consider the total needs of a country's development program;

(*g*) the holding of pledges of surplus foods committed by surplus-owning countries for utilization for development through multilateral channels, and the administration to recipient countries of food aid so pledged;

(*h*) evaluation and reporting, in co-operation with recipient and donor countries, on programs of surplus food utilization.

23. FAO should be the focal point for contacts and co-ordination in the whole expanded program of surplus food utilization. FAO would work closely in this field with the United Nations and would, in particular, collaborate with the Regional Economic Commissions of the United Nations in assisting countries in their development programing. The existing close co-operation between FAO and the United Nations Children's Fund (UNICEF) could be further strengthened, especially in promoting supplementary feeding programs.

24. Where surplus food is to be combined with additional financial aid, FAO would work with the United Nations and such financial agencies as the International Bank for Reconstruction and Development (IBRD) and the International Development Association (IDA), and other national and regional agencies as appropriate. It could also assist in determining the extent to which the debt repayment capacity of a country could be improved with food aid. For the provision of technical assistance required, action might be taken also in collaboration with the United Nations Expanded Program of Technical Assistance and the United Nations Special Fund. The other specialized agencies may be involved from time to time in specific activities arising from this program.

25. The implementation of an expanded program of world food aid to underdeveloped countries raises problems of co-ordination which may be studied by the Administrative Committee on Co-ordination of the United Nations, on which all United Nations bodies are represented by their administrative heads.

26. In addition to co-ordination between intergovernmental organizations, the co-ordination of multilateral and bilateral activities is envisaged, not only at the policy level but also in the field.

27. The proposal of the United States Government to set up a fund of $100 million in contributions of commodities and cash with a view to initiating action under multilateral auspices is a significant step in the context of the United Nations Resolution which forms the basis of this report.

28. Since the report was written, a specific FAO/UN proposal has been formulated, and has been approved in principle by both the FAO Conference and the United Nations General Assembly. After further development of plans and arrangements, and the pledging of contributions of food, cash and possibly services by governments, the World Food Program is expected to go into operation about the middle of 1962.

[1] All dollar references are to the U.S. dollar.
[2] Appendix 1, page 275.

I. FOOD AS AID

1. The basic ideas underlying the United Nations Resolution are stated in the preamble. It acknowledges that the ultimate solution to hunger lies in an acceleration of economic development and that food surpluses should help to make this possible.

2. The concept of food as aid is not new. It has been debated and accepted in specialized international groups, and embodied in many bilateral food transfer agreements over recent years. But in the United Nations Resolution the concept has been expressed as the consensus of world opinion, and as the guiding philosophy for the use of surplus food. This is new. In principle, the Resolution has ended the days of "surplus food disposal", and ushered in a period of "surplus food food utilization" for economic and social development in the world at large. Whether this will be realized in practice will be determined by the extent of action by governments in the future.

International inequality in food supplies and incomes

3. Data available to FAO indicate that more than one half of the population of the world is undernourished or malnourished. Hunger, for certain periods of the year at least. is still a grim reality for millions of people. Far larger numbers lack protein and protective foods necessary for health and full development, especially of children. The basic cause is poverty, resulting from low productivity and lack of economic development.

4. The range of food supplies available per head in different countries is well illustrated by the case of cereals (see Table 1). In North America where average incomes are high, the use of cereals per head is around 700 to 900 kilograms per year. Only about 70 kilograms of this is for direct human consumption. The rest is fed to livestock for the production of human food in the form of dairy products, meat and eggs. In countries with low income levels, e.g., Brazil, Japan, Mexico, and the United Arab Republic, the esti-

mated total annual use of cereals is only around 200 kilograms per head, and the quantity fed to livestock is very small. In the very low income countries, such as India and Pakistan, where very large populations are involved, total annual usage falls to 150 to 175 kilograms per head, nearly all consumed direct. The other side of this picture is that the animal protein food available per head in India and Pakistan is one ninth of the North American level and one sixth of the level in Western European countries.

5. If the present populations of India and Pakistan were to utilize cereals at the rate per head current in Japan, which is still low, their annual

Table 1. Income and consumption of cereals per head in selected countries 1957/58

Country	Income	Total consumption of cereals as food, feed, etc. in terms of grain and husked (or milled) rice	Cereals for direct human consumption in terms of flour and milled rice	Protein for human consumption	
				Animal	Total
	(1)	(2)	(3)	(4)	(5)
	U.S. $	...... *kg. per year*		.... *g. per day*	
United States	2,164	646	67	66	94
Canada	1,431	929	71	62	95
United Kingdom	960	413	85	51	87
France	839	375	110	49	96
Italy	406	304	142	25	76
Japan	250	218	157	15	67
Mexico	234	218	147	16	66
Brazil	218	214	106	18	67
U.A.R.: Syria	169	257	162	12	73
Egypt	112	235	188	13	79
Pakistan	77	173	151	8	45
India	60	144	124	6	47

SOURCES: (1) UN: *Yearbook of national accounts 1959*, and UN: *Monthly bulletin of statistics*, January 1961; (2) to (5) FAO: *Food balance sheets*.

NOTE: Data in column (2) refer to "domestic disappearance", that is, to production *plus* opening stocks and imports and *minus* exports and closing stocks.

requirements would go up by 33 million tons. If Italy were the standard, an additional 74 million tons would be needed. To reach the United States level of use per head, India and Pakistan would require an additional 238 million tons. It must be admitted that the world food situation is one of deficiencies, rather than surpluses. This is so, even if due allowance is made for the existence of food stocks.

6. The contrast in levels of human welfare between the developed countries of the world and those where the development process has barely begun is strikingly reflected in annual income levels per head of some $1,500 to $2,100[1] in North America in 1957-58; $700 to $1,000 in northwestern European countries; around $250 in Japan and Mexico; $100 to $150 in most countries of Latin America and the Near East, and less than $100 in most parts of Asia and tropical Africa.

7. These international inequalities are not being reduced. In fact, the gap is widening. Gross income in the underdeveloped regions of the world grew at the average rate of 3 percent per year between 1950 and 1959. Because of the growth of population, the increase in income per person was only about 1 percent per year – that is, about $1 per year. These are the food-deficient areas. In the United States and in the six countries of the European Economic Community, average incomes during the same period rose by over $20 per head per year. The gap in incomes is a reflection of low productivity in underdeveloped countries. As already noted, the problem in these countries is increasing in intensity with the rising rate of population growth which is in the nature of an explosion never before experienced in human history. As a result of the pressure of population on consumption, little is left for investment.

Need for international aid

8. Equality of opportunity, full employment, and at least something better than a minimum of subsistence are among the social goals of most of mankind. They have largely been achieved in the economically advanced countries for all sections of their populations. The task now is to speed up progress towards these goals for the world as a whole.[2] The vicious circle of hunger, poverty and stagnation can be broken by raising production and productivity.

9. It is recognized in the world community that the less developed countries have the possibility of providing most of the means for their own salvation, by mobilizing their own resources and using them more efficiently. But to allow this possibility to be realized without intolerable

sacrifices, outside aid is indispensable. On their own efforts, their increase in income cannot average very much more than the rate of one U.S. dollar per person per year achieved during the last decade. The awakening of the vast masses of underprivileged people all over the world, whose demand for political independence is only one aspect, cannot be contained by this slow rate of progress. The progress must be faster if the world as a whole is to avoid disaster.

10. Though its scale has increased and its allocation improved in recent years, the amount of foreign aid is still small, both in relation to the needs of the poor countries and in relation to the incomes of the developed countries. According to the United Nations[3] over the period 1957/58 to 1958/59, only one developed country contributed more than 0.4 percent of its gross national product as public economic aid[4] for bilateral economic assistance to underdeveloped countries (France, 1.4 percent). These figures do not include aid through multilateral organizations, which is relatively small. For some developed countries, not even one tenth of this fraction was attained. In spite of the recent increase in the volume of aid and in aid commitments, the basic proportions have not changed radically. There is evidence, however, that the developed countries are now taking advantage of the high levels of economic growth which they have attained, and that they will make a larger volume of resources available for economic assistance to underdeveloped countries. This is the context in which to review the use of surplus food as aid, and the possibilities of corresponding additional contributions in other forms of aid.

11. Despite all the attention that has been given to the expansion of world trade and the marked progress that has been made in the trade of the highly developed countries, it is disappointing how much slower the progress has been in increasing the volume and value of exports of the underdeveloped countries. Many of these countries are at present carrying surplus stocks of their export commodities which represent an investment they can ill afford. With all its vicissitudes, however, the export trade of the underdeveloped countries represents eight times the value of international public economic aid they receive. Therefore, even relatively small fluctuations in the value of their export trade can have great impact on their foreign exchange resources, and hence on their development programs, often nullifying the effect of the aid they receive.

12. Apart from measures to expand aid, the stabilization of world market prices of the exports of the less developed countries, and the elimination of barriers to these exports need greater attention, if the development of the less developed countries is not to be impeded. Measures are necessary also

in this context for the relief of the stock-carrying burden of the less developed countries.

Past international efforts: a history of frustration

13. A most significant feature of the postwar decade has been the growing awareness among the developed countries of the problem of inequality between nations. This awakening has been expressed with particular vigor in the meetings of the United Nations and its specialized agencies. It has led to considerable study of the ways in which the less developed countries could be helped to help themselves. It has also promoted intensified bilateral action, but the grim reality of poverty and hunger for millions is, as I have noted, still with us.

14. It may be asked why the impact of past efforts has been so small. There was certainly no shortage of advice. Various groups of experts appointed by the United Nations have dealt directly or indirectly with the problems of poverty and underdevelopment. A group appointed in 1951 had these as its main concern. It advocated a host of measures to be undertaken by the underdeveloped countries themselves; more positive trade policies (including due regard to price stabilization), and a flow of aid to the less developed countries of about $10,000 million per annum (that is, $13,000 million at 1962 prices) to achieve an annual increase in income of 1.5 percent per head.

15. The problems of food supply and commodity price stabilization were also dealt with extensively by FAO. The establishment of a World Food Board was discussed in 1946. The functions of this Board would have been to stabilize prices, secure a world food reserve and provide means for the disposal of surplus agricultural products where the need for them was most urgent. This proposal was found to be much too ambitious and wide in character. Other schemes, such as an International Commodity Clearing House, were not pursued to clear conclusions though the principle of sales from hard currency countries "for local currencies" was adopted in the bilateral agreements between the United States and some other countries and continues in operation. At its 1949 Session, the FAO Conference, while rejecting the clearing house proposal, decided to establish a purely advisory Committee on Commodity Problems (CCP) which is still functioning.[5]

16. Considerable attention was also given in FAO meetings to emergency food shortages, and a formal international procedure for dealing with them was approved in 1951. This procedure was employed only once, for

Yugoslavia in 1952. International action to help meet emergency situations in Chile (1960) and in the Congo (1960-61) was developed by less formal FAO procedures.

17. In 1953, proposals were developed by FAO for the establishment of an international emergency food reserve. These were relatively modest, and were characterized by maximum flexibility.[6] No positive action was taken on them. The FAO recommendations of 1958 for the establishment of national food reserves, which were endorsed by ECOSOC, have thus far been acted upon only in a very few countries.

18. The main reason for lack of progress appears to have been the reluctance of governments to undertake measures which might weaken their national initiative and national powers of control. In other words, the climate was against multilateral action in operational fields as distinct from advisory or informational roles.

[1] All dollar references are to the U.S. dollar.

[2] Appendix 2, page 278.

[3] *International economic assistance to the less developed countries* – UN Department of Economic and Social Affairs, United Nations, New York, 1961. Report of the Secretary General to the Economic and Social Council, 30th Session. E/3395 Revision I. Measurements of international aid are extremely difficult. The basic definition used by the United Nations includes as economic assistance all public grants and loans of over five years' duration, excluding direct military aid.

[4] Public economic aid excludes loans to governments or to individuals through normal commercial channels.

[5] The Committee within its broad terms of reference fulfills the useful function of serving as an intergovernmental clearing house for information on the commodity situation generally, and as a body for the formulation of policy recommendations on major commodity problems. Specific commodities are studied by means of study groups.

[6] One suggestion, known as the Three Circles Plan, provided for the participation of donor countries with different types of pledges; some were to be on a continuous basis, either in money or in kind, finally others on an *ad hoc* system (paragraphs 104-109).

II. NATIONAL PROGRAMS REQUIRING FOOD AID

Economic development

19. Within the context of national development plans, the use of food as aid can help in meeting the increased demands for food arising in the implementation of current development programs. The availability of more food as aid, however, might also permit the current development programs to be modified in various ways, with a view to speeding up the pace of economic and social progress and the advance of welfare – always assuming that adequate complementary resources of nonfood aid are made available to these countries at the same time. It may be convenient, therefore, to consider the use of food aid in relation to current programs first, and then look at the possibility of changes.

CURRENT DEVELOPMENT PROGRAMS

20. Investment expenditure raises domestic incomes through the payment of wages, the purchase of local raw materials and the stimulus to economic activity generally. The increase in incomes causes an increase in demand for consumer goods, including food. At the average level of incomes per head in underdeveloped countries, a large proportion of the increment in income, from an effective employment of partially or totally unemployed labor, will be spent on food, particularly food-grains. This proportion may, under special circumstances, be as high as 50 percent. If adequate additional supplies of food are not available, food prices will rise sharply. This could lead to inflation and jeopardize the whole development program. The governments of underdeveloped countries undergoing development must, therefore, deal with the problem of the balance between additional investment and additional supplies of food.

21. The increase in food supplies needed for an investment program may come from the expansion of domestic agriculture, commercial imports or aid, including food aid. The scarce foreign exchange earnings of under-

developed countries are urgently needed for the importation of machinery, equipment and raw materials for the development program. If these earnings are used to import large amounts of food the whole development program may be retarded. If without causing a curtailment of other essential parts of the program domestic agriculture can supply the additional food required, or if the flow of exports can easily be increased, there may be only a limited need for food aid. But production of food crops in most underdeveloped countries is likely to respond only sluggishly to increased demand; and the expansion of exports of these countries is, in most cases, beyond their control. Furthermore, sharp fluctuations in output are usual. Nor is it always possible to foresee correctly the extent to which a given rate of investment will cause the demand for food to rise. Many countries have, therefore, found it essential to seek food aid – mostly from the United States – at crucial times, to enable them to maintain the planned rate of development, or at least to minimize a reduction. [1]

22. This need for food aid as a balancing factor between supply and demand will continue, and will increase as the developing countries launch – as they must – more ambitious plans.

23. Surplus food for economic development purposes is usually channeled to the global food supply within the recipient country, following the same physical procedures as commercial imports. Individuals pay for their purchases of the commodities in the same way as for home-grown products. Since these payments are not made to domestic producers, they do not directly generate expenditure for personal consumption. They constitute a withdrawal of purchasing power from the community, and thus have a counter-inflationary effect. The government is now in the same position as if there had been additional proceeds from taxation or larger voluntary savings. It may therefore increase its expenditure, after due consideration of all the other factors determining the monetary balance, on the purchase of goods or services, either for economic development or for other purposes, such as social services or defence. Thus, food aid enables the government to finance expansion.

24. The whole operation should be carefully timed. If the increase in expenditure lags considerably after the sale of surplus foods, there may well be an interim period in which the demand for domestic agricultural output may fall, with adverse effects. Conversely, if a high rate of investment expenditure precedes the sale of surplus foods for a fairly long period, the monetary balance may be disturbed.

25. The use of food aid in this way is naturally limited to countries where large sections of the population consume the food-grains which are in

significant surplus, namely wheat, barley, maize and millets at the present time.

26. Some underdeveloped countries, while normally relying on commercial imports for part of their supply of staple foodstuffs, are major exporters of other primary products, notably of tropical foodstuffs, including beverages, and of various raw materials. The world prices of these exports are apt to be highly unstable, seriously affecting the foreign exchange earnings of these underdeveloped countries. This, in turn, has repercussions on their import capacity, and their development programs may be severely hit during periods of sharp decline in their export proceeds. A good deal of thought has been given recently to possible ways of compensatory financing which would help to mitigate the adverse effects of such sharp downward fluctuations of export returns. A UN Expert Group, in a report just published on the subject, has referred briefly to the possible compensating functions of surplus utilization, while cautioning against schemes for compensatory financing being tied directly to particular commodity supplies. My expert consultants, while refraining from going into detail since the other group was considering this matter, stated that: "By the same token that surplus food can serve to enlarge development programs of underdeveloped countries, it can also serve to prevent development programs from being cut down or dislocated, e.g., when external buying power is suddenly reduced as a result of an unforeseen sharp decline in the world market price of a country's main export product."[2] This is a point which, in my view, calls for serious consideration.

CHANGES IN DEVELOPMENT PROGRAMS

27. The essence of the development process in underdeveloped countries is putting more people to productive work, through capital investment, organization and incentive. Food products are an important part of capital in its original sense of a subsistence fund. Additionally employed workers have to be fed during the construction period, that is, before the fruits of investment can supply their needs or enable them to buy their subsistence. Food surpluses used for economic development will enable hungry people to produce either their own food, or commodities which may be sold to buy food.[3] These considerations open up the possibility of underdeveloped countries modifying their current development programs, if an expanded flow of food aid were assured for a reasonable period under suitable conditions. Several types of modifications may be considered.

A faster over-all rate of development

28. I have already explained the implications of the current rates of growth in underdeveloped countries, with their national income increasing at an average rate of only one dollar per person per year . Very few, if any, of these countries have yet reached the stage at which they can be independent of external aid and maintain a satisfactory rate of growth.

29. The rate of development can be raised by increasing investment. A higher rate of investment will also step up the demand for food and, for the reasons given in paragraph 21 above, at a faster rate than food supplies could be expanded. The countries are then faced with a dilemma: should the over-all rate of growth be restricted to the rate of growth of food supplies with a balanced allocation of development resources (including imports) to that sector, or should the over-all rate of growth be raised but strict measures taken to restrict demand. The alternatives are *inaction* despite mounting demographic pressure, or *action* involving sacrifices which would lower even the present inadequate standards of living. Both alternatives are likely to lead to greater social tensions.

30. Under certain conditions, an expanded flow of food aid may release the country from this dilemma, allowing a faster rate of development, including agricultural development, to be programed.

31. Of the required conditions, the basic one is an expansion of total aid. Manifestly, a faster rate of over-all development will call for additional supplies of other resources, as well as more food. My expert consultants considered that surplus food for economic development uses could not reasonably be expected to amount, on the average, to more than one sixth to one fifth[4] of the total capital aid required by underdeveloped countries. In certain countries the proportion might turn out to be higher – in others less. Thus, unless total aid is increased, the prospects for a greatly expanded use of surplus food for economic development must remain limited. Fortunately, many steps are being taken to enlarge the volume of such financing, including the creation of the Organisation for Economic Co-operation and Development (OECD) and of the Inter-American Bank and the recently-announced decision of the Government of the Federal Republic of Germany to participate in international economic assistance on a greatly enlarged scale over the next five years.

Employment promotion and rural capital formation

32. It is likely in many underdeveloped countries that development plans drawn up in the past did not take fully into account the availability of

food aid. It may now be possible for them to enlarge the whole development program by incorporating some additional worth-while projects or measures, which would require for their implementation mainly increased supplies of food. Projects which could be carried out simply by putting large numbers of unemployed persons to work would be particularly suitable.

33. There is much scope for such labor-intensive or food-intensive projects in underdeveloped countries where capital and skills are the scarce resources for development. Labor is relatively abundant and usually not fully utilized. This applies to both urban and rural areas. It is in agriculture, however, that the great manpower reserve exists. Underemployment in agriculture may be visible in the form of idleness; or disguised in the form of work of very low intensity and productivity. Farm operators may be affected, as well as farm family workers and hired labor. Underemployment may occur throughout the year in some districts, or only during the season of low labor demand for farm operations. The degree of underemployment may increase in the future, as more efficient agricultural production techniques are adopted.

34. Moreover, the absolute size of the labor force available in agriculture will continue to increase further in most underdeveloped countries over the next decade at least. This is because in most such countries the absolute growth in the nonagricultural sectors cannot in the near future be sufficient to draw enough workers out of agriculture to offset the growth in rural population, and thus hold the agricultural labor force stable, let alone cause it to decline.

35. The utilization in the development process of underemployed manpower is one of the great challenges in economic and agricultural planning in the underdeveloped regions. There is much labor-intensive and food-intensive development work to be done, in cities and in rural areas, for which relatively little domestic capital and even less foreign capital is required. Simple house construction in cities may be an instance. The opportunities for capital formation in rural areas through labor-intensive work are great.[5] Tree planting, land clearance, soil conservation work, terracing, road building, bunding, dam construction, the digging of irrigation and drainage channels are types of productive activities urgently needed in most areas. Of course, wherever possible, such projects should be considered within the framework of a general economic development program.

36. In many countries, an approach is being made on a voluntary basis under community development and similar schemes. Much useful capital-building work has been done in this way, but the potentialities would

appear to have been barely tapped so far. In particular, the contribution to land improvement under these schemes seems to have been very small up to date. The poorer peasants and laborers can hardly be expected to make much response to appeals for voluntary labor on projects which improve land belonging to others. Their inducement to work would be strong if they could be remunerated in cash or in kind. Wages paid to them would generate increased demand for goods that would be concentrated on food and clothing. Projects that provide employment for them are, therefore, particularly suited for inclusion in an extended development program aimed at absorbing surplus commodities, bearing in mind the availability of surplus cotton as well as food.[6]

37. The use of food aid to promote employment, particularly for rural capital formation, offers great possibilities which should be fully explored country by country in regions where one or other of the main surplus grains (wheat, maize or millet) is consumed.[7] Those possibilities could be broadened by conversion of feed grains into other foods. Operations of this kind would go far to implement the purpose of the United Nations Resolution, of using surplus food to raise productivity and speed economic development in food-deficient areas.

38. Many of the required development operations might be planned as local public works. In fact, this has been adopted in some Asian countries for soil conservation schemes. The work is planned by public works engineers, and the labor is put in by cultivators and agricultural laborers in the off-season for money wages. The farmers pay a slight increase in land revenue since their land has been made more productive. In some countries where representative local authorities exist it might be feasible to empower them to levy a small tax for local development works which, at the option of the taxpayer, could be paid in personal labor. Local co-operative societies or village councils might handle the necessary additional supplies of production requisites and consumer goods, including foods. This would help them to gain in economic strength and in acceptance.

39. It must be stressed that food aid for these purposes should not usually be tied to individual projects. It will be for the recipient country, reacting to the possibility of additional food aid, to include in its accelerated over-all development program the particular labor-intensive capital building projects which it favors. Only in this way can they be integrated into the national plan, so that the measures and allocations of supplementary resources required for their implementation may be provided. In countries where no general development plan has yet been formulated, however, a start might be made with selected projects of evident productive promise.

40. Increased food aid, with appropriate additions of matching financial aid, could enable some countries to include in their development programs more long-term investment, especially in the agricultural sector from which the increase in output may be very long-term. Some of the types of work mentioned above may come in this category, e.g., forestry, longer-range soil conservation construction, land clearing and resettlement, tidal land reclamation.

Livestock industries

41. The development of livestock industries is an istance of long-term investment in agriculture. It is singled out for special mention for several reasons. First is the fact, already noted, that diets in underdeveloped countries are seriously deficient in animal proteins. Over large regions the supply of livestock products is not sufficient to meet, even at present low levels, the additional requirements due to the growth of population. The second factor is the availability, at least for a transitional period, of large surplus stocks of feed grains, mainly maize and millet, with some barley and oats.

42. There appears to be a number of ways in which surplus feed grains, which form a large part of the available surpluses, could be used as a transitional supply to promote improvements in the livestock industries of the underdeveloped countries. In some countries – in the Near East and North Africa, for instance – the increasing demand for cereals for human consumption and livestock feeding has led to the extension of grain production in lands submarginal for cropping, which formerly were used for grazing purposes. Crop yields are very low and the lands are declining in fertility as a result of erosion and bad cultural methods. It is difficult for the farmer to change his practices, as he is dependent on the poor cereal crop. Pilot projects indicate that, in at least some areas of this type, it would be possible, if outside supplies of grains could be pledged to enable the farmer to return submarginal lands to grass for a long enough period, to build them up as a base for sound livestock production. After rehabilitation it might be possible to resume cereal cultivation in some areas under a grassland rotation and with higher yields. There may also be important instances in these and other regions where feed grains supplied as aid could be used to hasten the implementation of national plans for better range management and grazing control. Such grains could be used to help maintain the livestock off the range until the recovery of the vegetation, after which sometimes even twice the number of animals might eventually be carried under controlled grazing. Measures of this kind might also contribute to improved watershed management and soil conservation in many ways.

43. There are also many countries where cattle populations are large – as in Asia and Africa – but of very low productivity because of poor feeding. The addition of small quantities of feed grains to their diet could increase their output, especially if more nitrogenous local by-products such as oil cakes are included. The establishment of milk colonies[8] in a number of countries or of feed mixing plants, could provide a controlled channel for the distribution of the surplus feed grains.

44. The poultry industry in many less developed countries might similarly be stimulated, as has already happened in a few cases. The establishment of poultry feed mixing units could channel distribution, and continue to function later with local products. Such schemes could fit in well with the FAO/UNICEF Expanded Aid to Nutrition Program, which includes poultry production.

Land reform

45. In many underdeveloped countries, land reform is a necessary condition for the provision of incentives to farmers to adopt improved techniques and raise their productivity.[9] Where land reform means the subdivision of large estates and the distribution of land to small tenants or agricultural laborers, the immediate effect may be a fall in production and particularly in deliveries to the market. This may last several years, until the provision of credit, farm requisites, and technical advice to the new farmers is operating satisfactorily and production increases.

46. A few years of reduced market deliveries of food crops could cause severe inflation or necessitate the expenditure of overseas reserves of foreign exchange on food imports. Such a prospect might well deter a developing country from actually introducing measures of reform which it would be otherwise ready and willing to undertake. The firm assurance of the availability of food aid in a suitable form over the transitional period to offset such shortages, if needed, could be a deciding factor in such a country, and this use should be authorized by the surplus-owning countries.

47. It must be realized, however, that land reform does not pose only economic and administrative problems. In many countries it assumes a highly political character, sometimes involving international relations. This aspect of land reform is for the countries directly concerned to deal with, and other bodies, including the United Nations or any other multilateral system, must keep aloof. Only thus can international organizations operate free from political controversies.

National food reserves

48. The Member Governments of the United Nations, through resolutions passed in the Economic and Social Council, the General Assembly and the FAO Conference, have already stressed their unanimous support for national food reserve programs in underdeveloped countries, in line with recommendations presented by me in 1958.[10] There is, therefore, no need for me to seek further endorsement for such programs. Rather I would urge governments of underdeveloped and surplus-owning countries to give more attention to co-operative action for establishing such reserves.

49. In the framework of any arrangements for promoting greater use of food surpluses for world development, the establishment of national food reserves should have high priority.[11] Such reserves may serve a number of purposes according to the needs of particular countries. Two of the most important purposes are:

(a) to buffer natural and emergency fluctuations in supply of basic foods, due to vagaries of weather, and shortages or famine due to drought, flood or other disasters. In good years part of the crop would be purchased for the reserve at minimum prices. In bad years or times of disaster or famine, stocks would be released from the reserve to maintain the normal flow of supplies to consumers;

(b) to provide stocks for the implementation of domestic price and income policies. These policies should pay particular attention to the provision of stable prices as incentives to food producers to raise productivity and the protection of consumers against sharp increases in the cost of living.

50. There is an important relief element involved in the provision of stocks to cover emergency, as discussed later. But in underdeveloped countries where variations in climatic conditions are sizable and speculative activity is widespread, I regard national food reserves as one of the cornerstones of development policy. In some regions, reductions in output from one year to the next may be as much as one third, and the changes in marketed supplies could be much greater. The resultant price changes could jeopardize the continuity of a development program unless countered by a dependable reserve.

51. It might be thought that, if reserves were available on call in the surplus-producing countries, the need for nationally-held stocks in underdeveloped countries would be obviated. The advantages to the latter countries in cost reduction are obvious, but such a policy is not fully satisfactory. Reserves are needed in the food-producing areas of the food-deficient

countries, to enable producer prices to be protected from wild fluctuations. There is good evidence that, in some countries, a bumper food harvest may reduce the farmer's money income, as a result of the sharp price fall, while a short crop may raise this income. Naturally the incentive to higher productivity is blunted. The provision of incentives to larger output is one of the main foundations for an agricultural development program.

52. Absolute price fixation is not desirable, and selective price changes may be necessary to guide farm production. Furthermore, some reduction in price with a large crop, and some increase with a small one, are necessary in underdeveloped countries to prevent severe inflationary or deflationary effects on the whole economy. Nevertheless, I consider that, in general, floor prices to farmers should be established for at least one or two years in advance, at a level somewhat below expected average prices. Effective measures should be taken also to ensure that individual cultivators can count on getting the minimum prices. These policies are essential if domestic agriculture is to be stimulated to greater productivity.

53. In fact, in most cases a system of floor prices in the recipient country must be regarded as a basic precondition for any great expansion of surplus food utilization. This applies also to the establishment of food stock-managing organizations in the recipient countries that have not already developed them. This may raise many administrative and economic problems which must be faced in each country, with outside technical assistance where desired.

54. Since underdeveloped countries with accelerated development programs can seldom build up an adequate food reserve from domestic production (unless they are food exporters) and cannot afford to buy the necessary quantities on commercial terms, it is recognized by world authorities that the establishment and maintenance of such reserves should qualify for food aid on especially easy terms or in grant form.

55. Other costs are involved, particularly for shipping and the construction of storage facilities. To the extent that underemployed local resources can be used for the latter purpose, no serious problem is involved. Such additional outside resources as are required must be provided as increased aid, on a grant or loan basis. In a number of developed countries shipping is in surplus – such countries could participate in a broadened international program of food aid by providing transport.

56. Needless to say, the establishment of a national food reserve should be carefully planned in each country, and integrated in the over-all development program where one exists or can be formulated.

Social development and welfare

57. The formation of "human capital" in underdeveloped countries by raising the proportion of total manpower that is trained, educated, and experienced in the manifold tasks of economic and social development is as basic, as necessary, and as productive as physical capital formation, though it requires a longer period.[12] The urgency of this problem in Africa has already attracted international attention. But the problem exists in all underdeveloped countries. There is no doubt that economic and social progress would also be hastened by the better feeding of the young, as well as by improvements in the coverage of education at all levels. Better nutrition for workers could in many cases directly increase their productivity. Activities aimed at the achievement of these ends must be classed as social development rather than welfare.

58. The inclusion in over-all programs of well-prepared schemes of this kind would lead to a greater utilization of food aid. The organization of these schemes should be such as to enable the recipient countries to take over full responsibility for them in the course of time. Furthermore, they should be so managed as to strengthen rather than diminish the incentives for higher domestic agricultural output.

59. Schemes for supplementary meals could contribute to the achievement of development objectives in several ways. The provision of free school lunches and the extension of existing schemes, where they could be organized, would be an important and productive social investment. Quite apart from raising the nutritional levels of the young, it would also act as an incentive to school attendance. The provision of two nourishing meals a day or "food fellowships" to students at secondary and university level and to vocational trainees would similarly be a sound long-term investment, since it would enable more youths to take such training. Other programs of this kind might be advantageous in some countries. One instance could be the serving of meals in workers' canteens, as a part of the wage or on some similar basis, or the improvement of food levels in existing canteens.

60. Food distribution to the old, destitute and handicapped falls outside the scope of economic and social development and reaches into the humanitarian field.[13] However, it does come within the provision of food for the needy and the raising of nutritional levels for which FAO has a general international responsibility.

61. Surplus and other foods are already flowing into such social programs in many underdeveloped countries, mostly from the United States.

Grants are, and should remain, the recognized basis for food aid of this kind; its distribution must also continue to be direct to the recipients rather than through market sales. In some countries there may be scope for some variation of a "food stamp plan" for distribution in areas or among citizen groups (such as landless rural workers) suffering from chronic or acute malnutrition.

62. A number of less developed countries have initiated school lunch or supplementary meal programs. UNICEF has considerable experience in this field. So have a number of charitable and religious organizations, and FAO itself. These various bodies could no doubt assist countries to develop suitable schemes where desired or to expand existing ones, if sufficient resources were made available to them. It will also be necessary to give more attention than in the past to the needs of children of preschool age and of expectant mothers.

63. Supplies of surplus cereals (other than rice) are likely to be more than adequate for all the social development and welfare projects that can be soundly initiated in underdeveloped countries over the next five years, after allowing for economic development programs. However, such programs will also require large quantities of protein and protective foods, the supply of which is not in surplus. Such foods would, in the long term, be best provided by expansion in the livestock industries in the recipient countries themselves. In the transitional period, however, donor countries who have grain surpluses might consider converting part of their surplus into meat or milk, as discussed later. Other donor countries might consider making a contribution in cash so that the required supplementary food could be purchased commercially. Some countries which have a highly developed trade in livestock products might be concerned that a short-term expansion of capacity in developed countries for increasing supplies of animal protein food might have adverse effects on their trade. These fears are not borne out by experience so far gained. The demand from less developed countries for ordinary commercial imports of protein foods rather tends to be stimulated by such aid programs, as indeed has already happened in relation to school milk schemes.

64. However, the problem of destitution in the greater part of the world is staggering in its proportions, and can only be solved permanently by economic development. In this, both agriculture and industry have essential roles. Welfare measures which do not help in raising the productive capacity of the recipient areas are palliatives, and may tend to perpetuate the need for outside aid.

65. This is why, in line with the United Nations Resolution, I should like to keep the attention of the world focused primarily on the uses of food

aid for the promotion of economic and social development. It is evident that there are great needs and opportunities in this direction. At the same time, it is essential that the resources necessary to make a contribution to humanitarian relief are also made available.

[1] In the *World economic survey 1959*, the United Nations noted that in underdeveloped food-importing countries, deficiencies in domestic food production have often adversely affected the level of investment through limiting imports of capital goods.

[2] Appendix 2, page 289.

[3] Appendix 2, pages 280-81.

[4] According to the expert consultants, total food aid (that is, food aid including other uses than economic development) would be $2,400 to $2,700 million per year. This is at C.C.C. cost, and the experts suggest that for purposes of aid calculations this should be valued at $1,600 to $1,800 million. These figures represent about one third of the total aid flow which they suggest should be $5,000 to $6,000 million on their definition of aid (Appendix 2, pages 284 and 287).

[5] Appendix 2, page 288.

[6] The United Nations Resolution is specially concerned with surplus food, and its utilization to eliminate hunger and promote economic development in food-deficient areas. The present report reflects a similar concentration on food surpluses. However, the problem of agricultural surpluses, with which FAO has long been concerned, covers cotton and tobacco as well as food products. Surplus cotton, along with surplus food, has a current and potential role as aid in the development of underdeveloped countries. In countries where the pace of accelerated development might lead to increased demand for cotton textiles beyond the limits of the raw cotton supply normally available, and where textile spinning and weaving capacity is not fully utilized, there could be a case for utilizing surplus cotton as aid. In underdeveloped countries, cotton cloth probably ranks next to food in order of priority of expenditure out of additional income that becomes available to consumers. This use of cotton may raise the proportion of additional investment expenditures which can be covered by surplus commodities.

[7] See *Uses of agricultural surpluses to finance economic development in underdeveloped countries - A pilot study in India*, FAO Commodity Policy Studies, No. 6. FAO, Rome, 1955. See also this publication, pages 91-222.

[8] "Milk colonies" - concentrations of milk animals in one or more units, of a size consisting usually of 2,000 or more animals. Such colonies have already been established in some cases with the help of UNICEF and FAO, or under municipal initiative on a large scale in some countries, e.g., in Bombay, India.

[9] Appendix 2, page 297.

[10] *National food reserve policies in underdeveloped countries*, FAO Commodity Policy Studies, No. 11; FAO, Rome 1958.

[11] Appendix 2, page 289 *et seq.*

[12] Appendix 2, page 296.

[13] Appendix 2, pages 302-303.

III. REQUIREMENTS FOR AN EXPANDED PROGRAM OF FOOD AID TO ECONOMIC DEVELOPMENT

66. I have already indicated that food aid has an important part to play in the acceleration of economic and social progress in the less developed regions. Surplus food can play this part whether it flows into use through bilateral or multilateral transactions, provided certain practical requirements are met.

In recipient countries

67. Over the next five years many million dollars' worth of these commodities - roughly estimated in this report at $12,500 million[1] - may flow into stockpiles or become available for use outside normal market channels. The responsibility for determining the uses to which the surplus foods are to be put rests with the recipient countries, since it is their development which is to be promoted. It is for them to establish the policies, institutions and measures necessary in their own countries; to provide assurance that the food aid will be used effectively to achieve the progress they have in mind, without detriment to their own agricultural development, and in accordance with internationally accepted principles. This will involve the recipient countries in many tasks, some of which will be new to some of them and for which they may require technical assistance.

ECONOMIC DEVELOPMENT PROGRAMING

68. The governments in recipient countries will need to initiate or improve the integrated programing of their over-all economic development, with special attention to the rate of growth to be aimed at, the role of domestic agriculture, and the best uses to be made of increased quantities of surplus food for accelerated development. Many complicated questions will arise. Those relating to the utilization of surplus foods might include: the objectives of development; how much demand for food can be expanded; the extent and location of unemployed workers; the relative importance

of employment promotion; prospects for agricultural exports; long-term changes needed in domestic agriculture in the light of external market prospects and the relative advantages of producing various products; the selection of labor-intensive projects for inclusion in the plan; foreign exchange prospects; local resources needed for utilizing surplus food; supplementary foods or matching aid needed for utilizing surplus food; other countries likely to be affected; the implications in terms of resources of establishing necessary institutions. These questions could best be answered in the context of a comprehensive review of over-all development objectives, and of the place of agriculture and under-utilized rural workers in the country's over-all program or plans for its economic development.

69. A national development plan must be considered as a charter of policy which has to outline not only what the people may expect in time, but also the duties and the sacrifices which they have to undertake in order to achieve their objectives. It must receive general support from the community as a whole. More specifically, the plan must be comprehensive. It should give not only a clear picture of the economy and the possible targets, but it should describe also the institutions and policies designed to ensure that the plan is implemented and the targets reached. Moreover, the relationships between broad objectives, policies, sectors, individual projects and measures have to be carefully studied. The more closely the whole pattern can be co-ordinated, the wider will be the limits to which demand might be safely permitted to expand, and consequently the larger the amount of aid and of surplus food that could be utilized. If the rate of over-all investment is low, the receipt of a certain quantity of food as aid might displace some domestic production or commercial imports. But if total investment is pushed up, say by an increase in financial aid, the same quantity of food aid might be absorbed as additional consumption in view of the expansion of demand, without harmful effects on commercial production and trade. Thus, an increase in nonfood aid might create the conditions for a concurrent increase in food aid.

70. In this context it may be noted, as my consultants have stated, that foreign aid capital (including food aid) increases the range of the whole development program.[2] Since aid may require changes in several projects or a review of over-all priorities, a single loan or grant of food aid cannot with any exactness be said to be given to one specific project alone. It should rather be considered as a contribution to the development program as a whole, and evaluated accordingly.

71. Closely integrated programing requires adequate and fairly reliable statistical data on the functioning of the economy, and suitably skilled statistical and economic personnel. Where some form of integrated program-

ing is not yet established, it should nevertheless not be too difficult to select a few projects needing food aid that would merit inclusion in any national plan and make a permanent contribution to development. In such cases, commonsense, a close study of past trends, insight into the institutional framework, trial and error, and a sense of social priorities can show the way. However, as soon as the program so initiated assumes importance, and the volume of aid increases beyond a bare minimum, a comprehensive review becomes advisable.

72. Each country must work out for itself the main features and priorities of its development plan and the economic and social pattern at which it desires to aim. However, the technical elaboration of these programs may well profit from assistance from abroad.

DOMESTIC AGRICULTURAL DEVELOPMENT

73. Once the role of domestic agriculture in national development has been assessed, with objectives stated and plans formulated, the policies and measures for implementing the plans will need to be clearly specified. It is desirable that these policies and measures include, as already indicated, appropriate price and income policies and the strengthening or establishment of institutions designed to provide incentives to agricultural development, and to ensure that the incentives reach down to the farmers.

74. It cannot be emphasized too strongly that the utilization of food aid must not be allowed to discourage the progress of agriculture in the recipient country or the latter could be reduced to continued charity or eventual greater misery. Some countries might wish to ask for international technical assistance to help them to establish the appropriate policies and institutions to speed their own agricultural progress, but the initiative must be theirs.

NATIONAL FOOD AGENCY

75. As discussed previously, some type of national food agency is needed to handle food stocks under public control.[3] The operations involved may include the management of the national food reserve; the importation of food supplies for distribution or for enlarging or replenishing the reserve; the purchase of food from local farmers, particularly in good seasons, at floor prices; supervision of storage and transport of government food stocks; the fixing of maximum and minimum prices; releases of stocks for sales to consumers at controlled prices after a poor harvest; distribution

under emergency relief measures or for use in supplementary feeding schemes. Not all these functions would necessarily be needed in every country.

76. A number of underdeveloped countries have already established national food agencies and have been operating them for many years. Some modifications might be needed if a much larger utilization of surplus food were to be programed.

77. This would certainly be the case if it were decided to increase stocks, under food aid, to constitute an adequate national reserve. Additional storage space would be needed; functions of the reserves would need to be defined; policies for guaranteeing minimum prices to domestic producers might have to be strengthened; the procedures and methods of operation might have to be changed, and management reorganized to allow more freedom of action within statutory directives.

In donor countries

78. The term donor countries as used in this report includes developed countries which are present producers and donors of surplus foods, countries which could be potential donors of food, and countries which could be donors of resources other than food. These categories are not mutually exclusive. It should be pointed out that, in some of the developed countries which could be included in the classification above in one or more categories, there exists unused capacity to produce commodities, e.g., steel, electrical equipment, machine tools, fertilizers, pesticides and farm machinery, which are required for development purpose in some food-deficient areas at least as urgently as food. There is also idle capacity in freight or other services to match surplus food in recipient countries' development programs.

79. Important responsibilities rest with the donor or aid-giving countries, if the desired expansion of surplus food utilization is to be realized. I should like to state here that in my view the basis for the distribution of aid should conform with the principles of the United Nations Resolution which refers to "areas of greatest need". The experts, perhaps as a result of their concentration on the five-year period immediately ahead, take their stand on the principle that aid should favour areas where it can have the maximum "catalytic effect".[4] It follows that the basis of the distribution of aid might be taken to be the proximity to the stage of economic independence. This is, as the experts stress, a more generous criterion than the granting of aid according to the return per dollar. But it still remains a restrictive test. In my view, the distribution of aid will have to be based on

the principle of assuring, as much as possible, equal opportunity for eventual self-help through increase in income and investment capacity for all countries. This will mean that the poorer among the less developed countries would need relatively more attention than those which have richer resources and more immediate development possibilities.

80. The responsibilities of the donor countries can be analyzed under the following heads.

AVAILABILITY OF SURPLUSES AS AID

81. The expansion of food aid is limited by the amounts which individual governments have budgetary authority to appropriate for the purpose of promoting economic and social development in underdeveloped countries, whether through bilateral or multilateral arrangements. Enabling or amending legislation may be necessary to expand the food aid programs and ensure continuity, and broaden their uses.

PRIMACY OF RECIPIENT COUNTRY'S DEVELOPMENT

82. If underdeveloped countries are to seek additional food aid, they need to feel assured that the requirements of their development programs are recognized by donors as the main consideration. In other words, surplus food aid must flow in accordance with the over-all programs and orders of priority in economic and social development established by the recipient countries themselves. This rules out the project approach to which I have already referred, except where the recipient country has not yet formulated any over-all development program or plan. Under this approach, the donor country agrees with the recipient country on the particular development project or projects to which the food aid is to apply. If such agreement were made a condition of the aid, it could cause misunderstanding and perhaps involve, at times, some undue pressure from outside on the recipient country's desires.

COUNTRY-BY-COUNTRY STUDY OF NEEDS

83. The emphasis in my recommendations – accepting the suggestions of my expert consultants – is on country planning. Perhaps the weakness of earlier approaches was in the global single-pattern approach, as distinct from the country-by-country multi-pattern approach which I would advocate. The requirements of different countries differ widely, and there is a

correspondingly wide range of constructive uses to which food aid can be put. The matching of requirements and uses will have to be done country by country and will result in many different patterns of food aid.

RECOGNITION OF NEED FOR NONFOOD AID AND ADEQUATE CO-ORDINATING ARRANGEMENTS

84. It is most important for donor countries to recognize that the capacity of food-deficient countries to utilize surplus food aid for development purposes is limited, unless matching aid in other forms is also available. This fact indicates the value of having some co-ordinating arrangements among the donor countries, such as the Organisation for Economic Co-operation and Development (OECD) is now trying to work out. Consultation with the United Nations system, which has invaluable knowledge and experience of the problems of underdeveloped countries, has already been initiated and should also be helpful in this connection. In the field of food and agriculture, especially while developing the program of food aid, FAO can well be called upon to act as a clearing house for information and to assist co-ordination.

CONTINUITY OF AID AND COMPOSITION OF SURPLUSES

85. Aid, including food aid for development purposes, needs to be continued over a minimum transitional period of at least five to ten years. Unless some continuity of aid is assured, the developing country may hesitate to embark on certain projects. This would apply with particular force to projects with a large content of food aid in the form of, say, dried milk, which has ceased to be in significant surplus. A country may not feel safe to start a school milk scheme unless supplies can be assured for a reasonable period ahead. This problem may suggest to grain surplus countries the desirability of modifying the commodity content of the surplus "basket" to make that basket, as a whole, more useful and acceptable to potential recipients. Thus donor countries might convert part of their supplies of surplus grains into livestock products such as milk and meat and prepare them in forms suitable for surplus distribution. Greater acceptability of food surpluses achieved in this way should also result in an increase in total economic aid to underdeveloped countries. As I have stated before, assistance to underdeveloped countries in expanding their own livestock output with the use of surplus feedstuffs, would be an additional method of increasing their levels of protein consumption; it would, however, require a reorganization of their basic rural economy and, hence, be much slower to get into action.

86. In view of the very low repayment capacity of the less developed countries, a considerable proportion of food aid should be available as grants, and the remainder as long-term, low interest loans. Grants would be most appropriate where the recipient country is at the beginning of the development process with great poverty and very low income per head. For countries in a better position, combinations of the two may be used, with greater emphasis on loans as their economic condition improves. It is to be pointed out that, to the extent that goods and services are made available by the recipient country before the aid begins to yield results, the total aid resulting from a surplus transaction is reduced. In this report all the figures relating to the financing of economic development through food aid relate solely to the amount of commodities supplied in excess of any such use of local resources replacing foreign exchange.

COUNTRY PREFERENCES FOR MULTILATERAL CHANNELS

87. Some or many underdeveloped countries may prefer a multilateral channel for certain types of food aid. Such countries might be able to participate more fully in surplus food utilization in their development programs if the surplus countries recognized this preference, and were ready to commit or earmark an adequate amount of their surpluses to or for such channels or arrangements, if established. Unless the surplus-owning countries are willing to do this, there will be no scope for any such multilateral action.

88. Deficiencies as regards some of the points mentioned above in relation to potential recipient and donor countries may explain why surplus food disposal programs up to date have lagged behind the existing availabilities of surpluses. Some of the obstacles indicated may be removed by national action. In other cases there may be a role for multilateral assistance and arrangements. This aspect will be examined in the next chapter, after some broad issues have been stressed.

Size and distribution of total aid

89. The experts estimated that, on their definitions, the present level of aid is $3,600 million per year. They defined aid as consisting of "those parts of capital inflow which normal market incentives do not provide".[5] They consider, on the basis of their estimate of absorptive capacity in the lesser developed countries and of contributions from donor countries, that

total economic aid for all underdeveloped countries should run at $5,000 to $6,000 million per year. This would represent an increase of two fifths to two thirds over the present levels. In their opinion, this would enable the less developed countries to achieve an average income increase per head of 2 percent per year, and eventually to reach self-sustained growth. The more commonly held view is that total aid should run at 100 percent or more above the current rate in order to achieve this result which, considering the present low living standards, is very modest.

90. The point I wish to stress is that the larger the total flow of aid, the larger the quantity of surplus food that can be utilized for economic and social development in underdeveloped countries, in accordance with the FAO Principles, and without harmful repercussions on commercial markets for exporters of the same products. The greatest quantity of food aid must be used, as already indicated, to support higher rates of investment in such countries, particularly in promoting fuller employment, rural capital formation and longer-range economic and social investment. The total investment that can be achieved by a developing country will depend on the amount of the financial aid it receives, plus the food aid for economic and social development. On the basis of the data contained in the report by the expert consultants, the amount of food aid necessary for such purposes would be about 20 to 30 percent of total capital aid on the average – the actual figure in any country can be determined only in the context of its development plan, its income elasticity of demand and the range of surplus commodities available.

91. There has been much discussion about the absorptive capacity of an underdeveloped country for total aid. I have no doubt that at any particular time there is some limit. However, I know of very few countries which are at present receiving external aid up to the limit of their capacity to use it. As additional aid is received, especially if it is utilized under a carefully formulated over-all development program, a country's absorptive capacity for further aid will rise.

92. I believe that with enlarged programs there should be some more equitable sharing of the cost of total aid, both food and nonfood aid, than has prevailed in the past. Many developed countries are giving attention to this problem and some important steps are being taken. So far there seems to be no general agreement on a suitable basis for sharing in economic assistance. The expert consultants attempted to formulate some general guiding principles in the matter and mentioned a progressive rate of contribution rising from one half to three quarters of one percent of gross national product in developed countries.[6] However, some recent official statements have suggested one percent as the figure to be adopted.

93. The basis on which surplus food aid should be valued in the aid pro-grams has not yet been decided. Certainly, it would seem more reasonable to use world market prices rather than domestic prices in the aid-supplying country.

94. Given the need for resources other than foodstuffs in an expanded aid program, surplus-giving countries might, in collaboration with other countries contributing to international assistance, be expected to balance their agricultural surplus product aid with additional matching aid, in inconvertible or convertible currencies, or in the form of industrial prod-ucts which would otherwise have to be purchased by the developing coun-tries with foreign exchange.

Some wider implications

95. A successful food aid program will depend on the solution of several far-reaching problems. I would mention here the maintenance of expan-sion in the world economy, and the growth and stability of world trade.

EXPANSION AND STABILITY IN DEVELOPED COUNTRIES

96. It is a key condition for the success of an expanded program of inter-national aid that it should be co-ordinated with measures designed to main-tain a steady expansion in the world economy. This, in turn, would pro-mote an expansion of the trade of the underdeveloped areas, helping their eventual attainment of economic independence. Setbacks in richer coun-tries, which might cause only slight disturbances and minor social hard-ships in their own economies, have a disproportionate effect on the trade and prosperity of less developed countries. Those setbacks induce fluc-tuations in the export earnings of some underdeveloped countries which, as I have mentioned frequently, offset the total international assistance these countries may be receiving from all sources. Thus there is, also in this context, urgent need for further reinforcing of arrangements to maintain stable growth in the world economy as a whole.

97. The rise in production and trade in the less developed countries, which will have been stimulated by foreign aid, will in time also contribute to stability in the economies of the developed countries. Furthermore, the developed countries might, in times of recession, make extraordinary ad-ditional grants of industrial products and goods and materials for capital formation for which they have unused capacity. Although the effect of such extra grants on total production in the developed countries might be small,

they might, for some sensitive sectors in these countries, be helpful in maintaining a larger volume of activity. The recipient countries might be encouraged and assisted to store these goods until needed, so that fluctuations in the arrivals of capital goods would not prevent their steady expansion of employment and production. These extraordinary grants should not be allowed to influence the hard core of the plans of the less developed countries. Rather, they should be used for projects which might be on the periphery of their development plans, and be taken up as their expanding resources permit.

STABILITY AND CO-ORDINATION OF TRADE

98. Underdeveloped countries have often shown a tendency to plan for self-sufficiency. In view of the uncertainties of international trade, especially with respect to demand for agricultural products, this is understandable. Moreover, the increase in agricultural production and productivity in developed countries, and the rise in production of synthetics, threaten to narrow the markets for many agricultural exports of underdeveloped countries. Nevertheless, overemphasis on self-sufficiency in particular products may lead to dis-economies in the use of resources, and cause hardship and retarded growth to other underdeveloped countries, as in the case of rice. The development pace might in many cases be speeded up to common advantage, if the possiblities of developing complementarity with other suitable countries were fully considered when programs of economic growth were being formulated. Measures for promoting the stable expansion of trade in the products exported by underdeveloped countries would strongly reinforce the effect of surplus food and other aid on their rate of development.

---

[1] The estimates of the expert consultants are reviewed in more detail in Chapter VI, page 271.
[2] Appendix 2, page 288.
[3] See also Appendix 2, pages 291-95.
[4] Appendix 2, page 284.
[5] Appendix 2, pages 286-87.
[6] With World Bank loans counted in the aid. Appendix 2, pages 290-91.

IV. INTERNATIONAL EMERGENCY FOOD RELIEF

99. I have so far dealt with food mainly as aid for economic development, though I have referred to the need for emergency relief in connection with national reserves. The occurrence of natural disasters has always found human sympathy everywhere, and relief has been provided though not always in time.

100. There are various kinds of disasters and natural calamities. Some give sufficient warning for international action to be taken in time – others come suddenly, leaving death and suffering behind. Also there are pockets of acute malnutrition or chronic hunger scattered over the world where slow starvation takes a heavy toll of human life, unnoticed and uncared for.

101. The General Assembly and ECOSOC resolutions on food relief and reserves have mostly covered the case of disasters that could be foreseen to some extent, such as an impending crop shortage or possible famine. For disasters such as earthquakes, which happen suddenly and call for immediate action, adequate provision has not been made.

102. There is no doubt that the maintenance of an adequate national reserve of basic foods would provide a country with the means to withstand the first impact of either predictable or sudden emergencies. In such an event, national reserve stocks, if they exist, might well be drawn down by emergency distributions to a level that is beyond the possibility of replenishment from national food production. For the same reason that it is recognized that national food reserves of underdeveloped countries should be established by grants of food aid, so it may be agreed that the rebuilding of stocks depleted as a result of such emergencies may require further food aid as grants. To assure all countries that relief would be immediately available to replenish national reserves depleted by emergencies, it would be desirable, as my expert consultants recommended,[1] to establish an international emergency food reserve. This would involve FAO having an irrevocable option on some of the available food surpluses. In this sense, an international reserve may be regarded as the complement of national food reserves.

103. Very few underdeveloped countries have yet established national food reserves. This strengthens rather than weakens the case for an international arrangement for emergency relief, especially to meet cases of sudden, unforeseen disaster.

104. Much thought has been given to this subject by FAO in the past, and several alternative plans evolved. One, called the Three Circles Plan[2] was found by the Member Governments to be technically sound, but was not pursued. The United Nations Resolution, which also covers emergency relief, indicates that the time may have come for further world action in this matter. If the Resolution is to be implemented and emergency relief placed on a sound working basis, some definite plan must be adopted.

105. The Three Circles Plan was designed to combine speed and flexibility of relief operations with the acceptance and use of all kinds of contributions in a permanent plan. The arrangement proposed consisted of:

(a) an inner circle of financial contributors to provide the nucleus of the plan and to constitute a relief fund proper, based on renewable financial contributions on an agreed scale;

(b) contributors in kind constituting a second circle of "fixed value commitment" contributors, providing an additional reserve: this was to be used on terms which would allow for somewhat less operating flexibility than the "inner circle" fund;

(c) an outer circle of *ad hoc* participants linked to the plan by their recognition of its objectives, and by financial contributions to its administrative expenses, but without any other advance commitments.

106. It is recognized that the workability of such a plan as a system would depend largely on the inner circle's size, willingness and determination to adhere to its own more rigid rules.

107. The arrangements for operating the plan were adequately worked out at the time, but might need some modification in the present context. There was to be:

(a) an international authority, which might be merged with an existing organization such as FAO. The authority would consist of representatives of the contributing governments – the rights of representation might not be the same for each of the circles. The authority would decide the scale, kind, sources and terms of procurement; and the eligibility of countries for relief and the scale, kind and terms of relief operations. These functions were to be delegated to a general manager.

(b) a small executive committee, which would act for the authority in case of emergency. It would also keep in touch with participating governments, negotiate contributions in kind, and supervise the manager and the FAO famine unit.

(c) an FAO famine unit, the functions of which would be to keep the world situation under review for early signs of famine anywhere; to organize missions to study alleged famine conditions; and to prepare proposals for relief operations as regards scale, kind and sources, as a basis for intergovernmental decision.

108. Procedures were worked out in detail, covering in relation to any case of emergency relief the preliminary period, the period of warning, the period of alert, the period of action and the post-emergency period.

109. In considering more adequate use of surplus foods for both relief and development purposes, nations might care to re-examine this proposal, to see if action along these lines might now be agreed upon as one sector of the expanded surplus disposal and relief activities.

[1] Appendix 2, page 307.
[2] FAO: *Report of a group of experts on an emergency food reserve.* Document C 53/19; Rome, March, 1953 (Chapter IV).

V. MULTILATERAL FUNCTIONS AND ARRANGEMENTS

110. My basic conclusion is that the utmost use should be made of existing national and international institutions. This assumes the continuance and indeed the enlargement of bilateral aid and bilateral surplus transactions. It assumes also that the international agencies who have a role to play should make their respective contributions.

111. Nevertheless, in the light of the analysis so far undertaken with the aid of the experts whom I consulted, I have also come to the conclusion that there is a need for some important additional activities and functions to be conducted on a multilateral basis. These are summarized below. If they are carried out efficiently and on an adequate scale, they would, in my opinion, greatly promote the expanded utilization of surplus food in food-deficient areas and accelerate economic and social development.

112. It will be noted that the recommended multilateral activities include assistance, where desired, in the preparation of additional bilateral surplus transactions, through contacts with recipient and donor countries concerned. Such assistance would be based on the application of the FAO Principles and the ideas contained in this report, if endorsed. It would also be given in collaboration, as appropriate, with the United Nations and its agencies which had a contribution to make. The development of this activity would, therefore, have the effect of providing a multilateral setting for bilateral transactions in surplus utilization. In addition, I propose that food aid should be made available multilaterally to those recipient countries which might prefer that channel. This will depend upon the readiness of countries owning food surpluses to allocate a proportion of their surpluses for utilization through such a channel.

Activities and functions

113. The experts whom I consulted proposed the following activities and functions for intergovernmental agencies – that is, FAO, in co-operation with the United Nations and other agencies, as appropriate.

(a) Assistance and advice to potential recipient countries, on their request, in the programing of surplus food utilization for economic and social development, integrated with their general economic development programs.

Important aspects of this assistance and advice would be:

(i) Aiding countries to examine the role of agriculture in their national development, including the prospects of foreign trade, and the possibilities of complementary development with other countries.

(ii) Drafting realistic and constructive proposals for the use of surplus food, in consultation with the potential recipient and donor countries, taking into account the FAO Principles and the interests of other countries. These proposals might take the form of draft bilateral agreements where appropriate. This activity might extend to all types of surplus food utilization, including use in connection with land reforms and for social development and welfare, to meet emergency needs, or to raise chronically low levels of nutrition for specific groups or areas, as well as for expanding economic development.

(iii) Assessing, in consultation with the countries concerned, the additional aid required to balance the surplus food aid.

(iv) Where another underdeveloped country may be adversely affected by food aid which is nevertheless desirable on balance, conducting special consultations with that country and potential aid-giving countries, with a view to exploring the possibilities of easing the situation.

(b) Assistance and advice to recipient countries, on their request, in the establishment and operation of institutions and policies required for enlarged programs of surplus food utilization.

This would relate mainly to food and agricultural price policies, establishment or improvement of a national food agency and establishment and, in rare cases, operation of a national food reserve.

(c) Advice, on request, to potential donor countries, regarding the needs and requirements of recipient countries in terms of kinds and quantities of surplus foods and matching aid.

This activity might extend to assistance in developing proposed bilateral arrangements, and assurances regarding compatibility with the FAO Principles of Surplus Disposal.

(d) Appraisal, on request, of emergency or chronic food shortages in individual countries, and reporting to prospective donor countries on such situations requiring emergency assistance, and arranging with them for appropriate aid, or meeting such emergencies from reserve stocks already pledged to FAO.

(e) Control and administration of international emergency food reserves, constituted by pledges given by participating countries, to be used for

the purpose of supporting and replenishing national food reserves after emergencies, and in meeting emergency food shortages caused by crop failures or other disasters.

The functions would cover surpervision of the composition of the reserve to ensure flexibility, and the calling up of pledges in emergencies.

(f) Liaison and collaboration with international lending agencies, and *consortia* (or committees) including national agencies, which consider the total needs of a recipient country's development program.

The purpose of this function would be to ensure that the possibilities of food aid for economic development were fully taken into account in determination of the debt-carrying capacity of individual underdeveloped countries, and in allocations of financial aid among countries.

(g) The holding of pledges of surplus foods committed by surplus-owning countries for utilization for development through multilateral channels, and the administration to recipient countries of food aid so pledged.

Recipient countries preferring this channel would also on request be provided with multilateral assistance in the formulation of their surplus utilization programs. To the extent that sufficient supplies have been pledged, this would allow all underdeveloped countries who wished to do so, to participate without discrimination in an expanded program of surplus food use on a basis of equality, that is, solely on the basis of the technical requirements of their economic development plans and their readiness to use surplus food effectively.

(h) Evaluation and reporting, in co-operation with recipient and donor countries, on programs of surplus food utilization.

Such reports should cover the operation of the programs, including any multilateral programs, and record and appraise their economic and nutritional effects, particularly with reference to the state of agricultural development in recipient countries and the impact, if any, on domestic agriculture and on commercial imports, of the surplus food utilization. The agreements with recipient countries would indicate what information each country would collect and supply as a basis for these studies and evaluation.

The United Nations system

114. In line with the view of the experts,[1] it seems to me that FAO should be the focal point for contacts and co-ordination in the whole expanded program of surplus food utilization proposed. My further views are also in line with theirs. FAO is fully competent as regards assistance to

countries in the programing of agricultural development in the broader economic framework. However, in planning the use of food surpluses by incorporation in the general development plans of underdeveloped countries, and advising them on their general economic requirements, I envisage that FAO would work closely with the United Nations. In the field work of assistance to countries in their programing of development, collaboration might be particularly close with the Regional Economic Commissions of the United Nations. In many aspects of the work at country level, especially in relation to promoting supplementary feeding schemes, the present close co-operation between FAO and UNICEF could be further strengthened. I would also envisage that both FAO and the United Nations would work closely with such financial agencies as the International Bank for Reconstruction and Development, and the International Development Association and regional or national agencies, as appropriate, to help implement programs where food aid is combined with money aid, and to assist in determining the extent to which the debt repayment capacity of an underdeveloped country would be improved as a result of receiving food aid.

115. The program will certainly call for technical assistance to recipient countries in fields related to national economic programing and the utilization of surplus foods for development purposes; also for the training of their personnel. In many cases there may be a need for pilot projects and preinvestment surveys. These requirements could well lead to action by the United Nations Expanded Program of Technical Assistance and the United Nations Special Fund. Other specialized agencies may be involved from time to time in specific activities related to this program.

116. The use of the United Nations system to implement, along with national agencies, an expanded program of world food aid to underdeveloped countries, obviously raises the problem of co-ordination. This problem may be studied by the Administrative Committee on Co-ordination of the United Nations, on which all United Nations bodies are represented by their administrative heads.

Co-ordination with bilateral aid

117. I assume that the largest part of total aid resources, including food aid, will continue to flow to underdeveloped countries bilaterally. This is likely to be so, even if multilateral aid is expanded considerably. It is particularly important for the success of the world food aid program that co-ordination be improved between the multilateral agencies and national aid-administering agencies – also with intergovernmental bodies such as the Colombo Plan and the Organisation for Economic Co-operation and De-

velopment. I have already referred to this point in discussing co-ordinating arrangements between food aid and general economic assistance.

Co-ordination at the country level

118. The problem of co-ordination is posed not only at the policy level, but also in the field. Most of the recipient countries have established some type of machinery for co-ordinating foreign aid in relation to their over-all needs. There may be some scope for stronger joint working arrangements among the international and bilateral agencies within recipient countries *vis-à-vis* the recipient government, as regards particular special fields.

119. The interests of different types of countries in the expanded program of food aid would not all be the same. I agree with my expert consultants "that the international organizations and their staffs, working under proper government control and subject to the usual checks, must be trusted to reconcile these interests without elaborate new machinery or mechanisms."[2]

Implications for FAO

120. It may be found, as my expert consultants recommended, that the execution of this program of world food aid, if endorsed by the international community, would require a strong executive unit in FAO. In this case, it might be useful to bring all the international activities under the program into one focal point in FAO, as they also recommended. The daily operations would be greatly assisted and speeded up, if other international agencies with a major co-operative role related to its efforts could second officials to work closely with this unit. Likewise, FAO might find it helpful to outpost officials to establish close working relations with some other participating agencies.

121. Within FAO, the present intergovernmental machinery concerned with surplus disposals need not be changed.[3] The Committee on Commodity Problems, the Consultative Subcommittee on Surplus Disposal and other interested bodies, such as the FAO Group on Grains, would continue their activities. Their work would be strengthened by the availability of the evaluation reports mentioned in paragraph 113 *(h)*. The Committee on Commodity Problems, along with the FAO Council and Conference would be concerned with the broad lines of the world food aid program. The actual day-to-day activities of the program would be conducted under my direction, in co-ordination with other United Nations agencies.

---

[1] Appendix 2, page 304.
[2] Appendix 2, page 309.
[3] Appendix 2, page 308.

VI. A FIVE-YEAR PROGRAM

122. In arriving at the activities and arrangements proposed above, I have had in mind certain rough magnitudes of the possible availability and utilization of surplus food over a five-year period. These were presented to me by the expert consultants.[1]

123. On their assumptions,[2] in the United States alone over a five-year period, a total of about $12,500 million[3] worth of surplus food would be or become available for use outside commercial channels. They envisaged uses in underdeveloped countries over the same period amounting to about the same figure – $8,000 to $8,800 million in economic programs (including land reform) and $4,000 to $4,500 million in social development (excluding land reform) and welfare distribution. These totals of availability and utilization represent an annual rate about two thirds above the recent rate of disposal at $1,500 million per year (foods only, all countries, C.C.C. cost). If recent United States disposals of foods to underdeveloped countries only were taken into account, the increase, of course, would be much larger.

124. It seems to me reasonable to think in terms of a five-year program. Surplus food utilization activities would, in my view, be necessary and desirable for a longer period than this. But it is difficult to make any definite plans over a longer period. The situation could be reviewed later, with special reference to the degree of progress in underdeveloped countries and the trends in food production in surplus countries.

125. In estimating availabilities over five years, it would, of course, be desirable to include potential supplies from surplus countries other than the United States, although it is not at present known to what extent their stocks may become available for distribution on special terms as aid. The amounts estimated are probably, therefore, minimum figures of total availability over the next five years. However, they are sufficient to indicate the extent of the transitional opportunity for food aid.

126. As regards the total utilization that can actually be achieved during five years, I do not wish to hazard a forecast. The needs in the underdeveloped countries dwarf the available stocks. But in many cases it may take time for their governments to formulate sound proposals and to establish the institutions and policies necessary to ensure that food aid contributes, as intended, to the permanent advance of their countries. The world problem of attaining the required expansion of total financial aid is also a factor in determining how rapidly food aid can be safely expanded, without harmful repercussions on commercial trade.

[1] Appendix 2, pages 283-84.
[2] Appendix 3, page 312.
[3] Valued at assumed cost to the U.S. Commodity Credit Corporation - values at world prices would be about 70 percent of these.

VII. UNITED STATES PROPOSAL FOR A $100 MILLION FUND

127. At the meeting of the Intergovernmental Advisory Committee set up by the FAO Council, the Delegate of the United States proposed that an initial food utilization program aiming at a fund of $100 million in commodities and cash contributions be established. He declared that, for its part, the United States would be prepared to offer $40 million in commodities, with the possibility of a supplementary cash contribution.[1] He emphasized that the United States favored a multilateral approach as a supplement to bilateral arrangements, with the widest possible contribution by member countries. This proposal, it is hoped, will provide a basis for discussion and decision so that a beginning can be made with a multilateral program without delay.

[1] Appendix 4, page 315.

VIII. CONCLUSION

128. The objective of the UN Resolution, in the broad setting of FAO's Freedom from Hunger Campaign, is to ensure conditions which may allow man everywhere to live in dignity. In this age of science which every day brings countries and nations closer, with political consciousness stirring the vast masses who till now had accepted poverty and hunger as pre-ordained, against the background of unprecedented population growth which threatens even the present meager supplies of the necessities of life, the problem can no longer be left to be dealt with by each nation according to its capability. International resources must be mobilized to assist the developing countries. We must be warned that in the present situation lie the seeds of unlimited progress or unlimited disaster, not only for individual nations but for the whole world.

129. The proposals I have made go beyond what have been found feasible and acceptable in past; yet they can hardly be described as revolutionary. The goal we aim at is high. We can attain this goal only by determined and sustained effort.

APPENDIX 1

United Nations General Assembly Resolution 1496 (XV)

Provision of food surpluses to food-deficient peoples through the United Nations system [1]

THE GENERAL ASSEMBLY,

Considering that the peoples in many of the less developed countries suffer from serious shortages of food,

Noting with approval that the Food and Agriculture Organization of the United Nations in co-operation with the United Nations, appropriate specialized agencies, governments of Member States and non-governmental organizations, has launched a Freedom from Hunger Campaign designed as a concerted attack on the problem of providing adequate food for food-deficient peoples,

Recalling General Assembly resolutions 827 (IX) of 14 December 1954 and 1025 (XI) of 20 February 1957 and Economic and Social Council resolutions 621 (XXII) of 6 August 1956 and 685 (XXVI) of 18 July 1958 concerning international co-operation in the establishment of national food reserves,

Bearing in mind the existing opportunities for consultation and exchange of information provided by the Food and Agriculture Organization through its Consultative Subcommittee on Surplus Disposal,

Recognizing that the Principles of Surplus Disposal [2] and Guiding Lines [3] of the Food and Agriculture Organization are a valuable instrument for guidance to governments in transactions, programs, policies, and consultations relating to the disposal and utilization of agricultural surpluses,

Recognizing further that the ultimate solution to the problem of hunger lies in an effective acceleration of economic development allowing the underdeveloped countries to increase their food production and enabling them to purchase more food through normal channels of international trade,

Convinced of the impelling need to solve the problem of hunger and malnutrition among many peoples and of the role which the United Nations system can play in actions designed to help solve this critical problem,

Further convinced that assistance to food-deficient peoples will help raise productivity and thus contribute to the improvement of their standard of living,

1. *Endorses* the Freedom from Hunger Campaign launched by the Food and Agriculture Organization of the United Nations and urges all States Members of the United Nations and members of the specialized agencies to support this campaign in every appropriate way;

2. *Appeals* to States Members of the United Nations and members of the specialized agencies to take suitable measures to relieve the suffering of food-deficient people in other nations and assist them in their economic development and in their efforts towards a better life;

3. *Expresses the belief* that international assistance in the establishment of national food reserves in food-deficient countries is one effective transitional means of assisting accelerated economic development in the less developed countries;

4. *Invites* the Food and Agriculture Organization, after consulting governments of Member States, the Secretary-General and appropriate specialized agencies, to establish without delay procedures – in particular for consultation and the dissemination of information – by which, with the assistance of the United Nations system, the largest practicable quantities of surplus food may be made available on mutually agreeable terms as a transitional measure against hunger, such procedures to be compatible with desirable agricultural development as a contribution to economic development in the less developed countries and without prejudice to bilateral arrangements for this purpose and compatible with the principles of the Food and Agriculture Organization;

5. *Further invites* the Food and Agriculture Organization, in consultation with Governments of Member States, the Secretary-General, appropriate specialized agencies and other international bodies (such as the International Wheat Council, the Wheat Utilization Committee, etc.), to undertake a study of the feasibility and acceptability of additional arrangements, including multilateral arrangements under the auspices of the Food and Agricul-

ture Organization, having as their objective the mobilization of available surplus foodstuffs and their distribution in areas of greatest need, particularly in the economically less developed countries;

6. *Requests* the Director-General of the Food and Agriculture Organization to report on action taken to the Economic and Social Council at its thirty-second session;

7. *Requests* the Secretary-General, in consultation with the Director-General of the Food and Agriculture Organization and after such other consultations as he may deem necessary, to report to the Economic and Social Council at its thirty-second session on the role which the United Nations and the appropriate specialized agencies could play in order to facilitate the best possible use of food surpluses for the economic development of the less developed countries;

8. *Recommends* that the Secretary-General, in preparing, in consultation with the Director-General of the Food and Agriculture Organization, the provisional program for the joint session of the Commission on International Commodity Trade and the Committee on Commodity Problems of the Food and Agriculture Organization which will examine a report on the prospects of the production of, and demand for, primary commodities, include the question of the production of, and demand for, food in relation to the problem of hunger;

9. *Stresses* that any action taken or contemplated under the present resolution proceed in accordance with the Principles of Surplus Disposal and Guiding Lines of the Food and Agriculture Organization, and, specifically, with adequate safeguards and appropriate measures against the dumping of agricultural surpluses on the international markets and against adverse effects upon the economic and financial position of those countries which depend for their foreign exchange earnings primarily on the export of food commodities, and in the recognition that the avoidance of damage to normal trading in foodstuffs will best be assured by multilateral trading practices.

[1] At 908th Plenary Meeting, United Nations General Assembly, 27 October 1960.
[2] *Functions of a world food reserve – scope and limitations*, FAO Commodity Policy Studies, No. 10. FAO, Rome, 1956. Appendix III.
[3] *Ibid.*, para. 300.

APPENDIX 2

Report by the Expert Group
to the Director-General of FAO

February 1961

Dr. B. R. Sen
Director-General
Food and Agriculture Organization
of the United Nations
Rome, Italy

Dear Dr. Sen,

We have the honor to submit to you herewith our Report on an Expanded Program of Surplus Food Utilization, in accordance with the terms of reference communicated to us.

We wish to express to you personally and to your colleagues in FAO our warm appreciation of the assistance extended to us in our task. In particular, we should like to convey our thanks to our secretary, Mr. E.M. Ojala, and his staff.

Yours sincerely,

H.W. Singer
(Chairman)

M.R. Benedict   J. Figueres
V.K.R.V Rao   P.N. Rosenstein-Rodan

1. Introduction

The matters to which this Expert Group has been asked to give its attention were raised by the United Nations General Assembly in the latter part of 1960. On 27 October, the Assembly passed Resolution 1496 (XV) on the Provision of Food Surpluses to Food Deficient Peoples through the United Nations System.

The FAO Council in a Resolution of the same month took note with gratification of the United Nations Resolution. The Council authorized the Director-General of FAO to get studies and consultations under way in line with the mandate given to FAO, and in particular to arrange, if he considered this desirable, for a small "*ad hoc* group of high-level independent experts" to aid him in his task. Under this authorization and in this context the present Expert Group was constituted.

Our terms of reference are therefore derived from the General Assembly Resolution and the relevant Resolution of the FAO Council.

In addition, we have been guided by the statement made by the Director-General, Dr. B.R. Sen, at our first session. Dr. Sen summarized the main ideas in the UN Resolution as follows:

(a) The Freedom from Hunger Campaign, the essence of which is the increase of agricultural productivity, was basic to the Resolution.

(b) The expanded use of surplus foods for food-deficient areas should be seen as a transitional measure.

(c) The ultimate solution was the acceleration of economic progress in the underdeveloped countries.

(d) National food reserves in food-deficient countries could be an effective transitional means to assist their economic development.

(e) FAO was asked to do two things: to establish procedures, and to study the feasibility and acceptability of additional arrangements, including multilateral arrangements – the main emphasis being on the UN system, but without prejudice to bilateral arrangements.

Dr. Sen emphasized that the problem of surplus use was inseparable from problems of economic development, domestic agriculture and trade. He also said that the international climate for aiding underdeveloped countries was now more favorable than it had been in the past. Therefore, the experts and FAO could and should be bolder in their approach to the problem of use of surpluses than would have been possible earlier. While international aid to underdeveloped countries should be treated as a whole, the experts should specially concern themselves with food surpluses as an important part of that international aid.

We commenced our work at FAO Headquarters, Rome, on 23 January 1961 and concluded our report to the Director-General on 11 February 1961. We were unanimous in the expression of our views.

We were fully informed regarding the FAO Principles of Surplus Disposal and Guiding Lines, and all our recommendations are believed to be in accord with them.

2. Basic considerations

It is believed by FAO from the information available to it that over one half of the population of the world is either undernourished or malnourished. Often both these conditions occur together. In the light of this fact, and making allowance for the existence of stocks currently unused, the world food problem must be seen basically as one of deficiencies, not surpluses. As the United Nations Resolution has recognized, the basic cause is underdevelopment.

Poverty for many beside plenty for few used to be a general phenomenon, both national and international. For about one third of the world's people it is a memory, fading rapidly or gradually; but for the other two thirds it is still a grim reality. Underdeveloped countries within the world economy are the counterpart of underprivileged low-income classes within a national economy. With the growth of wealth within the developed countries, inequalities of income between different classes have diminished. Equality of opportunity, full employment and a minimum of subsistence are an accepted part of their social philosophy. Nothing similar obtains as yet within the international community. With the growth of wealth in the world, inequalities of income between nations have not diminished – equality of opportunity, full employment and a minimum of subsistence are still an ideal rather than a reality. The task of our generation is to apply the principles of social progress accepted within the rich countries to the world as a whole. Only if this is done can we talk of an international community.

The resources to implement such a program are available. A transfer of two thirds to three quarters of one percent of the gross national product of the developed countries over the next five years, and probably less for another decade would, in our opinion, provide sufficient means for helping people in the underdeveloped countries to help themselves. It would represent a very much smaller international redistribution of income than the national redistribution of income achieved by progressive taxation within most of the developed countries, when they were less rich than they are today. To think that the developed world cannot spare three quarters of one cent from each dollar of its income for an international program of economic aid is to show failure of imagination and failure of will.

Surplus food represents an important part – from one sixth to one quarter – of the external resources required for economic development in the underdeveloped countries. Far from being a waste it can be a blessing, if it is matched by other resources and used as an essential part of a coherent program of aid.

In fact, food products form an important part of capital in its original sense of a subsistence fund. Additionally employed workers have to be fed during the construction period, i.e., before the fruits of investment can supply their needs or enable them to buy their subsistence. Without such a fund additional investment would be impossible. Food surpluses used for economic development will enable hungry people to produce either their own food or other products to buy food. Freedom from hunger can ultimately be achieved only by freedom from poverty.

We have not considered that it was within our terms of reference to examine why surpluses of foods developed. The fact is that stocks exist above normal requirements. It is possible to say that around 12,500 million dollars' worth of agricultural commodities of known types is now available or will become available for use outside normal market channels over the next five years. It also appears that countries owning stocks are willing to use them to promote economic development in underdeveloped countries, through bilateral arrangements or through the United Nations system where appropriate. We have therefore concentrated our attention on analyzing different types of possible uses of the surplus foods, in the context of the needs and opportunities for expanded economic and social development in the underdeveloped parts of the world during the next five years. The principles that should guide such an operation of surplus food utilization have also been examined, and proposals are made regarding the role of the international agencies.

It is realized that surplus food utilization programs may need to be continued for longer than five years. However, we have not tried to look in detail further ahead than this, because it is not possible to foresee at this stage how much and what kinds of foods might be available for special uses, nor to what extent the needs of developing countries for outside aid may have changed. Moreover, much will depend upon the type of multilateral functions that are developed in this field during the next five years, how they are carried out and the extent to which they prove acceptable to potential supplying and recipient countries. By 1965, or earlier, if would be possible and no doubt desirable to review the situation with regard to a further period, and we trust that the continuing need for international development aid would be recognized and met.

It must be emphasized that surplus food utilization programs are essentially transitional in relation to any individual recipient country. This follows from the fact stressed in the United Nations Resolution and in the Director-General's statement to us, that the long-run solution to the food problem is economic development. Programs for agricultural development must be featured strongly in the economic development plans of the countries seeking surplus foods. The receipt of foodgrain aid should not be allowed to divert recipient countries from their long-term task of making the fullest use of their own agricultural resources, and raising the productivity and incomes of their farm producers. For this task, not only surplus foods are needed – other essential requirements are fertilizers, fertilizer manufacturing plants, agricultural machinery and equipment and other production requisites.

It would be incongruous in a world concerned about the utilization of the surpluses of richer countries to overlook the surplus problems of poorer nations. In recent years a case in point was rice, but at the present moment the worst affected commodities are coffee and cocoa. Underdeveloped countries cannot afford to carry surpluses of those export products on which they depend for their livelihood. Given the weak bargaining power of such countries, surpluses in their possession depress the market to a serious extent, limiting economic development and sometimes causing actual reduction in standard of living. It seems fair for the developed countries which can afford to give aid to help the poorer countries in carrying the burden of surpluses. The absorption of such surpluses by the stronger economies as a transitory or emergency measure would help in creating a healthier situation in the markets. The price of the commodities for such transfers could be very low, since the selling countries would be the beneficiaries of such a transaction. The increase in incomes of the producing countries could be several times the amounts invested by the buying countries in the purchase of surpluses. The value of such surpluses could be credited to outstanding debts.

Concurrently with the application of such emergency measures, the producing countries should undertake vigorous plans to reduce future production of commodities like coffee, for which it will probably be difficult to expand consumption to the level of the amounts now being produced. Furthermore, the Group notes that coffee has its principal markets in the developed countries, and that some of these countries are restricting consumption by high tariffs and excise duties. Since these developed nations are likely to increase their contribution to international aid, their most direct measure of help to the coffee-producing countries would be to forego part of the fiscal revenues which are now restricting consumption.

3. Broad estimates of availability and possible utilization of surplus foods over a five-year period

AVAILABILITY

On the basis of assumptions indicated in Appendix 3 it is estimated that United States surplus foods alone to the values indicated in the following table are or could become available for utilization annually over a five-year period.

The total availability over five years may be estimated at around $12,500 million.

Actual food disposals overseas to all countries (not only underdeveloped countries) in 1959/60 under current United States special programs amounted to approximately $1,500 million at C.C.C. cost (excluding ocean transportation).

Product	Quantity	Value at current [1] C.C.C. cost
	million m. tons	*U.S. $ million*
Wheat and wheat flour	15.35	1,380
Coarse grains	11.0	710
Rice (milled)	0.4	60
Dairy products:		
skim powder	0.3 ⎫	200
butter and cheese	0.1 ⎭	
Fats and oils, oilseeds		200
Total		2,550

[1] World market prices are currently about 70 percent of Commodity Credit Corporation (C.C.C.) cost.

UTILIZATION

The needs and possibilities for utilizing surplus foods in underdeveloped countries, in the framework of national programs for accelerated economic and social development, are foreseen as shown in the following table over a five-year period.

It will be evident that the utilization in underdeveloped countries of surplus foods for programs of the above order, which represents about 175 percent of the 1959/60 rate of United States surplus food disposals to all countries, would not exceed the total supplies of United States surplus foods which are available or considered likely to become available during a five-year period. The figures refer to estimated possibilities of total utilization, whether under bilateral agreements as at present or partly under multilateral arrangements such as those recommended in this report.

A more detailed discussion of the main types of utilization envisaged is presented in the following sections of the report.

Type of use	Assumed United States C.C.C. cost	
	Per year	Total - 5 years
	.... *million* $	
Economic development	1,200 - 1,300	6,000 - 6,500
Establishment of national food reserves	200	1,000
Establishment and replenishment of international emergency food reserves	150	750
Total - Economic programs	1,550 - 1,650	7,750 - 8,250
Social development		
Land reform	50 - 100	250 - 500
Supplementary meals:		
school children	500	2,500
higher students and trainees	100 - 200	500 - 1,000
Relief and welfare	200	1,000
Grand total	2,400 - 2,650	12,000 - 13,250

4. Use in promoting economic development

Economic development takes time and requires a tremendous effort of will and action by the countries themselves. This effort can be decisively strengthened and the time to reach the goal drastically shortened, by international aid to underdeveloped countries. The purpose of aid is to accelerate those countries' economic development up to a point where a satisfactory rate of growth can be achieved on a self-sustaining basis. Aid is needed for a transition period of one to two decades. Some countries can achieve the goal in the next decade; most of them in the next 15 years. Some few may require 20 years or more. If action which is well within our means is taken, freedom from poverty can be achieved for most of the world in one generation's time.

GENERAL PRINCIPLES

The general aim of aid (loans, grants, and technical assistance) is to provide in each underdeveloped country a positive incentive for maximum national effort to increase its rate of growth. Ideally, aid should be allocated where it will have the maximum catalytic effect of mobilizing additional national effort or preventing a fall in national effort. The primary criterion is thus to maximize additional effort, not to maximize income per dollar of aid.

Aid should be offered wherever there is reasonable assurance that the country's national effort is or will be adequate, and that capital will be effectively used. A positive incentive for increased national effort will be present only if it is believed that all requests which meet functional criteria of productivity will be granted. It would be highly desirable therefore that appropriations for aid should be higher (say by one third) than prospective disbursements. Knowledge that capital will be available over a decade or more up to the limits of the capacity to absorb it, will act in many cases as an incentive to greater effort on the part of the underdeveloped countries. Assurance of continuity of aid is as important as the amount of aid.

The main function of foreign capital inflow is to increase the rate of domestic capital formation up to a level (e.g., 12 percent) sufficient to yield an increase in income of 2 percent per head per year, which could then be maintained without further aid. Additional resources and know-how provided by foreign capital inflow produce an additional product. The proportion that can be saved out of this additional product can be very much higher than average savings at the pre-existing income level. While the *average* rate of savings is, for instance, 7 percent in Asia, the *marginal* rate of savings can be stepped up to 20 percent.

ABSORPTIVE CAPACITY

A marginal rate of savings which is much higher than the average rate is the main lever of a development program, and should be the principal condition of aid to underdeveloped countries. The extent to which increased investment with a high marginal rate of savings can be realized depends on the country's technical absorptive capacity. The capacity to absorb capital is more limited on a low level of development, where a high proportion of technical assistance must precede a large capital inflow. With a rising level of development the marginal rate of savings will increase.

While the capacity to absorb capital is a limiting factor, it can, within a few years, be stepped up in many underdeveloped countries by 20 to 30 percent above the presently realized level of investment. There are, however, narrow limits to the pace and extent at which a country's absorptive capacity can be expanded. Education in the long run and revolution of habits in the short run may widen the scope. But it is not true to say that absorptive capacity – in the short run of five to ten years at any rate – entirely depends on the amount to effort one is willing to put into massive technical assistance.

Technical absorptive capacity should determine the amount of aid, while the capacity to repay should largely determine the method of financing it. Where the capacity to repay in low-income, underdeveloped countries is below their absorptive capacity, a proportion of aid will have to be given in grants or soft loans. In principle, it should not make any difference which particular portions of aid are allocated in grant or soft loan form. All that matters is that the proportion of grants be decided according to the total economic situation of the country, not according to the "bankable" or "not bankable" nature of the individual projects which comprise the development program. The narrower criterion of whether a single project can repay from its own revenue is, at best, irrelevant and at worst may be seriously misleading. In those cases in which a part of aid will be in the form of food surpluses, and in which a proportion of aid equal to or higher than that part which is in food surpluses has on general considerations to be given in grant or soft loan form, it will be appropriate to contribute surplus food on a grant or soft loan basis.

TERMINOLOGY: WHAT IS "AID"?

"Foreign capital inflow" and "aid" are not synonymous terms. We feel that aid should refer only to those parts of capital inflow which normal market incentives do not provide. It consists of:

(a) Long-term loans repayable in foreign currency. "Long-term" conventionally means loans of more than 10 years' maturity (preferably, however, 20 years or more).

(b) Grants and "soft" loans (very long-term loans with a long grace period and possibly also a low rate of interest), including loans repayable in local currency.

(c) Grants or sales of surplus products for local currency payments (Public Law 480 in the United States) or on some other "soft" loan basis. Not only capital (equipment) goods, but also consumption goods can constitute capital. In fact, as already observed, agricultural products can and must form an important part of capital in its original sense of a subsistence fund. If sufficient foodstuffs could not be supplied in a country to meet the increased demand from the additionally employed workers on construction or other investments, then either more resources (circulating capital) would have to be spent for imports, or the amount of additional investment would have to be reduced. Surplus food is a most important part of capital aid – and economic development is the most important and largest part of a productive use of surplus foods. It cannot be said in reality, however, that the whole of imported surplus food products will be used for additional investment. A good economic development policy can see to it that a major part is used for raising investment, but a part will merely bolster domestic consumption. This latter part incidentally satisfies demand for consumption due to the multiplier effects of investments and is a valuable antidote to inflation. A withdrawal of surplus food would in practice lead to a reduction in both consumption and investment. We assume that *two thirds* of surplus products offered to underdeveloped countries may be considered as investment aid, while one third goes into increased consumption.[1] Even on that basis between one fifth and one quarter of total aid to underdeveloped countries can be rendered in this form. In the United States two thirds of Public Law 480 sales may form up to one third of the United States aid to underdeveloped countries. We assume an annual surplus products investment aid figure of $700 to $800 million, which implies total per year Public Law 480 sales of $1,200 million (at C.C.C. cost).

(*d*) Technical and preinvestment assistance generally are undoubtedly a most important part of aid to underdeveloped countries; they must form part – and an increasing part – of appropriations for aid; but since they are not capital in the strict terminological sense, they are not counted as foreign capital inflow.

Since economic aid is defined as that part of capital inflow which normal market incentives do not provide, neither short- or medium-term loans, nor private foreign investment are counted as aid. They are trade, not aid. Differences in definition may account for differences in estimates of the present amount of aid to underdeveloped countries.

AMOUNT OF AID REQUIRED

On the basis of the above-mentioned general principles the amount of aid required for all underdeveloped countries, other than Mainland China, North Korea, North Viet-Nam and Albania, has been roughly estimated at $4,300 million per year over the next ten years, to which $400 million per year for technical assistance and $300 million for an emergency fund should be added. Total economic aid expenditure would thus amount to $5,000 million per year. This would represent an increase of 60 percent over and above the present level of aid. Since a margin of error of at least plus or minus 25 percent is inherent in these estimates, the aid required should be asumed at $5,000 to $6,000 million per year.[2]

On slightly different assumptions – namely, a wider definition of aid including also some medium-term loans, a slightly higher capital output ratio of 3:1 instead of 2.8:1, and excluding Yugoslavia, Greece, Spain and Portugal, which are included in the previous calculation – Mr. Paul Hoffman,

288

Managing Director of the United Nations Special Fund, estimates that a doubling of the present flow of aid up to a level of $7,000 million per year is required.[3]

SURPLUS FOODS AS PART OF AID

Surplus foods are assumed to constitute from one sixth ($700 million per year) to one fifth ($850 million) of the total capital aid of $4,300 million per year. This takes account of the two thirds of surplus food products which directly increase investment. The other third, which is in joint supply, bolsters consumption and amounts to an additional $350 to $430 million per year, so that the total amount of surplus products imported by underdeveloped countries would amount to $1,050 to $1,300 million (at C.C.C. cost).

The use of food for additional investment can only be determined within the framework of the total development program of a country. The composition of the development program (sector allocation) should notably take account of the existence of disguised (and seasonal) unemployment and availability of surplus foods. Projects which would cover costs at shadow prices[4] of labor and food should be included in the development program.[5] Shadow prices of food may be assumed at one quarter to one third of the United States C.C.C. cost, or one third to one half of the world market price. This may notably increase employment at low wages in rural capital formation projects like terracing, bunding, fencing, digging, etc., as well as road building, which use no (or very little) capital. If organizational difficulties are solved, surplus food requirements in overpopulated countries may rise by 10 to 20 percent. On this assumption $1,300 million per year (at C.C.C. cost), rather than $1,050 million per year, represents perhaps a reasonable estimate of the surplus food requirements for economic development.

SURPLUS PRODUCTS IN THE DEVELOPMENT PROGRAM

To estimate what part surplus products can form of total investment and of total aid is only possible within the framework of a country's development program. The various projects comprising a development program are interrelated and reinforce each other. This balance depends on whether complementary activities have been planned on the required scale. It is therefore practically impossible to judge the soundness of any particular project without knowledge of the whole program of which it is a part. A program approach, not a project approach, must determine the criteria of productive use of aid capital. Foreign aid capital increases the range of the program as a whole. Since this may require a reshuffle and changes in several projects, a single loan cannot with any exactness be said to have been given to one specific project only – it should be considered as a contribution to the whole program.

The incorporation of food surpluses in economic development programs, where they can be seen in conjunction with other available resources, is clearly the most desirable way of programing their use. However, many underdeveloped countries do not have a full development program as yet, and are not likely to be in a position to develop one at short notice. In such cases it is nevertheless possible to go ahead with projects which would obviously have high priority in any program.

Furthermore, previous economic policy or development programs may not have fully taken into account additional availabilities of surplus food. A widening of the development program will then be appropriate, by adding additional "food-intensive" and "labor-intensive" projects which require a minimum of other matching resources, have a low import content and have, if possible, a short gestation period. Construction and improvement of rural roads, terracing, fencing, and bunding would be illustrations of such types of additional projects. The over-all development program may be readjusted to allow for the small additional matching resources for such projects. Apart from surplus food, the inflationary effects of such additional projects may be mitigated by other measures, such as introducing a third shift in textile industries. The degree of inflation may thus be minimized, while additional employment, e.g., through community development programs, may yield both human and economic gains. In many underdeveloped countries, especially in Africa, which are in transition from a subsistence to a money economy, the availability of additional surplus foods may facilitate a division of labor and accelerate the process of monetization.

Economic growth itself increases the demand for agricultural products. For technical, psychological and institutional reasons it is hardly ever possible to speed up domestic agricultural production to the same extent to which it is possible to proceed with social overhead and industrial activities. Most development programs foresee, and see to it, that agriculture should catch up later. The interval must be filled by additional food supplies, if possible economic growth is not be to stifled. Obviously, only specific country studies will show more precisely the proportion of additional foodstuffs required for that purpose. On the basis of several underdeveloped countries' development programs, it appears that from one sixth to one fifth of total aid should, on the average of all underdeveloped countries (not for every one of them), consist of food products.

SAFEGUARDING EXISTING DEVELOPMENT PROGRAMS

By the same token that surplus food can serve to enlarge development programs of underdeveloped countries, it can also serve to prevent development programs from being cut down or dislocated, e.g., when external buying power is suddenly reduced as a result of an unforessen sharp decline in the world market price of a country's main export product. Since a United Nations Committee of Experts on Compensatory Financing was sitting at the same time as our Group, we have refrained from considering this matter in any detail. But if surplus food can be useful in enlarging current programs, it would be incongruous to deny that it might also conceivably be a part of international action designed to safeguard existing programs.

While we recognize that such action may in some cases be in conflict with the principle of "additionality," we feel that help of this kind is so important to economic growth in some underdeveloped countries that it may be considered to come within the provision foreseen in paragraph 5 of the FAO Principles of Surplus Disposal.[6]

SHARING OF AID

General principles of how the burden of international aid should be divided between developed countries have not yet been agreed upon. The social philosophy of our generation provides nonetheless some clear indications.

(a) All developed countries – say those with income per head above $600 per year – should contribute to aid a proportion of the gross national product – perhaps one half to three quarters of one percent per year. Preferably their contributions, which should add up to the total aid required,[7] should be computed by applying the United States income tax progression to the number of families of each developed country, counting a family's income as four times the country's income per head. A "real" gross national product indicating the purchasing power of the gross national product compared with United States prices may be computed instead of the nominal one.

Neither short- nor medium-term loans nor private foreign investment should be included in aid. Long-term loans of the International Bank are certainly aid, but they are not included in the computation of each country's contribution.

Appropriations for aid should, if possible, be at least one third higher than the amount which will probably be disbursed, for reasons mentioned above. In our calculation only prospective disbursements, not the desirable appropriations, are counted.

(b) All long-term loans and grants should, in principle, be untied.

(c) Up to one third of each country's contribution to aid can be tied, however, to the grant or sale of surplus production for local currency

repayments. Only two thirds of each country's total surplus product grants or sales are counted as capital aid.

(d) During a year of balance of payments difficulties, a contributing country may be given the right to invoke a special clause, analogous to the General Agreement on Tariffs and Trade (GATT) provisions tying her loans and grants – for other than surplus product sales – during that year.

On such principles the United States share would amount to around 64.4 percent of total aid, that of Western Europe to 30 percent, of Canada 3.7 percent, of Oceania 1.9 percent. If the U.S.S.R. were to participate in this program its share, on the same principles, would amount to 9 percent. The shares of the other countries would then be reduced accordingly.

5. National food reserves and international emergency food reserve

NATIONAL FOOD RESERVES

Conditions vary greatly as among the underdeveloped countries. A uniform plan of operation is therefore neither desirable nor possible. But in all of them there are certain basic aims that should govern food reserve policy. In broad terms, these may be stated as follows.

(a) To even out short-term fluctuations in supply and price, which are detrimental to both producers and consumers.

(b) To provide incentives to producers that will cause them to strive vigorously and continuously for increased production. One of the measures that is particularly important is the establishment of floor prices for two or more years in advance, so that producers will not hold back on production for fear of disastrous price declines.

(c) To protect consumers against shortages of supply and the sharp increases in cost of living which result from them. Changes of that kind not only cause hardship to consumers, but are a serious impediment to steady progress in economic development. They also give rise to speculative activities that tend to accentuate the price fluctuations in both directions.

Objectives *(b)* and *(c)* may at times be somewhat in conflict. In such cases, it is important not to sacrifice incentives to producers for full production. The price to consumers should, of course, be as low as possible, consistent with a sound production program for increasing domestic output.

Well-managed food reserves maintained within or in close proximity to the underdeveloped country can be very helpful in achieving the objectives outlined above. They will contribute to stability, promote confidence, discourage speculation, and help in making the best use of surpluses that may arise in years when production is above normal. The importance of mechanisms for stabilizing supplies and prices is, of course, much greater in those countries which are subject to extreme variations in output than in those where production is more stable.

Most of the countries that are subject to extreme variations in output are aware of the advantages that could result from the maintenance of food reserves, and would like to build up stabilizing stocks. They find this difficult because of the large expense involved and the fact that investments in such stocks lock up capital that is much needed in their development programs. On the other hand, the surplus-producing countries, particularly the United States and Canada, have large amounts of capital locked up in surplus stocks that are neither well located nor efficient as contributors to worldwide food stabilization activities. Once established, food reserves can be maintained in the countries desiring them at manageable cost, particularly as they can be part of a multiple purpose operation. The conditions now existing in the world food economy are especially favorable for the building up of such reserves, wherever adequate plans for using them have been developed or, where that is not the case, as soon as suitable plans can be devised. Such reserves must, of course, consist of nonperishable products that can be stored and rotated at minimum expense.

For the carrying out of such a program most countries will need some type of stock-managing organization, though the particular form of such an agency may vary from country to country, depending on existing institutional arrangements and the preferences of the country concerned. The United States Commodity Credit Corporation, which has been in continuous operation since 1933, carried on many of the types of activity here envisioned and may warrant study as a type of multi-purpose organization which, with modifications, could provide the services needed.

Despite certain defects of organization and flexibility, the Commodity Credit Corporation has performed many useful services under a great variety of conditions, including those of extreme depression, war, and high-level economic activity. It has been the means of absorbing heavy oversupplies resulting from sharp increases in production, as with the cotton crop of 1937; of releasing needed supplies in time of shortage, as in the case of corn in 1934 and of wheat and corn in the second world war. In addition, it has been the mechanism for distributing part of the foods used in school lunches, and in institutional and other special group food programs. It has also acted as an agency for acquiring and forwarding supplies to other nations in wartime and for block purchases of sugar.

Principal criticisms of the Commodity Credit Corporation have centered around the fact that its holdings have increased to undesirable size (partly as a result of overrigid policies prescribed by the United States Congress) and that it lacks the autonomy and flexibility needed for optimum functioning as a stabilizing agency. Both of these defects could be avoided in a food-deficit country by appropriate planning and legislation. A principal problem there would be to avoid undue depletion of rotating stocks, rather than to prevent accumulation of excess stocks. This difficulty could be overcome by additional planned transfers from surplus areas in prolonged periods of less than normal production.

The activities mentioned above, and others, could be very helpful in a number of the food-deficit countries as a means of bringing about more orderly management of the food supply schemes. For maximum usefulness, such an agency should be managed by highly qualified people with broad and flexible powers.

With these considerations in mind, it is suggested, as part of the expanded program of surplus food use here recommended, both for economic and social development and for relief, that the food-deficit countries be encouraged to establish appropriate organizations for creating and maintaining food reserves, and that such amounts of storable foodstuffs as may be needed in initiating such reserves be supplied out of existing surplus stocks on a grant-in-aid basis. This would call for very little, if any, new expense to the supplying countries since the capital represented by these stocks is already tied up and inactive. The reduction in storage costs would, in any case, go a long way toward covering the transportation costs incurred.

Such a program does imply initial costs to the receiving country for construction of a suitable network of storage and handling facilities, and a continuing cost for management and rotation of stocks. Many of the underdeveloped countries are not at present in a position to afford the heavy outlay required for the creation of adequate storage facilities. To the extent that underemployed local resources can be used for this purpose no serious problem is involved, but such additional outside resources as are required must be provided on a loan or grant basis.

The amounts of aid needed for establishing food reserves have not been included in the economic development chapter. The burden of this aid should be shared on similar principles to those mentioned there. The developed countries who do not supply surplus food should provide the other outlays (for storage facilities, etc.) necessary for establishing food reserves.

Assuming acceptance and implementation of this proposal, or something similar, the functions of the stock-managing organization or national food reserve agency, would be as follows.

(a) To acquire, by way of an international food reserve program or bilaterally, a stock of storable foods adequate to meet shortages resulting from drought, flood or other disaster, and to be in a position to release such stocks in sufficient quantity in time of need to maintain an approximately normal flow of food to consumers at about normal prices.

Crops of approximately normal size would move by way of existing commercial channels without intervention by the food reserve agency. Parts of very large crops would be absorbed by it with a view to preventing any large decline in prices to producers. Deficits in outturn would be offset by release of stocks held by the agency into commercial channels, in such a way as to prevent speculation and hoarding or any significant amount of increase in cost to consumers. If significant upward or downward trends in food production or consumption should develop, these would be taken into account and the flows into and out of stocks adjusted accordingly. Sizable or continuing changes in the value of money would also need to be taken into account.[8]

There are precedents for these procedures, not only in the activities of the United States Commodity Credit Corporation and in the program of the British Ministry of Food in the second world war, but also in some of the underdeveloped countries. In general, the commercial processing and distributing industries seem to have been able to adjust to such stabilizing actions without serious difficulty.

(b) To serve as a channel for distribution of such quantities of surplus foods as may be made available internationally, or otherwise, for meeting temporary relief needs, improving diets, or carrying out programs of economic and social betterment.

(c) A number of other functions could be assigned to such an agency if that is considered desirable and if funds are available. For example, it could be used as a mechanism for providing incentives to producers of commodities for which special expansion programs are planned (by buying at one price and reselling to the trade at a lower price). Such an agency can also be used as a form of crop insurance for producers if so desired. This would imply absorption of excess production at a price somewhat below normal in years of heavy production (but not so as to return a smaller income for a large crop than for a small one), and resale for consumption at about normal prices. Profits arising from these transactions could be used in supplementing incomes of producers in years of low production or crop failure. The compensating action should not, of course, be so complete as to destroy incentives for producing as large an output as can be achieved.

The plan here suggested contemplates that, in times of normal domestic production, ordinary imports would move through regular commercial channels, despite the fact that the national food reserve agency would serve as a cushioning device both against excessively low prices or incomes to producers and excessively high prices to consumers. Some moderate variations in price could, of course, be tolerated without compromising the basic objectives of the scheme. The agency would require wise and skilful handling, and financing on a wider or narrower basis, depending upon the resources made available to it. If a country chooses to go far in this direction, the capital fund required will be rather large. Specific details of operation should not be written into law, but should be left to carefully selected and very able administrators having rather wide discretion as to the measures to be taken in any specific situation, so long as these are in keeping with the basic objectives which should, of course, be prescribed by law.

It is here proposed that surplus storable foods be made available by the surplus-producing countries for the initial stocks of such food reserve agencies in the underdeveloped countries, to the extent that the latter can equip themselves with appropriate facilities and institutional arrangements, and wish to take advantage of the opportunity thus provided. For any given country this would be a one-shot operation, though that need not preclude later contributions by way of the same mechanism (to offset prolonged periods of subnormal production or for programs of economic and social betterment), provided the surplus-producing countries are willing to make supplies available.

As to inputs required for the initial phase of creating food reserves, quantitative estimates are difficult because of uncertainty as to how many countries may wish to take advantage of such an opportunity if it is provided and how fast plans and facilities can be developed. A very tentative estimate is that over the next five years an average contribution of roughly $200 million per year at C.C.C. cost would be sufficient to implement the program. This, however, would not be uniform from year to year. It undoubtedly would be much smaller in the earlier years, with the number of participating countries and the size of operations increasing as the program matures.

INTERNATIONAL EMERGENCY FOOD RESERVE

The quantitative estimate given above related only to amounts needed in creating basic food reserves. The same mechanism could and probably should be used in handling relief grants made to offset famines and other physical disasters. Since these obviously would draw down reserves, probably on a scale larger than could be offset by normal types of acquisition, relief grants, to the extent that they are made available, could be used to rebuild stocks depleted as a result of such emergencies. Such grants have been made rather freely in the past, and have been of the order of $100 to $150 million per year on the part of the United States.

It is suggested that an item of some $150 million per year over the next five years be included in estimates of the amounts needed in implementing the surplus food utilization program as a whole.

6. Use in promoting social development

The preceding sections relate primarily to economic programs. These, according to our estimates could, if vigorously implemented, make use of $1,550 million to $1,650 million annually (at C.C.C. cost) in surplus United States foodstuffs, over a five-year period, following initiation of an expanded program. This is in terms of estimated average annual usage. In nearly all cases, there will be time lags because of the need for developing plans and institutional arrangements, carrying out negotiations, etc. Hence, the amounts used in the early years of an expanded program would certainly be smaller than in later years and smaller than the average annual amounts here proposed.

Use for the above purpose would account for a total of $7,750 to $8,250 million of the $12,500 to $13,500 million supply estimated to be firmly available over a five-year period under conservative estimates. This means that sizable additional amounts could be committed for more broadly conceived programs of human betterment here designated as social programs. Since the current concessional sales by the United States do not ease the burden on the United States Treasury,[9] the channeling of a sizable portion of these additional amounts into constructive uses would not involve a further drain on the United States Treasury, except for costs of transportation. It might in fact reduce the net burden by lessening the very considerable outlay now being made for storage.

The channeling of surpluses into such uses is not detrimental to local production schemes, since it represents additional consumption, and the effects of added and improved nutrition can be striking.

It is suggested, therefore, that vigorous efforts be made with a view to putting these stocks into use in a series of social development programs, i.e., land reform, and supplementary meals for school children, higher students and trainees, and that surplus food countries be urged to make stocks available to the extent that they can be used effectively in that way. Among the steps contemplated are a greatly expanded use of such foods in school meals for children and young adults in low-diet countries throughout the world, and in special aid to the aged and other destitute groups wherever practical programs for such aid can be devised. While the enormous gap in dietary levels between the people of the poorer countries and those of the wealthier countries could not be bridged even by the very large stocks now in hand or in prospect, it is practically certain that current and prospective surpluses are adequate to carry out most if not all of the projects of this kind that the poorer countries will be able to get into operation over the next five years.

In launching schemes of this kind, the plans should be very carefully worked out with a view to *(a)* moving gradually toward a situation in which the underdeveloped countries will be able to take over this function themselves;

(b) avoiding action that will depress prices to domestic producers or lessen incentives for maximum food production within the countries concerned.

With respect to *(a)*, if a program of improved feeding should have to be abandoned after being established and built up, the longer-term situation might be worse than if it had not been launched. We propose that definite commitments be made for a five-year period, for which stocks are clearly available. We have reason to think, moreover, that they will be available for a longer period. We suggest that the position be reappraised at the end of five years, but with full expectation that, if schemes are functioning well, the contributing nations will not be found wanting in their willingness to continue aid to the extent of their abilities. That attitude will unquestionably be strengthened materially if in the meantime there is clear evidence that the countries aided are making progress in the development of their own programs looking to the above ends. A program which contemplates indefinitely the continuance of outside aid on a gift basis is not, we believe, in accord with the desires of underdeveloped countries or in their best interest. Nevertheless, there is every reason for optimism as to the feasibility of continuing such aid, possibly on a smaller scale, for a period considerably longer than the next five years.

LAND REFORM

The use of surplus foods to facilitate land reform, in those countries that need it and want it, may be considered equally as an aid to economic development and to social development.

In many underdeveloped countries land reform is a precondition for a rise in agricultural productivity, for the application of incentives, and generally for economic development. However, some underdeveloped countries are deterred from introducing measures which they really want and need, partly for fear of the temporary risks involved in any disturbance of the *status quo,* and partly because of the short-term adverse effects which land reform may entail.

Particularly where reform means the break-up of large estates and the distribution of land to small tenants or agricultural laborers, the immediate effect, for two or three years, may well be a reduction rather than an increase in production, until agricultural organization, and the supply of the required tools and other instruments of production have adjusted themselves to the new situation. Even more likely, there may be a transitional period, lasting perhaps for several years, during which an increase in production may be offset by an even larger increase in consumption by the farm families themselves, so that deliveries to the towns – which are the "food capital" of industrialization – are actually reduced.

The anticipated fear of such temporary difficulties may prevent otherwise desirable reforms from being introduced. Moreover, the actual experience of such difficulties may wrongly discredit sound reform, and may cause inflation, with permanently harmful effects.

For these reasons, we recommend that over a five-year period, surplus food to the extent of $250 to $500 million be set aside to help in the launching of justified land reforms.

This sum is small in relation to total surpluses but its impact on economic and social development could be great. Moreover, there is no danger that the use of surplus food in this direction could be harmful to the farmers of the receiving country – quite the contrary, it permits the introduction of an important reform, for their own benefit.

It seems to us desirable that such activity should be under international administration. We recommend, therefore, that FAO be given control, by irrevocable options on the part of the surplus-giving countries, over supplies up to a specified upper limit of, say, $500 million, to be used over a five-year period for the support and encouragement of approved and desirable land reform programs.

No new organization seems necessary for this purpose. FAO should be in the best position to certify that the difficulties encountered are the transitional results of a land reform, or that the anticipation of such difficulties is justified, and in turn justifies the earmarking of surplus food.

SUPPLEMENTARY MEALS

School children

Economists and other competent observers of conditions in underdeveloped countries are coming more and more to agree that the formation of "human capital" is as basic, as necessary, and as productive as physical capital formation. Feeding the young is investment; feeding the old is relief. Moreover, the improved feeding of school children and other young people undergoing education and training should appeal strongly to the generosity and consciences of the more developed countries – not only those having surplus food, but also those able to provide monetary aid in supplementing the very limited diets that can be provided by way of surplus foods alone. The better feeding of school children and of young people in the higher educational institutions is a move in the direction of "equality of opportunity" which is a basic concept in fostering self-help toward economic development. Foods so used are not likely to be wasted and such uses satisfy the criterion of additionality.

To feed all children between the ages of 5 and 14 in the underdeveloped countries of Africa, Asia and Latin America, a single meal per day of even as little as 60 grams of wheat or its equivalent and 25 grams of dried skim milk would cost around $7,000 million per year – $2,500 million for food-stuffs and $4,500 million for transport and distribution – or half as much if the program were restricted to those actually in school. The availability of meals would encourage school attendance. It seems clear that the amounts of cereals available are fully adequate to supply as many programs as the underdeveloped countries are likely to be able to get into practical opera-tion over the next five years.

The most serious lack is in supplemental protein foods, particularly dried milk. There are no large stocks of dried milk on hand nor are they likely to arise as a result of current developments in the advanced coun-tries. This lack of balance is likely to be one of the important limiting fac-tors in the implementation of a greatly expanded program of school meals. There are three possible approaches to the easing of this problem.

(a) Increased production of protein supplements, particularly milk, should be strongly stressed in the production plans of the underdeveloped countries, wherever conditions are such that this type of production is practically feasible. This is in line with the best long-term interests of these countries and will contribute to best use of the kinds of surplus foods that can readily be made available to them. Furthermore, dairy products and other needed supplements must for the most part be pro-duced locally. They are less transportable and storable than are the cereals which are now in long supply. [10]

(b) It is suggested that FAO be authorized to explore with the surplus-pro-ducing countries the possibility and practicability of modifying their domestic agricultural programs in such a way as to provide more pro-tein supplements, particularly dried milk, without material increase in the over-all costs of the programs. For some countries, particularly the United States, a shift in that direction, if feasible, would apparently be desirable domestically in some areas. It is conceivable also that sev-eral of the specialized dairy countries could modify their production programs in such a way as to make more dried milk available.

(c) The approach contemplated calls for a concerted attack on the problem of hunger and poor diets by all of the countries, both advanced and underdeveloped, each contributing in the ways best suited to its abil-ities. This implies cash grants by some of the wealthier countries that do not have agricultural surpluses. Such grants, if available, could be of crucial importance in rounding out and making effective and accept-able the kind of school feeding program here proposed.

In a number of underdeveloped countries there may be a need for additional help in the planning and actual operation of school meal programs. This is a field in which international agencies such as the United Nations Children's Fund (UNICEF) and many voluntary societies have a great deal of experience. Young people in developed countries who wish to make a personal contribution to world betterment might well find an opportunity to be of service through working for a period with one or other of these organizations. We cannot think of a better employment of volunteer workers than in the processing and distribution of surplus food made available to children in underdeveloped countries through experienced organizations, where this arrangement is acceptable to an underdeveloped country concerned. Not least in importance is the possibility of developing improved food habits on the part of the coming generations of citizens in these countries.

Higher students and trainees

In the above comments, emphasis has been primarily on the 5- to 14-year age group. The possibility of extending some aid of this kind to the poorer students at the secondary and college levels should be explored. This is a very important foundation group in economic development. In some countries a major stumbling block in initiating and carrying out needed programs of development is a lack of trained personnel. Aid in overcoming that shortage is obviously a long-term matter, but it may well be one of the most fruitful investments that can be made. Where inability to finance their subsistence while in training is a limiting factor in the progress of capable students through secondary school and college, the provision of some resources for institutional feeding may well be considered, at least on a modest scale.

The cost of providing two simple but nourishing meals to half of the students and trainees in higher education and vocational training during the working year would be $1,500 million per year even on their present numbers – and their numbers ought to be rapidly increasing. We suggest that $500 to $1,000 million be devoted to such "food scholarships" over the five-year period (or $100 to $200 million per year).

USE OF GRAINS IN LIVESTOCK DEVELOPMENT PROGRAMS

One of the urgent needs in improving diets in many of the underdeveloped countries is an increased production of animal protein to round out customary diets, which in almost all cases consist too largely of starchy foods. This is of particular interest because the major portion of the surpluses available consists also of starchy foods. The problem of supplementing cereal foods made available for school meals and similar purposes has already been mentioned.

The most desirable solution of this problem is to build up the production of foods of animal origin in the underdeveloped countries themselves, but this is a long-term program that will require extensive technical and institutional changes – education, improved strains of livestock, new processing and distributing facilities and changes in land use.

As already mentioned, there is need for vigorous exploration of the possibility that some of the advanced countries may be able to modify their production, in such a way as to supply larger quantities of these supplemental foods that are so necessary in bringing low-diet countries up to a more satisfactory level of nutritional adequacy. This, however, is a transitional measure. The ultimate solution must be sought in improved and better balanced agricultural production programs in the underdeveloped countries themselves.

Surplus grains which are now in long supply can, however, be used constructively in encouraging and speeding up this longer-term program of livestock development in a number of the underdeveloped countries, where such action is desirable and feasible. In many of these countries, the need for larger cereal output has resulted in an extension of grain production into submarginal lands (for crop production) which formerly were used for grazing purposes. Here, yields are very low and the lands are declining in fertility as a result of erosion and bad cultural methods. The situation degenerates into a vicious circle from which it is very hard for the farmer to escape. He cannot divert land to other uses for a long enough period to make possible the shift over to a more constructive type of agriculture, because he is dependent on the low and uneconomic yield of cereals he is now able to obtain.

Pilot studies and projects now being carried on indicate that in at least some areas of this type very encouraging results could be obtained, if outside supplies of grains could be pledged for a long enough period to enable the farmer to return submarginal crop lands to grass, and build them up as a base for livestock production.

Changes of this kind may well be included, where appropriate, in the economic plans of the underdeveloped countries, and the provision of modest amounts of surplus grains for that purpose may well be a very constructive way of using them. The amounts that can be so used in the immediate future will not be large, as such a program is by nature a long-term and slowly developing one. However, to the extent that it can be implemented it is one of the most fundamental and desirable types of economic development in agriculture.

While the above comments relate mainly to areas in which much submarginal crop land is now being used for cereal production – as in the Near

East – the type of program suggested may well be considered in different form for other animal deficient economies, such as Africa, in those places where livestock or poultry production is feasible and practical.

7. Use in relief and welfare

We cannot leave the subject of the use of surplus foods in social programs without mentioning one other group, in some ways the most tragic part of the world's underfed population, namely, the old, the handicapped and the destitute in underdeveloped countries. Such contribution as they have been able to make is in the past, but they have a humanitarian claim on the workers of the present. As of now, there are few well thought-out schemes whereby these people could be assisted. There is a possibility, however, that some additional aid can be provided for them by way of the surplus food program.

Schemes for such uses go beyond what is customarily envisioned as economic and social development and reach into the humanitarian field. They do not solve but only mitigate the problem of poverty. They are not ultimate but at best proximate solutions, which will make the whole development operation less hard and painful.

Few of the underdeveloped countries have institutional arrangements whereby expanded programs of this kind could be put into effect. Considerable preparation and some experimenting will be necessary if they are to come into being. Hence they must be thought of in terms of a longer period than the next five years, though it is to be hoped that some substantial progress in this important aspect of nutritional improvement can be achieved in five years. Machinery for organizing assistance in this field will have to be adjusted to the conditions and needs of individual countries. Pilot operations and more adequate organization will be required.

Some experience exists in the international organizations, particularly FAO and UNICEF. In the main the responsibility for organization and operation of these programs is national, but the international agencies can provide encouragement, advice and technical assistance, and can foster interest in such efforts by arranging for interchange of ideas and experience or organizing pilot projects. In some cases, it may be not only necessary but wholly acceptable to the underdeveloped countries to have an international agency administer a national scheme in its early stages, until local experience and organization have been developed.

UNICEF and many private voluntary bodies are currently engaged in food relief and welfare operations in the underdeveloped countries. They channel at present over $100 million worth of foodstuffs into these programs. We propose to double that amount, and suggest accordingly $1,000 million over five years.

With all due priority to economic development and to the future, the availability of surplus food should enable us to spare a thought for those whose contribution to development is in the past, or who are unable through no fault of their own to make further contributions.

8. International machinery

The foregoing parts of our report have mainly outlined what is to be done. The means chosen may, however, significantly influence the degree to which desired ends can be achieved. We have now to consider how it is to be done.

GENERAL PRINCIPLES

Two general principles underlie our conclusions.

Functionality

All the existing and prospective international and national aid agencies are considered to be means to the end of achieving economic and social development of underdeveloped countries.

Pragmatism

We do not live in an ideal world. The better should not be the enemy of the good. Even if it were thought desirable or logical that only international agencies should handle all economic and social development aid, the acceptance of this principle would mean considerable delays and smaller contributions. A "practical" or "second best" form of organization, which can operate more quickly and have greater aid resources should be adopted.

We propose accordingly to use existing institutions rather than to create new ones, but envisage some additional functions and some changes in the division of labor between them. We also assume that a *de facto* co-ordination of the bilateral and multilateral aid activities will be achieved by consultation both within and outside the United Nations framework, between nations extending and receiving aid; by *consortia* (or committees) which discuss the total needs of a country's development program, and by agreement on common principles according to which individual agencies extend their aid. A consultative, multinational organization can assure that the national and international aid activities will fit the jig-saw puzzle of coherent and consistent country development programs. A major part of international aid may continue to be administered bilaterally, but it will be bilateral aid within a multinational framework.[11] There is no dogmatic reason to assume that either bilateral or multilateral operation is preferable or more effective in itself. There is good reason to assume that the multilateral framework for bilateral action which we propose is better than bilateral action without such a multilateral framework. There is also good reason to make provision for multilateral action where such action is desired.

GENERAL ROLE OF INTERNATIONAL AGENCIES

As far as international agencies are concerned, we shall not describe the detailed distribution of functions as between FAO and the other international organizations. It stands to reason that FAO would be the focal point for contacts and co-ordination in this whole program. For incorporating the use of food surpluses in general development programs and advising on the general economic requirements of the various underdeveloped countries, we would expect that FAO would work closely with the United Nations, particularly perhaps with its Regional Economic Commissions. Where surplus food is to be combined with additional money aid in related "packages", obviously both FAO and the United Nations would work closely with such financial agencies as the International Bank and the International Development Association. Much of the technical and training work involved, as well as the undertaking of pilot projects and the necessary surveys, may well lead to action by the United Nations Special Fund and the Expanded Program of Technical Assistance.

The program for expanded use of surplus foods recommended in this report will entail responsibilities for FAO covering five main fields:

(a) A heightened activity will be called for in the traditional functions of FAO, i.e., advice, information, intergovernmental consultation, etc.

(b) A good deal of technical assistance work in the ordinary sense will be required, i.e., the sending of individual experts to work with the governments of underdeveloped countries in setting up the necessary national machinery, helping to construct storage facilities, the training of people abroad, the organization of seminars to exchange experience, etc.

(c) It seems to us of the greatest importance that FAO, together with other international and national agencies, should play a key role, working with individual countries, in studying the role of agriculture in the framework of general development; and helping countries to develop realistic and constructive programs for the use of surplus food. This activity should preferably be taken to the stage of drafting agreements ready for execution, provided – in the case of bilateral transactions – that the surplus-giving country accepts them.

(d) FAO would have an important role in making the needs and potentialities of receiving countries known to possible contributors of surplus food and related monetary supplements, and in making the underdeveloped countries aware of the possibilities and various methods of
taking advantage of them.

(e) Additional operational responsibilities would also be placed upon
FAO, ranging from decision taking (e.g., calling on irrevocable options
on the international emergency reserve), through co-operation in administration, up to full operation of school meal programs.

Of these five functions the first two should not raise any new problems,
except that it must be recognized that they may require strengthening of
the staff and of technical assistance funds for this purpose. The third function, that of country programing, appears so vital to us that something more
should be said about it.

The purposes of an additional surplus use program would be diverse, as
discussed in earlier sections of this report. The situations of different countries vary widely. Some underdeveloped countries have development programs and others have not. Some underdeveloped countries have a high
immediate absorptive capacity for further capital for additional projects,
while others would need longer time for preparation and greater technical
and preinvestment assistance of all kinds. Some underdeveloped countries
are themselves major producers of surplus commodities, or of their substitutes, while others are not. Some underdeveloped countries in different
degrees are interwoven with other countries who may be affected by surplus use transactions. Some individual countries have already made considerable use of surplus disposal under existing programs, while others
have not.

While this list of diverse circumstances could be augmented, it will be
sufficient to establish the point that additional use of food surpluses can
only be programed on a country-by-country basis. The suggestion of general schemes, such as a world food bank or world food reserve or similar
description, would not amount to much more than a different name or
label for what we call here the additional food surplus utilization program.
The essential step would still be the translation of the program into concrete action, which can only be done at the country level.

It is essential that the country programing should be approached entirely
with the interest of the recipient underdeveloped countries in mind. It is
equally essential that in the very process of forming the country program,
the interest of other countries which might be adversely affected should be
fully borne in mind by the international organization, of which they are as
full members as the potential beneficiary. It is important that the individual potential recipients of the additional surplus foods be treated on a
basis of equality, notwithstanding the great diversity of individual circum-

stances and needs, so that each country has the same opportunity to participate, however widely the final forms and sizes of the national programs
may differ. The international organizations are in a good position to apply
uniform and high standards in assuring the use of additional surplus food
only for constructive and important objectives.

While the giving countries will naturally not be bound to approve all
proposals for surplus food use presented by an international organization
on behalf of the receiving countries, it is likely that they will welcome such
proposals, since they are interested in a coherent program of productive use
of food surpluses.

The individual country program drawn up with the help of the international organization should normally include a financial assessment specify-
ing the types of additional financial assistance, other than surplus food, as
well as technical assistance, which would further enhance the value of the
program. This would apply both to action by international lending agencies
and to technical assistance and preinvestment assistance of all kinds.

In order to undertake country-by-country planning and programing of
additional use of surplus foods, it is necessary for the international organizations concerned to be able to approach the countries with an approximate
idea of the amounts of aid available, provided that good and acceptable
programs for their use can be formulated. We therefore suggest that the
surplus-giving countries should indicate their willingness to earmark surplus food for aid to underdeveloped countries. Since it is not known what
part of total requirements will be handled multilaterally – this will result
from the preferences of individual countries – part of the total earmarkings
should be made available on a flexible basis for multilateral transactions.

ROLE OF INTERNATIONAL AGENCIES IN THE SPECIFIC TYPES OF USE

Economic development activities

The role of agriculture in the development programs of underdeveloped
countries will require careful studies based on an overall program approach
rather than a single project approach. Technical assistance and co-operation will be needed for these purposes in greater amounts and intensity
than has hitherto been the case. The compatibility of the amounts of food
surplus requested with the criterion of additionality should be certified by
FAO. Representatives of the major agricultural exporting countries and of
agricultural deficit countries might plan co-operative arrangements whereby
surplus commodity disposal would be related to economic development.
It is notably on the point of duplications and complementarities in the
development programs of various countries (besides giving help in con-

structing them) that FAO, in consultation with regional economic commissions of the United Nations, should be particularly effective.

In many underdeveloped countries where no development program exists, or where the use of surplus foods can only be undertaken by the formulation of additional projects, the international organizations will have to work very closely with the governments of the underdeveloped countries to prepare sound projects which do not merely serve the purpose of utilizing food surpluses, but may be a durable contribution to the economic development of the receiving country.

National food reserves and international emergency food reserve

FAO should lend technical assistance in studying the needs, the optimum location and the costs involved. It should also propose and initiate joint arrangements by several states in order to minimize costs of transport, storage and handling. Only in some cases where the countries ask for direct FAO administration should FAO be willing, for a transition period, to operate food reserves. Some food reserves may in addition be stored in distant countries which are earmarked as another country's property. FAO might be the guardian of such property, having an irrevocable right of disposal irrespective of the food reserves location.

To cover emergency famine relief, a considerable part of the food reserve can be located in one or very few centers. Today already various countries have a reasonable expectation of obtaining surplus foods for famine emergency from the United States under Public Law 480, Title II. It is advisable that FAO should hold an irrevocable option for some emergency food surpluses which would convert reasonable expectation into perfect certainty. That would allow countries to store less in dispersed form without risk, and save on costs of storage and handling. The first needs in case of famine may be met from national food reserves. Countries may then replenish their reserves by drawing on central national or international reserves. Again, FAO might hold irrevocable options, which would give assurance to the holders of national food reserves that they can replenish their necessary inventories.

SOCIAL DEVELOPMENT

Land reform

Countries which want to carry out land reform but are prevented from doing so from fear of diminished food availabilities may obtain food surpluses for such purposes. It is desirable that such activities should be under international administration. FAO may hold irrevocable options on surplus foods for such purposes and be responsible for their allocation.

Supplementary meals

An immense activity of study and organization will be needed in this case. Studies will be needed on amounts required and on changes in agricultural production to be proposed. Organization will have to be adjusted to various countries' needs and administrative capabilities. In some countries the task of operation can be delegated to a national organization and suitable international control and reporting will be the only international task. In other countries partial or full operating activity will have to be organized. This will require a new department or subsidiary of FAO.

ORGANIZATIONAL IMPLICATIONS FOR FAO

Where FAO and other international organizations are actively participating in the planning and possibly in the execution of surplus disposal schemes, we see no need, as has been stressed above, for any elaborate new intergovernmental machinery. The main responsibility for carrying out the program and negotiations as required must rest with the Director-General or his designated representative. The Director-General would, of course, as with all FAO activities, be bound by his directive and basic resolutions, and he would have to report at least annually on his activities under the program. If the Director-General feels the need for this, he might possibly be assisted in his task by a governmental advisory group and/or by a small group of experts.

Given such arrangements, the present intergovernmental machinery of co-ordination and harmonization (Committee on Commodity Problems of FAO, the Subcommittee on Surplus Disposal and other interested bodies such as the FAO Group on Grains) need not be affected, since we expect bilateral programs to continue and broaden rather than contract. In fact, the existing intergovernmental machinery – as with the FAO Principles themselves – provide an adequate basis for lending added support to the positive task of promoting food aid as a means of economic and social development. We assume that these existing bodies would welcome the possibility of developing the more positive aspects of this work, since they have already done a great deal in the past toward developing the general ideas on which a forward-looking program of food aid should be based. Their annual general debate on these questions, which already form part of their regular agenda, could now be greatly strengthened by the background of field studies and detailed programing work for which resources and machinery may have been lacking up to now. The main annual debate in the Committee on Commodity Problems, based on the Director-General's annual report should be concerned with the broad lines of the main sectors of the food-aid program and with the philosophy underlying it, in line with the Principles. The existing bodies should *not,* however, get involved in any of the detailed programing work, which should be the direct responsibility of the Director-General in his year-round activities. As the work of existing bodies is given new possibilities for positive action, this may also be reflected in the level of representation by governments in these bodies. If this is the case, the continued advice of independent experts, which we have suggested may possibly not be necessary.

While we recognize that many conflicting interests of different types of countries are involved in the expanded program of food aid here suggested, we feel that the international organizations and their staffs, working under proper government control and subject to the usual checks, must be trusted to reconcile these interests without elaborate new machinery or mechanism. This seems to us the whole *raison d'être* of international organizations. The ultimate sanction of governments, if they are dissatisfied with the operation of multilateral agencies, will be to indicate a preference for bilateral dealings, as they are fully entitled to do. But we believe that multilateral mechanism and, in proper cases, multilateral operation, should be given a chance of demonstrating their value and superiority over the purely bilateral approach.

Aid-giving international bodies (such as the International Bank for Reconstruction and Development, the International Development Association, the United Nations Special Fund, the Colombo Plan Organization, the Organisation for Economic Co-operation and Development, the European Community Funds for Investment in Overseas Territories, etc.) should all consider to what extent aid given by them can be enlarged or made more effective by combining aid in terms of surplus commodities with monetary aid. Requests which otherwise would have to be rejected may become feasible if the requesting country would simultaneously receive surplus food aid. Receipt of food aid, like the receipt of other grants, might raise the debt-servicing capacity of an underdeveloped country to a level where it could become eligible for additional aid on hard monetary terms. Organizationally, this would mean that FAO should be ready to respond to all requests for information from financial international bodies, and would be free to approach either international or national agencies with proposals and suggestions.

We consider that the execution of this program would certainly require a strong special unit of FAO. It would seem to us good to bring all the FAO and other international activities under this program together in one focal point in FAO. We assume that the necessary full co-ordination between FAO, the United Nations, the United Nations financial agencies and the other specialized agencies involved would be secured through the normal administrative machinery of the Administrative Committee on Co-operation, with the Economic and Social Council of the United Nations serving as the organ for governmental policy co-ordination.

9. Concluding remarks

From the data which we have before us, from the expert advice which we have received, and from our own enquiries, we have derived a picture of an available surplus of very considerable magnitude. Even our figure, which relates to the United States alone over the next five years to the extent of $12,500 to $13,500 million – formidable as this magnitude is – may yet turn out to be an underestimate. The chief limiting factor to a surplus food utilization program which could make major contributions to world economic development lies *not* so much, in our view, in the available supplies but rather in the capacity of the underdeveloped countries to absorb these supplies into their economies at the high standards of effectiveness on which the giving countries and they themselves will rightly insist. A related limiting factor also lies in the necessity, in which again the food surplus-owning countries as well as the underdeveloped countries are equally concerned, for the underdeveloped countries to provide the correlated domestic efforts. Without impressive evidence of such correlated domestic efforts the beneficial effects of this opportunity will be lost, or be purely transitory at best. Moreover, the present willingness of surplus-owning and other developed countries to place these resources at the disposal of underdeveloped countries cannot be indefinitely counted upon. It should be emphasized that in the program we envisage, the utilization of the surplus food would not be entirely costless to the donating countries, since it would involve them in supplementary action.

Perhaps we may be permitted a further development of this conclusion, casting our minds beyond the immediate problems of surplus food. The readiness to give additional aid may appear in future in many different forms and variations, depending on the specific situation and availabilities in the aiding countries. Thus, the willingness of richer countries holding surplus stocks to use these as an instrument of world economic development is only one example of different types of opportunities which may arise in the future. It therefore seems to us that, quite apart from the present case, it would be unfortunate if the planning and programing machinery in the underdeveloped countries, in the international organizations, and among the aid-giving countries were not better developed to take better and more immediate advantage of such opportunities. The improvement of development planning machinery in the broader sense inside the underdeveloped countries; the improvement of the facilities available in international organizations to render assistance to underdeveloped countries in the creation, improvement and operation of such machinery; and the more systematic anticipation and organization of different types of opportunities by the aid-giving countries as well, ought to place us in a better position for the future than we seem to be in at the moment.

[1] Since the world market price of surplus wheat is at the level of around two thirds of the C.C.C. cost in the United States, two thirds of the C.C.C. cost counted as contribution to investment happens also to represent the value at world market prices of the total United States surplus products contribution.

[2] *International aid for underdeveloped countries*, P.N. Rosenstein-Rodan, Cambridge, Massachusetts Institute of Technology.

[3] *One hundred countries, one and one quarter billion people.* Albert D. and Mary Lasker Foundation, Committee for International Economic Growth, Washington, D.C., 1960.

[4] Shadow prices measure the true social cost, i.e., the value of opportunities foregone to use the resources in an alternative way.

[5] For an important example of an agricultural program of this type, *see* the section on "Use of Grains in Livestock Development Programs" on pages 300-301.

[6] Paragraph 5 states: "In weighing the advantages to countries benefiting from special disposal measures against the possible harm done to other countries, account must be taken of the relationship of possible sacrifices to the economic capacity of the countries concerned, and in particular to the effects of such sacrifices on their rates of development."

[7] For instance, for each of the years 1961-1966, $3,800 million of capital aid plus $400 million for Technical Assistance, plus $300 million for emergencies – making $4,500 million per year, assuming that the International Bank / International Development Association will supply $500 million per annum.

[8] In the above comments we do not wish to be understood as suggesting a policy of absolute price stabilization since that involves some dangers. In years of bumper crops, if prices are held more or less steady, farmers' incomes might be suddenly increased markedly and their additional demand might create strong inflationary pressures in the economy, especially in the underdeveloped countries where farmers constitute a large proportion of the population. Surplus food could not be helpful in coping with this type of inflationary pressure, since the situation contemplated would itself be one of abundance of crops. It would be more logical to require that policies of price stabilization should be combined with adequate compensatory fiscal and monetary policies, and that appropriate saving facilities be provided. Generally speaking, price stabilization requires cautious and skilled handling. This is not an argument for failing to utilize the powers of price stabilization to unlock the potential productive powers of agriculture. It is, however, an argument for proceeding cautiously and for taking skilled advice. In this latter connection, the various international organizations concerned could be helpful to underdeveloped countries in their respective fields of competence.

[9] The commodities have already been paid for in dollars and the foreign currencies acquired do not contribute to a balancing of the United States budget.

[10] For a fuller elaboration, see the section on "Use of Grains in Livestock Development Programs" on pages 300-301.

[11] See, for example, *The objectives of United States economic assistance programs*, a study by the Center for International Studies, Massachusetts Institute of Technology, for the Special Committee to Study the Foreign Aid Program, U.S. Senate: Washington, D.C., 1957. Chapter V.

APPENDIX 3

Assumptions of the Expert Group regarding the availability of surplus foods in the United States of America

WHEAT

During the last three years (1 July 1957 to 30 June 1960) the United States disposed of 27 million metric tons[1] as surplus and accumulated 11 million tons of additional stocks. That is, the average accretion of surplus was $38:3 = 12.6$ million tons.

Take United States stocks at 1 July 1953 as representing normal United States stocks, i.e., 16.5 million tons, as against stocks at 1 July 1960 of 35.7 million tons. That is, the availability in the reduction of stocks

$$= 35.7 - 16.5 \text{ million tons}$$
$$= 19.2 \text{ million tons.}$$

Over the five years, 1 July 1960 to 30 June 1965, assume:

(a) changes in United States annual production, consumption and commercial exports of wheat resulting in an average annual accretion of surplus of 11.5 million tons (i.e., 1 million tons less than in the period 1957/58 to 1959/60);

(b) United States stocks could be reduced to the level of July 1953.

Then the total availability of surplus United States wheat would be:

$$(11.5 \times 5) + 19.25 \text{ million tons}$$
$$= 76.7 \text{ million tons}$$
$$\text{or } 15.36 \text{ million tons per year}$$

$$\text{at \$90 per ton assumed C.C.C. cost}$$
$$= \$1,382 \text{ million per year}$$

COARSE GRAINS

During the three years 1957/58 to 1959/60 the United States disposed of 7.6 million tons as surplus, and accumulated 23.4 million tons as additional stocks. That is, the average annual accretion of surplus was $31:3 = 10.3$ million tons.

Take United States stocks in 1953 representing normal United States stocks, i.e., 24.3 million tons, as against 67.5 million tons in 1960. That is, the availability in the reduction of stocks

$$= 67.5 - 24.3 \text{ million tons}$$
$$= 43.2 \text{ million tons}$$

Over the five years 1960-65, assume:

(a) annual United States production does not exceed 1959/60 level;

(b) United States consumption may increase by 7 percent annually;

(c) United States commercial exports run at 7 million tons annually but might increase to 7.5 million tons;

(d) United States stocks may be reduced to level of 1953.

Then concessional exports should reach at least 2.5 million tons annually to prevent stock accumulation; and total availability of United States coarse grains for annual utilization as surplus would be:

$$2.5 + 43.2:5$$
$$= 11.1 \text{ million tons}$$
at \$65 per ton assumed C.C.C. cost
$$= \$722 \text{ million per year.}$$

RICE

The flow of surplus disposals over the three years 1957/58 to 1959/60 averaged 394,500 tons (milled) annually, and there are no abnormal stocks. Assuming no change in United States production, consumption and commercial exports over the next five years, approximately 400,000 tons of United States rice might be available for export under special programs, as an annual average. Assuming \$150 per ton as C.C.C. investment cost, the average annual value would be \$60 million.

DAIRY PRODUCTS

Surpluses do not accumulate. The flow of surplus disposals abroad over the three years 1957/58 to 1959/60 has been nil for butter, dwindling for cheese, and an average of 213,000 tons annually for skim powder. Expectations are for slightly larger surpluses of butter and skim milk.

Assume butter 50,000 tons, cheese 50,000 tons and skim powder 300,000 tons will be available as surpluses annually for the next five years. At C.C.C. cost, these would amount to $200 million.

FATS AND OILS

Surplus stocks have not been accumulated, and the annual flow of surplus disposals has averaged $150 million recently. Increases in production are expected without corresponding increases in consumption and commercial trade, so that the annual availability of surplus over the next five years may be assumed at $200 million.

[1] All references in this appendix to tons signify metric tons.

APPENDIX 4

Intergovernmental advisory committee

Statement by the Honorable George S. McGovern, Delegate of the United States of America,[1] on 10 April, 1961

1. The United States favors a multilateral approach for the use of agricultural commodities as a supplement to bilateral arrangements.

2. We think FAO should have a major role in such a program, in co-operation with other UN organizations.

3. We believe this should be a truly multilateral program with the widest possible contribution by member countries.

4. We recognize that countries are here to advise the Director-General on his report – not to take government positions on subjects covered in his report. Because of the need to move to the consideration of specific action proposals, however, we have been in touch with our Government over the weekend.

5. As a result, we are authorized to propose that an initial program on a multilateral basis might aim at a fund of $100 million in commodities and cash contributions. For its part, the United States would be prepared to offer $40 million in commodities, and the possibility of a supplementary cash contribution will be explored in Washington.

6. The $100 million total would be available for use over a fixed period. We are thinking of three years.

7. We recognize the desire of the Director-General to make the widest possible use of commodities in alleviating malnutrition. However, we continue to believe that the primary aim of the program in its initial stage should be to meet emergency needs. At the same time, we should support use of the program fund for pilot activities in other fields such as school

316

lunch or labor-intensive projects, in order to develop some diversified experience.

8. Specifics including additional staffing would have to be worked out for consideration by governments. This could be the responsibility of the Director-General in informal consultation with individual countries.

9. The purpose of our proposal is to help in launching a multilateral program utilizing food and to test approaches. After such experience, we could then examine the question of future additional work.

[1] Director of the Food for Peace Program, Executive Office of the President.

APPENDIX 5

United Nations Economic and Social Council Resolution 832 (XXXII)

Provision of food surpluses to food-deficient peoples through the United Nations system

THE ECONOMIC AND SOCIAL COUNCIL,

Recognizing that the effective utilization of available surplus foodstuffs, in ways compatible with the Food and Agriculture Organization principles of surplus disposal, provides an important transitional means for relieving the hunger and malnutrition of food-deficient peoples, particularly in the less developed countries, and for assisting these countries in their economic development,

Believing that the progress being made toward these objectives through bilateral arrangements could be further advanced by the use of supplementary multilateral arrangements which would provide for the mobilization and distribution of available surplus foodstuffs through the United Nations system,

Recalling General Assembly Resolution 1496 (XV) of 27 October 1960 on the provision of food surpluses to food-deficient people through the United Nations system, and paragraph 4 (d) of General Assembly Resolution 1515 (XV) of 15 December 1960 which *inter alia* reaffirms the need for additional development capital,

Having considered the two reports prepared in accordance with General Assembly Resolution 1496 (XV), namely the report of the Director-General of the Food and Agriculture Organization, entitled *Development through food – A strategy for surplus utilization*[1] and the report by the Secretary-General entitled *The role of the United Nations and its related agencies in the use of food surpluses for economic development,*[2]

Noting the helpful views presented in these reports as to how and under what conditions surplus food can be effectively used to promote economic and social development of the less developed countries,

Noting further that only preliminary consideration has been given in these reports to the formulation of procedures through which the United Nations and the Food and Agriculture Organization, in consultation with other appropriate specialized agencies, could most effectively carry out a program for the multilateral utilization of food surpluses in conformity with General Assembly Resolution 1496 (XV),[3]

Recognizing that the effective use of food aid depends upon the readiness of recipient countries to use such aid as an appropriate element in their plans for social and economic development, and also upon the readiness of the more developed countries so to program their contributions to the economic development of the less developed countries as to recognize an appropriate over-all relationship between food and other aid,

Affirming that assistance in the form of food to promote economic and social development should not adversely affect international trade and, in particular, trade of less developed countries who export foodstuffs, nor adversely affect their plans for economic development,

1. *Appreciates* the proposal for an initial program aiming at a fund of $100 million in commodities and cash contributions, as made before the Food and Agriculture Organization Council and recommends to governments that they be prepared to take positions respecting it and the principal measures for its implementation at the forthcoming sessions of the General Assembly and Food and Agriculture Organization Conference;

2. *Requests* the Secretary-General of the United Nations and the Director-General of the Food and Agriculture Organization to consult further with one another and with other agencies concerned, taking into account the discussions at the Thirty-second Session of the Economic and Social Council, with a view to formulating more fully proposals regarding procedures and arrangements through which a multilateral program for the mobilization and distribution of surplus food for the relief of hunger and malnutrition including the proposals for national and international emergency food reserves, and for the use of surplus food in connection with economic and social development programs, could be most effectively carried out in conformity with General Assembly Resolution 1496 (XV), particularly paragraph 9,[4] and to submit such proposals to the General Assembly and the Food and Agriculture Organization Conference respectively, and to report thereon to the Thirty-fourth Session of the Council;

3. *Recommends* that the General Assembly take into account the discussions and any decisions taken at the Eleventh Session of the Food and Agriculture Organization Conference when considering these proposals.

1179th Plenary Meeting
2 August 1961

[1] E / 3462 and FAO publication, Rome, 1961.
[2] E / 3509.
[3] Appendix 1, pages 275-277.
[4] *See* Appendix 1, pages 276-277.

APPENDIX 6

FAO/UN proposals regarding procedures and arrangements for the multilateral utilization of surplus food

In conformity with the United Nations General Assembly Resolution 1496 (XV) and Economic and Social Council Resolution 832 (XXXII)

I. Introduction

1. The following specific proposals for multilateral action on surplus food utilization have evolved from successive discussions in the General Assembly, in October, 1960; in the FAO Council, in October 1960, and June, 1961; and related discussions in subordinate bodies such as the FAO Committee on Commodity Problems; and finally in the 32nd Session of the Economic and Social Council, in July-August 1961. The Resolution adopted by the Economic and Social Council requests the Secretary-General of the United Nations and the Director-General of FAO to consult with one another and with other agencies concerned, to formulate more fully "proposals regarding procedures and arrangements" for a multilateral program for surplus food mobilization and distribution, including national and international emergency food reserves, and the use of surpluses for economic and social development programs.[1] The Resolution invites governments to be prepared to take positions respecting the United States proposal for an initial program aiming at a fund of $100 million, in commodities and cash contributions, as made before the FAO Council, and the principal measures for its implementation at the forthcoming sessions of the General Assembly and FAO Conference. It also recommends that the General Assembly, in considering these proposals, take into account the discussions and any decisions taken at the 11th Session of the FAO Conference, so that the matter would be considered first by FAO, and then by the United Nations Assembly in the light of the FAO action.

2. In agreement between the Secretary-General of the United Nations and the Director-General of FAO, and after consultation with representatives of the specialized and other international agencies concerned, the fol-

lowing proposal for procedures and arrangements is submitted for consideration and action by the FAO Council and Conference and the United Nations General Assembly, respectively.

3. The subject is presented first in terms of *arrangements* to be made by countries in providing the resources needed, and by FAO and other co-operating international organizations in creating the mechanisms for handling those resources; and then secondly in terms of *procedures* to be followed by recipient countries, contributing countries, and international organizations, respectively.

II. Arrangements by governments for providing the resources

A preliminary outline of the arrangements suggested for establishing the initial fund was given in a paper tabled by the United States representative at the FAO Council on 19 June, 1961. After considering these suggestions, and the suggestions made by delegations at the FAO Council and at the ECOSOC discussions, arrangements for providing the resources are suggested as follows.

ESTABLISHMENT OF SURPLUS UTILIZATION FUND

1. The FAO Conference will decide on establishing the Surplus Utilization Fund (hereafter called "the Fund") to be administered by a joint FAO/UN Surplus Utilization Division (hereafter referred to as SUD, see paragraph III. 3). Matters of United Nations participation would be approved subsequently at the United Nations General Assembly, and any necessary action on co-operation by other international agencies would be considered by their governing bodies in due course. These discusssions would take into consideration the decisions of the 35th FAO Council, the 32nd Session of ECOSOC,[2] and the resolution of the 15th Session of the United Nations General Assembly,[3] and the relevant sections of the reports of the Committee on Commodity Problems.

2. The initial subscription goal would be $100 million. Operations could commence, however, as soon as more than half of the amount had been pledged.

USES OF THE FUND

3. The Fund would be used to help finance emergency relief and international food reserves; national food reserves; relief of chronic malnutrition, infant, preschool and school feeding, educational fellowships, and

other social development activities; labor-intensive and other economic development activities.

TERMS OF CONTRIBUTIONS, IN CASH OR IN KIND

4. The pledges would be in terms of surplus commodities or in currencies, or both, acceptable to the Director-General of FAO. The over-all goal would be two thirds in commodities, and one third in cash, with commodity contributions valued at world market prices for commercial shipments.[4]

5. The Director-General would be authorized to accept contributions from all member countries of the United Nations or of the specialized agencies. The Director-General would also be authorized to invite additional contributions to meet famine or food emergencies, if the resources set aside for these purposes (paragraph IV. B 7) have been exhausted.

6. The Director-General would be authorized to accept contributions in tems of services in special cases (such as for ocean transport) where he deemed it to the advantage of the program to accept and utilize them.

7. The contributions to the initial subscriptions would be available for commitment to recipient countries and delivery to them until three years after operations began. If any country found itself, by reason of unexpected developments, in serious difficulty in completing the commodity deliveries it had offered, it would be free to cancel unused portions at the end of any calendar year, but only to the extent that such unused portions had not yet been committed for distribution.

CONDITIONS ON COMMODITY CONTRIBUTIONS

8. (a) The commodity contributions would be held in the contributing country until called for by SUD and then delivered at export ports f.o.b., at the cost of the contributing country.

(b) Costs of ocean freight and ocean insurance to the port of the recipient country and, in the absence of such a port, the costs of unloading in the port of call and of transport to the border of the recipient country will be paid from the Fund. Normally, the contributing or recipient countries would make the shipping arrangements in agreement with SUD at the Fund's expense.

(c) Costs of unloading and internal transport and distribution would normally be borne by the recipient country. SUD might, in exceptional circumstances, assist these arrangements, through helping to arrange surplus utilization projects, to create needed additional physical resources for handling storage or distribution.

BASIS FOR CONTRIBUTIONS

9. Contributions would be on a voluntary basis, to be announced, for example, at a pledging conference at a subsequent agreed time.

III. Arrangements for administering the resources

1. FAO would be the focal point for administering the Fund jointly with the UN and in collaboration with other specialized agencies and other international institutions concerned in the manner set forth below. The center for administration will be at FAO Headquarters in Rome.

2. The Fund will be administered in accordance with the Financial Regulations of FAO in so far as applicable. In case of need, special regulations will be developed for approval by the FAO Conference.

The accounts of the Fund's operations will be subject to the internal and external audit of FAO and will be presented through the Finance Committee and the Council to the Conference for approval.

3. Activities concerning the Fund shall be carried out in a new joint FAO/UN Surplus Utilization Division (SUD). It will operate under the supervision of the Director-General of FAO and the Secretary-General of the United Nations.

FUNCTIONS OF THE SURPLUS UTILIZATION DIVISION

4. The functions of the Surplus Utilization Division will include:

(i) preparing and executing agreements with countries concerning the supply and utilization of surplus commodities from the Fund for emergency relief, national and international food reserves, for relief of chronic malnutrition, and social and economic development through the promotion of labor-intensive and other appropriate projects;

(ii) estimating the capacity of a given country to absorb additional food surpluses in connection with programs and plans for social and economic development, with due regard to existing conditions of nutrition and food supply, the need for developing domestic agricultural production, and patterns of international trade;

(iii) advising countries on measures needed to ensure that the development of indigenous production will not suffer as a result of the utilization of surpluses (introduction of minimum price systems, setting up of national food reserve and national institutions to handle food policy matters, storage and marketing facilities, etc.);

(iv) insuring that surplus utilization operations are planned and operated in accord with the FAO Principles of Surplus Disposal and Guiding Lines;

(v) aiding, as appropriate and on request, in the multilateral co-ordination of bilateral arrangements and activities.

In carrying out the above functions, SUD would consult or work with other units of FAO and the United Nations, including the United Nations regional economic commissions, as well as other specialized agencies and other international institutions, as specified in paragraphs III. 8-10 and IV. B 2.

STRUCTURE OF THE SURPLUS UTILIZATION DIVISION

5. SUD will be a joint FAO/UN division with its staff composed in part of FAO officials and in part of United Nations officials stationed at Rome for this purpose.

6. SUD will be financed entirely from the Surplus Utilization Fund. It will start on as small a scale as needed to handle the essential initial activities, and grow with the operation.

7. Although the exact scope and nature of the work cannot at this stage be forecast, it is contemplated that SUD might be composed of three branches: a planning and research branch, an operations branch, and an appraisal branch.

CO-OPERATION OF SUD WITH OTHER FAO AND UNITED NATIONS UNITS

8. SUD would consult with, and seek advice from, the appropriate units of FAO and of the United Nations including its regional economic commissions.

9. The financial administration of the Fund will be the responsibility of the Department of Administration and Finance of FAO. To the extent feasible, SUD would also utilize other technical, administrative and general ser-

vices of the Organization. The additional costs involved would be charged to the Fund.

CO-OPERATION WITH OTHER SPECIALIZED AGENCIES AND UNICEF

10. WHO, ILO, UNESCO and UNICEF will be closely associated in the examination and planning of appropriate portions of the over-all program, and will assist countries, at their request, in the implementation of individual projects or aspects of them coming within their respective fields of competence. IBRD, IDA and IFC will be kept fully informed and will be consulted on all aspects of programs of interest to them. These organizations may also submit proposals leading to the support of the Fund in implementing appropriate projects in their own programs.

GOVERNMENT SUPERVISION OF THE PROGRAM

11. Government supervision of the program would be exercised by a committee for surplus utilization consisting of representatives of 18 states members of the United Nations or the specialized agencies.

12. The committee would provide general policy guidance on the administration and operations of the Fund. It would examine programs of work submitted to it jointly by the Director-General of FAO and the Secretary-General of the United Nations and authorize the implementation of such programs. The committee would meet twice a year.

13. All members of the committee would be elected by ECOSOC, or alternatively half by the Economic and Social Council and half by the FAO Council. There would be equal representation on the committee of economically more developed countries, on the one hand, having due regard to their contributions to the Surplus Utilization Fund, and of less developed countries, on the other hand, taking into account the need for equitable geographical distribution among the latter members.

14. The Council of FAO and the Economic and Social Council would review the operations of the Surplus Utilization Fund on the basis of the annual reports submitted by the Committee for Surplus Utilization.

15. The Washington Consultative Subcommittee on Surplus Disposal (CSD) would receive periodic reports on the progress and results of the program.

16. The financial operations of the Fund will be reviewed by the FAO Finance Committee which will report to the Council thereon.

IV. Procedures to be followed in regard to the Fund

A. BY CONTRIBUTING COUNTRIES

1. The time and place for contributing countries to pledge or announce their contributions will be established by the Secretary-General of the United Nations and the Director-General of FAO in joint consultation.

2. Countries will pay their contributions in cash, or deliver their goods or services in kind, normally in three equal annual installments, except as the country concerned and the Director-General may agree otherwise.

3. Countries providing economic aid or assistance will help the development of the operations by making available to the Director-General, upon request, any relevant information concerning their current and proposed bilateral aid program for given countries where the FAO is contemplating a food utilization program, to assist FAO in co-ordinating its proposed multi-lateral activities with those bilateral activities.

B. BY RECIPIENT COUNTRIES AND SUD IN DEVELOPING AND OPERATING PROJECTS

Initiation of projects

1. Countries desiring to establish surplus food aid programs or projects will inform the Director-General through the United Nations Resident Representative, keeping the FAO Country Representative fully informed.

2. If, after examination of the application or the draft project in SUD it appears feasible within the resources available, SUD will proceed to collect additional information necessary for its consideration. It may then, if necessary, dispatch a survey team to examine the project on the ground in consultation with the country concerned. Such a team should normally include a United Nations general economist and also a representative of each of the other United Nations agencies which may be directly concerned and may wish to be represented. After study and consultation on the spot, supported by consultation with the Secretariat of the United Nations Regional Economic Commission, the survey team will prepare a draft report and submit it to SUD.

Completion of project agreement

3. Upon approval of a proposed project an agreement will be prepared by SUD in consultation with the country concerned. It will cover the terms and conditions of the proposed surplus activities; will indicate any supplementary aid for the program being provided by other agencies or institutions; the obligations of the country with respect to ways the food aid is to be utilized, including the use of any local currencies arising therefrom; domestic mechanisms to be created, if any, for storage, price support, internal transport and distribution; conditions concerning data to be collected on the manner, the repercussions and effects of food distribution, including the possible impact on the improvement of the nutrition status of the country on a longer-term basis and other conditions mutually agreed upon as necessary.

Execution of project

4. As the agreement is carried into effect, the recipient country will give full co-operation to SUD and other co-operating organizations, where appropriate, in observing the operations from time to time, in checking their effects, and ultimately in completing their appraisal of the results of each operation. These analysis reports will, in each case, be submitted to the recipient country concerned for its comments before the final revised report is submitted to the Surplus Utilization Committee.

5. For cases involving emergency and disaster relief, a briefer procedure would be utilized, based on previous FAO studies and procedures.

Terms for surplus utilization

6. Where surplus utilization activities involve the direct distribution of the products concerned, without payment in cash (as for infant, preschool or school feeding, food fellowships, improving nutrition, or most emergency relief operations) the commodities will be donated to the country as grants. Where the products received as grants are sold to the consumers in the recipient countries for local currencies, the net proceeds from the sale of the food in local currencies will be retained by the government to help finance, in a manner to be agreed, additional domestic expenditures involved in economic and social development programs.

Maintenance of an international emergency reserve

7. The Director-General of FAO is authorized to earmark 25 percent of the Fund for emergency use, including national and international food reserves, and if those earmarked quantities are exhausted during the initial

period, to appeal to member countries for additional food contributions to build up the emergency reserve at his disposition. Operations from this emergency reserve could be initiated at any time by the Director-General of FAO after consulting with the Secretary-General of the United Nations.

Continuation of activities

8. The Secretary-General of the United Nations and the Director-General of FAO shall maintain a review of the allocation and use of the Fund's resources and may jointly recommend to the appropriate FAO and United Nations organs that arrangements be made for the necessary discussions as to whether, and in what manner, the multilateral surplus utilization program should be continued.

[1] Appendix 5, pages 317-319.
[2] Appendix 5, pages 317-319.
[3] Appendix 1, pages 275-277.
[4] The Director-General would be authorized to use a portion of the cash for the purchase of surplus commodities and other products from countries not in position to contribute them.

APPENDIX 7

Extract from the report of the Eleventh Session of the FAO Conference with Resolution 1/61

Utilization of food surpluses for economic and social development

1. The Conference considered this item on the basis of the Report of the Director-General, *Development through food – A strategy for surplus utilization,* and the Joint Report of the Secretary-General and the Director-General, "FAO/UN proposals regarding procedures and arrangements for multilateral utilization of surplus Food" (C 61/18).[1] As stated in the Joint Report, this proposal

> "evolved from successive discussions in the General Assembly, in October 1960; in the FAO Council, in October 1960 and June 1961; and related discussions in subordinate bodies such as the FAO Committee on Commodity Problems; and finally in the 32nd session of the Economic and Social Council, in July-August 1961. The Resolution adopted by the Economic and Social Council requests the Secretary-General of the United Nations and the Director-General of FAO to consult with one another and with other agencies concerned, to formulate more fully 'proposals regarding procedures and arrangements' for a multilateral program for surplus food mobilization and distribution, including national and international emergency food reserves, and the use of surpluses for economic and social development programs... The Resolution invites governments to be prepared to take positions respecting the United States proposal for an initial program aiming at a fund of $100 million in commodities and cash contributions,... and the principal measures for its implementation at the forthcoming sessions of the General Assembly and FAO Conference. It also recommends that... the matter... be considered first by FAO, and then by the United Nations Assembly in the light of the FAO action."

2. The Director-General's report to ECOSOC, *Development through food – A strategy for surplus utilization,* had delineated the part that food surpluses might be capable of playing over the ensuing five years in a greatly expanded program of international assistance in order to speed up the rate

of development in less developed countries, and so help correct the current situation where increase in food production was only barely exceeding population growth in less developed countries generally. While the report indicated the part multilateral food disposal might play in such expanded surplus distribution, and some of the essential conditions that would need to be met to achieve maximum effectiveness, it recognized that distribution through bilateral arrangements would continue to be the dominant part of such a program.

3. The Director-General emphasized the dual role of food in development projects, pointing out that the distribution of food in the areas of need and use of food surpluses for economic development could not be separated from one another. Food aid and economic development are "two sides of the same coin." He advocated that these two elements should be planned and operated as an integrated activity, carefully balanced with each other, both as to timing and location.

4. Following consideration of the Director-General's report at the 35th Session of the FAO Council (June 1961) and at the 32nd Session of ECO-SOC (July 1961), the Secretary-General and the Director-General prepared the Joint Report requested in the ECOSOC Resolution. A preliminary debate on the Joint Report took place at the 36th Session of the FAO Council immediately prior to the present Conference Session. At this Session of the Conference the specific proposals for implementation of the initial program contained in that Report were discussed carefully. The joint proposals of the Director-General and Secretary-General aroused great interest and commanded widespread support.

5. There was general agreement as to the importance of raising the level of international assistance for the economic development of less developed countries, and for increased use of food surpluses for that purpose. There was general recognition of the desirability of establishing a multilateral approach for emergency relief and the use of food surpluses for economic development, on an initial experimental scale. While several countries questioned the desirability of agricultural production being deliberately expanded to provide products for such purposes, it was recognized that with the rapid increase in agricultural productivity in many countries and the limited possibilities for increased food consumption in developed countries even with continued improvement in the buying power of their people, substantial and possibly even increasing supplies of food would be generated that could be available for distribution on special terms.

6. There was wide support for the general proposal, and for a number of its specific elements:

(1) that the new activity would be an initial experimental program for three years, with subsequent multilateral activities to be determined in the light of this experience;

(2) that the program would be financed by voluntary contributions;

(3) that FAO should have a major role in the new activity;

(4) that guidance would be provided by a special intergovernmental committee.

7. There was also full agreement that the operations should be conducted in accordance with the FAO Principles of Surplus Disposal and Guiding Lines, so as to ensure that all foods so distributed went into increased consumption in the recipient countries and did not interfere with commercial imports or with the production plans of farmers in the recipient countries themselves. In this connection, it was noted that the proposed unit in the administering organization would assist materially in seeing that projects were carried out in full conformity with the FAO Principles. Consultations with countries whose normal marketing involved similar commodities in a country to which food aid was to be extended should be conducted through the machinery for consultation already established by FAO.

8. It was also agreed that any project developed under this program should be undertaken only on the request of the recipient country concerned. Projects for economic or social development should be related to and consistent with the country's plans or programs for its own development, and should be co-ordinated with other projects already under way or projected in that country, to make the aid most effective.

9. Many less developed countries stressed that as a result of the setting up of the multilateral program the flow of bilateral assistance to such countries as prefer that channel should not be affected. They in fact visualized that multilateral assistance would be distinct from and supplementary to bilateral arrangements which might even expand further.

10. Differences of opinion were expressed, however, on a number of other points. Some less developed countries stated that they had no need for food aid themselves, in as much as they were already food exporting countries with a reasonable level of diet within the country. There was particularly keen debate on the question of whether greater attention should be paid, in this initial program, to the use of surpluses for emergency and relief purposes, or for economic and social development. The majority took the latter view, particularly so far as development for rural welfare was concerned. Similarly, in regard to the proposal that the administrative unit be a joint FAO/United Nations unit, reporting jointly to the Director-General

and the Secretary-General, some countries favored an FAO unit merely co-operating with the United Nations, but a much larger number supported the joint operation. It was pointed out that there had been long experience and satisfactory results with the use of the technique of joint FAO/United Nations units, e.g., the Joint FAO/United Nations Agricultural Divisions that operate at each United Nations Economic Commission.

11. While it was generally agreed that pledges to the program should be voluntary, and composed of suitable commodities, services and cash, some countries questioned the effect that the donation of services might have on normal commercial practices, e.g., the charter terms for shipping freights.

12. There was general agreement that at least one third of the *total* contributions subscribed should be in cash. A number of delegates thought that a minimum proportion in cash should be required of each country contributing commodities or services, but most preferred the completely voluntary system proposed by the Secretary-General and the Director-General.

13. In this connection, the question of meeting the administrative expenses was discussed. Although a few countries had differing views, it was generally agreed that all expenses of both operation and administration of the new program should be met from the contributed funds.

14. Another subject given considerable attention was the suggestion in the Joint Report that part of the cash contributions could be used for the commercial purchase of foods not in surplus but needed to improve the dietary adequacy of food supplies furnished to recipient countries, particularly with regard to important components such as desirable proteins. While this was strongly supported by most countries, others had doubts as to the wisdom of the proposal.

15. The Conference also considered the steps by which the proposals would be approved and implemented, and the special problems of securing joint and agreed approval of the proposals from both FAO and the United Nations. As stated in Resolution No. 1/61,[2] the following sequence of steps was agreed upon, subject to the concurrence of the United Nations.

(1) Immediately following this Conference session, the FAO Council would elect the 10 FAO members of the Intergovernmental Committee.

(2) Immediately after the conclusion of the United Nations debate on this subject in the current (Sixteenth) United Nations General Assembly,

ECOSOC would elect the 10 United Nations members of the Inter-governmental Committee to be selected by the United Nations.

(3) If in the opinion of the Director-General, the conclusions and recommendations of the General Assembly regarding this program involved basic differences of policy from what had been approved by the FAO Conference, he would convene a special session of the FAO Council.

(4) After the General Assembly action, and action by such special session of the Council if found necessary, the Intergovernmental Committee would be called for its first session by the Director-General (and Secretary-General), to draw up procedures and make arrangements for the program. This session would take place in Rome early in 1962.

(5) When the report of this session of the Intergovernmental Committee was completed and submitted to the Director-General and Secretary-General, they would call concurrent meetings in April 1962 at New York of the FAO Council and the ECOSOC, to consider that report. The meetings of the two Councils would be alternated so that countries having membership of both could be represented by the one delegation. Every effort would be made by informal discussions between the members of the two Councils, meeting at the same location, to resolve any differences in their conclusions, so as to secure common recommendations and decisions.

(6) The Director-General and Secretary-General would then jointly convene a conference at which countries could announce their pledges.

(7) At their regular sessions, the FAO Council and ECOSOC would re-examine the list of countries representing them on the Intergovernmental Committee and make any changes deemed advisable following the Pledging Conference.

16. The Conference also made provision for an advance of funds to meet expenses in connection with these meetings and with any preparatory work for the program.

17. The outcome of the Conference's consideration of this matter is contained in the Resolution set out below. There is discussion of various factors that should be taken into account in determining the countries to be chosen as members of the Intergovernmental Committee. In addition to the obvious need for balance between developed and less developed countries, among other considerations would be geographic distribution, representation of commercial exporting countries, both developed and less developed, and representation of countries which are major contributors to the resources for the program. The phrase "other relevant factors" used in paragraph 1.4 of that Resolution covers all such factors, it being left to the

judgment of the two Councils what weight to attach to each in making their selection.

18. During the discussion, some delegates further expressed the view that the Committee should be composed only of countries actively participating in the program, either as contributing countries or as recipient countries, or as commercial exporters closely concerned. It would, however, be impossible at the start to tell which countries would in fact be contributors or likely recipients. It is for this reason that provision is made in the Resolution for the two Councils, after the Pledging Conference, to re-examine the country composition of the Committee.

19. Reference is also made in the Resolution to further studies on the use of food in multilateral programs. It was accepted that the Intergovernmental Committee might consider at its first meeting the nature of such studies, taking as a basis for selection the examples given in paragraph 33 of the Report of the 34th Session of the CCP. Such studies could be undertaken by the Organization and its subsidiary bodies, especially the CCP, by other United Nations agencies or other interested intergovernmental bodies.

20. The Resolution adopted by the Conference reads as follows:

Resolution No. 1/61
UTILIZATION OF FOOD SURPLUSES – WORLD FOOD PROGRAM

THE CONFERENCE

Having considered Resolution 1469 (XV) of the United Nations General Assembly[3] and Resolution 832 (XXXII)[4] of the United Nations Economic and Social Council,

Having studied the report of the Director-General on *Development through food – A strategy for surplus utilization,* and the joint proposals of the Secretary-General of the United Nations and the Director-General of the Food and Agriculture Organization, Document C 61/18, "FAO/UN proposals regarding procedures and arrangements for multilateral utilization of surplus foods"[5] and

Having reviewed the observations of the FAO Intergovernmental Advisory Committee, the Committee on Commodity Problems and the Council, as well as the relevant reports of the FAO Council and of other interested intergovernmental groups or agencies,

Records its appreciation for the documentation prepared by the Secretary-General and Director-General, for the full co-operation provided by the interested international agencies, and for the proposals put forward jointly by the Secretary-General and the Director-General,

Resolves, subject to the concurrence of the General Assembly of the United Nations, that:

I

(1) an initial experimental program for three years of approximately $100 million with contributions on a voluntary basis be undertaken jointly by the Food and Agriculture Organization and the United Nations, in co-operation with other United Nations agencies, and appropriate intergovernmental bodies;

(2) contributions to the program, to be known as the World Food Program, may be pledged by countries in the form of appropriate commodities, acceptable services, and cash, aiming in the aggregate at a cash component of at least one third of the total contributions, and countries should give due regard to the importance of achieving this over-all objective, when determining the cash element in their contribution;

(3) an Intergovernmental Committee of 20 nations which are members of FAO or the United Nations be established to provide guidance on policy, administration and operations, as outlined in paragraphs 11 and 12 of Part III of the Joint Report of the Secretary-General and the Director-General;

(4) the Committee be elected half by the FAO Council and half by the United Nations, taking into account the need for balanced representation of economically developed countries and of less developed countries and other relevant factors: in appointing its representative, each government should pay due regard to the complexities of the executive and operational planning required for the proposed program;

(5) the Intergovernmental Committee meet in Rome early in 1962 to develop detailed procedures and arrangements for the program on the basis of this resolution, taking due account of the Joint Report of the Secretary-General and the Director-General and giving consideration to the views expressed in reports of meetings related to this subject held under the auspices of FAO and the United Nations;

(6) the procedures and arrangements drawn up by the Intergovernmental Committee be reviewed and approved in concurrent sessions of the Council of FAO and the Economic and Social Council (ECOSOC) in New York in April 1962;

(7) a conference for contributing countries to pledge their contributions in accordance with paragraph I.2 above be convened by the Secretary-

General and the Director-General after the concurrent sessions of the FAO Council and ECOSOC;

(8) the FAO Council and the ECOSOC, at their next regular meetings following the Pledging Conference, should make any adjustment of country composition on the Intergovernmental Committee (of 20) that might be deemed desirable in view of the considerations mentioned in paragraph I.4 above;

(9) subject to the guidance of the Intergovernmental Committee, the program will be carried on by a joint FAO/UN administrative unit located at FAO Headquarters in Rome and reporting to both the Director-General and the Secretary-General, with the costs of administration and operation under this Resolution to be met from contributions to the program;

(10) in the administration of the program, attention should be paid to:

(a) establishing adequate and orderly procedures on a world basis for meeting emergency food needs and emergencies inherent in chronic malnutrition (this could include the establishment of food reserves),

(b) assisting in preschool and school feeding, and

(c) implementing pilot projects, with the multilateral use of food as an aid to economic and social development, particularly when related to labor-intensive projects and rural welfare;

(11) projects should be undertaken only in response to requests from the recipient country or countries concerned;

(12) the administration of the proposed program will require close co-operation, particularly on development projects, between FAO and the United Nations, as well as with appropriate United Nations agencies, and other appropriate intergovernmental bodies;

(13) the Intergovernmental Committee shall ensure that:

i. in accordance with the FAO Principles of Surplus Disposal and with the consultative procedures established by the CCP, and in conformity with United Nations General Assembly Resolution 1496 (XV), particularly paragraph 9,[6] commercial markets and normal and developing trade are neither interfered with nor disrupted,

ii. the agricultural economy in recipient countries is adequately safeguarded with respect both to its domestic markets and the effective development of food production,

iii. due consideration is given to safeguarding normal commercial practices in respect to acceptable services;

II

Requests the Director-General:

(1) to convene the special session of the FAO Council referred to in para. I.6 above;

(2) if required to resolve policy differences arising from decisions taken by the United Nations General Assembly at its Sixteenth Session, to convene, before the first session of the Intergovernmental Committee, a special session of the Council, which is hereby authorized to take decisions in this respect for FAO;

(3) in agreement with the Secretary-General, to convene the Pledging Conference referred to in paragraph I.7 above;

(4) in close co-operation with the Secretary-General and with interested groups or agencies and jointly where appropriate, to undertake as soon as feasible studies which would aid in the future development of multilateral food programs;

(5) to report to the Twelfth Session of the Conference on the operation of the program;

III

Authorizes the Director-General to implement the program under this Resolution as promptly as possible, in co-operation with the Secretary-General, and to take all necessary steps in line with the decisions taken by the FAO Conference, the United Nations General Assembly and the special session of the Council referred to in paragraph II.2 above;

IV

Decides to consider at its Twelfth Session the conditions under which a general review should be made of the results attained with a view to taking such action as may be deemed desirable and to recommend to the General Assembly of the United Nations the next steps to be taken.

[1] Appendix 6, pages 320-328.
[2] *See* pages 334-337.
[3] Appendix 1, pages 275-277.
[4] Appendix 5, pages 317-319.
[5] Appendix 6, pages 320-328.
[6] *See* Appendix 1, page 277.

APPENDIX 8

United Nations General Assembly Resolution 1714 (XVI)

Provision of food surpluses to food-deficient peoples through the United Nations system, World Food Program

THE GENERAL ASSEMBLY,

Recalling its Resolution 1496 (XV)[1] of 27 October 1960 and Economic and Social Council Resolution 832 (XXXII)[2] of 2 August 1960 on the provision of food surpluses to food-deficient peoples through the United Nations system,

Having considered the report of the Director-General of the Food and Agriculture Organization of the United Nations entitled *Development through food – A strategy for surplus utilization,*[3] the report of the Secretary-General on the role of the United Nations and the appropriate specialized agencies in facilitating the best possible use of food surpluses for the economic development of the less developed countries,[4] and the joint proposal by the United Nations and the Food and Agriculture Organization of the United Nations regarding procedures and arrangements for multilateral utilization of surplus food,[5]

Having reviewed the action taken at the Eleventh Session of the Conference of the Food and Agriculture Organization on the utilization of food surpluses and specifically its Resolution stating that, subject to the concurrence of the General Assembly of the United Nations, an initial experimental program for three years, to be known as the World Food Program, should be undertaken, having also noted in particular the reference to safeguards contained in paragraph 13[6] of the abovementioned Resolution of the Conference of the Food and Agriculture Organization,

Recognizing the existing facilities for consultation provided by the Food and Agriculture Organization through its Consultative Subcommittee on Surplus Disposals,

Bearing in mind its Resolution 1710 (XVI) of 19 December 1961 on the United Nations Development Decade, and, in particular, the reference in paragraph 4 *(d)* to the elimination of illiteracy, hunger and disease,

I

1. *Approves* the establishment of an experimental World Food Program to be undertaken jointly by the United Nations and the Food and Agriculture Organization of the United Nations, in co-operation with other interested United Nations agencies and appropriate intergovernmental bodies, bearing in mind that the establishment of such a program in no way prejudices the bilateral agreements between developed and developing countries, and accepts and endorses the purposes, principles, and procedures formulated in the first part of the Resolution approved by the Conference of the Food and Agriculture Organization on 24 November 1961, including the safeguards mentioned in that Resolution and General Assembly Resolution 1496 (XV) especially in paragraph 9 thereof;[7]

2. *Approves* specially the establishment of a United Nations/FAO Intergovernmental Committee of 20 States Members of the United Nations or members of the Food and Agriculture Organization to provide guidance on policy, administration and operations, and of a joint United Nations/FAO administrative unit reporting to the Secretary-General of the United Nations and the Director-General of the Food and Agriculture Organization;

3. *Requests* the Economic and Social Council at its resumed thirty-second session to elect, subject to the provisions of paragraph 9 below, ten States Members of the United Nations or members of the Food and Agriculture Organization to the United Nations/FAO Intergovernmental Committee, taking into account:

(a) the representation provided by the ten states that were elected to serve on the United Nations/FAO Intergovernmental Committee by the Council of the Food and Agriculture Organization;

(b) the need for balanced representation of economically developed and of developing countries, and other relevant factors such as the representation of potential participating countries, both contributing and recipient, equitable geographical distribution and the representation of both developed and less developed countries having commercial interests in

international trade in foodstuffs, especially those highly dependent on such trade;

4. *Calls upon* the Economic and Social Council at its thirty-third session, in co-operation with the Council of the Food and Agriculture Organization, to review and to take appropriate action on the procedures and arrangements for the World Food Program recommended by the United Nations/FAO Intergovernmental Committee;

5. *Decides* that pilot projects to be undertaken by the joint United Nations/FAO administrative unit, under the guidance of the United Nations/FAO Intergovernmental Committee, involving the use of food as an aid to economic and social development, shall be undertaken in agreement between the Secretary-General, acting on behalf of the United Nations, and the Director-General, acting on behalf of the Food and Agriculture Organization;

6. *Concurs* in the calling of a conference where States Members of the United Nations or members of the Food and Agriculture Organization will be invited to pledge contributions;

7. *Requests* the Secretary-General, in co-operation with the Director-General of the Food and Agriculture Organization, to convene such a conference at United Nations Headquarters as soon as feasible after the concurrent sessions of the Economic and Social Council and the Council of the Food and Agriculture Organization;

8. *Urges* States Members of the United Nations or members of the Food and Agriculture Organization, in considering their contributions, to make every effort to assure the early attainment, on a voluntary basis, of the $100 million program;

9. *Further requests* the Economic and Social Council, in co-operation with the Council of the Food and Agriculture Organization, at its next regular session following the pledging conference, to review the composition of the United Nations/FAO Intergovernmental Committee and to make by election for the balance of the three-year program any adjustments of membership that might be deemed desirable in the light of the considerations outlined in paragraph 3 above;

10. *Instructs* the United Nations/FAO Intergovernmental Committee, in preparing recommendations on the conditions and procedures for the establishment and operation of the program for the review and approval by the Economic and Social Council and the Council of the Food and Agriculture

Organization, to proceed on the basis of the present resolution and the resolution of the Conference of the Food and Agriculture Organization of 24 November 1961,[8] taking into account the joint proposal by the United Nations and the Food and Agriculture Organization of the United Nations regarding procedures and arrangements for multilateral utilization of surplus food,[9] statements made during the debates in the General Assembly and in the Conference of the Food and Agriculture Organization and such other conditions and procedures as may seem to it appropriate;

11. *Recommends* that Governments requesting assistance under this program, the United Nations/FAO Intergovernmental Committee, and the joint United Nations/FAO administrative unit responsible for the administration of the program keep the resident representatives fully informed about, and, within their field of competence, associated with, activities undertaken under the program;

12. *Invites* the Secretary-General of the United Nations and the Director-General of the Food and Agriculture Organization to insure that, in carrying out the program, the joint United Nations/FAO administrative unit rely to the fullest extent possible on the existing staff and facilities of the United Nations and the Food and Agriculture Organization, as well as other appropriate intergovernmental agencies;

13. *Requests* the United Nations/FAO Intergovernmental Committee to report annually to the Economic and Social Council and to the Council of the Food and Agriculture Organization on the progress made in the development of the program and its administration and operation;

14. *Decides* to undertake, not later than at its nineteenth session, a general review of the program, taking into account the objectives of its Resolution 1496 (XV);[10]

II

Recognizing that the experimental program outlined above constitutes a step towards the broader objectives outlined in its Resolution 1496 (XV),

Recognizing further that the ultimate solution to this problem of food deficiency lies in self-sustaining economic growth of the economies of the less developed countries to the point where they find it possible to meet their food requirements from their food-producing industries or from the proceeds of their expanding export trade,

Recognizing that the effective utilization of available surplus foodstuffs, in ways compatible with the principles of surplus disposal of the Food and Agriculture Organization of the United Nations, provides an important transitional means for relieving the hunger and malnutrition of food-deficient peoples, particularly in the less developed countries, and for assisting these countries in their economic development,

Recognizing further that food aid is not a substitute for other types of assistance, in particular for capital goods,

1. *Recognizes* that food aid to be provided under this program should take into account other forms of assistance and country plans for economic and social development;

2. *Requests* the Secretary-General of the United Nations, in close cooperation with the Director-General of the Food and Agriculture Organization and with interested groups or agencies and jointly where appropriate, to undertake, as soon as feasible, expert studies which would aid in the consideration of the future development of multilateral food programs;

3. *Expresses the hope* that, in the light of these studies and of the experience gained, the progress of the experimental program will be such as to permit the United Nations and the Food and Agriculture Organization to consider the possibility and advisability of increasing the program, taking into account the advantages to developing countries, the interests of the contributing States, the interests of the food-exporting countries, the effectiveness of the program and its contribution to the objectives of General Assembly Resolution 1496 (XV);

4. *Endorses again* the Freedom from Hunger Campaign launched by the Food and Agriculture Organization, and requests the Secretary-General of the United Nations and the Director-General of the Food and Agriculture Organization, simultaneously with the implementation of the present resolution, to pay particular attention to the necessity of improving and increasing local food production and to include, where appropriate, reference to this subject in the reports mentioned above, and requests the United Nations/FAO Intergovernmental Committee to consider the possibility of applying a reasonable proportion of resources resulting from the World Food Program to this purpose.

1084th Plenary Meeting
19 December 1961

[1] Appendix 1, pages 275-277.
[2] Appendix 5, pages 317-319.
[3] FAO publication, Rome, 1961.
[4] Official Records of the Economic and Social Council, Thirty-second Session Annexes, agenda item 8, document E / 3509.
[5] A / 4907 and Add. 1 and 2.
[6] Appendix 7, page 334.
[7] Appendix 1, pages 275-277: *see particularly*, pages 276-277.
[8] Appendix 7, pages 334-337.
[9] Appendix 6, pages 320-328.
[10] Appendix 1, pages 275-277.

WHERE TO PURCHASE FAO PUBLICATIONS LOCALLY

Algeria	Société nationale d'édition et de diffusion, 92, rue Didouche Mourad, Alger.
Argentina	Librería Agropecuaria S.A., Pasteur 743, 1028 Buenos Aires.
Australia	Hunter Publications, 58A Gipps Street, Collingwood, Vic. 3066: Australian Government Publishing Service, Sales and Distribution Branch, Wentworth Ave, Kingston, A.C.T. 2604. Bookshops in Adelaide, Melbourne, Brisbane, Canberra, Perth, Hobart and Sydney.
Austria	Gerold & Co., Graben 31, 1011 Vienna.
Bahrain	United Schools International, PO Box 726, Manama.
Bangladesh	ADAB, House No. 46A, Road No. 6A, Dhanmondi R/A, Dhaka.
Belgium	M. J. De Lannoy, 202, avenue du Roi, 1060 Bruxelles. CCP 000-0808993-13.
Bolivia	Los Amigos del Libro, Perú 3712, Casilla 450, Cochabamba; Mercado 1315, La Paz.
Botswana	Botsalo Books (Pty) Ltd, PO Box 1532, Gaborone.
Brazil	Livraria Mestre Jou, Rua Guaipá 518, São Paulo 05089; Fundação Getulio Vargas, Praia de Botafogo 190, C.P. 9052, Rio de Janeiro; A Nossa Livraria, CLS 104, Bloco C, Lojas 18/19, 70.000 Brasilia, D.F.
Brunei	SST Trading Sdn. Bhd., Bangunan Tekno No. 385, Jln 5/59, PO Box 227, Petaling Jaya, Selangor.
Canada	Renouf Publishing Co. Ltd, 61 Sparks St (Mall), Ottawa, Ont. KIT 56; toll-free calls in Canada: 1-800-267-4164; local and other call 613-238-8985.
China	China National Publications Import Corporation, PO Box 88, Beijing.
Congo	Office national des librairies populaires, B.P. 577, Brazzaville.
Costa Rica	Librería, Imprenta y Litografía Lehmann S.A., Apartado 10011, San José.
Cuba	Ediciones Cubanas, Empresa de Comercio Exterior de Publicaciones, Obispo 461, Apartado 605, La Habana.
Cyprus	MAM, PO Box 1722, Nicosia.
Czechoslovakia	ARTIA, Ve Smeckach 30, PO Box 790, 111 27 Prague 1.
Denmark	Munksgaard Export and Subscription Service, 35 Nørre Søgade, DK 1370 Copenhagen K.
Dominican Rep.	Fundación Dominicana de Desarrollo, Casa de las Gárgolas, Mercedes 4, Apartado 857, Zona Postal 1, Santo Domingo.
Ecuador	Su Librería Cía. Ltda., García Moreno 1172 y Mejía, Apartado 2556, Quito.
El Salvador	Librería Cultural Salvadoreña S.A. de C.V., Calle Arce 423, Apartado Postal 2296, San Salvador.
Finland	Akateeminen Kirjakauppa, 1 Keskuskatu, PO Box 128, 00101 Helsinki 10.
France	Editions A. Pedone, 13, rue Soufflot, 75005 Paris.
Germany, F.R.	Alexander Horn Internationale Buchhandlung, Friederichstr. 39, Postfach 3340, 6200 Wiesbaden.
Ghana	Fides Enterprises, PO Box 14129, Accra; Ghana Publishing Corporation, PO Box 3632, Accra.
Greece	G.C. Eleftheroudakis S.A., 4 Nikis Street, Athens (T-126); John Mihalopoulos & Son S.A., 75 Hermou Street, PO Box 73, Thessaloniki.
Guatemala	Distribuciones Culturales y Técnicas «Artemis», 5a. Avenida 12-11, Zona 1, Apartado Postal 2923, Guatemala.
Guinea-Bissau	Conselho Nacional da Cultura, Avenida da Unidade Africana, C.P. 294, Bissau.
Guyana	Guyana National Trading Corporation Ltd, 45-47 Water Street, PO Box 308, Georgetown.
Haiti	Librairie "A la Caravelle", 26, rue Bonne Foi, B.P. 111, Port-au-Prince.
Hong Kong	Swindon Book Co., 13-15 Lock Road, Kowloon.
Hungary	Kultura, PO Box 149, 1389 Budapest 62.
Iceland	Snaebjörn Jónsson and Co. h.f., Hafnarstraeti 9, PO Box 1131, 101 Reykjavik.
India	Oxford Book and Stationery Co., Scindia House, New Delhi 100 001; 17 Park Street, Calcutta 700 016; Oxford Subscription Agency, Institute for Development Education, 1 Anasuya Ave, Kilpauk, Madras 600 010.
Indonesia	P.T. Inti Buku Agung, 13 Kwitang, Jakarta.
Iraq	National House for Publishing, Distributing and Advertising, Jamhuria Street, Baghdad.
Ireland	The Controller, Stationery Office, Dublin 4.
Italy	Distribution and Sales Section, FAO, Via delle Terme di Caracalla, 00100 Rome; Libreria Scientifica Dott. Lucio de Biasio "Aeiou", Via Meravigli 16, 20123 Milan; Libreria Commissionaria Sansoni S.p.A. "Licosa", Via Lamarmora 45, C.P. 552, 50121 Florence.
Japan	Maruzen Company Ltd, PO Box 5050, Tokyo International 100-31.
Kenya	Text Book Centre Ltd, Kijabe Street, PO Box 47540, Nairobi.